Modern Standard Arabic Grammar

Modern Standard Arabic Grammar

A Learner's Guide

MOHAMMAD T. ALHAWARY

A John Wiley & Sons, Ltd., Publication

This edition first published 2011
© 2011 Mohammad T. Alhawary

Blackwell Publishing was acquired by John Wiley & Sons in February 2007. Blackwell's publishing program has been merged with Wiley's global Scientific, Technical, and Medical business to form Wiley-Blackwell.

Registered Office
John Wiley & Sons Ltd, The Atrium, Southern Gate, Chichester, West Sussex, PO19 8SQ, United Kingdom

Editorial Offices
350 Main Street, Malden, MA 02148-5020, USA
9600 Garsington Road, Oxford, OX4 2DQ, UK
The Atrium, Southern Gate, Chichester, West Sussex, PO19 8SQ, UK

For details of our global editorial offices, for customer services, and for information about how to apply for permission to reuse the copyright material in this book please see our website at www.wiley.com/wiley-blackwell.

The right of Mohammad T. Alhawary to be identified as the author of this work has been asserted in accordance with the UK Copyright, Designs and Patents Act 1988.

Library of Congress Cataloging-in-Publication Data

Alhawary, Mohammad T.
  Modern standard Arabic grammar : a learner's guide / Mohammad T. Alhawary.
    p. cm.
  Includes bibliographical references and index.
  ISBN 978-1-4051-5501-4 (hardcover : alk. paper) – ISBN 978-1-4051-5502-1 (pbk. : alk. paper)
  1. Arabic language–Textbooks for foreign speakers–English. I. Title.
  PJ6307.A386 2010
  492.7′82421–dc22

                                                                                    2010016184

A catalogue record for this book is available from the British Library.

Set in 11/13.5pt Sabon by Graphicraft Limited, Hong Kong

Printed in the UK

Contents

Introduction

The Aim of this Book

Enthusiasm and demand for Arabic language learning have risen dramatically since the mid-1990s. Yet the field of Arabic as a foreign language has not been keeping up with this demand, especially with respect to instructional materials and foreign language teacher-preparation programs. This book is an effort toward filling the gap in both areas. It is also a pedagogical guide to all the basic structures and grammar of the Arabic language needed in the first 4–5 years of learning the language, taking into consideration comprehensive coverage (while not being overly comprehensive), sequence of presentation (from the more basic and frequent to the less basic and frequent in the language), and communicative functional use (from the more essential for communication to the less essential), and presented holistically in terms of forms and functions (i.e., without being solely based on grammar items alone). Concomitantly, it is a resource book for the teacher to develop an awareness or a better conceptualization of the essentials of Arabic grammar and structures and how to present them to students of Arabic as a foreign language.

The book aims to develop adequate exposure to Arabic grammar in current standard use from beginner to advanced proficiency levels, covering phonological, syntactic, and morphological rules. I focus on essential aspects of the grammar rules and provide straightforward explanations and multiple examples. The book is pedagogically oriented and uses symbols, tables, and diagrams to further encapsulate the rules and make them easy to understand and remember.

In addition to being useful to learners of Arabic as a foreign language, other types of learners and users will equally benefit from the book as a resource or reference tool, such as heritage speakers, teachers, and linguists (who know Arabic script). Because of its balanced coverage of phonology, morphology, and syntax, the book can be used as a supplementary text for language courses during the first 4–5 years of Arabic language learning, a primary text for Arabic structure and grammar courses, or a reference book.

Why Learn/Teach Grammar?

The communicative approach is often misunderstood as implying that knowledge of the grammar and structure is not as important as other language skills, and therefore its role is often marginalized by teachers and learners. The view adopted here is similar to that of most foreign language theorists and practitioners: that grammar is one of the important composite skills for developing communicative *competence*:

> Communicative competence is composed minimally of grammatical competence, sociolinguistic competence, and communication strategies, or what we refer to as strategic competence. There is no strong theoretical or empirical motivation for the view that grammatical competence is any more or less crucial to successful communication than is sociolinguistic competence or strategic competence. The primary goal of a communicative approach must be to facilitate the integration of these types of knowledge for the learner, an outcome that is not likely to result from overemphasis on one form of competence over the others throughout a second language program. (Michael Canale and Merrill Swain, "Theoretical Bases of Communicative Approaches to Second Language Teaching and Testing," *Applied Linguistics* 1: 47, 1980, p. 27; see also Leech and Svartvik, *A Communicative Grammar of English*, 2002: p. 3)

Is the Arabic Language Difficult to Learn?

While Arabic may present some learning challenges because of some of its grammatical aspects or its diglossic nature (although diglossia is a characteristic of almost all languages), Modern Standard Arabic (MSA) is not difficult to learn. Consider the following facts that *are not* characteristic of Arabic:

- its script is not logographic requiring knowledge of tens of thousands of logographs or symbols in order to reach the level of an educated native speaker
- it exhibits no distinction between capital and lowercase letters
- it exhibits no distinction between cursive and noncursive styles, allowing only for one (cursive) style
- it is not a tonal language in which word meanings change with tone changes
- unlike English, it exhibits no complex intonation patterns reflecting the mood of the speaker, beyond simple rising and falling patterns.

Rather, MSA has many aspects that are easy and/or amenable to rigorous learning strategies (of guessing the meaning of words from contexts). Consider the following facts that *are* characteristic of Arabic:

- its script is phonetic
- its phonetic alphabet is transparent, with one-to-one correspondence between sound and symbol; i.e., each distinct sound has its own distinct symbol
- it has a simple vowel system: three long (high front, high back, and low) simple ones (aa, ii, uu) and three short (high front, high back, and low) corresponding ones (a, u, i)
- unlike English, stress is predictable and non-phonemic (such that if stress is misplaced it does not result in a change in meaning)
- word derivations and patterns allow us not only to identify the part of speech to which a word belongs, but also, in combination with knowledge of the root, can allow us to guess the meaning of the word.

Vocabulary may be one of the few areas that may present a learning challenge, especially for someone learning a second language (e.g., Arabic) which is a non-cognate language in relation to his or her native language (e.g., English), but this does not make Arabic uniquely difficult, since the same can be said about the learner's native language (English) when learned by someone whose native language is a non-cognate language.

The Organization and Content of the Book

The organization and content of the book are based on the author's experience of over fifteen years' teaching Arabic as a second/foreign language and acquisition research (from the learner's perspective) of Arabic as a second language. The organization also takes into consideration the development of language skills and sequencing due to complexity or formality of structure and communicative functional use (i.e., it is not just based on grammar items alone, such as presenting negation or the subjunctive particles isolated from the verbs/tenses).

The book consists of 22 chapters and five appendices. It begins with the most basic and fundamental aspects of the language and progresses as communicative needs dictate. The first four chapters of the book start with letter/sound level and progress to syllable level, word level, phrase level, and sentence level. The next eight chapters focus on Arabic prepositions, pronouns, question words, and the different adverbs available in Arabic. These items are important to solidify knowledge of the Arabic sentence. The next four chapters aim to help the learner gain deeper knowledge of verbs, nouns, adjectives, and quantifiers, respectively. Due to its complexity, the conditional sentence is then presented in an independent chapter. The last five chapters contain the most formal structures covered in the book, with the last chapter aiming to help the learner fine-tune their knowledge of case and mood endings.

In addition, three of the five appendices contain rules for the writing of the *hamza*, rules for the Arabic numbers, and rules for looking up words in the dictionary so that they are immediately accessible to both the student and the teacher. Depending on the level of the learner, especially in the first year of Arabic language learning, roughly represented in most of the contents of the first four chapters, the book is best covered in sequence. Beyond the first year, the learner can navigate between the chapters smoothly, as all necessary cross-references are provided. If used alongside a language textbook, items can be skipped until they are covered in the textbook.

For ease of reference and space constraints, a number of abbreviations and symbols (for transliteration) are used. A list of all transliteration symbols used is provided. The distinction between the long and short *back* low vowels [aa] and [a] and the long and short *front* low vowels [aa] and [a] is only maintained in Chapter 1, since one of the primary aims of the chapter is accuracy of the sound system. The [l] sound of the definite article ['al-] is assimilated whenever the sun letter rule applies throughout the text and examples. Beyond Chapters 1–2, all proper names are transliterated following conventional spellings (i.e., not according to the transliteration symbols provided). This makes such names easier to read and helps the learner understand how to connect Arabic names as they are typically transliterated in English with their correct spelling and pronunciation in Arabic.

Background Knowledge Required of the Reader

The first two chapters of the book do not presuppose any background knowledge of Arabic, since all Arabic texts and examples are transliterated fully in English. Beyond these two chapters, the examples presuppose knowledge of Arabic script only, since only occasional transliteration of the examples is provided, to help clarify and simplify the explanation. Arabic script is usually taught at the beginning of almost any first course in Arabic and should take only a few weeks to learn. Therefore, with knowledge of the script, the reader can follow the contents of the book independently. To help clarify the scope of the Arabic structures in question (and that of English), comparisons are occasionally made between Arabic and English (such as question formation, conjugation of the past tense, and active participles). The learner and teacher are encouraged to make further comparisons of other structures so that the full scope of both Arabic and English (or any other language) is explored and connections are made between the two.

In addition, linguistic jargon and terminology are kept to a minimum and the prose is simplified so that the book is accessible to as many second-language learners of Arabic as possible. Arabic terms are provided side by side with the English terms so that: (1) the contents are immediately accessible and easier to identify by students at all levels; (2) the book can be integrated with any classroom textbooks, most of which also use these terms; and (3) fourth- to fifth-year students and beyond can make the transition to reading Arabic grammar explanations written solely in Arabic.

Transliteration Symbols of Arabic Sounds

I. Consonants

Arabic	Symbol	Technical description	Examples of equivalent or closest equivalent sounds in English (in bold)
ب	b	voiced bilabial stop	**b**ank
ت	t	voiceless alveolar stop	**t**an
ث	th	voiceless interdental/dental fricative	**th**ank
ج	j	voiced alveo-palatal fricative	**j**ob
ح	H	voiceless pharyngeal fricative	no English equivalent
خ	kh	voiceless velar fricative	Ba**ch**
د	d	voiced alveolar stop	**D**an
ذ	dh	voiced interdental/dental fricative	**th**at
ر	r	voiced alveolar trill	**r**oad
ز	z	voiced alveolar fricative	**z**ebra
س	s	voiceless alveolar fricative	**s**ee
ش	sh	voiceless palato-alvealor fricative	**sh**oes

Arabic	Symbol	Technical description	Examples of equivalent or closest equivalent sounds in English (in bold)
ص	S	voiceless alveolar fricative emphatic	**s**aw
ض	D	voiced alveolar stop emphatic	**D**onna (closest English equivalent)
ط	T	voiceless alveolar stop emphatic	**t**ar
ظ	Z	voiced interdental/dental fricative emphatic	no English equivalent
ع	ʿ	voiced pharyngeal fricative	no English equivalent
غ	gh	voiced velar fricative	no English equivalent
ف	f	voiceless labio-dental fricative	**f**an
ق	q	voiceless uvular stop	**c**aw (closest English equivalent)
ك	k	voiceless velar stop	**k**ing
ل	l	voiced alveolar lateral	**l**ight
م	m	voiced bilabial nasal	**m**an
ن	n	voiced alveolar nasal	**n**ear
ﻫ	h	voiceless glottal fricative	**h**ere
و	w	voiced bilabial velar glide	**w**oman
ي	y	voiced palatal glide	**y**es
ء	ʾ	(voiceless) glottal stop	co**ʾ**operate

II. Vowels

Arabic	Symbol	Technical description	Examples
ﹷ	a	short front low	instant
ﹷ	a̲	short back low	interruptive
ا	aa	long front low	bat
ا	a̲a̲	long back low	bar
ﹹ	u	short high back rounded	full
و	uu	long high back rounded	fool
ﹻ	i	short high front unrounded	fill
ي	ii	long high front unrounded	feel

Abbreviations

Symbol	Meaning
1	first person
2	second person
3	third person
acc	accusative case
AP	active participle
CA	Classical Arabic
D	dual
F	feminine
gen	genitive case
H	human
M	masculine
MSA	Modern Standard Arabic
nom	nominative case
P	plural
PP	passive participle
VN	verbal noun
S	singular

Acknowledgments

I wish to thank the four anonymous reviewers for their careful reading and excellent comments on an earlier draft of this book. I am grateful to the former linguistics acquisition editor of Wiley-Blackwell, Ada Brunstein, who first adopted the book project, as well as to her successor, Danielle Descoteaux, for her unfailing support and encouragement until the very end. Many thanks to Danielle's editorial assistant, Julia Kirk, for her prompt help during the early stages of the preperartion of the book. Special thanks go to Juanita Bullough, the project manager, for her patience, diligent work, and all the prompt assistance. My special thanks also go to Emma Anderson – for reading the proofs and for her invaluable editorial suggestions on the English text – and to Professor Ghazi Al-Zanahreh for his super-fast reading of the proofs and suggestions on the Arabic text. I also benefited from valuable suggestions made by my colleague, professor Raji Rammuny. However, all errors remain mine alone. I thank all other Wiley-Blackwell staff who assumed the duties of project editor during the various stages of the book: Caroline Clamp, Charlotte Frost, and Tom Bates. In particular, special thanks go to Caroline Clamp, who located the more than competent typesetters, Graphicraft Limited, who did a fine job of both the Arabic and the English texts. Finally, I am indebted to my wife, Jennifer, and our four children, for their love and moral support, and for putting up with the countless hours of work on this book. In addition, my wife provided much needed valuable editing and proofreading remarks. This book is dedicated to her.

1

Arabic Script and Sounds

This chapter discusses the essentials of the Arabic writing and sound systems at sound/letter, syllable, word, and sentence level. The following will be covered:

- Arabic letters of the alphabet, writing method, and orientation
- Arabic sounds (consonants, vowels, diphthongs, and other sound combinations)
- gemination (or consonant doubling)
- stress
- variations in sounds and spelling
- additional symbols
- formal MSA vs. informal MSA (Modern Standard Arabic)
- definiteness and assimilation of the [l] sound of the definite article
- helping vowels
- the dropping and retention of the *hamza* and *'alif* seat of the definite article.

Due to the transparent nature of Arabic spelling, the terms *letter* and *sound* are used interchangeably.

Modern Standard Arabic Grammar: A Learner's Guide, First Edition.
© 2011 Mohammad T. Alhawary. Published 2011 by Blackwell Publishing Ltd.

1.1   Arabic Script: The Alphabet

Arabic has a phonetic alphabet consisting of distinct symbols for three long (pure) vowels and 26 consonants. Whether in handwriting or print, Arabic script only exhibits a cursive style and is written from right to left. It may be for reasons to do with this right-to-left writing orientation that Arabs abandoned their (Arabic) numeral system, which was based on a geometrical conceptual design of the number of angles in each number (see Appendix A):

10	9	8	7	6	5	4	3	2	1	0

and later adopted the Indian Sanskrit number system:

١٠	٩	٨	٧	٦	٥	٤	٣	٢	١	٠

Whereas most Indian Sanskrit numerals are written from right to left, most Arabic numerals are written from left to right.

Although Arabic script is characterized as cursive, not all letters can be connected to a letter following them, allowing them only to be connected to letters preceding them. These letters comprise a small number of the total letters (six out of the 29 letters) and are usually referred to as *non-connectors*. The remaining letters can be connected to letters before and after them and are usually referred to as *connectors*. The nature of cursive writing style necessitates that:

- each *connector* letter assumes four (slightly) different shapes
- each *non-connector* letter assumes two shapes
- each shape depends on whether it is in initial, medial after a connector, medial after a non-connector, final after a connector, or final after a non-connector (usually referred to as *independent* or dictionary shape) position
- the *initial* and *medial after a non-connector* shapes of all the letters are identical
- the *medial* and *final after a connector* shapes of the *non-connectors* are identical.

Table 1.1a shows the alphabet (in descending order), which consists of 29 letters, including the 26 consonants and three long vowels, the different shapes (initial, medial, final after connectors, and final after non-connectors), and the distinction of connectors vs. non-connectors.

Table 1.1a Shapes of Arabic letters according to their positions within the word

Name		Final after non-connectors	Final after connectors	Medial after non-connectors	Medial after connectors	Initial
أَلِف	'alif	ا	ـا	ا	ـا	ا *
باء	baa'	ب	ـب	بـ	ـبـ	بـ
تاء	taa'	ت	ـت	تـ	ـتـ	تـ
ثاء	thaa'	ث	ـث	ثـ	ـثـ	ثـ
جيم	jiim	ج	ـج	جـ	ـجـ	جـ
حاء	Haa'	ح	ـح	حـ	ـحـ	حـ
خاء	khaa'	خ	ـخ	خـ	ـخـ	خـ
دال	daal	د	ـد	د	ـد	د
ذال	dhaal	ذ	ـذ	ذ	ـذ	ذ
راء	raa'	ر	ـر	ر	ـر	ر
زاي	zaay	ز	ـز	ز	ـز	ز
سين	siin	س	ـس	سـ	ـسـ	سـ
شين	shiin	ش	ـش	شـ	ـشـ	شـ
صاد	Saad	ص	ـص	صـ	ـصـ	صـ
ضاد	Daad	ض	ـض	ضـ	ـضـ	ضـ
طاء	Taa'	ط	ـط	طـ	ـطـ	طـ
ظاء	Zaa'	ظ	ـظ	ظـ	ـظـ	ظـ
عَيْن	ʿayn	ع	ـع	عـ	ـعـ	عـ
غَيْن	ghayn	غ	ـغ	غـ	ـغـ	غـ
فاء	faa'	ف	ـف	فـ	ـفـ	فـ

Table 1.1a   Continued

Name		*Final after non-connectors*	*Final after connectors*	*Medial after non-connectors*	*Medial after connectors*	*Initial*
قاف	*qaaf*	ق	ـق	قـ	ـقـ	قـ
كاف	*kaaf*	ك	ـك	كـ	ـكـ	كـ
لام	*laam*	ل	ـل	لـ	ـلـ	لـ
ميم	*miim*	م	ـم	مـ	ـمـ	مـ
نون	*nuun*	ن	ـن	نـ	ـنـ	نـ
هاء	*haa'*	ه	ـه	هـ	ـهـ	هـ
واو	*waaw*	و	ـو	و	ـو	و *
ياء	*yaa'*	ي	ـي	يـ	ـيـ	يـ *
هَمْزَة	** *hamza*	ء / ؤ / أ / ئ	ـئ / ـؤ / ـأ / ء	ـئ / ؤ / أ / ء	ـئـ / ـؤ / ـأ	إ / أ

Note: Names of letters in bold = non-connectors; * = (pure) long vowels which never occur in word initial position; ** = *hamza* which has certain writing rules (see Appendix B).

Table 1.1b gives examples of the letter *baa'* [b] occurring in initial position, in medial position following a connector, in medial position following a non-connector, in final position following a connector, and in final position following a non-connector.

Table 1.1b

Name	*Final after non-connectors*	*Final after connectors*	*Medial after non-connectors*	*Medial after connectors*	*Initial*
baa'	ب	ـب	بـ	ـبـ	بـ
Examples	تاب *taab* "he repented"	حَليب *Haliib* "milk"	رِبح *ribH* "profit"	حَبل *Habl* "rope"	بَعيد *ba'iid* "far"

Table 1.1a shows the letters according to the most widely known alphabetical order, usually referred to as التَّرْتيب الأَلِفْبائيّ "the *'alifbaa'iyy* or alphabetical order." Another (earlier) order exists and is usually used for arranging headings and subheadings within a text. The latter order is based on the first alphabet invented by the Phoenicians and is usually referred to as التَّرْتيب الأَبْجَديّ "the *'abjadiyy* order." The order is combined in the following words:

كَلَمُن				حُطّي			هَوَّز				أَبْجَد		
ن	م	ل	ك	ي	ط	ح	ز	و	هـ	د	ج	ب	أ
n	m	l	k	ii	T	H	z	w	h	d	j	b	a

ضَظَغ			ثَخَذ			قَرَشَت				سَعْفَص			
غ	ظ	ض	ذ	خ	ث	ت	ش	ر	ق	ص	ف	ع	س
gh	Z	D	dh	kh	th	t	sh	r	q	S	f	ᶜ	s

It is the same Phoenician alphabet that the Greeks relied on for their alphabet. Hence the order of the Greek alphabet proceeds in a similar fashion, as A, B, Γ, Δ, etc. (see Appendix C for the oldest extant tablet of the Phoenician alphabet, the first real phonetic alphabet).

Note: The *'alif* here stands for two sounds: the long vowel [aa] and the *hamza* [']. This makes the total number of characters in the Arabic alphabet 29: 26 consonants and three (long) vowels. As for the meaning of the words containing the letters arranged according to the التَّرْتيب الأَبْجَديّ "'*abjadiyy* order," traditional Arabic sources state that the words refer to names of ancient kings of *Madyan* tribes (in the Arabian Peninsula) who invented the Arabic alphabet, except for the last two words, containing the letters [th], [kh], [dh], [D], [Z], and [gh], which were added later.

1.2 Arabic Sounds

1.2.1 Vowels and Grammatical Vowel Endings

From the above explanation of the letters of the Arabic alphabet, note that only the long vowels are included in the alphabet and the representation of the short vowels is left out. MSA has a symmetrical vowel system: three long vowels [aa], [uu], and [ii]; and three corresponding short ones: [a], [u], and [i]. These are explained in Tables 1.2 and 1.3.

Table 1.2   Arabic long vowels

Name	Symbol	Sound	*Examples (from English)*	*Examples (from Arabic)*
'alif	١	[aa]	as "a" in fan	"mortal" *faan* فان
waaw	و	[uu]	as "oo" in fool	"beans" *fool* فول
yaa'	ي	[ii]	as "ee" in feel	"elephant" *fiil* فيل

Table 1.3   Arabic short vowels

Name	Symbol	Sound	*Examples (from English)*	*Examples (from Arabic)*
fatHa	´	[a]	as "a" in instant	"art" *fan* فَن
Damma	ُ	[u]	as "u" in full	"jasmine" *ful* فُل
kasra	ِ	[i]	as "i" in fill	"cent" *fils* فِلْس

Long vowels are twice as long as short vowels. Thus, if we assume the short vowel to equal one beat, the long vowel equals two beats of its corresponding short vowel. Pure long and short vowels as such never occur at the beginning of a word, occurring only in medial or final word position. However, unlike the symbols for the long vowels, the short vowel symbols are not written as part of the MSA word but rather as diacritical marks above or under the consonants. Thus, a short vowel is written above or below the consonant that follows it in speech. For this reason, short vowels are usually left out for adult readers but usually retained for children and adolescents (kindergarten to 12th grade) until they are able to read and spell words without the short vowels.

Arabic script has four additional symbols, one signifying the absence of any vowel (long or short), called *sukuun* سُكون "stillness," and three (formal ones) usually referred to as *tanwiin* تَنْوين or *nunation*, signifying indefiniteness (equivalent to the indefinite article "a" in English), signaled by the sound [n] attached to the grammatical (case) endings [a], [u], and [i] (to be discussed in subsequent chapters, particularly Chapter 22). These are illustrated in Table 1.4:

Table 1.4 Arabic nunation and grammatical endings and *sukuun*

Name	Translation and function	Symbol	Sound	Examples
تَنْوِين الفَتْح (مَنْصوب)	nunation of fatH (accusative)	◌ً	[an]	"a boy" *walad-an* وَلَداً
تَنْوِين الضَّمّ (مَرْفوع)	nunation of Damm (nominative)	◌ٌ	[un]	"a boy" *walad-un* وَلَدٌ
تَنْوِين الكَسْر (مَجْرور)	nunation of kasr (genitive)	◌ٍ	[in]	"a boy" *walad-in* وَلَدٍ
سُكُون	sukuun	◌ْ	[ø]	"a rope" *Habl* حَبْل

As shown in Table 1.4, the nunation, together with the three grammatical endings [an], [un], and [in], only occur in word final position, whereas the *sukuun* occurs in medial or final position but never in word initial position nor following a consonant in initial position, since MSA does not allow consonant clusters in word initial position, unlike English and some other languages. Thus, the word *street* in English contains the three-consonant cluster [str] with no vowels separating the first [s] and second [t] consonants. The absence of consonant clusters in word initial position in MSA is illustrated in the example below:

"he concealed"	*satara*	سَتَرَ
"concealing"	*satrun*	سَتْرٌ
"concealing"	*satr*	سَتْر

Sukuun is not allowed in initial position in any of the three words. Rather, in *satara* "he concealed," Arabic exhibits short syllables (or chunks of a word) consisting of a consonant [s] + a vowel [a], hence the short word consists of three syllables (*sa + ta + ra* ➜ *satara*). In *satrun* "concealing" Arabic allows *sukuun* in the middle of the word following a consonant (following a consonant and a vowel in word initial position), allowing for a longer first syllable, consisting of a consonant [s], a vowel [a], and a consonant [t] and a similar second syllable; hence the short word consist of two syllables (*sat + run* ➜ *satrun*). In *satr* "concealing," which is similar to *satrun* "concealing" (except that the former occurs in pause form; i.e., without the grammatical *un* at the end), *sukuun* occurs in the middle of the word after the consonant [t] and at the end of the word. A good way to conceptualize the *sukuun* in Arabic, if a word contains *sukuun*, is to consider it the point at which a word can be broken into parts/syllables.

1.2.2   Consonants

As stated above, Arabic has 26 consonants. Most of these have equivalent consonant sounds in English and other languages, although a few do not. Below is a brief description of all Arabic consonants, examples, and, where there is little or no similarity between Arabic consonants and those of the English language, an explanation.

1. ب   b   [voiced bilabial stop] produced with the two lips: as "b" in *bank*.

2. ت   t   [voiceless alveolar stop] produced with the tip of the tongue and the alveolar ridge at the base of the upper incisors (with the back of the tongue lowered): as "t" in *tan*.

3. ث   th   [voiceless interdental/dental fricative] produced with the tip of the tongue and the tip of the incisors (with the back of the tongue lowered): as "th" in *thank*.

4. ج   j   [voiced alveo-palatal fricative] produced with the tip of the tongue against the alveolar ridge and the middle of the tongue raised against the palate in this sequence: as "j" in *judge*.

5. ح   H   [voiceless pharyngeal fricative] produced in the middle of the windpipe by constricting it (so as to constrict the air passage without complete closure), just as producing a steam/breath with a *sound*; not to be confused with "h" as in *hat*, which is produced in the larynx.

6. خ   kh   [voiceless velar fricative] produced with the back of the tongue raised against the back of the roof of the mouth: as "ch" in the name of the German composer *Bach*.

7. د d [voiced alveolar stop] produced with the tip of the tongue and the alveolar ridge at the base of the upper incisors (with the back of the tongue lowered): as "d" in *Dan*.

8. ذ dh [voiced interdental/dental fricative] produced with the tip of the tongue and the tip of the incisors (with the back of the tongue lowered): as "th" in *that*.

9. ر r [voiced alveolar trill] produced with the tip of the tongue and the alveolar ridge above the upper incisors with the back of the tongue lowered: as "r" in *read* or with the back of the tongue raised, as "r" in *rust*.

10. ز z [voiced alveolar fricative] produced with the tip or blade of the tongue against the alveolar ridge (with the back of the tongue lowered): as "z" in *zebra*.

11. س s [voiceless alveolar fricative] produced with the tip or blade of the tongue against the alveolar ridge (with the back of the tongue lowered): as "s" in *see*.

12. ش sh [voiceless palato-alveolar fricative] produced with the middle of the tongue and that of the palate (without complete closure): as "sh" in *shoes*.

13. ص S [voiceless alveolar fricative emphatic] produced with the tip or blade of the tongue against the alveolar ridge (with the back of the tongue raised): as "s" in *saw*. **Note:** The consonant [S], as well as [s] and [z] above, are usually referred to as "alveolar." Another accurate articulation is where the tip of the tongue is behind the back of the lower incisors.

14. ض D [voiced alveolar stop emphatic] produced with the tip of the tongue and the alveolar ridge at the base of the upper incisors (with pressure applied from both sides of the tongue against the inner sides of the upper molars, so that the sound produced is not just the empathic/heavy/deep version of the voiced alveolar stop [d]; the closest English sound is "d" in *Donna*.)

15. ط T [voiceless alveolar stop emphatic] produced with the tip of the tongue and the alveolar ridge at the base of the upper incisors (with the back of the tongue raised): as "t" in *tar*.

16. ظ Z [voiced interdental/dental fricative emphatic] produced with the tip of the tongue and the tip of the incisors (with the back of the tongue raised): as "th" in *though* (with the additional effect of the back of the tongue raised).

17. ع   ᶜ   [voiced pharyngeal fricative] produced in the middle of the windpipe by constricting it (so as to constrict the air passage without complete closure) to produce a voiced throat sound; not to be confused with the *hamza* "glottal stop" ['] as in *co'opt*, which is produced in the larynx.

18. غ   gh   [voiced velar fricative] produced with the back of the tongue raised against the back of the roof of the mouth, resembling gurgling, or the French [r].

19. ف   f   [voiceless labio-dental fricative] produced with the tip of the upper incisors and the upper, inner part of the lower lip: as "f" in *fan*.

20. ق   q   [voiceless uvular stop] produced with the back of the tongue against the uvular: the closest English equivalent is "c" in *caw* if it were to be produced from the very back of the mouth.

21. ك   k   [voiceless velar stop] produced with the back of the tongue against the soft palate/velum: as "k" in *king*.

22. ل   l   [voiced alveolar lateral] produced with the front sides and tip of the tongue and the alveolar ridge above the upper incisors: as "l" in *list*.

23. م   m   [voiced bilabial nasal] produced with the two lips: as "m" in *man*.

24. ن   n   [voiced alveolar nasal] produced with the tip of the tongue and the alveolar ridge above the upper incisors (with the back of the tongue lowered): as "n" in *near*.

25. ﻪ   h   [voiceless glottal fricative] produced in the larynx: as "h" in *hear*.

26. ء   '   [voiceless glottal stop] produced in the larynx: as the catch ['] between the two syllables in *co'opt* (when the word is pronounced with the catch; i.e., when the glottal stop/catch in the middle is not elided/dropped in speech).

1.2.3   Variations in Consonants and Vowels

Of the 26 consonants, seven have an emphatic or deep/heavy quality. These are [kh], [S], [D], [T], [Z], [gh], and [q]. Of these, five have somewhat roughly light counterpart consonants: [S] vs. [s], [D] vs. [d], [T] vs. [t], [Z] vs. [dh], and [q] vs. [k]. However, all seven consonants both influence and are influenced by the quality of the vowels adjacent to them; in particular, the vowels following them. Thus, the deep/heavy consonants are generally:

- deepest/heaviest when followed by *'alif* [aa] or *fatHa* [a]
- less deep/heavy when followed by *waaw* [uu] or *Damma* [u]
- least deep/heavy when followed by *yaa'* [ii] or *kasra* [i].

With respect to their effect on the vowels, most distinctly, the *'alif* [aa] and *fatHa* [a] are pronounced as deep (back) vowels following any of these seven consonants, whereas *'alif* [aa] and *fatHa* [a] are pronounced as light (front) vowels following any of the remaining consonants. The examples below illustrate the distinction between the [S] and [s].

[S] as in saw/sauce:

Saa	صا		*Sa*	صَ
Suu	صو		*Su*	صُ
Sii	صي		*Si*	صِ

[s] as in see/seem/Sam:

saa	سا		*sa*	سَ
suu	سو		*su*	سُ
sii	سي		*si*	سِ

In addition, another consonant, the voiced alveolar trill [r]:

- is treated as a deep/heavy sound when followed by *'alif* [aa] and *fatHa* [a] or *waaw* [uu] and *Damma* [u] by raising the back of the tongue: as "r" in *rust*
- is not treated as a deep/heavy sound following *yaa'* [ii] or *kasra* [i] by lowering the back of the tongue: as "r" in *read*.

Note: Some dialects do not treat [kh] and [gh] as heavy/deep consonants, for example, Damascene, Syria, but others do, such as the dialect of Aleppo, Syria. According to the former, a following *'alif* [aa] or *fatHa* [a] sound is produced as a light/front vowel. Thus, the *'alif* [aa] in the proper name Khalid [khaalid] is pronounced as a long front vowel (as "a" in *fan*) rather than as a long back vowel (as "a" in *far*). Similarly, some dialects do not treat [r] as a heavy/deep consonant (when preceding *'alif* or *fatHa* and *waaw* or *Damma*). Hence, *'alif* in such dialects is pronounced as a long front vowel, as "a" in *rat* with [r] more rolled.

Finally, the voiced alveolar lateral consonant [l] is always pronounced light (as "l" in list) except for the name الله ['al-laah] "God," where it is pronounced dark/heavy (somewhat as "l" in *light*), as long as it is not preceded by a word ending with *yaa'* [ii] or *kasra* [i]. The following examples illustrate the variations of the consonant [l]:

"God"	*'al-laah* ("l" as in *law*)	الله	←	dark/heavy [l]
"to God"	*'ilaa l-laah* ("l" as in *law*)	إلى الله	←	dark/heavy [l]
"I worship God"	*'aᶜbudu l-laah* ("l" as in *law*)	أَعْبُدُ الله	←	dark/heavy [l]
"in the name of God"	*bismi l-laah* ("l" as in *lamp*)	بِسْمِ الله	←	light [l]

1.2.4   Diphthongs and other Sound Combinations

In addition to the 29 consonants and vowels of the Arabic alphabet, MSA has at least 16 diphthongs, glides/semi-vowels, and basic sound combinations. These are illustrated in Table 1.5:

Table 1.5   Diphthongs and other sound combinations

"spouse"	*zawj*	زَوْج	←	[aw]	وْ
"the Faw (Port)"	*'al-faaw*	الفاوْ	←	[aaw]	ا وْ
"Zayd"	*zayd*	زَيْد	←	[ay]	يْ
"tea"	*shaay*	شايْ	←	[aay]	ا يْ
"hand"	*yad*	يَد	←	[ya]	يَ
"measurement"	*qiyaas*	قِياس	←	[yaa]	يا

Table 1.5   Continued

"to honor"	*yukrim*	يُكْرِم	←	[yu]	يُ
"Joseph"	*yuusuf*	يوسُف	←	[yuu]	يو
"minister"	*waziir*	وَزير	←	[wa]	وَ
"valley"	*waadii*	وادي	←	[waa]	وا
"sin"	*wizr*	وِزْر	←	[wi]	وِ
"amateur"	*haawii*	هاوي	←	[wii]	وي
"roses"	*wuruud*	وُرود	←	[wu]	وُ
"peacock"	*Taawuus*	طاوُوس	←	[wuu]	وُو
"Zaayid"	*zaayid*	زايِد	←	[yi]	يِ
"decoration"	*tazyiin*	تَزْيِين	←	[yii]	يِ ي

1.3   Gemination

Gemination refers to consonant doubling (termed in Arabic *tashdiid* تَشْديد),
or the occurrence of two identical consonants with no vowel, short or
long, between them. Unlike English, where gemination only occurs in
medial word position (e.g., as "pp" in *appear*, "mm" in *immoral*, and "rr"
in *irrational*), in MSA gemination occurs in medial or word final positions, but never in initial position. For reasons of economy (keeping Arabic
script neat and simple) and because gemination occurs widely, gemination
is represented by a single consonant and a *shadda* symbol which resembles a slanted "w" shape ّ placed over the consonant. Below are examples
of gemination *tashdiid* in different positions of the word followed and
preceded by short and long vowels:

"he deliberated"	*tadabbar*	تَدَبَّر	←	بَّ	=	بْ + بَ
"deliberation"	*tadabbur*	تَدَبُّر	←	بُّ	=	بْ + بُ
"deliberator"	*mutadabbir*	مُتَدَبِّر	←	بِّ	=	بْ + بِ

"Mass"	quddaas	قُدّاس	←	دّا	=	دْ + دا
"the Sanctified"	qudduus	قُدّوس	←	دّو	=	دْ + دو
"saint"	qiddiis	قِدّيس	←	دّي	=	دْ + دي
"a mole"	Dabb	ضَبّ	←	بّ	=	ب + ب
"young man"	shaabb	شابّ	←	بّ	=	ب + ب
"to love each other"	taHaabbaa	تَحَابّا	←	بّ	=	ب + ب

In addition, gemination in Arabic occurs with diphthongs and glides/semi-vowels (see also Table 1.5) followed by any of the short or long vowels. The following examples illustrate such possible gemination combinations:

"he changed"	taghayyar	تَغَيَّر	←	[yya]	يَّ	=	يْ + يَ
"pilot"	Tayyaar	طَيَّار	←	[yyaa]	يّا	=	يْ + ي + ا
"changing"	taghayyur	تَغَيُّر	←	[yyu]	يُّ	=	يْ + يُ
"the Sustainer"	qayyuum	قَيّوم	←	[yyuu]	يّو	=	يْ + ي + و
"he got married"	tazawwaj	تَزَوّج	←	[wwa]	وَّ	=	وْ + وَ
"doorman"	bawwaab	بَوّاب	←	[wwaa]	وّا	=	وْ + و + ا
"he was married"	zuwwij	زُوّج	←	[wwi]	وِّ	=	وْ + وِ
"she/it strengthens"	tuqawwii	تُقَوّي	←	[wwii]	وّي	=	وْ + و + ي
"getting support"	tazawwud	تَزَوّد	←	[wwu]	وُّ	=	وْ + وُ
"Mister"	sayyid	سَيِّد	←	[yyi]	يِّ	=	يْ + يِ

1.4 Stress

The very first fact to keep in mind with respect to stress النَّبْر (or emphasis on a syllable within a word) in Arabic is that it is predictable and not phonemic. In other words, absence or presence and even misplacement of stress do not lead to a change in word meaning. This is unlike English where, for example, the placement of stress at the beginning of a word such as ′reject makes the word a noun, whereas placement of stress on the second syllable (i.e., before [j]), as in re′ject, renders the word a verb. However, there are certain stress rules in Arabic which can be very helpful in mastering the Arabic script and sound system more quickly and efficiently. The most basic and most useful stress rules to know are those observed in the presence or absence of long vowels, since in Arabic stress is generally associated with vowel length.

1.4.1 Presence of a Long Vowel

Stress falls on the syllable with the long vowel, whether the syllable is in initial, medial, or final position of the word. The following examples illustrate stress accordingly:

Long vowel in the initial syllable:

"he said"	*qaala*	قالَ
"student"	*Taalib*	طالِبْ
"worms"	*duudun*	دودٌ

Long vowel in the middle syllable:

"he meets"	*yuqaabil*	يُقابِل
"negotiator"	*mufaawiD*	مُفاوِض
"borders"	*Huduudun*	حُدودٌ

Long vowel in the final syllable:

"they both"	*humaa*	هُما
"both studied"	*darasaa*	دَرَسا
"borders"	*Huduud*	حُدودْ

1.4.2   Presence of Two Long Vowels

Since stress is generally associated with vowel length, stress is distributed between the two syllables where the long vowels occur; that is, with the word containing two stresses, as in the following words:

"negotiations"	*mufaawaDaat*	مُفاوَضات
"high"	*ᶜaalii*	عالي
"both got lost"	*Daa͟ᶜaa*	ضاعا

1.4.3   Absence of a Long Vowel

In the absence of a long vowel in a word, stress generally falls on the first syllable (i.e., the beginning of the word) except when *gemination* occurs, then stress falls on the first part/syllable where gemination occurs as in the following examples:

"he"	*huwa*	هُوَ
"we"	*naHnu*	نَحْنُ
"office"	*maktab*	مَكْتَبْ
"office"	*maktabun*	مَكْتَبٌ
"he taught"	*ᶜallama*	عَلَّمَ
"he learned"	*taᶜallama*	تَعَلَّمَ

Note: There are a few exceptions to the stress rules here, including أنا "I" pronounced with word initial stress. However, the word أنا "I" is pronounced ['ana] with a final *fatHa* [a] but written orthographically with a final *'alif* (to be distinguished from أنْ ['an] "to").

A useful implication of the above stress rules, especially for the beginner, is that when a long vowel and a short vowel occur within a word and we are not sure which of the two vowels is the long one, stress provides the answer: stress falls on the syllable with the long vowel. Similarly, if two long vowels occur in two syllables within a word, we can determine the presence of two long vowels, since stress is distributed; that is, there are two stresses within a word.

1.5 Spelling Variations of *'alif*

The symbol of the *'alif* [١] explained as part of the Arabic alphabet above has two additional variant shapes in word medial and final positions. Remember that *'alif* does not occur at the beginning of the word as a vowel (see Appendix C for an explanation of rules of the *hamza* and silent *'alif* occurring at the beginning of the word and elsewhere as merely a seat for the *hamza* consonant). The medial form of *'alif* is also represented by a shorthand form (as part of a CA spelling convention) where *'alif* is not actually connected within the word but rather appears as a short vertical line raised to the level of the dots and the short vowels. This form of the *'alif* is usually referred to as الأَلِف الخِنْجَرِيَّة *'al-'alif 'al-khinjariyya* "dagger *'alif*" or الأَلِف الصَّغِيرَة *'al-'alif 'aS-Saghiira* "the small *'alif*." Sometimes this *'alif* does not appear in handwritten or printed texts but occurs in a few words that are quite common, hence perhaps the reason for this short-form *'alif*. Below is a list of such common words both with and without the dagger *'alif*:

"God"	*'al-laah*	الله	=	الله
"the Merciful"	*'ar-raHmaan*	الرَّحْمـن	=	الرَّحْمـٰن
"a god"	*'ilaah*	إلـه	=	إلـٰه
"but"	*laakinna*	لكِنَّ	=	لـٰكِنَّ
"but"	*laakin*	لكِنْ	=	لـٰكِنْ
"this [masculine]"	*haadhaa*	هذا	=	هـٰذا
"this [feminine]"	*haadhihi*	هـذِهِ	=	هـٰذِهِ
"that [masculine]"	*dhaalika*	ذلِكَ	=	ذٰلِكَ
"these [human]"	*haa'ulaa'i*	هـؤلاءِ	=	هـٰؤلاءِ
"those [human]"	*'ulaa'ika*	أُولـئِكَ	=	أُولـٰئِكَ

The other variant form of the *'alif* occurs in word final position and is represented by the same shape of the final *yaa'* (final after a connector or non-connector) without the two dots ى . Both final *'alif* shapes (١ and ى) are pronounced the same. Arab grammarians refer to *'alif* in final position, whether it has the shape ١ or ى , as الأَلِف المَقْصورَة *'al-'alif 'al-maqSuura*. However, today only the latter is referred to as *'al-'alif 'al-maqSuura*. The variations in the spelling of the final *'alif* depend on the derivation rules of such words (rules of words ending with *'al-'alif 'al-maqSuura* will be discussed in Chapter 2). To distinguish the final *'alif* shape ى from that of the *yaa'* ي (although only the latter has dots beneath it), the symbol of *'al-'alif 'al-khinjariyya* "the dagger *'alif*" or *'al-'alif 'aS-Saghiira* "the small *'alif*" is written above, although it may not be provided in some texts. Below are examples of words ending with final *'alif* ى with and without *'al-'alif 'al-khinjariyya* "the dagger *'alif*":

"to"	*'ilaa*	إلى	=	إلىٰ
"on"	*ʿalaa*	عَلى	=	عَلىٰ
"he cried"	*bakaa*	بكى	=	بَكىٰ
"he spent"	*qaDaa*	قَضى	=	قَضىٰ
"hospital"	*mashfaa*	مَشْفى	=	مَشْفىٰ
"café"	*maqhaa*	مَقْهى	=	مَقْهىٰ
"Layla"	*laylaa*	لَيْلى	=	لَيْلىٰ
"Salma"	*salmaa*	سَلْمى	=	سَلْمىٰ
"Moses"	*muusaa*	موسى	=	موسىٰ
"Jesus"	*ʿiisaa*	عيسى	=	عيسىٰ
"Mustafa"	*musTafaa*	مُصْطَفى	=	مُصْطَفىٰ

1.6   *taa' marbuuTa*

A suffix (word ending) referred to as *'at-taa' 'al-marbuuTa* التَّاء المَرْبوطة "the tied [t]" ـة results from literally tying up the Arabic letter ت. The latter is referred to as التّاء المَبْسوطة *'at-taa' 'al-mabsuuTa* "the flat [t]." There are two shapes of *taa' marbuuTa*, depending on whether it occurs following a connecting letter or a non-connecting letter, as the two examples below illustrate:

"a female dog"	*kalb-ah*	كَلْبَة	←	ـَة	following a connector
"a female cow"	*baqar-ah*	بَقَرَة	←	ة	following a non-connector

The suffix is a feminine gender, as Arabic refers to humans, animals, and any inanimate objects as having either the masculine gender "he" or the feminine gender "she" (see Chapter 2). The *taa' marbuuTa* is always preceded by the vowel [a]. In pause form (where no grammatical ending is produced) in formal MSA (and CA), *taa' marbuuTa* is pronounced as a voiceless glottal fricative [h] so that it is pronounced, together with the vowel [a] preceding it, as [-ah]. However, in spoken and informal MSA, speakers do not usually produce the voiceless glottal fricative [h], and instead just produce the vowel [a], so that the *taa' marbuuTa* is simply pronounced as [a] in word final position to indicate the feminine gender marking of the word. Below are examples of masculine and feminine human, animal, and inanimate objects in pause form:

"a female teacher"	*'ustaadh-a*	أُسْتَاذَة	"a male teacher"	*'ustaadh*	أُسْتَاذ
"a female dog"	*kalb-a*	كَلْبَة	"a male dog"	*kalb*	كَلْب
"a library"	*maktab-a*	مَكْتَبَة	"an office"	*maktab*	مَكْتَب

In full (formal) MSA form (where grammatical endings are produced), *taa' marbuuTa* is produced as [t] with the only distinction that feminine forms do not require the *'alif* as a seat (i.e., the *'alif* is written but not pronounced) for the nunation of *fatH* [˝], but masculine forms require the *'alif*, as shown in the following examples (see also Table 1.4 above):

"a student F"	*Taalib-at-an*	طَالِبَةً	"a student M"	*Taalib-an*	طَالِباً
"a student F"	*Taalib-at-un*	طَالِبَةٌ	"a student M"	*Taalib-un*	طَالِبٌ
"a student F"	*Taalib-at-in*	طَالِبَةٍ	"a student M"	*Taalib-in*	طَالِبٍ

Finally, a small number of words may end with a *taa' marbuuTa* following *'alif*. In full MSA form, *taa' marbuuTa* is produced as [t] followed by any of the grammatical endings, as in the above examples. In pause form in formal MSA (and CA), *taa' marbuuTa* following *'alif* is pronounced as a voiceless glottal fricative [h] so that it is pronounced, together with the *'alif* [aa] preceding it, as [-aah]. However, in spoken and informal MSA, it is usually pronounced as [t], so that it is pronounced, together with the *'alif* preceding it, as [-aat]. Below are examples illustrating both uses:

"a channel"	*qanaa-t*	قَنَاة	"a channel"	*qanaa-h*	قَنَاهْ
"life"	*Hayaa-t*	حَياة	"life"	*Hayaa-h*	حَياهْ
"a girl"	*fataa-t*	فَتَاة	"a girl"	*fataa-h*	فَتَاهْ

1.7   Definiteness

At the word level, a word (noun or adjective) is by default indefinite whether in pause (with no *nunation* attached) or full form (with *nunation*) (see Table 1.4 above). On the other hand, definiteness is signaled by attaching the definite article اَلْ ['al-] "the" to the beginning of the word. The *fatHa* [´] that appears on the *hamza* (itself seated on a silent *'alif*) is not usually provided in texts, nor is the *hamza* itself, nor is the *sukuun* on لْ, since the definite article occurs quite frequently. Therefore, the definite article appears simply as الـ.

Note: The *hamza*, the *fatHa*, and the *sukuun* are provided on the definite article اَلْ ['al-] "the" in this chapter and whenever appropriate in order to clarify the rules involved. Due to orthographic conventions, the *hamza* and the *fatHa* أ ['a] are widely misunderstood as being merely a *fatHa* on a silent *'alif* ا rather than a *hamza* and a *fatHa* on a silent *'alif* أ ['a]. As a glottal stop, the *hamza* originates from the larynx, as opposed to a *fatHa*, which would originate from the mouth alone. The latter would be hard to pronounce at the beginning of a word starting with a vowel (without a glottal stop), at least for Arabic and English speakers. In English, every word that starts with a vowel also starts with a *hamza* "glottal stop." However, English does not require a special symbol to represent it, since it rarely occurs in the middle of a word (e.g., co'ordinate and co'operate), and even then it is often elided/dropped (see 1.2.2 for a description of the *hamza* and how it is articulated/pronounced). Similarly, in Arabic the *hamza* of the definite article belongs to the هَمْزَة الوَصْل "connecting/eliding *hamza*" category, which, in certain contexts, is elided/dropped (in speech) (see 1.9–10 below and Appendix B).

With respect to pronunciation, the [l] sound of the article may undergo assimilation with the initial sound of the word following it, depending on whether such a sound is a *sun letter* or *moon letter*. When the definite article is added to a word beginning with a *moon letter*, the [l] sound of the article is not assimilated; hence, the definite article and the word attached to it are pronounced normally. Except for [j], all *moon letters* are produced without involving the tip of the tongue. This makes it easy to remember and we can apply it intuitively by feeling the position of the tongue before applying the rule. Table 1.6 lists all the *moon letters*, with examples for each in indefinite and definite words:

Table 1.6 *Moon letters* in indefinite and definite words

"the Earth"	'al-'arD	الأَرْض	←	'arD	أَرْض + الـ	أ
"the door"	'al-baab	الباب	←	baab	باب + الـ	ب
"the mountain"	'al-jabal	الجَبَل	←	jabal	جَبَل + الـ	ج
"the milk"	'al-Haliib	الحَليب	←	Haliib	حَليب + الـ	ح
"the bread"	'al-khubz	الخُبْز	←	khubz	خُبْز + الـ	خ
"the eye"	'al-ᶜayn	العَيْن	←	ᶜayn	عَيْن + الـ	ع
"the deer"	'al-ghazaal	الغَزال	←	ghazaal	غَزال + الـ	غ
"the cent"	'al-fils	الفِلْس	←	fils	فِلْس + الـ	ف
"the moon"	'al-qamar	القَمَر	←	qamar	قَمَر + الـ	ق
"the dog"	'al-kalb	الكَلْب	←	kalb	كَلْب + الـ	ك
"the salt"	'al-milH	المِلْح	←	milH	مِلْح + الـ	م
"the crescent"	'al-hilaal	الهِلال	←	hilaal	هِلال + الـ	هـ
"the paper"	'al-waraqa	الوَرَقَة	←	waraqa	وَرَقَة + الـ	و
"the hand"	'al-yad	اليَد	←	yad	يَد + الـ	ي

Note: As shown, the *hamza* and the *fatHa* [ᵃ] on the silent *'alif* seat are not provided in texts.

However, when the definite article is added to a word beginning with a *sun letter*, the [l] sound of the article is assimilated. The [l] sound becomes silent (i.e., not pronounced). The loss of the [l] sound (in pronunciation only) is compensated for by doubling the *sun letter* beginning the word. Like gemination, as discussed above, this is represented by a *shadda* symbol placed on the *sun letter*. All *sun letters* are produced using the tip of the tongue, so it is easy to remember and apply the rule intuitively (by feeling the position of the tongue). Table 1.7 lists all the *sun letters*, with examples in indefinite and definite words:

Table 1.7 *Sun letters* in indefinite and definite words

"the berries"	'at-tuut	التّوت	←	tuut	توت	+ الـ	ت
"the snow"	'ath-thalj	الثّلج	←	thalj	ثَلج	+ الـ	ث
"the house"	'ad-daar	الدّار	←	daar	دار	+ الـ	د
"the corn"	'adh-dhura	الذّرَة	←	dhura	ذُرَة	+ الـ	ذ
"the leg"	'ar-rijl	الرّجْل	←	rijl	رِجْل	+ الـ	ر
"the button"	'az-zar	الزّر	←	zar	زَر	+ الـ	ز
"the sugar"	'as-sukkar	السُّكَّر	←	sukkar	سُكَّر	+ الـ	س
"the sun"	'ash-shams	الشَّمْس	←	shams	شَمْس	+ الـ	ش
"the patience"	'aS-Sabr	الصّبر	←	Sabr	صَبْر	+ الـ	ص
"the mole"	'aD-Dabb	الضّبّ	←	Dabb	ضَبّ	+ الـ	ض
"the medicine"	'aT-Tibb	الطّبّ	←	Tibb	طِبّ	+ الـ	ط
"the shade"	'a Z-Zill	الظّلّ	←	Zill	ظِلّ	+ الـ	ظ
"the night"	'al-layl	اللّيْل	←	layl	لَيْل	+ الـ	ل
"the fire"	'an-naar	النّار	←	naar	نار	+ الـ	ن

Note: As shown, the *hamza* and the *fatHa* [ﺀ] on the silent *'alif* seat are not provided in texts.

It is worth noting here that Arab grammarians who came up with the terms *moon letters* الْحُروف القَمَريَّة and *sun letters* الْحُروف الشَّمْسِيَّة did so as they chose the words قَمَر *qamar* "moon" and شَمْس *shams* "sun" to exemplify the rule and to remind the speaker of the intuitive nature of the rule: it is applied intuitively by first feeling the position of the tongue in a somewhat conscious manner, and eventually by applying it unconsciously. Alternatively, to apply and learn the *sun* and *moon letter* rule, one can memorize the *moon letters* (a total of 14 letters) and *sun letters* (a total of 15 letters) which are distributed somewhat evenly between letters of the alphabet. With practice and exposure over time, applying the rule will become automatic (see Tables 1.6–1.7 above).

1.8 Formal MSA vs. Informal MSA

Formal MSA style is marked by the production of grammatical and vowel (as part of the spelling and pronunciation) endings of words in a sentence, except for the last word in the sentence, which should be in pause form. "Pause form" means that no grammatical or short vowel ending of any kind is produced (except for a few one-letter words usually used in CA). Hence, formal MSA means providing the full form of each word with its ending, whether the ending is grammatical or has to do with its fixed spelling at the end of the word. The following sentence is an example of full formal MSA style:

الرَّئيسُ الجَزائريُّ في زِيارَةٍ رَسْمِيَّةٍ مَعَ نائِبِهِ إلى سوريَّة .

'ar-ra'iisu l-jazaa'iriyyu fii ziyaaratin rasmiyyatin ma'a naa'ibihi 'ilaa suuriyya
"The Algerian president is on an official visit with his vice-president to Syria."

Note that every word in the sentence is fully vowelled; that is, every word has the grammatical and vowel endings on the end except the last word سوريَّة .
Informal MSA style, on the other hand, is marked by the production of words in the sentence in pause form, just as one would produce the last word of the sentence in formal MSA in pause form. This means that all grammatical endings are dropped (i.e., not produced altogether). Below is the same sentence in pause form, as an example of informal MSA style at sentence level:

الرَّئيس الجَزائريّ في زِيارَة رَسْمِيَّة مَعَ نائِبِه إلى سوريَّة .

'ar-ra'iis 'al-jazaa'iriyy fii ziyaara rasmiyya ma'a naa'ibih 'ilaa suuriyya
"The Algerian president is on an official visit with his vice-president to Syria."

Unlike grammatical endings, short vowel endings that constitute part of the spelling/pronunciation of a word may or may not be produced in pause form. The preposition *ma^aca* "with" in the sentence above is the only word which is produced with the *fatHa* ending here. The ending is part of the pronunciation of the word (prepositions have no grammatical endings) and it may also be produced as *ma^c* without the *fatHa* in pause form.

However, the presence of two MSA styles, formal and informal, does not mean that Arab speakers use one style restrictively to the exclusion of the other. This is especially evident in formal speech, where some speakers may tend to produce full forms and pause forms selectively within the same sentence due to running out of breath or some other consideration, some of which may be idiosyncratic. Below is the same sentence again, restated with words produced selectively both in full and pause forms:

الرَّئيسُ الجزائريّ في زيارَةٍ رَسْميَّة مَعَ نائِبِهِ إلى سوريَّة .

'ar-ra'iisu 'al-jazaa'iriyy fii ziyaaratin rasmiyya ma^ca naa'ibihi 'ilaa suuriyya
"The Algerian president is on an official visit with his vice-president to Syria."

الرَّئيس الجزائريّ في زيارَةٍ رَسْميَّة مَعَ نائِبِه إلى سوريَّة .

'ar-ra'iis 'al-jazaa'iriyy fii ziyaaratin rasmiyya ma^ca naa'ibih 'ilaa suuriyya
"The Algerian president is on an official visit with his vice-president to Syria."

Thus, full mastery of MSA skills, especially that of listening, necessitates learning and practicing the use of grammatical and vowel endings.

1.9 Helping Vowels and Dropping the *hamza* of the Definite Article

When full or mixed full and pause forms are used in MSA, Arabic resorts to dropping the *hamza* of the definite article together with the *fatHa* [a] vowel that occurs with it [أ] and to inserting certain vowels to help merge words smoothly, so that words in a stretch of speech in full form style can be pronounced with less effort than in pause form. Many languages resort to similar methods, probably for ease of pronunciation. English, for example, allows the insertion of [n] with the indefinite article before words starting with a vowel (e.g., *a banana* vs. *an apple*). This allows the glottal stop (equivalent to the *hamza* in Arabic) occurring with the vowel to be elided/dropped, since any English word that starts with a vowel necessarily starts with a glottal stop (to make vowels easier to pronounce in word initial position). Similarly, some

English dialects allow the insertion of [r] when words preceding the preposition *of* end with a vowel (*idea of* → *idea-r-of*). In Arabic, vowels inserted to help smooth the merger between words are referred to as "helping vowels" that include [a], [u], and [i] and the occurrence is explained due to اِلْتِقاءُ السّاكِنَيْن "the meeting of the quiescent/still sounds."

1.9.1 The *fatHa* Helping Vowel [a]

The *fatHa* [a] helping vowel is inserted after the preposition مِنْ *min* "from" when a word following it contains the definite article ـٱلْ ['al-] "the." Inserting the vowel [a] is also accompanied by the dropping of the *hamza* and the *fatHa* of the definite article أ ['a] (in speech only) so that only the sound [l] is produced/heard in words beginning with a *moon letter*, whereas the entire definite article is dropped in words beginning with a *sun letter* (see 1.7 above). The following are examples of both phenomena taking place at the same time:

	After helping vowel [a]		Before helping vowel [a]	
"from the moon"	*mina l-qamar*	مِنَ الْقَمَر ←	*min 'al-qamar*	مِنْ أَلْقَمَر
"from the sun"	*mina sh-shams*	مِنَ الشَّمْس ←	*min 'ash-shams*	مِنْ أَلْشَّمْس

1.9.2 The *Damma* Helping Vowel [u]

The *Damma* [u] helping vowel is inserted after the personal pronouns and pronoun suffixes for second- and third-person masculine plural when a word following it contains the definite article ـٱلْ ['al-] "the." Inserting the vowel [u] is also accompanied by the dropping of the *hamza* and the *fatHa* of the definite article أ ['a] (in speech only) so that only the sound [l] is produced/heard in words beginning with a *moon letter*, whereas the entire definite article is dropped in words beginning with a *sun letter* (see 1.7 above). The following are examples of both phenomena taking place at the same time:

After helping vowel [u]		Before helping vowel [u]	
qaabala-kumu l-waziir قابَلَكُمُ الْوَزير ←		*qaabala-kum 'al-waziir* قابَلَكُمْ أَلْوَزير	
"The minister met you all."			

After helping vowel insertion [u]	Before helping vowel insertion [u]
wadda'a-humu r-rajul وَدَّعَهُمُ الرَّجُلِ ← *wadda'a-hum 'ar-rajul* وَدَّعَهُمْ أَلرَّجُلِ	
"The man bade them farewell."	

1.9.3   The *kasra* Helping Vowel [i]

The *kasra* [i] helping vowel is inserted after any word ending in a consonant sound (i.e., *sukuun*/no vowel) when a word following it begins with the definite article أَلْ ['al-] "the" or with a (light) *hamza 'i* (see also Appendix B on the different types of *hamza*). Inserting the vowel [i] is also accompanied by the dropping of the *hamza* and the *fatHa* of the definite article أ ['a] (in speech only) so that only the sound [l] is produced/ heard in words beginning with a *moon letter*, whereas the entire definite article is dropped in words beginning with a *sun letter* (see 1.7 above). Accordingly, the *kasra* helping vowel is the most frequent of the three "helping vowels" [a], [u], and [i]. The following are some examples of the *kasra* "helping vowel":

		After helping vowel [i]	Before helping vowel [i]
"Is the moon ...?"	*hali l-qamar*	هَلِ الْقَمَرَ...؟ ←	*hal 'al-qamar*	هَلْ أَلْقَمَرَ...؟
"Is the sun ...?"	*hali sh-shams*	هَلِ الشَّمْسِ...؟ ←	*hal 'ash-shams*	هَلْ أَلْشَّمْسِ...؟
"the sun rose"	*Tala'ati sh-shams*	طَلَعَتِ الشَّمْسَ ←	*Tala'at 'ash-shams*	طَلَعَتْ أَلْشَّمْسَ
"take* the book"	*khudhi l-kitaab*	خُذِ الْكِتَابَ ←	*khudh 'al-kitaab*	خُذْ أَلْكِتَابَ
"take* the notebook"	*khudhi d-daftar*	خُذِ الدَّفْتَر ←	*khudh 'ad-daftar*	خُذْ أَلدَّفْتَر
"who is the man"	*mani r-rajul*	مَنِ الرَّجُلَ؟ ←	*man 'ar-rajul*	مَنْ أَلْرَّجُلِ؟

Note: * = second-person singular masculine

Thus, in addition to the "helping vowels," the rules of the *sun letters* and *moon letters* apply (see 1.7 above). In the case of a definite word containing a *sun letter* following the definite article, not only are the *hamza*, *fatHa*, and *'alif* seat of the definite article أ ['a] silent, but also the [l] sound; that is, the whole definite article is silent, with gemination giving the clue as to the position of the definite article. However, in the case of the definite word containing a *moon letter* following the definite article, only the *hamza* and its *fatHa* أ ['a] are silent.

Of course, no "helping vowel" is needed if the word preceding the definite article already contains a vowel (long or short). However, an additional rule applies when a long vowel is present. In this case, the long vowel is shortened (e.g., عَلى "on" *ʿalaa* → *ʿala* and في "in" *fii* → *fi*), as in the following examples:

		After two words are combined		Before two words are combined	
"on the moon"	*ʿala-l-qamar*	عَلى الْقَمَر	←	*ʿalaa 'al-qamar*	عَلى أَلْقَمَر
"and the moon"	*wa-l-qamar*	وَالْقَمَر	←	*wa 'al-qamar*	وَ أَلْقَمَر
"in the sun"	*fi-sh-shams*	في الشَّمْس	←	*fii 'ash-shams*	في أَلشَّمْس
"and the sun"	*wa-sh-shams*	وَالشَّمْس	←	*wa 'ash-shams*	وَ أَلشَّمْس

1.10 Dropping the *hamza* and *'alif* Seat of the Definite Article in Writing

In none of the above phenomena is any letter or symbol deleted in *writing*. The only occasion when an actual letter or symbol is deleted in writing (as well as in speech) is when a word containing the definite article is preceded by the preposition particle لِ *li-* "for." In this case, the *hamza* of the definite article, its *fatHa*, and its silent *'alif* seat أ ['a] are dropped in both speech and writing. Other particles, such as the preposition *bi-* "with/in/by" and *fa-* "so/but," when attached to a word containing the definite article, do not require the deletion of the *hamza* and its *fatHa* in writing – requiring only the *hamza* and its *fatHa*, together with the *'alif* seat, to be silent. The following examples illustrate the dropping in both speech and writing of the *hamza* (together with its *fatHa* and *'alif* seat) of the definite article with the particle *li-* and its retention in writing with other particles, such as *bi-* "with/in/by" and *fa-* "so/but":

	After two words are combined			Before two words are combined	
"for the moon"	*li-l-qamar*	لِلْقَمَر	←	*li- 'al-qamar*	لـ ألْقَمَر
"for the sun"	*li-sh-shams*	لِلشَّمْس	←	*li- 'ash-shams*	لـ ألشَّمْس
"so, the moon ..."	*fa-l-qamar*	فَالْقَمَر	←	*fa- 'al-qamar*	فَـ ألْقَمَر
"so, the sun ..."	*fa-sh-shams*	فَالشَّمْس	←	*fa- 'ash-shams*	فَـ ألشَّمْس
"by train"	*bi-l-qitaar*	بِالْقِطار	←	*bi- 'al-qitaar*	بـ ألْقِطار
"by car"	*bi-s-sayyaara*	بِالسَّيّارة	←	*bi- 'as-sayyaara*	بـ ألسَّيّارة

1.11 Summary

This chapter discussed the basic facts relevant to the Arabic writing and sound systems. Remember:

- Arabic script proceeds from right to left
- Arabic allows only cursive-style writing, with each letter having a slightly distinct shape to fit five word positions: initial, medial after a connector, medial after a non-connector, final after a connector, and final after a non-connector
- Arabic has a straightforward phonetic alphabet consisting of 26 consonants and three long vowels, in addition to three corresponding short vowels represented as floating symbols above the consonants
- each distinct sound is represented by a distinct symbol, except for the symbol of the long vowel *'alif* [aa], which has three variants
- Arabic has a simple, symmetrical vowel system: with three simple, long vowels [aa], [uu], and [ii] and three short corresponding ones [a], [u], and [i], respectively – allowing for additional semi-vowels, diphthongs, and sound combinations which are simple and which almost all have English equivalents
- Arabic adopts an economical system of writing where gemination/consonant doubling is represented by a special symbol over the doubled consonant, since gemination occurs frequently in many words and in both medial and final word positions

- Arabic stress generally follows straightforward intuitive patterns, as stress is associated with vowel length: where there is a long vowel there is stress
- Arabic has a special symbol, *taa' marbuuTa*, attached to the end of the word to indicate the feminine gender of the word (whether noun or adjective)
- Arabic indefiniteness is signaled by the default form of the word and/ or nunation [n] sound at the end of the word, usually attached together with a grammatical (short vowel) ending
- Arabic definiteness is formed by attaching the definite article *'al-* "the" to the beginning of the word following an intuitive assimilation rule, for ease of pronunciation
- Arabic, at the sentence level, is produced both in pause form (informally) and full form (formally)
- Arabic employs three helping vowels for ease of pronunciation
- The *hamza*, together with its *'alif* seat belonging to the definite article, is dropped in speech as well as writing only with the preposition ل *li-* "for."

2

Word Structure

This chapter discusses the basic components of the Arabic word. It also discusses particles or suffixes that are attached to words as part of their essential, individual makeup. The chapter deals with aspects of Arabic words that any given word necessarily consists of and covers:

- the basic components of the Arabic word: root and pattern
- gender markings: masculine and feminine
- the dual: masculine and feminine
- the regular masculine plural
- the regular feminine plural
- the irregular plural: masculine and feminine.

2.1 The Basic Components of the Arabic Word: Root and Pattern

As in other Semitic languages, Arabic words have a unique underlying form–meaning relationship. Words are derived from combining a pattern وَزْن with core root جَذْر consonants. Patterns consist of vowels (and sometimes additionally auxiliary consonants), while roots mostly consist of three consonants in a specific order. The complete meaning of a given word obtains only from combining both, since root consonants carry the core meaning and a given pattern modifies the core meaning by making it more specific. Examples (1)–(3) show that the words are formed by combining the root س - ر - د *d-r-s* "that which has to do with studying" with certain patterns.

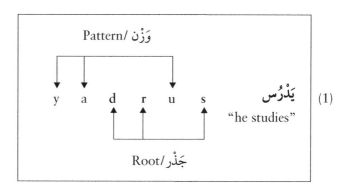

Literally speaking, *daaris* دارِس means "a studier"; hence the gloss given: "researcher."

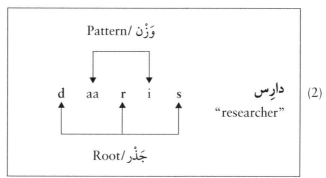

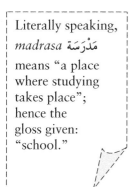

Literally speaking, *madrasa* مَدْرَسَة means "a place where studying takes place"; hence the gloss given: "school."

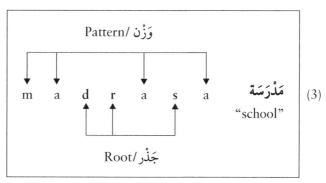

Accordingly, a given word can have a large number of related words which share the same core root consonants. Thus, from the root د - ر- س *d-r-s* (in this order: [d], then [r], then [s]) we can derive a large number of related words such as those listed below:

"he studied"	*darasa*	دَرَسَ
"he studies"	*yadrusu*	يَدْرُسُ
"studying/a study"	*diraasa*	دِراسَة
"studies"	*diraasaat*	دِراسات
"a lesson"	*dars*	دَرْس
"lessons"	*duruus*	دُروس
"a researcher"	*daaris*	دارِس
"researchers"	*daarisuuna*	دارِسونَ
"studied"	*madruus*	مَدْروس
"a teacher"	*mudarris*	مُدَرِّس
"teachers"	*mudarrisuuna*	مُدَرِّسونَ
"a school"	*madrasa*	مَدْرَسَة
"two schools"	*madrasataani*	مَدْرَسَتانِ
"schools"	*madaaris*	مَدارِس

Literally speaking, *mudarris* مُدَرِّس means "someone who causes to study"; hence the gloss given: "teacher."

There is a large number of patterns (which may also be called "infixes" or "circumfixes"), but at this point only certain patterns are useful to learn. As for root consonants, the vast majority of words (nouns, verbs, adjectives, and adverbs) have three root consonants; a small number (of nouns and verbs and adjectives) have four; and a smaller number (of nouns and adjectives) have five. Table 2.1 gives examples of words having three root consonants (called "triliteral root" الجَذْر الثُّلاثِي), four root consonants (called "quadriliteral root" الجَذْر الرُّباعِي), and five root consonants (called "quinqueliteral root" الجَذْر الخُماسِي :):

Table 2.1

"he studies"	*yadrusu*	يَدْرُسُ	d-r-s	د - ر - س	الثُّلاثِي triliteral
"a man"	*rajul*	رَجُل	r-j-l	ر - ج - ل	الثُّلاثِي triliteral
"beautiful"	*jamiil*	جَميل	j-m-l	ج - م - ل	الثُّلاثِي triliteral
"in the morning"	*SabaaHan*	صَباحاً	S-b-H	ص - ب - ح	الثُّلاثِي triliteral
"he rolled"	*daHraja*	دَحْرَجَ	d-H-r-j	د - ح - ر - ج	الرُّباعِي quadriliteral
"a penny"	*dirham*	دِرْهَم	d-r-h-m	د - ر - هـ - م	الرُّباعِي quadriliteral
"a translator"	*mutarjim*	مُتَرْجِم	t-r-j-m	ت - ر - ج - م	الرُّباعِي quadriliteral
"quince"	*safarjal*	سَفَرْجَل	s-f-r-j-l	س - ف - ر - ج - ل	الخُماسِي quinqueliteral
"false"	*khuzaᶜbil*	خُزَعْبِل	kh-z-ᶜ-b-l	خ - ز - ع - ب - ل	الخُماسِي quinqueliteral

There is also a small subset of words consisting of fewer than three root consonants which, instead, may consist of one or two consonants with one or two vowels. Such words include a few connectors, a few prepositions, a few question words, and a few negation particles. Table 2.2 shows examples of words consisting of fewer than three consonant roots:

Table 2.2

Word			Root / جذر	
"and"	*wa*	وَ	w	و
"then"	*fa*	فَ	f	ف
"in"	*fii*	في	f-ii	ف - ي
"with"	*maʿa*	مَعَ	m-ʿ	م - ع
"about"	*ʿan*	عَنْ	ʿ-n	ع - ن
"who"	*man*	مَنْ	m-n	م - ن
"how many"	*kam*	كَمْ	k-m	ك - م
"will not"	*lan*	لَنْ	l-n	ل - ن
"did not"	*lam*	لَمْ	l-m	ل - م

In the eighth century Arab grammarians came up with an ingenious way or scale of representing this relationship between the root and the pattern, to make word meanings and patterns easier to learn. To represent the root consonants, they came up with three consonants which they used as variables in the following order: ف - ع - ل / f - ʿ -l. Then, any non-root letters (including consonants and vowels) are added according to the pattern of the word while keeping the sequence of the variable letters. Thus, for example, the ف - ع - ل pattern of the examples (1)–(3) above can be captured as in examples (4)–(6), as follows:

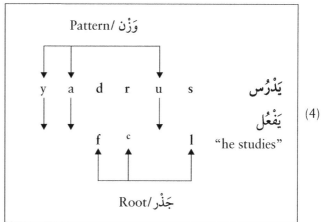

يَدْرُس
يَفْعُل (4)
"he studies"

يَفْعُل is a present-tense pattern.

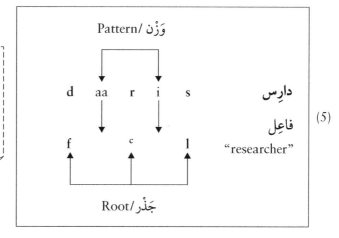

دارِس
فاعِل (5)
"researcher"

فاعِل is a "doer" pattern equivalent to the English suffix {-er} when attached to the verb in English.

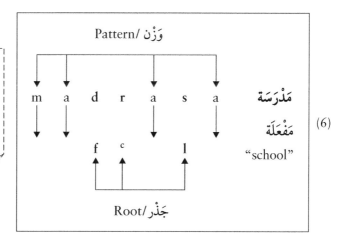

مَدْرَسَة
مَفْعَلَة (6)
"school"

مَفْعَلَة is a noun of place pattern; i.e., a place where the act of studying takes place.

Thus, the ف - ع - ل pattern of يَدْرُس *yadrus* "he studies" is يَفْعُل *yaf ʿul*, of دارِس *daaris* "researcher" is فاعِل *faa ʿil*, and of مَدْرَسَة *madrasa* "school" is مَفْعَلَة *maf ʿala*.

As mentioned above, there is a large number of patterns, such as يَفْعُل *yaf ʿul*, فاعِل *faa ʿil*, and مَفْعَلَة *maf ʿala*, but it is only useful to learn certain patterns. In this chapter, as well as in subsequent ones, patterns making up words (including verbs, nouns, and adjectives) that are useful to learn will be discussed in detail, and over the course of the book it will be possible to tease apart root consonants from non-consonants and vowels (see Appendix D for rules on reducing the word to its essential root, which is necessary for looking up words in root-based Arabic dictionaries).

Beyond the two basic components of Arabic words, root and pattern, Arabic words exhibit other basic markings, such as gender and number. These are discussed in the sections immediately below.

2.2 Gender الجِنْس

Verbs, nouns, and adjectives are marked for gender: masculine and feminine. Pronouns are also marked for masculine and feminine gender (see Chapter 5). All other parts of speech, such as prepositions, adverbs, question words, negation particles, conditional particles, and other particles, are not marked for gender. The gender distinction can sometimes be *natural*, referring to humans and animals with biological gender traits as males and females, or *grammatical*, when referring to inanimate objects that exhibit no biological gender traits and which are marked in Arabic as masculine or feminine. Verbs are marked for gender in distinct ways from nouns and adjectives, as explained in the sections below.

2.2.1 Gender in Verbs

Arabic verbs are marked for masculine and feminine gender either by means of a prefix or a suffix or both, depending on whether the verb is in the present or past tense. Specifically, the masculine–feminine distinction is marked in the second-person singular, second-person plural, third-person singular, third-person dual, and third-person plural (for more on verbs, see Chapter 13). Tables 2.3–2.4 display all the gender markings of all the conjugated verb forms. The example given here is the verb يَدْرُس "he studies" and دَرَسَ "he studied" in the present and past tense, respectively.

Table 2.3

Plural feminine	Plural masculine	Dual feminine	Dual masculine	Singular feminine	Singular masculine	Person
يَدْرُسْنَ ya-drus-na "they all F study"	يَدْرُسُونَ ya-drus-uuna "they all M study"	تَدْرُسَانِ ta-drus-aani "they both F study"	يَدْرُسَانِ ya-drus-aani "they both M study"	تَدْرُسُ ta-drusu "she studies"	يَدْرُسُ ya-drusu "he studies"	3rd
تَدْرُسْنَ ta-drus-na "you all F study"	تَدْرُسُونَ ta-drus-uuna "you all M study"	تَدْرُسَانِ ta-drus-aani "you both study"		تَدْرُسِينَ ta-drus-iina "you F study"	تَدْرُسُ ta-drusu "you M study"	2nd
نَدْرُسُ na-drusu "we study"				أَدْرُسُ 'a-drusu "I study"		1st

Table 2.4

Plural feminine	Plural masculine	Dual feminine	Dual masculine	Singular feminine	Singular masculine	Person
دَرَسْنَ daras-na "they all F studied"	دَرَسُوا daras-uu "they all M studied"	دَرَسَتَا daras-ataa "they both F studied"	دَرَسَا daras-aa "they both M studied"	دَرَسَتْ daras-at "she studied"	دَرَسَ daras-a "he studied"	3rd
دَرَسْتُنَّ daras-tunna "you all F studied"	دَرَسْتُم daras-tum "you all M studied"	دَرَسْتُمَا daras-tumaa "you both studied"		دَرَسْتِ daras-ti "you F studied"	دَرَسْتَ daras-ta "you M studied"	2nd
دَرَسْنا daras-naa "we studied"				دَرَسْتُ daras-tu "I studied"		1st

As can be seen from Tables 2.3–2.4, verbs are marked for the masculine or feminine gender except for the first-person singular, first-person plural, and second-person dual in both past and present tenses.

Note: The third-person singular feminine form of the verb in the present tense is identical to that of the second-person singular masculine, and so is the third-person dual feminine to that of the second-person dual (masculine and feminine).

2.2.2 Gender in Nouns

Not unlike verbs, Arabic nouns are marked for masculine or feminine gender. Gender markings in nouns are either natural (biological) or grammatical. Natural gender refers to the natural assignment of gender (masculine and feminine) to words according to the biological distinction of humans and animals as males and females, whereas grammatical gender refers to the assignment of masculine or feminine gender to words whose referents may not exhibit any apparent reason for the distinction. Accordingly, nouns in Arabic fall into one of two categories: masculine or feminine. In other words, a human, animal, or thing/object/entity is treated as either "he" or "she" (for more on nouns, see Chapter 14). Arabic does not exhibit neutral gender, such as the English "it." Below are some examples:

Natural Gender:

إِنْسانَة	إِنْسان
'insaan-a	*'insaan*
"a female human"	"a male human"

كَلْبَة	كَلْب
kalb-a	*kalb*
"a female dog"	"a male dog"

Grammatical gender:

مَكْتَبَة	مَكْتَب
maktab-a	*maktab*
"a library F"	"an office M"

However, feminine words need not be derived from the masculine forms, especially in (non-human) animals and inanimate objects, as in the following examples:

Natural Gender:

بَقَرَة	ثَوْر
baqar-a	*thawr*
"a cow"	"a bull"

ناقَة	جَمَل
naaq-a	*jamal*
"a female camel"	"a male camel"

Grammatical gender:

طاوِلَة	كُرْسِيّ
Taawil-a	*kursiyy*
"a table F."	"a chair M"

In the vast majority of Arabic nouns, a word is marked for the feminine gender by use of the suffix {-a} تاء مَرْبوطَة *taa' marbuuTa* ـَة (usually pronounced [a], as explained in the previous chapter) and for the masculine gender by absence of this suffix (as shown in the examples above).

However, there are three small sub-classes of nouns that deviate somewhat from this rule:

(A)   a small sub-class of animals that exhibit the feminine ending {-a} where the gender may not be immediately evident. Such words can be used as feminine or masculine, depending on the intended (natural) gender of the animal, such as:

حَيَّة	بَطَّة	حَمامَة	نَحْلَة	جَرادَة	بومَة
Hayy-a	*baTT-a*	*Hamaam-a*	*naHl-a*	*jaraad-a*	*buum-a*
"a snake"	"a duck"	"a pigeon"	"a bee"	"a grasshopper"	"an owl"

(B)   a small sub-class of nouns that do not exhibit the feminine gender suffix but can be used as either feminine or masculine, such as:

روح	طَريق	سوق	سِكّين	خَمْر	فَرَس
ruuH	*Tariiq*	*suuq*	*sikkiin*	*khamr*	*faras*
"spirit"	"road"	"market"	"knife"	"wine"	"horse"

(C)   two extremely common feminine nouns that end with a suffix {-t}
تاء مَبْسوطة rather than {-a} : تاء مَرْبوطَة

بِنْت	أُخْت
bin-t	*'ukh-t*
"a girl"	"a sister"

There are two other feminine suffixes not quite different in principle from {-*a*}. (Remember: the masculine form is always signaled by the default or bare-stem form; i.e., the lack of any additional suffix beyond the bare essentials of the root and pattern.) These are أَلِف التَّأْنيث المَقْصورة *'alif 'at-ta'niith 'al-maqSuura* {-*aa*} ى and *'al-'alif 'al-mamduuda* with *hamza* {-*aa'*} ء اء ; the latter is referred to as أَلِف التَّأْنيث المَمْدودَة *'alif 'at-ta'niith 'al-mamduuda*, as in the following words:

أُنْثى	عَصا	حُمَّى	مُنى	لَيْلى
'unth-aa	*ʿaS-aa*	*Humm-aa*	*mun-aa*	*layl-aa*
"a female F"	"a stick F"	"a fever F"	"Mona"	"Layla"

صَحْراء	خُنْفُساء	حَسْناء	هَيْفاء	حَمْراء
SaHr-aa'	*khunfus-aa'*	*Hasn-aa'*	*hayf-aa'*	*Hamr-aa'*
"a desert F"	"a ladybug F"	"pretty one F"	"Hayfaa'"	"red F"

Note: To be treated as feminine, a word ending with the suffix *'alif 'at-ta'niith 'al-mamduuda* {-*aa'*} should consist of three root consonants or more in addition to the suffix {-*aa'*}. Otherwise, such words are usually masculine, such as ماء *maa'* "water M," داء *daa'* "an epidemic M," and دَواء *dawaa'* "medicine M."

In addition, a conventional use of the feminine marking is exhibited in some words referring to body parts. Although some body parts do not end with a feminine marking, they are treated as feminine. The general rule is that body parts that have a pair are treated as feminine. The following words all behave as feminine words since each is part of a pair, as opposed to, for example, رَأْس *ra's* "head M," لِسان *lisaan* "tongue M," ظَهْر *dhahr* "back M," and بَطْن *baTn* "abdomen M," which behave as masculine nouns, since there is only one such body part:

عَيْن	أُذُن	سِنّ	كَتِف	ذِراع
ʿayn	*'udhun*	*sin*	*katif*	*dhiraaʿ*
"an eye F"	"an ear F"	"a tooth F"	"a shoulder F"	"an arm F"

يَد	فَخِذ	ساق	رِجْل	قَدَم
yad	*fakhidh*	*saaq*	*rijl*	*qadam*
"a hand F"	"a thigh F"	"lower leg F"	"a leg F"	"a foot F"

Note: There are a few exceptions to this rule, such as عَضُد *'aDud* "upper arm" and ساعِد *saa'id* "forearm," both of which are treated as masculine, although they belong to a pair.

In addition, the names of countries are treated as feminine. Although many country names may or may not end with a feminine suffix, they all refer to the word أَرْض *'arD* "land," which is feminine, such as the following:

(أَرْض) ليبيا	(أَرْض) سوريَّة	(أَرْض) مِصر
('arD) liibyaa	*('arD) suuriyya*	*('arD) miSr*
"(the land F of) Libya F"	"(the land F of) Syria F"	"(the land F of) Egypt F"

(أَرْض) كَنَدا	(أَرْض) نيجيريا	(أَرْض) الصين
('arD) kanadaa	*('arD) niijiiryaa*	*('arD) 'aS-Siin*
"(the land F of) Canada F"	"(the land F of) Nigeria F"	"(the land F of) China F"

This applies to non-Arabic as well as Arabic countries, except for the following names, which are treated as masculine:

العراق	لُبْنان	السُّودان
'al-'iraaq	*lubnaan*	*'as-suudaan*
"Iraq M"	"Lebanon M"	"Sudan M"

المَغْرِب	اليَمَن	الأُرْدُنّ
'al-maghrib	*'al-yaman*	*'al-'urdunn*
"Morocco M"	"Yemen M"	"Jordan M"

However, when modified in a sentence by the word بَلَد *balad* "country," which is masculine, names of countries are treated as masculine, as the following examples show:

مِصر غَنيَّة بالآثار.

"(The land F of) Egypt F is rich F with ruins."

مِصر بَلَد غَنيّ بالآثار.

"Egypt M is a rich M country M with ruins."

Similarly, names of cities are treated as feminine, since the words that they refer to, مَدينَة *madiina* "city" and بَلْدَة *balda* "town," are feminine in Arabic (both ending with the *taa' marbuuTa*), such as the following examples:

مَدينَة) واشِنطون)	مَدينَة) طَنْجَة)	مَدينَة) بَغْداد)
waashinTun	*Tanja*	*baghdaad*
"(city of) Washington F"	"(city of) Tangier F"	"(city of) Baghdad F"

Finally, note that not all words that end with *taa' marbuuTa* are words marked for the feminine gender. A very small sub-class of plural masculine words may end with *taa' marbuuTa*, as in the following examples:

"male teachers"	*'asaatidh-a*	أَساتِذَة	←	"a male teacher"	*'ustaadh*	أُسْتاذ
"misters"	*saad-a*	سادَة	←	"mister"	*sayyid*	سَيِّد
"brothers"	*'ikhw-a*	إِخْوَة	←	"a brother"	*'akh*	أَخ

A notable exception to the suffix gender rules explained above is a small sub-class of words which are treated as feminine even though they do not exhibit any gender marking, as in the following words:

نَفْس	نار	حَرْب	جَهَنَّم	أَرْض	شَمْس
nafs	*naar*	*Harb*	*jahannam*	*'arD*	*shams*
"self F"	"fire F"	"war F"	"Hell F"	"Earth F"	"sun F"

فَأْس	بِئْر	يَمين	شِمال	كَأْس	دار
fa's	*bi'r*	*yamiin*	*shimaal*	*ka's*	*daar*
"ax F"	"well F"	"right hand F"	"left hand F"	"glass F"	"house F"

Note: Other synonymous words for "cup" and "house" are كوب *kuub* "cup" and بَيْت *bayt* "house" and are treated as masculine.

Another notable exception includes some proper names in Arabic that have a masculine ending but are used as female names, and some proper names that end with a feminine suffix used as male names, as in the following examples:

زَيْنَب	سُعاد	هِنْد	حَمْزَة	أُسَامَة	يَحْيَى
zaynab	*su'aad*	*hind*	*Hamz-a*	*'usaam-a*	*yaHy-aa*
"Zaynab F"	"Suad F"	"Hind F"	"Hamza M"	"Usama M"	"John M"

Similarly, not all words that end with an *'alif maqSuura* {-aa} or *'alif mamduuda* with hamza {-aa'} are treated as feminine. A small sub-class of plural masculine words may also end with *'alif maqSuura* or *'alif mamduuda* with hamza, as in the following examples:

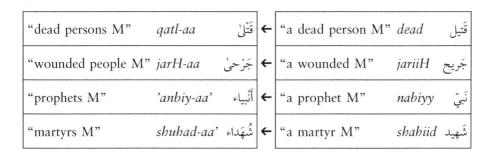

"dead persons M"	*qatl-aa*	قَتْلَى	←	"a dead person M" *dead*	قَتيل
"wounded people M"	*jarH-aa*	جَرْحَى	←	"a wounded M" *jariiH*	جَريح
"prophets M"	*'anbiy-aa'*	أَنْبِيَاء	←	"a prophet M" *nabiyy*	نَبِيّ
"martyrs M"	*shuhad-aa'* شُهَدَاء		←	"a martyr M" *shahiid*	شَهيد

Finally, derived words (i.e., words consisting of more than three root consonants) such as nouns of place (see 14.5) and passive participles (see 14.4) may end with an *'alif maqSuura* {-aa} but are treated as masculine by default (e.g., مَقْهى *maqhaa* "café M" and مُصْطَفى *muSTafaa* "chosen one M" as opposed to مُصْطَفاة *muSTafaat* "chosen one F."

2.2.3 Gender in Adjectives

Like nouns, adjectives are marked for masculine or feminine gender, which may be either natural (biological) or grammatical. Adjectives are characterized by similar grammatical regularity with respect to gender markings, exhibiting the same types of gender suffixes as nouns. Thus, adjectives can be marked for the feminine gender by means of التّاء المَرْبوطَة *'at-taa' 'al-marbuuTa* {-a}, أَلِف التَّأْنيث المَقْصورة *'alif 'at-ta'niith 'al-maqSuura* {-aa}, and أَلِف التَّأْنيث المَمْدودَة *'alif 'at-ta'niith 'alif 'al-mamduuda* (with hamza) {-aa'} suffixes and for the masculine gender by the absence of any of these endings (for more on adjectives, see Chapter 15).

The vast majority of Arabic adjectives are marked for the feminine gender with the تاء مَرْبوطَة *taa' marbuuTa* {-a} feminine suffix, as illustrated by the following words:

كَبيرَة	كَبير	كَريمَة	كَريم
kabiir-a	*kabiir*	*kariim-a*	*kariim*
"big F"	"big M"	"generous F"	"generous M"

مَرِحَة	مَرِح	قَلِقَة	قَلِق
mariH-a	*mariH*	*qaliq-a*	*qaliq*
"joyful F"	"joyful M"	"worried F"	"worried M"

In addition, certain adjectives are feminine by default, depending on the noun they are used to qualify. Therefore, words for languages are all feminine, since the noun they qualify, لُغَة *lugh-a* "language," is feminine in Arabic (ending with a *taa' marbuuTa*). Below are some examples:

(اللُّغَة) الإسْبانيَّة	(اللُّغَة) الإنْجِليزيَّة	(اللُّغَة) العَرَبيَّة
'al-'isbaaniyy-a	*'al-'injiliiziyy-a*	*'al-ʿarabiyy-a*
"the Spanish language F"	"the English language F"	"the Arabic language F"

A sub-class of Arabic adjectives are marked for the feminine gender by means of the الأَلِف المَقْصورة *'al-'alif 'al-maqSuura* {-aa} suffix, especially those having the pattern فُعْلَى *fuʿlaa*, as in the following examples:

عُظْمَى	فُضْلَى	مُثْلَى	حُبْلَى
ʿuZm-aa	*fuDl-aa*	*muthl-aa*	*Hubl-aa*
"greatest F"	"best F"	"ideal F"	"pregnant F"

صُغْرَى	كُبْرَى	قُصْوَى	دُنْيا
Sughr-aa	*kubr-aa*	*quSw-aa*	*duny-aa*
"smallest F"	"biggest F"	"highest F"	"worldly F"

Another small sub-class of Arabic adjectives are marked for the feminine gender by means of the الأَلِف المَقْصورة *'al-'alif 'al-maqSuura* {-aa} suffix. The masculine forms of such adjectives have the pattern فَعْلان *faʿlaan* so that the feminine version of this pattern is, by default, فَعْلَى *faʿlaa'*. However, a modern accepted MSA trend is to mark such forms as feminine by the التّاء المَرْبوطَة *'at-taa' 'al-marbuuTa* {-a} suffix, as illustrated in the following examples:

<table>
<tr><td></td><td></td><td>فَعْلىٰ</td><td>فَعْلان</td></tr>
<tr><td>عَطْشانَة</td><td>=</td><td>عَطْشىٰ</td><td>عَطْشان</td></tr>
<tr><td>ʿaTshaan-a</td><td></td><td>ʿaTsh-aa</td><td>ʿaTshaan</td></tr>
<tr><td>"thirsty F"</td><td></td><td>"thirsty F"</td><td>"thirsty M"</td></tr>
<tr><td>سَكْرانَة</td><td>=</td><td>سَكْرىٰ</td><td>سَكْران</td></tr>
<tr><td>sakraan-a</td><td></td><td>sakr-aa</td><td>sakraan</td></tr>
<tr><td>"drunk F"</td><td></td><td>"drunk F"</td><td>"drunk M"</td></tr>
</table>

A third small sub-class of Arabic adjectives, including adjectives of color and bodily defects/beauties, are marked for the feminine gender by means of the أَلِف التَّأْنِيث المَمْدودَة *'alif 'at-ta'niith 'al-mamduuda* (with hamza) {-aa'} suffix. The masculine forms of such adjectives have the pattern أَفْعَل *'afʿal* so that the feminine version of this pattern is, by default, فَعْلاء *faʿlaa'*, as illustrated in the following examples:

<table>
<tr><td>فَعْلاء</td><td>أَفْعَل</td><td>فَعْلاء</td><td>أَفْعَل</td></tr>
<tr><td>حَمْراء</td><td>أَحْمَر</td><td>صَفْراء</td><td>أَصْفَر</td></tr>
<tr><td>Hamr-aa'</td><td>'aHmar</td><td>Safr-aa'</td><td>'aSfar</td></tr>
<tr><td>"red F"</td><td>"red M"</td><td>"yellow F"</td><td>"yellow M"</td></tr>
<tr><td>عَرْجاء</td><td>أَعْرَج</td><td>صَلْعاء</td><td>أَصْلَع</td></tr>
<tr><td>ʿarj-aa'</td><td>'aʿraj</td><td>Salʿ-aa'</td><td>'aSlaʿ</td></tr>
<tr><td>"limping F"</td><td>"limping M"</td><td>"bald-headed F"</td><td>"bald-headed M"</td></tr>
</table>

An exception to the rules above is a small sub-class of adjectives that do not exhibit the feminine gender marking, since they are restrictively female adjectives. The following are the most common of these:

<table>
<tr><td>حامِل</td><td>حائِض</td><td>طالِق</td><td>طامِث</td><td>مُرْضِع</td></tr>
<tr><td>Haamil</td><td>Haa'iD</td><td>Taaliq</td><td>Taamith</td><td>murDiʿ</td></tr>
<tr><td>"pregnant"</td><td>"menstruating"</td><td>"divorced"</td><td>"menstruating"</td><td>"nursing mother"</td></tr>
</table>

although such words are also acceptable MSA words if marked by the feminine *taa' marbuuTa* {-a} suffix, as follows:

<table>
<tr><td>حامِلَة</td><td>حائِضَة</td><td>طالِقَة</td><td>طامِثَة</td><td>مُرْضِعَة</td></tr>
<tr><td>Haamil-a</td><td>Haa'iD-a</td><td>Taaliq-a</td><td>Taamith-a</td><td>murDiʿ-a</td></tr>
<tr><td>"pregnant"</td><td>"menstruating"</td><td>"divorced"</td><td>"menstruating"</td><td>"nursing mother"</td></tr>
</table>

Finally, it is worthy of note here that the تاء مَرْبوطَة *taa' marbuuTa* {-a}
suffix can occur with certain adjectives for emphasis, having nothing to
do with the masculine–feminine gender distinction. In this case, such
words can be used for the feminine or masculine, for example:

رَحّالَة   ←   رَحّال

raHHaal-a   *raHHaal*

"widely traveled M/F"   "traveler M"

راوِيَة   ←   راوي

raawiy-a   *raawii*

"consummate narrator M/F"   "narrator M"

عَلّامَة   ←   عالِم

ᶜallaam-a   *ᶜaalim*

"knowledgeable scholar M/F"   "scholar M"

2.3 Number العَدَد

In addition to gender, Arabic verbs, nouns, and adjectives are marked
for number: singular (i.e., for one person/thing), dual (i.e., for two
persons/things), and plural (i.e., for three or more persons/things). Pronouns are also marked for these number features; they are explained
in Chapter 5.

2.3.1 The Dual المُثَنّى

Verbs are marked for the dual number feature by means of the suffix
{-aa} [ا] for the third-person past tense, {-aani} [انِ] for the second-
and third-person present tense, and {-tumaa} [تُما] for the second-person
past tense. Naturally, there is no dual marking for the first person (see
Tables 2.3–2.4 above).

As for nouns and adjectives, the dual number is conflated with case.
As explained in Chapter 1, case in Arabic has three forms: مَرْفوع nominative, مَنْصوب accusative, and مَجْرور genitive (for more on case, see Chapter 22). Thus, there are two dual endings that appear on Arabic nouns
and adjectives: انِ {āni} in the nominative and َيْنِ {-ayni} in the accusative
and genitive; the latter two are conflated together, as shown in the
masculine and feminine examples (of nouns and adjectives) below:

Dual acc / مَنْصوب and gen / مَجْرور	Dual nom / مَرْفوع	Singular
مُدَرِّسَيْنِ *mudarris-ayni* "two teachers M"	مُدَرِّسانِ *mudarris-aani* "two teachers M"	مُدَرِّس *mudarris* "one teacher M"
مُدَرِّسَتَيْنِ *mudarrisat-ayni* "two teachers F"	مُدَرِّسَتانِ *mudarrisat-aani* "two teachers F"	مُدَرِّسَة *mudarris-a* "one teacher F"
كَبيرَيْنِ *kabiir-ayni* "big DM"	كَبيرانِ *kabiir-aani* "big DM"	كَبير *kabiir* "big SM"
كَبيرَتَيْنِ *kabiirat-ayni* "big DF"	كَبيرَتانِ *kabiirat-aani* "big DF"	كَبيرَة *kabiir-a* "big SF"

The dual suffix follows a watertight rule (i.e., with hardly any exceptions) in the Arabic language for both nouns and adjectives. However, there are certain cases where certain words undergo an assimilation (i.e., change) word finally before the dual suffix is attached. These include: the three kinship terms أب *'ab* "father," أخ *'akh* "brother," and حَم *Ham* "father/brother-in-law"; words ending with أَلِف التَّأْنيث المَمْدودة *'alif 'at-ta'niith 'al-mamduuda* (with hamza) {-aa'}; and words ending with الأَلِف المَقْصورَة *'al-'alif 'al-maqSuura* {-aa}, as in the examples below.

First, when changing any of the three kinship terms into the dual, the vowels [a–w] must be inserted in word final position, as in the following (see also 14.10):

Dual acc / مَنْصوب and gen / مَجْرور	Dual nom / مَرْفوع	Singular
أَبَوَيْنِ *'ab-a-w-ayni* "two fathers"	أَبَوانِ *'ab-a-w-aani* "two fathers"	أب *'ab* "father"
أَخَوَيْنِ *'akh-a-w-ayni* "two brothers"	أَخَوانِ *'akh-a-w-aani* "two brothers"	أخ *'akh* "brother"

حَمَوَيْنِ	حَمَوانِ	حَم
Ham-a-w-ayni	*Ham-a-w-aani*	Ham
"two fathers-in-law"	"two fathers-in-law"	"father-in-law"

Second, when changing a noun or adjective ending with the *'alif 'at-ta'niith 'al-mamduuda* {-aa'} suffix into the dual, the *hamza* "glottal stop" ['] assimilates/changes into [w], as in:

Dual acc / مَنْصوب and gen / مَجْرور	*Dual nom / مَرْفوع*	*Singular*
صَحْراوَيْنِ	صَحْراوانِ	صَحْراء
SaHr-aa-w-ayni	*SaHr-aa-w-aani*	*SaHr-aa'*
"two deserts F"	"two deserts F"	"a desert F"
حَسْناوَيْنِ	حَسْناوانِ	حَسْناء
Hasn-aa-w-ayni	*Hasn-aa-w-aani*	*Hasn-aa'*
"two pretty ones F"	"two pretty ones F"	"pretty one F"

This rule applies only to feminine words whose feminine suffix *'alif 'at-ta'niith 'al-mamduuda* {-aa'} is not part of the (usually triliteral) root consonants. Hence, the following words follow the dual rule without any changes to the *hamza* occurring at the end of each word, since the *hamza* in these words is part of the (triliteral) root consonants:

Dual acc / مَنْصوب and gen / مَجْرور	*Dual nom / مَرْفوع*	*Singular*
ماءَيْنِ	ماءانِ	ماء
maa'-ayni	*maa'-aani*	*maa'*
"two waters M"	"two waters M"	"a water M"
داءَيْنِ	داءانِ	داء
daa'-ayni	*daa'-aani*	*daa'*
"two diseases M"	"two diseases M"	"a disease M"
دواءَيْنِ	دَواءانِ	دَواء
dawaa'-ayni	*dawaa'-aani*	*dawaa'*
"two medicines M"	"two medicines M"	"a medicine M"

Third, when changing a noun or adjective ending with *'alif maqSuura* {-aa} into the dual, three sub-rules are observed, depending on whether the word is derived or non-derived:

(A) If a word is derived (i.e., consists of more than three root consonants), then the *'alif maqSuura* {-aa} changes into the vowel sequence [a–y], as in the following (see also Chapters 14–15 for more on derived nouns and adjectives):

Dual acc / مَنْصوب *and gen /* مَجْرور	*Dual nom /* مَرْفوع	*Singular*
مُصْطَفَيَيْنِ	مُصْطَفَيانِ	مُصْطَفى
muSTaf-a-y-ayni	*muSTaf-a-y-aani*	*muSTaf-aa*
"two chosen ones M"	"two chosen ones M"	"chosen one M"
مَقْهَيَيْنِ	مَقْهَيانِ	مَقْهى
maqh-a-y-ayni	*maqh-a-y-aani*	*maqh-aa*
"two cafés M"	"two cafés M"	"café M"
حُبْلَيَيْنِ	حُبْلَيانِ	حُبْلى
Hubl-a-y-ayni	*Hubl-a-y-aani*	*Hubl-aa*
"two pregnant ones F"	"two pregnant ones F"	"pregnant F"

(B) If a word is non-derived (i.e., consists of only three root consonants) but the underlying root consonant of the *'alif maqSuura* {-aa} is [ii], then the *'alif maqSuura* {-aa} changes into the vowel sequence [a–y], as in the following words:

Dual acc / مَنْصوب *and gen /* مَجْرور	*Dual nom /* مَرْفوع	*Singular*
فَتَيَيْنِ	فَتَيانِ	فَتى
fat-a-y-ayni	*fat-a-y-aani*	*fat-aa*
"two young men M"	"two young men M"	"young man"
هُدَيَيْنِ	هُدَيانِ	هُدى
hud-a-y-ayni	*hud-a-y-aani*	*hud-aa*
"two Hodas F"	"two Hodas F"	"Hoda F"

(C)   If a word is non-derived (i.e., consists of only three root consonants) but the underlying root consonant of the *'alif maqSuura* {-aa} is [uu], then the *'alif maqSuura* {-aa} changes into the vowel sequence [a–w], as in the following words:

Dual acc / مَنْصوب and gen / مَجْرور	Dual nom / مَرْفوع	Singular
عَصَوَيْن	عَصَوانِ	عَصا
ᶜaS-a-w-ayni	*ᶜaS-a-w-aani*	*ᶜaS-aa*
"two sticks F"	"two sticks F"	"a stick F"
قَفَوَيْن	قَفَوانِ	قَفا
qaf-a-w-ayni	*qaf-a-w-aani*	*qaf-aa*
"two backs of the neck M"	"two backs of the neck M"	"back of the neck M"

Note: The *'alif* [aa], whether in final or medial word position, is never a root consonant. When a word or root appears to consist of two consonants and an *'alif*, then the *'alif* is underlyingly either a *yaa'* [ii] or a *waaw* [uu] (see Appendix D for rules on reducing the word to its root).

Although a few changes are involved in the dual suffix (at the end of words) before it is attached to the noun or adjective, the dual suffix itself remains unchanged in all cases so that it remains distinct from other types of endings.

2.3.2   The Plural الجَمْع

Arabic verbs are also marked for the plural with respect to the first- and second-person masculine and feminine, and the third-person masculine and feminine (see Tables 2.3–2.4 above). As for nouns and adjectives, there are two main types of plural markings: the irregular or *broken* plural and the regular or *sound* plural. The former is a much larger class than the latter. The regular plural has distinct markings for the plural masculine (hence the name *sound masculine plural*) and the plural feminine (hence the name *sound feminine plural*), whereas no such distinct feminine or masculine markings for the irregular plural exist. In the *broken* plural, it is as if the word were broken from the middle, with resulting changes to the vowels of the word from within.

2.3.2.1 *Regular/Sound Plural Masculine* جَمْع المُذَكَّر السّالِم

Like dual markings, the markings of the regular or *sound masculine plural* جَمْع المُذَكَّر السّالِم *jamᶜ ’al-mudhakkar ’as-saalim* on nouns and adjectives are conflated with case endings. Accordingly, there are two sound plural endings: ونَ {-*uuna*} for the nominative مَرْفوع and ينَ {-*iina*} for the accusative مَنْصوب and genitive مَجْرور (for more on case, see Chapter 22). The most useful rules of the sound plural masculine to remember include:

(A)   the plural of human proper names:

Plural acc / مَنْصوب and gen / مَجْرور	*Plural nom* / مَرْفوع	*Singular*
مُحَمَّدينَ *muHammad-**iina*** "Muhammads M"	مُحَمَّدونَ *muHammad-**uuna*** "Muhammads M"	مُحَمَّد *muHammad* "Muhammad M"
سَليمينَ *saliim-**iina*** "Salims M"	سَليمونَ *saliim-**uuna*** "Salims M"	سَليم *saliim* "Salim M"

(B)   adjectives denoting human attributes:

Plural acc / مَنْصوب and gen / مَجْرور	*Plural nom* / مَرْفوع	*Singular*
قَلِقينَ *qaliq-**iina*** "worried ones M"	قَلِقونَ *qaliq-**uuna*** "worried ones M"	قَلِق *qaliq* "worried M"
طَيِّبينَ *Tayyib-**iina*** "good-hearted ones M"	طَيِّبونَ *Tayyib-**uuna*** "good-hearted ones M"	طَيِّب *Tayyib* "good-hearted M"

(C)   derived words denoting human attributes, such as active participles, passive participles, and the comparative form having the أَفْعَل *’af ᶜala* pattern (for more on participles and the comparative form, see Chapters 14–15):

Plural acc / مَنْصوب and gen / مَجْرور	Plural nom / مَرْفوع	Singular
قاتِلينَ	قاتِلونَ	قاتِل
qaatil-**iina**	qaatil-**uuna**	qaatil
"killers M"	"killers M"	"killer M"
مَقْتولينَ	مَقْتولونَ	مَقْتول
maqtuul-**iina**	maqtuul-**uuna**	maqtuul
"killed ones M"	"killed ones M"	"killed M"
أَكْرَمينَ	أَكْرَمونَ	أَكْرَم
'akram-**iina**	'akram-**uuna**	'akram
"more generous ones M"	"more generous ones M"	"more generous"

Usually, and as evident in the above examples, the addition of the regular masculine plural suffix forces no changes to the word. However, there are certain cases where certain derived words, such as active and passive participles (see Chapters 14–15 for more on derived nouns and adjectives), undergo assimilation/change word finally before the regular masculine plural suffix is attached. These include words ending with the أَلِف مَقْصورة *'alif maqSuura* {-aa} and (defective) words ending with *yaa'* [ii], as follows:

(A)   The أَلِف مَقْصورة *'alif maqSuura* {-aa} suffix shortens to a *fatHa* [a] and, as a result, the long vowel of the plural masculine suffix changes into [w] in the nominative مَرْفوع and [y] in the accusative مَنْصوب and genitive مَجْرور (i.e., {aa-uuna} → {a-wna} and {aa-iina} → {a-yna}, respectively), as in:

Plural acc / مَنْصوب and gen / مَجْرور	Plural nom / مَرْفوع	Singular
مُصْطَفَيْنَ	مُصْطَفَوْنَ	مُصْطَفىٰ
muSTaf-a-**yna**	muSTaf-a-**wna**	muSTaf-aa
"chosen ones M"	"chosen ones M"	"chosen one M"

مُسْتَثْنَيْنَ	مُسْتَثْنَوْنَ	مُسْتَثْنَى
mustathn-a-yna	*mustathn-a-wna*	*mustathn-aa*
"excepted ones M"	"excepted ones M"	"excepted one M"

(B) The *yaa'* {-*ii*} suffix is dropped before the regular plural masculine suffix is attached, as in:

Plural acc / مَنْصوب and gen / مَجْرور	Plural nom / مَرْفوع	Singular
القاضِينَ	القاضُونَ	القاضِي
'al-qaaD-iina	*'al-qaaD-uuna*	*'al-qaaD-ii*
"the judges M"	"the judges M"	"the judge M"
المُدَّعينَ	المُدَّعونَ	المُدَّعي
'al-mudda^c-iina	*'al-mudda^c-uuna*	*'al-mudda^c-ii*
"the claimants M"	"the claimants M"	"the claimant M"

2.3.2.2 *Regular/Sound Plural Feminine* جَمْع المُؤَنَّث السّالِم

Unlike dual and sound masculine plural markings, the markings of the regular or sound feminine plural جَمْع المُؤَنَّث السّالِم *jam^c 'al-mu'annath 'as-saalim* on nouns and adjectives are not conflated with case. Accordingly, the sound feminine plural has one marking: ات {-*aat*}. The most useful rules of the sound feminine plural to remember include:

(A) the plural of human proper names (note: if the name ends with the singular feminine suffix *taa' marbuuTa* {-*a*}, then the singular feminine suffix is dropped):

Plural	Singular
عائِشات	عائِشة
^caa'ish-aat	*^caa'ish-a*
"Ayshas F"	"Aysha F"
هِنْدات	هِنْد
hind-aat	*hind*
"Hinds F"	"Hind F"

(B)   the plural of singular feminine words ending with the singular feminine suffix *taa' marbuuTa* {-a} (in this case, the singular feminine suffix is dropped):

Plural	Singular
أُسْتاذات	أُسْتاذَة
'ustaadh-aat	*'ustaadh-a*
"teachers F"	"a teacher F"
جامِعات	جامِعَة
jaamiᶜ-aat	*jaamiᶜ-a*
"universities F"	"a university F"
عَزيزات	عَزيزَة
ᶜaziiz-aat	*ᶜaziiz-a*
"dear ones F"	"dear F"

(C)   the plural of singular feminine words ending with the singular feminine suffix *'alif maqSuura* {-aa} (in this case, the singular feminine suffix *'alif maqSuura* is changed into an {a–y} vowel sequence):

Plural	Singular
ذِكْرَيات	ذِكْرىٰ
dhikr-a-y-aat	*dhikr-aa*
"memories F"	"a memory F"
كُبْرَيات	كُبْرىٰ
kubr-a-y-aat	*kubr-aa*
"biggest ones F"	"biggest F"

(D) the plural of singular feminine words ending with the singular feminine suffix *'alif 'at-ta'niith 'al-mamduuda* with hamza {-aa'} (in this case the "glottal stop" ['] of the suffix changes into [w]):

Plural	Singular
حَسْناوات	حَسْناء
Hasn-aa-w-aat	*Hasn-aa'*
"pretty ones F"	"a pretty one F"
حَمْراوات	حَمْراء
Hamr-aa-w-aat	*Hamr-aa'*
"red ones F"	"red F"

(E) the plural of the names of the letters of the alphabet:

Plural	Singular
أَلِفات	أَلِف
'alif-aat	*'alif*
"*alif* letters"	"a letter *'alif* M/F"
باءات	باء
baa'-aat	*baa'*
"*baa'* letters"	"a letter *baa'* M/F"
تاءات	تاء
taa'-aat	*taa'*
"*taa'* letters"	"a letter *taa'* M/F"

(F)   the plural of derived gerund/verbal nouns (for more on verbal nouns, see Chapter 14):

Plural	Derived singular gerund/verbal noun
تَدْريبات	تَدْريب
tadriib-aat	*tadriib*
"exercises"	"an exercise/exercising M"
إرْشادات	إرْشاد
'irshaad-aat	*'irshaad*
"directions"	"guidance/direction M"
اِسْتِخْدامات	اِسْتِخْدام
'istikhdaam-aat	*'istikhdaam*
"uses"	"a use M"

(G)   the plural of borrowed nouns and certain Arabic nouns:

Plural	Singular
رادارات	رادار
raadaar-aat	*raadaar*
"radars"	"a radar M"
كَرْنَفالات	كَرْنَفال
karnavaal-aat	*karnavaal*
"carnivals"	"a carnival M"
حَمّامات	حَمّام
Hammaam-aat	*Hammaam*
"bathrooms"	"a bathroom M"

2.3.2.3 *Irregular/Broken Plural* جَمْع التَّكْسير

Perhaps the single most important reason for the presence of the جَمْع التَّكْسير *jamᶜ 'at-taksiir* irregular/broken plural in Arabic is word length, since Arabic favors short word length. Although it can apply to words consisting of fewer than four letters (including triliteral roots), the broken plural most frequently occurs in words of four or more letters (especially quadriliteral and quinqueliteral roots). Such words would become rather long if the regular/sound plural suffix {-*uuna*}/{-*iina*} or regular/sound feminine suffix {-*aat*} were added. Hence, most such words undergo a change to the internal makeup of their vowels according to certain patterns while preserving the root consonants and their sequence within a word. Examples of broken plurals include the following:

(A) words with three letters:

Plural	Singular
جِبال	جَبَل
jibaal	*jabal*
"mountains"	"a mountain M"
أَرْجُل	رِجْل
'arjul	*rijl*
"legs"	"a leg F"

(B) words with four letters:

Plural	Singular
كُتُب	كِتاب
kutub	*kitaab*
"books"	"a book M"
أُسَر	أُسْرَة
'usar	*'usr-a*
"families"	"a family F"

(C) words with five letters:

Plural	Singular
صَناديق	صُنْدوق
Sanaadiiq	Sunduuq
"boxes"	"a box M"
مُدُن	مَدينَة
mudun	madiin-a
"cities"	"a city F"

(D) words with five and six letters (including words with five root consonants, in which case even the final root consonant is deleted to preserve word length):

Plural	Singular
سَفارِج	سَفَرْجَل
safaarij	safarjal
"quinces"	"a quince M"
عَنادِل	عَنْدَليب
ᶜaanadil	ᶜandaliib
"nightingales"	"a nightingale M"

(E) words that belong to اِسْم الجِنْس الجَمْعيّ "genus collective nouns" (referring to names of plants, insects, and animals) whose singular form is derived by simply adding the *taa' marbuuTa* feminine suffix {-a}:

Plural	Singular
حَبّ	حَبَّة
Habb	Habb-a
"seeds"	"a seed F"

شَجَر	شَجَرَة
shajar	shajar-a
"trees"	"a tree F"
نَمْل	نَمْلَة
naml	naml-a
"ants"	"an ant F"
بَقَر	بَقَرَة
baqar	baqar-a
"cows"	"a cow F"
دَجاج	دَجاجَة
dajaaj	dajaaj-a
"hens"	"a hen F"

(F) a word that belongs to اِسْم الجِنْس الجَمْعيّ "genus collective nouns" additionally has a regular feminine plural ending {-aat} (usually used to express quantity; e.g., ٣ شَجَرات "3 trees"; ٥ شَجَرات "5 trees"):

Plural	Plural	Singular
حَبّات	حَبّ	حَبَّة
Habb-aat	Habb	Habb-a
"seeds"	"seeds"	"a seed F"
شَجَرات	شَجَر	شَجَرَة
shajar-aat	shajar	shajar-a
"trees F"	"trees F"	"a tree F"
بَقَرات	بَقَر	بَقَرَة
baqar-aat	baqar	baqar-a
"cows"	"cows"	"a cow F"

(G) a word may have two plurals (following CA): a plural denoting 3–10 items and another denoting more than 10, although MSA speakers hardly make a distinction in their use of plural forms accordingly, as in:

Plural: more than 10	Plural: 3–10	Singular
شُهور	أَشْهُر	شَهْر
shuhuur	*'ash-hur*	*shahr*
"months"	"months"	"a month M"
ثِياب	أَثْواب	ثَوْب
thiyaab	*'athwaab*	*thawb*
"dresses"	"dresses"	"a dress M"
صِبْيان	صِبْية	صَبِيّ
Sibyaan	*Sibya*	*Sabiyy*
"boys"	"boys"	"a boy"

Accordingly, there can be as many as three or more plural forms (regular and irregular) available for a word:

Plural	Plural	Plural	Singular
كُتّاب	كَتَبة	كاتِبونَ	كاتِب
kuttaab	*kataba*	*kaatib-uuna*	*kaatib*
"writers M"	"writers M"	"writers M"	"a writer M"
أَشْجار	شَجَر	شَجَرات	شَجَرة
'ashjaar	*shajar*	*shajar-aat*	*shajar-a*
"trees"	"trees"	"trees"	"a tree F"
حُبوب	حَبّ	حَبّات	حَبَّة
Hubuub	*Habb*	*Habb-aat*	*Habb-a*
"seeds"	"seeds"	"seeds"	"a seed F"

The irregular/broken plural words constitute a great number of words – much greater than those of the sound (masculine and feminine) plural. In fact, except in cases where sound plural words are recognized due to their distinct endings and the few rules governing them, it is not possible for a beginner to distinguish in an a priori fashion between words that take regular/sound plural endings and those that do not. It almost amounts to the distinction between the so-called regular plural suffix {-s} in English and other non-regular plural forms. To illustrate this point, when encountering the word *desk* English learners will probably learn the plural regular form ➜ *desks* and *note* ➜ *notes*; similarly, *foot* ➜ *feet*, *tooth* ➜ *teeth*; however, the plural of *book* is *books* and of *booth* is *booths*, not *beek* nor *beeth*, respectively. Therefore, at an early point in the learning process, Arabic plural words may be better learned on an individual basis (i.e., learning each singular word together with its particular plural form). Later, it will be become easier to recognize the many patterns governing broken plurals, together with their exceptions.

2.4   Summary

This chapter discussed the basic facts relevant to the structure of the Arabic word and the basic elements that comprise the word. Remember:

- the two most basic elements that any Arabic word consists of are the root and the pattern
- the meaning of a given word obtains from combining both the root, which carries the basic meaning, and the pattern, which carries an additional specific meaning
- most words are derived from triliteral roots, fewer from quadriliteral roots, and much fewer from quinqueliteral roots; a very small number of words consist of fewer than three root consonants
- gender marking is another basic feature of a word structure at word level, represented word finally
- verbs are marked for masculine and feminine gender with respect to the second-person singular, second-person plural, third-person singular, third-person dual, and third-person plural
- the singular masculine, in nouns and adjectives, is marked by the default form of the word (i.e., the absence of any specific marking)
- the singular feminine, in nouns and adjectives, is marked by the feminine gender suffix {-a} *taa' marbuuTa;* fewer words are marked by the *'al-maqSuura* {-aa} and *'alif mamduuda* with the *hamza* {-aa'} suffixes

- number marking is another basic feature of a word structure, represented word finally
- verbs are marked for the dual number by means of the suffix {-aa} for the third-person past tense, {-aani} for the second- and third-person present tense, and {-tumaa} for the second-person past tense
- nouns and adjectives are marked for the dual number by means of the suffixes {-aani}(in the nominative مَرْفوع) and {-ayni}(in the accusative مَنْصوب and genitive مَجْرور) for both masculine and feminine
- Arabic words are marked for the plural number
- verbs are marked for the feature number with respect to the first, second, and third person
- Arabic nouns and adjectives have a regular/sound plural and an irregular/broken plural
- the biggest class of nouns and adjectives in the plural is by far the irregular/broken plural, since Arabic favors short words
- regular/sound masculine plural nouns and adjectives are marked by means of the suffixes {-uuna}(in the nominative مَرْفوع) and {-iina}(in the accusative مَنْصوب and genitive مَجْرور)
- regular/sound feminine plural nouns and adjectives are marked by means of the suffix {-aat}.

3

Noun Phrase Structure

This chapter discusses four types of Arabic noun phrase, including الصِّفة والمَوْصوف the noun–adjective phrase, الإضافة the *'iDaafa* phrase, the adjective *'iDaafa* phrase, and the demonstrative phrase. As the name suggests, a phrase in Arabic comprises a chunk of words forming part of a sentence. An Arabic phrase consists minimally of two words or more. The chapter covers the four basic types of noun phrase, including the following:

- the component parts of each of the four types of Arabic noun phrase
- agreement between the noun and adjective (in a noun–adjective phrase)
- agreement between the demonstrative pronoun and the noun (in a demonstrative phrase)
- the definiteness status of the first noun of an *'iDaafa* phrase
- the dropping of the nunation and the [n] ending of the dual and plural of the first noun of an *'iDaa fa* phrase
- the definiteness status of the adjective (in an adjective *'iDaafa* phrase)
- case endings in each of the four types of Arabic noun phrase.

3.1 Noun–adjective Phrase الصِّفَة والمَوْصوف

As the name suggests, a noun–adjective phrase consists minimally of two component parts: a noun, called in Arabic المَوْصوف "that which is described," and الصِّفة "the adjective."

Modern Standard Arabic Grammar: A Learner's Guide, First Edition.
© 2011 Mohammad T. Alhawary. Published 2011 by Blackwell Publishing Ltd.

3.1.1 Real Attributive Adjective النَّعْت الحَقيقيّ

Unlike English, in a straightforward Arabic noun–adjective phrase, the adjective always comes after the noun and agrees with it in gender, number, definiteness, and case. In semi-formal and informal Arabic (or pause form), both parts must agree minimally in gender, number, and definiteness. The examples below are of noun–adjective phrases where the noun and adjective agree in gender (i.e., both are either feminine or masculine), number (i.e., both are singular, dual, or plural), and definiteness (i.e., both are either indefinite or definite).

	Plural masculine	*Dual masculine*	*Singular masculine*
Indefinite	طُلّاب جُدُد "new students M"	طالبانِ جَديدانِ "two new students M"	طالِب جَديد "a new student M"
Definite	الطُّلّاب الجُدُد "the new students M"	الطّالبانِ الجَديدانِ "the two new students M"	الطّالِب الجَديد "the new student M"

	Plural feminine	*Dual feminine*	*Singular feminine*
Indefinite	طالِبات جَديدات "new students F"	طالِبتانِ جَديدَتانِ "two new students F"	طالِبة جَديدَة "a new student F"
Definite	الطالِبات الجَديدات "the new students F"	الطالِبتانِ الجَديدَتانِ "the two new students F"	الطّالِبَة الجَديدَة "the new student F"

Whereas dual masculine nouns are followed by dual masculine adjectives and dual feminine nouns are followed by dual feminine adjectives, non-human plural nouns, regardless of whether they are feminine or masculine, are followed by adjectives in the singular feminine (similar to the occurrence of non-human plural with verbs and nouns; see 4.1.2, 5.4, and 22.2.2), as in:

	Plural (non-human)	*Dual masculine*	*Singular masculine*
Indefinite	كُتُب جَديدَة "new books"	كِتابانِ جَديدانِ "two new books M."	كِتاب جَديد "a new book M"
Definite	الكُتُب الجَديدَة "the new books"	الكِتابانِ الجَديدانِ "the two new books M"	الكِتاب الجَديد "the new book M"

	Plural (non-human)	*Dual feminine*	*Singular feminine*
Indefinite	سَيّارات جَديدَة "new cars"	سَيّارَتانِ جَديدَتانِ "two new cars F"	سَيّارة جَديدَة "a new car F"
Definite	السَّيّارات الجَديدَة "the new cars"	السَّيّارَتانِ الجَديدَتانِ "the two new cars F"	السَّيّارة الجَديدَة "the new car F"

An exception to the non-human plural rule is the non-human (irregular) plural belonging to اِسْم الجِنْس الجَمْعيّ "genus collective nouns" (referring to the names of plants, insects, and animals) whose singular (feminine) form is derived by adding the *taa' marbuuTa* feminine suffix {-a} and whose regular (feminine) plural is formed by adding the {-aat} suffix (see 2.3.2.3). The irregular plural of collective nouns is usually treated in MSA as masculine, whereas the regular feminine plural is treated as feminine, as in:

	Plural (irregular)	*Plural (regular)*	*Dual*	*Singular*
Indefinite	شَجَر جَميل "pretty M trees"	شَجَرات جَميلَة "pretty F trees"	شَجَرَتانِ جَميلَتانِ "two pretty trees F"	شَجَرَة جَميلَة "a pretty tree F"
Definite	الشَّجَر الجَميل "the pretty M trees"	الشَّجَرات الجَميلَة "the pretty F trees"	الشَّجَرَتانِ الجَميلَتانِ "the two pretty trees F"	الشَّجَرَة الجَميلَة "the pretty tree F"

Indefinite	دَجاج صَغير "small M hens"	دَجاجات صَغيرة "small F hens"	دَجاجَتانِ صَغيرَتانِ "two small hens F"	دَجاجة صَغيرة "a small hen F"
Definite	الدَّجاج الصَّغير "the small M hens"	الدَّجاجات الصَّغيرة "the small F hens"	الدَّجاجَتانِ الصَّغيرَتانِ "the two small hens F"	الدَجاجَةالصَّغيرة "the small hen F"

A noun–adjective phrase may contain one noun and more than one adjective describing the noun. In this case, and unlike English, the adjectives are not separated by the conjunction وَ "and," as in the following (note here, also, that the noun and adjectives are either both indefinite or definite):

طالب مُجْتَهِد ذَكيّ

"a (male) hardworking [and] (male) smart (male) student"

الطّالِب المُجْتَهِد الذَّكيّ

"the (male) hardworking [and] (male) smart (male) student"

طالِبَة مُجْتَهِدة ذَكيَّة

"a (female) hardworking [and] (female) smart (female) student"

الطّالِبَة المُجْتَهِدة الذَّكيَّة

"the (female) hardworking [and] (female) smart (female) student"

In full formal MSA (i.e., with full vowel endings), the adjective must also agree in case with the noun it follows. That is, both must be either مَرْفوع nominative, مَنْصوب accusative, or مَجْرور genitive. The examples below are of noun and adjective phrases in the singular masculine and singular feminine forms and in both the indefinite and definite forms. Indefinite adjectives (and nouns) occur with nunation (with a final [n] sound).

	Genitive / مَجْرور	*Accusative /* مَنْصوب	*Nominative /* مَرْفوع
Indefinite	طالِب جَديد "a new student M"	طالِباً جَديداً "a new student M"	طالِبٌ جَديدٌ "a new student M"
Definite	الطّالِب الجَديد "the new student M"	الطّالِبَ الجَديدَ "the new student M"	الطّالِبُ الجَديدُ "the new student M"

	Genitive / مَجْرور	*Accusative* / مَنْصوب	*Nominative* / مَرْفوع
Indefinite	طالِبَةٍ جَديدَةٍ "a new student F"	طالِبَةً جَديدَةً "a new student F"	طالِبَةٌ جَديدَةٌ "a new student F"
Definite	الطّالِبَةِ الجَديدَةِ "the new student F"	الطّالِبَةَ الجَديدَةَ "the new student F"	الطّالِبَةُ الجَديدَةُ "the new student F"

The examples of phrases within sentences below include use of the case endings where, for example, the nominative مَرْفوع indicates the subject (i.e., the doer of the action), the accusative مَنْصوب indicates the object (i.e., the doee of the action), and the genitive مَجْرور indicates the object of a preposition (i.e., when a noun follows a preposition) functions of the noun phrase (for examples in the dual and the plural and more on case endings and their use, see 22.2.2).

حَضَرَ الطّالِبُ الجَديدُ .
"The new (male) student came."

حَضَرَ طالِبٌ جَديدٌ .
"A new (male) student came."

حَضَرَتْ الطّالِبَةُ الجَديدَةُ .
"The new (female) student came."

حَضَرَتْ طالِبَةٌ جَديدَةٌ .
"A new (female) student came."

قابَلْتُ الطّالِبَ الجَديدَ .
"I met the new (male) student."

قابَلْتُ طالِباً جَديداً .
"I met a new (male) student."

قابَلْتُ الطّالِبَةَ الجَديدَةَ .
"I met the new (female) student."

قابَلْتُ طالِبَةً جَديدَةً .
"I met a new (female) student."

سَلَّمْتُ عَلَى الطّالِبِ الجَديدِ .
"I greeted the new (male) student."

سَلَّمْتُ عَلَى طالِبٍ جَديدٍ .
"I greeted a new (male) student."

سَلَّمْتُ عَلَى الطّالِبَةِ الجَديدَةِ .
"I greeted the new (female) student."

سَلَّمْتُ عَلَى طالِبَةٍ جَديدَةٍ.
"I greeted a new (female) student."

3.1.2 Causative Attributive Adjective النَّعْت السَّبَبِيّ

Another kind of noun–adjective phrase is one that consists of a noun, an adjective, and another noun. In this case, the adjective is partly related to the preceding noun, but it occurs mainly to describe the noun that follows it. Hence, it is called النَّعْت السَّبَبِيّ "the causative adjective." In this structure, the adjective occurs always in the singular, agrees with the preceding noun in definiteness and case, and agrees with the noun that follows it in gender; the noun that follows the adjective is always in the مَرْفوع nominative case, as in:

جاءَ طالِبٌ مُمَزَّقٌ قَميصُهُ .

"A (male) student [with] a torn shirt came."

جاءَتْ طالِبَةٌ مُمَزَّقٌ قَميصُها .

"A (female) student [with] a torn shirt came."

جاءَ الرَجُلُ المُحَطَّمَةُ سَيّارَتُهُ .

"The man [with] the smashed car came."

جاءَتْ المَرْأَةُ المُحَطَّمَةُ سَيّارَتُها .

"The woman [with] the smashed car came."

رَأَيْتُ طالِباً مُمَزَّقاً قَميصُهُ .

"I saw a (male) student [with] a torn shirt."

رَأَيْتُ طالِبَةً مُمَزَّقاً قَميصُها .

"I saw a (female) student [with] a torn shirt."

رَأَيْتُ الرَجُلَ المُحَطَّمَةَ سَيّارَتُهُ .

"I saw the man [with] the smashed car."

رَأَيْتُ المَرْأَةَ المُحَطَّمَةَ سَيّارَتُها .

"I saw the woman [with] the smashed car."

نَظَرْتُ إلى طالِبٍ مُمَزَّقٍ قَميصُهُ .

"I looked at a (male) student [with] a torn shirt."

نَظَرْتُ إلى طالِبَةٍ مُمَزَّقٍ قَميصُها .

"I looked at a (female) student [with] a torn shirt."

نَظَرْتُ إلى الرَجُلِ المُحَطَّمَةِ سَيّارَتُهُ .

"I looked at the man [with] the smashed car."

نَظَرْتُ إلى المَرْأَةِ المُحَطَّمَةِ سَيّارَتُها .

"I looked at the woman [with] with smashed car."

3.2 Demonstrative Phrase

A demonstrative phrase consists minimally of a demonstrative pronoun or اِسْم إشارة "noun of referring" (see Chapter 5 on demonstrative pronouns أَسْماء الإشارة) and a definite noun, both agreeing in gender and number, as in:

Plural masculine	Dual masculine	Singular masculine
هٰؤُلاءِ الطُّلّاب "these students M"	هٰذانِ الطّالِبانِ "these two male students M"	هٰذا الطّالِب "this male student M"

Plural feminine	Dual feminine	Singular feminine
هٰؤُلاءِ الطّالِبات "these female students F"	هٰاتانِ الطّالِبَتانِ "these two female students F"	هٰذِهِ الطّالِبَة "this female student F"

A demonstrative phrase may consist of a demonstrative pronoun and a noun followed by a definite adjective (or more than one adjective, as shown in the preceding section), all of which need to agree in gender and number, as in:

Plural masculine	Dual masculine	Singular masculine
هٰؤُلاءِ الطُّلّاب الجُدُد "these new students M"	هٰذانِ الطّالِبانِ الجَديدان "these two new male students M"	هٰذا الطّالِب الجَديد "this new male student M"

Plural feminine	Dual feminine	Singular feminine
هٰؤُلاءِ الطّالِبات الجَديدات "these new female students F"	هٰاتانِ الطّالِبَتانِ الجَديدَتان "these two new female students F"	هٰذِهِ الطّالِبَة الجَديدَة "this new female student F"

In formal MSA (i.e., with full vowel endings), the demonstrative pronoun and the noun (as well as the adjective, if available) must also agree in case. That is, all elements must be either مَرْفوع nominative, مَنْصوب accusative, or مَجْرور genitive, as in the following (see also 22.2.2 on case endings):

	Plural masculine	*Dual masculine*	*Singular masculine*
Nominative مَرْفوع	هٰؤُلاءِ الطُّلَّابُ "these students M"	هٰذانِ الطّالِبانِ "these two students M"	هٰذا الطّالِبُ "this student M"
Accusative مَنْصوب	هٰؤُلاءِ الطُّلَّابَ "these students M"	هٰذَيْنِ الطّالِبَيْنِ "these two students M"	هٰذا الطّالِبَ "this student M"
Genitive مَجْرور	هٰؤُلاءِ الطُّلَّابِ "these students M"	هٰذَيْنِ الطّالِبَيْنِ "these two students M"	هٰذا الطّالِبِ "this student M"

	Plural feminine	*Dual feminine*	*Singular feminine*
Nominative مَرْفوع	هٰؤُلاءِ الطّالِباتُ "these students F"	هاتانِ الطّالِبَتانِ "these two Students F"	هٰذِهِ الطّالِبَةُ "this female student F"
Accusative مَنْصوب	هٰؤُلاءِ الطّالِباتِ "these students F"	هاتَيْنِ الطّالِبَتَيْنِ "these two students F"	هٰذِهِ الطّالِبَةَ "this female student F"
Genitive مَجْرور	هٰؤُلاءِ الطّالِباتِ "these Students F"	هاتَيْنِ الطّالِبَتَيْنِ "these two students F"	هٰذِهِ الطّالِبَةِ "this female student F"

3.3   *'iDaafa* Phrase الإِضافة الحَقيقيَّة

An *'iDaafa* phrase or الإِضافة الحَقيقيَّة "real *'iDaafa*," or simply إِضافة *'iDaafa*, expresses a possessive relationship between two or more things/nouns, but consists minimally of two nouns that make up a single (compound) noun. The best way to understand an إِضافة *'iDaafa* phrase is to consider its equivalent in English where two nouns occur together and are joined in one of three ways: (1) by means of the preposition "of" (e.g., "a member of parliament"), (2) by means of the apostrophe "'s" (e.g., "a teacher's book"), or (3) by nothing (e.g., "a jury member"). The Arabic إِضافة *'iDaafa* phrase resembles the third case (i.e., with nothing joining the two nouns), but with the word order reversed. Alternatively, to expel any word-order confusion, one can simply assume the Arabic إِضافة *'iDaafa* phrase resembles (1) above by keeping the English word order the same and *mentally* inserting the preposition "of" between the two Arabic nouns, as in:

عُضو [of] بَرْلَان   =   عُضو بَرْلَان
"a member of parliament"   =   "a parliament member"

نافِذَة [of] بَيْت   =   نافِذَة بَيْت
"a window of a house"   =   "a house window"

كِتاب [of] أُسْتاذ   =   كِتاب أُسْتاذ
"a book of a teacher"   =   "a teacher's book"

Unlike in other types of Arabic noun phrase, nouns within the إِضافة *'iDaafa* phrase do not agree in gender, number, case, or even definiteness. In fact, the first noun always occurs indefinite (i.e., without the definite article or a pronoun suffix attached to it), because definiteness is indicated only by means of the second noun. Thus, to treat the (whole) phrase as definite only the second noun must be definite; otherwise when indefinite both nouns occur indefinite, as in:

أُسْتاذ جامِعَة
"a (male) teacher of a university"/"a university teacher (male)"

أُسْتاذ الجامِعَة
"the (male) teacher of the university"/"the university teacher (male)"

أُسْتاذَة جامِعَة
"a (female) teacher of a university"/"a university teacher (female)"

أُسْتاذَة الجامِعَة
"the (female) teacher of the university"/"the university teacher (female)"

أُسْتاذ جامِعَتي

"my (male) teacher of the university"/"my university teacher (male)"

أُسْتاذَة جامِعَتي

"my (female) teacher of the university"/"my university teacher (female)"

Note: If the first noun is intended to be indefinite and the second definite, this can be expressed by modifying the first noun with a prepositional phrase consisting of the preposition مِن "from" followed by a noun in the plural, as in:

أُسْتاذ مِنْ أَساتِذَة الجامِعَة

"a (male) teacher/one of the teachers of the university"

شارِع مِنْ شَوارِع المَدينَة

"a street/one of the streets of the city"

مَكْتَبة مِنْ مَكْتَبات الجامِعَة

"a library/one of the libraries of the university"

An إضافة *'iDaafa* phrase may consist of more than two nouns (perhaps up to five), in which case the whole phrase is treated as definite when the last noun is definite, and as indefinite when all the nouns are indefinite, as in:

مَكْتَب أُسْتاذ جامِعَة

"an office of a (male) teacher of a university"

مَكْتَب أُسْتاذ الجامِعَة

"the office of the (male) teacher of the university"

بِناء مَكْتَب أُسْتاذ جامِعَة

"a building of an office of a (male) teacher of a university"

بِناء مَكْتَب أُسْتاذ الجامِعَة

"the building of the office of the (male) teacher of the university"

بِناء مَكْتَب أُسْتاذ جامِعَة دِمَشْق

"the building of the office of the (male) teacher of the university of Damascus"

An adjective may be used to describe a noun (and agrees with it in gender) within an إضافة *'iDaafa* phrase, although, to avoid ambiguity, this is usually restricted to a phrase consisting of two nouns, as in:

أُسْتاذ جامِعَة سوريّ

"a Syrian (male) teacher of a university"

أُسْتاذ جامِعَة سوريّة

"a (male) teacher of a Syrian university"

أُسْتاذ الجامِعَة السّوريّ

"the Syrian (male) teacher of the university"

أُسْتاذ الجامِعَة السّوريَّة

"the (male) teacher of the Syrian university"

أُسْتاذَة جامِعَة سوريّة

"a Syrian (female) teacher of a university"/
"a (female) teacher of a Syrian university"

أُسْتاذَة الجامِعَة السّوريَّة

"the Syrian (female) teacher of the university"/
"the (female) teacher of the Syrian university"

Note: The last two sentences (in their pause form) are ambiguous, as indicated in the English gloss, where the context would be relied on to clarify the exact intended meaning.

Two adjectives may be used to describe each of the nouns within an إضافة *'iDaafa* phrase (both of which would follow the nouns, with the adjective of the first noun occurring at the end, and each agreeing in gender with the noun it describes), although this structure may alternatively be expressed by means of two noun–adjective phrases joined by the preposition لِ "for," as in:

عُضو مُنَظَّمَة دَوْليّة دّائم

"a permanent (male) member of an international organization"

عُضو دائم لِمُنَظَّمَة دَوْليّة

"a permanent (male) member for an international organization"

نَدْوَة المُؤْتَمَر الشَّعْبِيّ الثَّامِنَة

"the eighth symposium of the people's conference"

النَّدْوَة الثَّامِنَة لِلمُؤْتَمَر الشَّعْبِيّ

"the eighth symposium for the people's conference"

Another rule that involves an إِضافة *'iDaafa* phrase is the deletion of the ن /[n] ending of the dual and the regular masculine plural, as in:

أُسْتاذانِ ← أُسْتاذا ← أُسْتاذا جامِعَة

"two (male) teachers of a university"/"two (male) university teachers"

أُسْتاذَتانِ ← أُسْتاذَتا ← أُسْتاذَتا جامِعَة

"two (female) teachers of a university"/"two (female) university teachers"

مُهَنْدِسونَ ← مُهَنْدِسو ← مُهَنْدِسو بِناء

"(male) engineers of construction"/"construction engineers (male)"

As for case, in formal MSA, the case ending of the first noun depends on its function in the sentence, whether مَرْفوع nominative, مَنْصوب accusative, or مَجْرور genitive (see 22.2.2 on case endings), and so does the adjective it describes; whereas all other nouns (and any adjective modifying a subsequent noun) occur in the مَجْرور genitive, as in:

حَضَرَ أُسْتاذُ الجامِعَةِ .	حَضَرَ أُسْتاذُ جامِعَةٍ .
"The (male) teacher of the university came."	"A (male) teacher of a university came."
قابَلْتُ أُسْتاذَ الجامِعَةِ .	قابَلْتُ أُسْتاذَ جامِعَةٍ .
"I met the (male) teacher of the university."	"I met a (male) teacher of a university."
تَكَلَّمْتُ مَعَ أُسْتاذِ الجامِعَةِ .	تَكَلَّمْتُ مَعَ أُسْتاذِ جامِعَةٍ .
"I spoke with the teacher of the university."	"I spoke with a teacher of a university."

هٰذا بِناءُ مَكاتِبِ أَساتِذَةِ جامِعَةٍ .

"This is a building of offices of teachers of a university."

هٰذا بِناءُ مَكاتِبِ أَساتِذَةِ الجامِعَةِ .

"This is the building of the offices of the teachers of the university."

هو عُضوُ مُنَظَّمَةٍ دَوْليَّةٍ دائِمٌ .

"He is a (male) permanent member of an international organization."

اِنْعَقَدَتْ نَدْوَةُ المُؤْتَمَرِ الشَّعْبِيِّ الثّامِنَةُ .

"The eighth symposium of the people's conference was held."

Note: In the same way that the ن /[n] ending of the dual and the regular masculine plural of the first noun is dropped, the nunation [n] of the first noun in the indefinite singular is also dropped, as shown in the above examples.

3.4 Adjective *'iDaafa* Phrase الإضافة اللَّفْظِيَّة

An adjective *'iDaafa* phrase or الإضافة اللَّفْظِيَّة "unreal *'iDaafa*" consists of an adjective followed by a noun and differs from a regular إضافة *'iDaafa* phrase (explained above) in two ways. First, when the adjective *'iDaafa* phrase is treated as indefinite, the adjective occurs in the indefinite, although the noun following it occurs definite. Second, when the adjective *'iDaafa* phrase is treated as definite, then both the adjective and the noun occur definite. Case-ending rules of the adjective *'iDaafa* phrase are the same as those of the regular إضافة *'iDaafa*. The examples below illustrate the uses of adjective *'iDaafa* phrase:

الحَسَنُ الخُلُقِ	حَسَنُ الخُلُقِ
"the good-mannered (male) ..."	"a good-mannered (male) ..."
الحَسَنَةُ الخُلُقِ	حَسَنَةُ الخُلُقِ
"the good-mannered (female) ..."	"a good-mannered (female) ..."
الجَميلُ الوَجْهِ	جَميلُ الوَجْهِ
"the beautiful (male) of face ..."	"a beautiful (male) of face ..."
الجَميلَةُ الوَجْهِ	جَميلَةُ الوَجْهِ
"the beautiful (female) of face ..."	"a beautiful (female) of face ..."

المَهْضُومُ الحَقِّ
"the stripped (male) of right . . ."

مَهْضُومُ الحَقِّ
"a stripped (male) of right . . ."

المَهْضُومَةُ الحَقِّ
"the stripped (female) of right . . ."

مَهْضُومَةُ الحَقِّ
"a stripped (female) of right . . ."

حَضَرَ الأُسْتاذُ الحَسَنُ الخُلُقِ .
"The well-mannered teacher came."

حَضَرَ أُسْتاذٌ حَسَنُ الخُلُقِ .
"A well-mannered teacher came."

قابَلْتُ الأُسْتاذَ الحَسَنَ الخُلُقِ .
"I met the well-mannered teacher."

قابَلْتُ أُسْتاذاً حَسَنَ الخُلُقِ .
"I met a well-mannered teacher."

تَكَلَّمْتُ مَعَ الأُسْتاذِ الحَسَنِ الخُلُقِ .
"I spoke with the well-mannered teacher."

تَكَلَّمْتُ مَعَ أُسْتاذٍ حَسَنِ الخُلُقِ .
"I spoke with a well-mannered teacher."

3.5   Summary

This chapter discussed all four types of Arabic noun phrase. Remember:

- in a noun–adjective phrase, the noun and adjective agree in gender, number, definiteness, and case
- more than one adjective can occur in a noun–adjective phrase
- in a demonstrative phrase, the demonstrative pronoun and the noun agree in gender, number, definiteness, and case
- the first noun of an *'iDaafa* phrase never occurs with a definite article or a pronoun
- the nunation of the singular [n] and the ن /[n] ending of the dual and plural of the first noun of an *'iDaafa* phrase is always dropped
- in an adjective *'iDaafa* phrase, the adjective (as the first item of *'iDaafa*) occurs both indefinite and definite.

4

Sentence Structure

This chapter discusses the structure of the two main types of Arabic sentence: الجُمْلة الفِعْليَّة the verbal sentence and الجُملة الإسْميَّة the nominal sentence. As the name suggests, a verbal sentence contains a verb (in initial position) followed by a subject (and an object as well as other parts of speech, if necessary), while a nominal sentence may or may not contain a verb (in second position). The chapter covers the two basic types of Arabic sentence, including the following:

- the component parts of each of the two types of Arabic sentence
- agreement between the verb and subject (in a verbal sentence)
- agreement between the subject and predicate (in a nominal sentence)
- tenses and negation of the verbal sentence
- past and future tenses and negation of the nominal sentence
- كانَ and its sisters
- إنَّ and its sisters
- mood and case endings of the different parts of verbal and nominal sentences.

4.1 The Verbal Sentence الجُمْلة الفِعْليَّة

4.1.1 Basic Structure of the Verbal Sentence

As the name suggests, a verbal sentence contains a verb. However, following the traditional analysis of Arab grammarians, the verb must also

Modern Standard Arabic Grammar: A Learner's Guide, First Edition.
© 2011 Mohammad T. Alhawary. Published 2011 by Blackwell Publishing Ltd.

occur at the beginning of the sentence. A verbal sentence may consist minimally of one word in the form of a verb with a subject pronoun suffix attached to it (see Chapter 5 on pronouns). It may also consist of two words (a verb with a subject pronoun suffix attached to it and an object), three words (a verb, an independent subject, and an object), or more (e.g., a verb, an independent subject, an object, a preposition, a noun phrase, an adverb, etc.), as in:

تَدْرُسُ .

"She studies."

تَدْرُسُ العَرَبِيَّةَ .

"She studies Arabic."

تَدْرُسُ صَديقَتي العَرَبِيَّةَ .

"My (female) friend studies Arabic."

تَدْرُسُ صَديقَتي العَرَبِيَّةَ في الجامِعَةِ .

"My (female) friend studies Arabic at the university."

تَدْرُسُ صَديقَتي العَرَبِيَّةَ في الجامِعَةِ كُلَّ يَوْم .

"My (female) friend studies Arabic at the university every day."

4.1.2 Verb–Subject Agreement

In a verbal sentence, with the verb occurring in sentence initial position, the verb agrees with the subject (or doer of the action) in gender but not number. That is, the verb occurs always in the singular but can be either feminine or masculine, depending on the gender of the subject, as in:

يَدْرُسُ الطّالِبُ في البَيْت .

"The (male) student studies at home."

تَدْرُسُ الطّالِبَةُ في البَيْت .

"The (female) student studies at home."

تَدْرُسُ الطّالِبَتانِ في البَيْت .

"The two (female) students study at home."

يَدْرُسُ الطّالِبانِ في البَيْت .

"The two (male) students study at home."

تَدرُسُ الطّالِباتُ في البَيْت .
"The (female) students study at home."

يَدرُسُ الطُّلّابُ في البَيْت .
"The (male) students study at home."

Otherwise, in a nominal sentence, with the verb occurring after the subject (see below for more on nominal sentences), the verb must agree with the subject in gender, number, and person, as in:

الطّالِبُ يَدرُسُ في البَيْت .
"The (male) student studies at home."

الطّالِبَةُ تَدرُسُ في البَيْت .
"The (female) student studies at home."

الطّالِبَتانِ تَدرُسانِ في البَيْت .
"The two (female) students study at home."

الطّالِبانِ يَدرُسانِ في البَيْت .
"The two (male) students study at home."

الطّالِباتُ يَدرُسْنَ في البَيْت .
"The (female) students study at home."

الطُّلّابُ يَدرُسونَ في البَيْت .
"The (male) students study at home."

Note: When non-human plurals occur as subjects/doers of the verb/action, the verb is used in the third-person singular feminine whether the verb precedes the non-human plural or follows it, as in:

مُحاضَراتي تَبْدَأُ صَباحاً .　　　=　　　تَبْدَأُ مُحاضَراتي صَباحاً .
"My lectures/classes start in the　　　　"My lectures/classes start in the
morning."　　　　　　　　　　　　　morning."

صُفوفي تَبْدَأُ صَباحاً .　　　=　　　تَبْدَأُ صُفوفي صَباحاً .
"My classes start in the morning."　　　"My classes start in the morning."

This is quite like the use of singular feminine adjectives of non-human plurals (regardless of the gender of the non-human plural nouns), as well as pronouns referring to non-human plurals (see 3.1, and Chapter 5). However, اِسْم الجِنْس الجَمْعيّ "genus collective nouns" (referring to names of plants, insects, and animals), whose singular is derived by adding the *taa' marbuuTa* feminine suffix {-a} (e.g., شَجَر "trees" → شَجَرَة "a tree," تَمْر "dates" → تَمْرَة "a date," ذُباب "flies" → ذُبابَة "a fly", and بَقَر "cows" → بَقَرَة "a cow"), are usually treated as singular masculine (see 2.3.2.3, 3.1, and Chapter 5), as in:

<table>
<tr><td>النَّمْرُ يَنْضَجُ في الخريفِ في كاليفورنيا .</td><td>=</td><td>يَنْضَجُ التَّمْرُ في الخريفِ في كاليفورنيا .</td></tr>
<tr><td>"Dates ripen in the fall in California."</td><td></td><td>"Dates ripen in the fall in California."</td></tr>
</table>

4.1.3 Tenses of the Verbal Sentence

Unlike English and other languages, Arabic does not have a complex tense system. Any given verb in Arabic has two basic forms (the perfect/past and the imperfect/present). Therefore, tenses in Arabic are expressed periphrastically, that is, by means of one of the two forms of the verb and additional, simple words.

4.1.3.1 *The Simple Present Tense and its Negation*

The simple present tense is expressed by the imperfect/present form of the verb (see also Table 2.3, Chapter 2) and one or more adverbs of time (see Chapter 8 on adverbs of time) expressing a habitual action in the present, as in:

تَدْرُسُ صَديقَتي كُلَّ يَوْم .
"My (female) friend studies every day."

يَعْمَلُ الطُّلّابُ في النَّهارِ ويَدْرُسونَ في المَساء .
"The students work during the day and study in the evening."

أَذْهَبُ إلى الجامِعَةِ في السّاعةِ الثّامِنَةِ صَباحاً .
"I go to the university at eight o'clock in the morning."

The simple present tense is negated by the placement of the negation particle لا "do not/does not" before the verb, as in:

لا تَدْرُسُ صَديقَتي كُلَّ يَوْم .
"My (female) friend does not study every day."

لا يَعْمَلُ الطُّلَّابُ في النَّهارِ ولا يَدْرُسونَ في المَساء .

"The (male) students do not work during the day and do not study
in the evening."

لا أَذْهَبُ إلى الجامِعَةِ في السّاعةِ الثّامِنةِ صَباحاً .

"I do not go to the university at eight o'clock in the morning."

The mood ending on the verb following the negation particle لا "do
not/does not" is that of المُضارِع المَرْفوع "the indicative," or simply the
default form of the verb ending in the imperfect/present, as illustrated
below:

لا يَفْعَلْنَ "they all F do not do"	لا يَفْعَلونَ "they all M do not do"	لا تَفْعَلانِ "they both F do not do"	لا يَفْعَلانِ "they both M do not do"	لا تَفْعَلُ "she does not do"	لا يَفْعَلُ "he does not do"
لا تَفْعَلْنَ "you all F do not do"	لا تَفْعَلونَ "you all M do not do"	لا تَفْعَلانِ "you both do not do"		لا تَفْعَلينَ "you SF do not do"	لا تَفْعَلُ "you SM do not do"
لا نَفْعَلُ "we do not do"				لا أَفْعَلُ "I do not do"	

4.1.3.2 *The Present Continuous Tense and its Negation*

The present continuous tense is expressed by the imperfect/present form
of the verb and an adverb (see Chapter 8 on adverbs) expressing a present
time, as in:

تَدْرُسُ صَديقَتي في البَيْتِ هٰذا الصَّباح .

"My (female) friend is studying at home this morning."

يَكْتُبُ الطُّلَّابُ واجِبَهُم و يَدْرُسونَ الآن .

"The (male) students are writing their homework and studying now."

تَصْعَدُ صَديقَتي الطّائِرَةَ في هٰذه اللَّحْظَة .

"My (female) friend is boarding the plane at this moment."

The present continuous tense is negated by the placement of the negation particle لا "is not/are not/am not" before the verb (and the negation particle ما can also be used though less frequently), as in:

لا / ما تَدْرُسُ صَديقَتي في البَيْتِ هٰذا الصَّباح .

"My (female) friend is not studying at home this morning."

لا / ما يَكْتُبُ الطُّلّابُ واجِبَهُم ولا / ما يَدْرُسونَ الآن .

"The (male) students are not writing their homework and are not studying now."

لا / ما أَدْرُسُ الآن .

"I am not studying now."

4.1.3.3 *The Present Perfect Tense and its Negation*

The present perfect tense is somewhat rare in MSA and is used only to indicate an event which has just occurred. It may be expressed by the perfective/past form of the verb, and the adverbial particle تَوّاً / تَوّ "just" or لِتَوِّ followed by a pronoun suffix referring to the subject/doer, as in:

حَضَرَتْ صَديقَتي تَوّاً / لِتَوِّها .

"My (female) friend has just come."

حَضَرَ صَديقي تَوّاً / لِتَوِّهِ .

"My (male) friend has just come."

حَضَرَ الطُّلّابُ لِتَوِّهِم .

"The (male) students have just come."

The present perfect tense is negated by the imperfect/present form of the verb and the placement of the negation particle لَمّا "has not yet/have not yet" before it, as in:

لَمّا تَحْضُرْ صَديقَتي .

"My (female) friend has not yet come."

لَمّا يَقْرَأِ الطُّلّابُ و لَمّا يَكْتُبوا .

"The students have not read or written yet."

Note: The verb takes the jussive مَجْزوم mood after the negation particle لَمّا "did not" (see 4.1.3.4 below for an explanation of the jussive مَجْزوم ending).

4.1.3.4 *The Simple Past Tense and its Negation*

The simple past tense is expressed by the perfect/past form of the verb (see also Table 2.4, Chapter 2) and an adverb (see Chapter 8) expressing a past time, as in:

دَرَسَتْ صَديقَتي أمْس .

"My (female) friend studied yesterday."

عَمِلَ أصْدِقائي في النّهارِ ودَرَسوا في المَساء .

"My (male) friends worked during the day and studied in the evening."

دَرَسْتُ في السّاعَةِ الثّامِنَةِ صَباحاً .

"I studied at eight o'clock in the morning."

The simple past tense is negated by the imperfect/present form of the verb and the placement of the negation particle لَمْ "did not" before it, as in:

لَمْ تَدْرُسْ صَديقَتي أمْس .

"My (female) friend did not study yesterday."

لَمْ يَعْمَلْ أصْدِقائي في النّهارِ و لَمْ يَدْرُسوا في المَساء .

"My (male) friends did not work during the day and did not study in the evening."

لَمْ أدْرُسْ في السّاعَةِ الثّامِنَةِ صَباحاً .

"I did not study at eight o'clock in the morning."

The mood ending of the verb following the negation particle لَمْ "did not" is that of المُضارِع المَجْزوم "the jussive," as illustrated below:

لَمْ يَفْعَلْنَ "they all F did not do"	لَمْ يَفْعَلوا "they all M did not do"	لَمْ تَفْعَلا "they both F did not do"	لَمْ يَفْعَلا "they both M did not do"	لَمْ تَفْعَلْ "she did not do"	لَمْ يَفْعَلْ "he did not do"
لَمْ تَفْعَلْنَ "you all F did not do"	لَمْ تَفْعَلوا "you all M did not do"	لَمْ تَفْعَلا "you both did not do"		لَمْ تَفْعَلي "you SF did not do"	لَمْ تَفْعَلْ "you SM did not do"
لَمْ نَفْعَلْ "we did not do"			لَمْ أفْعَلْ "I did not do"		

Alternatively, the simple past tense can be negated by the perfect/past form of the verb and the placement of the negation particle ما "did not" before it, although this carries extra emphasis, as in:

ما دَرَسَتْ صَديقَتي أمْس .

"My (female) friend did not study yesterday."

ما عَمِلَ أَصْدِقائي في النَّهارِ وما دَرَسوا في المَساءِ .

"My (male) friends did not work during the day and did not study in the evening."

ما دَرَسْتُ في السَّاعَةِ الثَّامِنَةِ صَباحاً .

"I did not study at eight o'clock in the morning."

4.1.3.5   *The Past Continuous Tense and its Negation*

The past tense is expressed by the verb كانَ "was/were," the imperfect/present form of the verb, and an adverb of time (see Chapter 8) expressing a past time, as in:

كانَتْ صَديقَتي تَدْرُسُ أمْس .

"My (female) friend was studying yesterday."

كانَ الطُّلَّابُ يَدْرُسونَ في المَكْتَبَةِ في الأُسْبوعِ الماضي .

"The (male) students were studying in the library last week."

كُنْتُ أَعْمَلُ في النَّهارِ وأَدْرُسُ في المَساءِ في الشَّهْرِ الماضي .

"I was working during the day and studying in the evening last month."

The past continuous tense is negated by the imperfect/present form of the verb يَكونُ and the placement of the negation particle لَمْ "did not" before it, as in:

لَمْ تَكُنْ صَديقَتي تَدْرُسُ أمْس .

"My (female) friend was not studying yesterday."

لَمْ يَكُنْ الطُّلَّابُ يَدْرُسونَ في المَكْتَبَةِ في الأُسْبوعِ الماضي .

"The (male) students were not studying in the library last week."

لَمْ أَكُنْ أَعْمَلُ في النَّهارِ في الشَّهْرِ الماضي .

"I was not working during the day last month."

Alternatively, the past continuous tense can be negated by the perfect/
past form of the verb كانَ and the placement of the negation particle ما
"did not" before it, although this carries extra emphasis, as in:

ما كانَتْ صَديقَتي تَدْرُسُ أمْس .

"My (female) friend was not studying yesterday."

ما كانَ الطُّلّابُ يَدْرُسونَ في المَكْتَبَةِ في الأُسْبوعِ الماضي .

"The (male) students were not studying in the library last week."

ما كُنْتُ أعْمَلُ في النَّهارِ في الشَّهْرِ الماضي .

"I was not working during the day last month."

Note: The verb to be يَكونُ "is" is a hollow verb which undergoes certain
changes in the jussive مَجْزوم and other forms (see Chapter 13.4.5 on hollow
verbs).

4.1.3.6 *The Habitual Past Tense and its Negation*

The habitual past tense is expressed by the verb كانَ "was/were," the
imperfect/present form of the verb, a clause or a phrase expressing a
habitual past event (e.g., equivalent to "when she was young," "when she
was a student," "when she was in Egypt," "during childhood days," etc.),
and, if needed, an adverb of time (see Chapter 8) expressing a habitual
action, as in:

عِنْدَما كانَتْ صَديقَتي صَغيرَةً كانَتْ تَدْرُسُ كُلَّ يَوْم .

"When my (female) friend was young, she used to study every day."

عِنْدَما كانَتْ صَديقَتي طالِبَةً كانَتْ تَعْمَلُ في المَكْتَبَة .

"When my (female) friend was a student, she used to work at
the library."

عِنْدَما كانَتْ صَديقَتي في مِصْر كانَتْ تَتَكَلَّمُ مَعَ أُسْرَتِها كُلَّ أُسْبوع .

"When my (female) friend was in Egypt, she used to speak with her family
every week."

في أيّامِ الطُّفولَةِ كانَتْ تُساعِدُ والِدَتَها في تَنْظيفِ البَيْت .

"During childhood days, she used to help her mother in
house cleaning."

Like the past tense, the habitual past tense can be negated by the two optional ways of لَمْ "did not" or ما "did not," as in:

عِنْدَما كانَتْ صَديقَتي صَغيرَةً لَمْ تَكُنْ تَدْرُسُ كُلَّ يَوْم .

"When my (female) friend was young, she did not use to study every day."

عِنْدَما كانَتْ صَديقَتي صَغيرَةً ما كانَتْ تَدْرُسُ كُل يَوْم .

"When my (female) friend was young, she did not use to study every day."

في أَيّامِ الطُّفولَةِ لَمْ تَكُنْ تُساعِدُ والِدَتَها في تَنْظيفِ البَيْت .

"During childhood days, she did not use to help her mother in house cleaning."

في أَيّامِ الطُّفولَةِ ما كانَتْ تُساعِدُ والِدَتَها في تَنْظيفِ البَيْت .

"During childhood days, she did not use to help her mother in house cleaning."

4.1.3.7 *The Past Perfect Tense and its Negation*

The past perfect tense (i.e., expressing two events/verbs in the past, one having happened before the other) in Arabic can be expressed in three ways, as follows:

(1) by means of both events in the perfect/past forms with the adverbial بَعْدَ أن "after":

حَضَرَ إلى الفَصْلِ بَعْدَ أنْ كَتَبَ الواجِب .

"He came to class after he had written the homework."

(2) by means of the first event in the perfect/past form and the second event in the imperfect/present form preceded by قَبْلَ أن "before":

كَتَبَ الواجِبَ قَبْلَ أنْ يَحْضُرَ إلى الفَصْل .

"He had written the homework before he came to class."

(3) by means of both events in the perfect/past forms with the verb كانَ "was/were" and the particle قَدْ preceding the first event and عِنْدَما "when" preceding the second event:

عِنْدَما حَضَرَ إلى الفَصْلِ كانَ قَدْ كَتَبَ الواجِب .

"When he came to class, he had already written the homework."

Like the past tense, the past perfect tense can be negated by the two optional ways of لَمْ "did not" or ما "did not," as in:

لَمْ يَحْضُرْ / ما حَضَرَ إلى الفَصْلِ بَعْدَ أنْ كَتَبَ الواجِبَ .

"He did not come to the class after he had written the homework."

لَمْ يَكْتُبْ / ما كَتَبَ الواجِبَ قَبْلَ أنْ يَحْضُرَ إلى الفَصْلِ .

"He had not written the homework before he came to class."

عِنْدَما حَضَرَ إلى الفَصْلِ لَمْ يَكُنْ قَدْ كَتَبَ الواجِبَ .

"When he came to class, he had not written the homework."

عِنْدَما حَضَرَ إلى الفَصْلِ ما كانَ قَدْ كَتَبَ الواجِبَ .

"When he came to class, he had not written the homework."

4.1.3.8 *The Simple Future Tense and its Negation*

The simple future tense is expressed by the future particles سَـ or سَوْفَ "will" (for *near* and *distant* future, respectively), the imperfect/present form of the verb, and an adverb of time (see Chapter 8) expressing a future time, as in:

سَتَدْرُسُ صَديقتي غَداً .

"My (female) friend will study tomorrow."

سَوْفَ تَدْرُسُ صَديقتي في الأُسْبوع القادِمِ .

"My (female) friend will study next week."

سَيَعْمَلُ أَصْدِقائي في النَّهارِ وسَيَدْرُسونَ في المَساءِ غَداً .

"My (male) friends will work during the day and will study
in the evening tomorrow."

سَوْفَ يَعْمَلُ أَصْدِقائي في النَّهارِ و يَدْرُسونَ في المَساءِ في الشَّهْرِ القادِمِ .

"My (male) friends will work during the day and will study
in the evening next month."

سَأُسافِرُ إلى الجَزائِرِ في الأُسْبوع القادِمِ إنْ شاءَ الله .

"I will travel to Algeria next week, God willing."

سَوْفَ أُسافِرُ إلى الجَزائِرِ في السَّنَةِ القادِمَةِ إنْ شاءَ الله .

"I will travel to Algeria next year, God willing."

The simple future tense is negated by the dropping of the future particles سَـ or سَوْفَ "will," the use of the imperfect/present form of the verb, and the placement of the negation particle لَنْ "will not" before it, as in:

لَنْ تَدْرُسَ صَديقَتي غَداً .

"My (female) friend will not study tomorrow."

لَنْ يَعْمَلَ أَصْدِقائي في النَّهارِ ولَنْ يَدْرُسوا في المَساءِ في الأُسْبوعِ القادِمِ .

"My (male) friends will not work during the day and will not study
in the evening next week."

لَنْ أُسافِرَ إلى الجَزائِرِ في السَّنَةِ القادِمَة .

"I will not travel to Algeria next year."

The mood ending of the verb following the negation particle لَنْ "will not" is that of المُضارِع المَنْصوب "the subjunctive," as illustrated below:

لَنْ يَفْعَلْنَ "they all F will not do"	لَنْ يَفْعَلوا "they all M will not do"	لَنْ تَفْعَلا "they both F will not do"	لَنْ يَفْعَلا "they both M will not do"	لَنْ تَفْعَلَ "she will not do"	لَنْ يَفْعَلَ "he will not do"
لَنْ تَفْعَلْنَ "you all F will not do"	لَنْ تَفْعَلوا "you all M will not do"	لَنْ تَفْعَلا "you both will not do"		لَنْ تَفْعَلي "you SF will not do"	لَنْ تَفْعَلَ "you SM will not do"
لَنْ نَفْعَلَ "we will not do"			لَنْ أَفْعَلَ "I will not do"		

4.1.3.9 The Future Continuous Tense and its Negation

There is no specific future continuous tense in Arabic. It may be expressed by the simple future tense or by the additional use of an adverb of time (see Chapter 8) expressing a duration of time, as in:

سَتَدْرُسُ صَديقَتي غَداً .

"My (female) friend will be studying/will study tomorrow."

سَوْفَ تَدْرُسُ صَديقَتي في الأُسْبوعِ القادِمِ .

"My (female) friend will be studying/will study next week."

سَيَقْرَأُ الطُّلَّابُ ويَكْتُبُونَ طِوالَ النَّهارِ غَداً .

"The (male) students will be reading and will be writing all day tomorrow."

سَوْفَ يَقْرَأُ الطُّلَّابُ و يَكْتُبُونَ طِوالَ العُطلَةِ في الأُسْبوعِ القادِم .

"The (male) students will be reading and will be writing during
all the holiday next week."

سَتَعْمَلُ صَديقَتي في المَكْتَبَةِ كُلَّ المَساء .

"My (female) friend will be working/will work in the library all evening."

سَوَفَ تَعْمَلُ صَديقَتي في المَكْتَبَةِ كُلَّ الصَّيْف .

"My (female) friend will be working/will work in the library all summer."

The future continuous tense is negated in the same way as simple future
negation (see 4.1.3.8), as in:

لَنْ يَقْرَأَ الطُّلَّابُ ولَنْ يَكْتُبوا طِوالَ النَّهارِ غَداً .

"The (male) students will not be reading and will not be writing
all day tomorrow."

4.1.3.10 *The Future Perfect Tense and its Negation*

The future perfect tense can be expressed by the future particles ـسَ or
سَوْفَ "will," the imperfect/present form of the verb يَكُونُ "will be" preceded
by the particle قَدْ , and the perfect/past form of the verb, and an adverb
of time (see Chapter 8) expressing a future time, as in:

في العامِ القادِم سَوْفَ تَكونُ قَدْ دَرَسَتْ العربيَّةَ خَمْسَ سَنَوات .

"Next year, she will have studied Arabic for five years."

غَداً سَتكونُ قَدْ دَرَسَتْ العربيَّةَ خَمْسَ سَنَوات .

"Tomorrow, she will have studied Arabic for five years."

The future perfect tense is negated in the same way as simple future
negation (see 4.1.3.8), as in:

في العامِ القادِم لَنْ تَكونَ قَدْ دَرَسَتْ العربيَّةَ خَمْسَ سَنَوات .

"Next year, she will not have studied Arabic for five years."

4.2 The Nominal Sentence الجُمْلة الإِسْمِيَّة

4.2.1 Structure of the Nominal Sentence

Three aspects characterize nominal sentences. First, a nominal sentence must contain two basic components. The first component is called المُبْتَدأ "that which the sentence starts with," or what is technically referred to (in the West) as "the topic" or "subject." (When a word occurs in sentence initial position, this indicates a focus on that word.) The second component is called الخَبَر "that which tells news [about the first component]," or what is technically referred to (in the West) as "the comment" or "predicate." The Arabic terms and their literal meanings must be borne in mind so that the nominal sentence structure can be distinguished from the noun phrase structure. Second, while the first part must be definite, the second part occurs mostly (though not always) in the indefinite. Third, while the first part may be a noun, a pronoun, a phrase, or a clause, the second part may be a verb, a noun, a pronoun, an adjective, a phrase, a clause, or even a sentence. Accordingly, there are six distinct types of nominal sentence: (1) nominal sentences containing a verb predicate, (2) nominal/verbless sentences containing an indefinite predicate, (3) nominal/verbless sentences containing a definite predicate, (4) nominal sentences containing an indefinite subject, (5) nominal sentences containing a sentence predicate, and (6) nominal sentences containing a clause predicate.

4.2.1.1 Nominal Sentences Containing a Verb Predicate

A sentence containing a noun, a pronoun, a proper noun, or a noun phrase in initial position followed by a verb is treated traditionally as a nominal sentence, rather than a verbal sentence. The difference between a verbal sentence (with a verb in initial position) and a nominal sentence containing a verb as its predicate is that the latter must consist minimally of two main parts, المُبْتَدأ "that which the sentence starts with" (or "subject/topic") and الخَبَر "that which tells news [about the first component]" (or "predicate/comment"), whereas the former may consist of one part/word (as explained in 4.1.1 above). Each part of the nominal sentence may consist of one word or more, with the first part always definite and both parts of the sentence agreeing in number and gender with each other, as in:

	الخَبَر	المُبْتَدَأ	
"The students studied."	دَرَسوا .	الطُّلّابُ	.1
"She was absent."	تَغَيَّبْتْ .	هِيَ	.2
"My (female) teacher was absent from class."	تَغَيَّبَتْ عَن الصَّفِ .	أُسْتاذَتي	.3
"Mustafa came to the market."	جاءَ إلى السّوقِ .	مُصطَفى	.4
"This woman came to the market."	جاءَتْ إلى السّوقِ .	هٰذِهِ المَرأَةُ	.5

4.2.1.2 *Nominal/Verbless Sentences Containing an Indefinite Predicate*

This is by far the most common type of nominal (verbless) sentence. Like all types of nominal sentence, a nominal (verbless) sentence consists of two parts: a definite subject المُبْتَدَأ (i.e., the first part) that can be a noun, pronoun, proper name, or noun phrase and an indefinite predicate الخَبَر (i.e., the second part) that can be an adjective, noun, or noun phrase. Both parts agree in number and gender with each other, as in:

	الخَبَر	المُبْتَدَأ	
"The students [are] American."	أمريكيّونَ .	الطُّلّابُ	.6
"She [is] a student."	طالِبَةٌ .	هِيَ	.7
"I [am] Arab (male)/Arab (female)."	عَرَبيٌّ / عَرَبِيَّةٌ .	أنا	.8
"Cairo [is] a city."	مَدينَةٌ .	القاهِرَةُ	.9
"Washington [is] a big city."	مَدينَةٌ كَبيرَةٌ .	واشِنْطن	.10
"George [is] a (male) student."	طالِبٌ .	جورج	.11
"George [is] a (male) American student."	طالِبٌ أمريكيٌّ .	جورج	.12
"Abdullah [is] a (male) student."	طالِبٌ .	عَبْدُ الله	.13
"Abdullah [is] a (male) Iraqi student."	طالِبٌ عِراقيٌّ .	عَبْدُ الله	.14
"The (female) teacher [is] Syrian."	سوريَّةٌ .	الأُسْتاذَةُ	.15
"My (female) teacher [is] Syrian."	سوريَّةٌ .	أُسْتاذَتي	.16
"This [is] a (female) teacher."	أُسْتاذَةٌ .	هٰذِهِ	.17
"This [is] a (female) Syrian teacher."	أُسْتاذَةٌ سوريَّةٌ .	هٰذِهِ	.18
"This (female) teacher [is] Syrian."	سوريَّةٌ .	هٰذِهِ الأُسْتاذَةُ	.19

This type is also referred to as an "equational sentence" (i.e., consisting of two main parts) or "verbless sentence" (i.e., where the present-tense verb *to be* is missing but is supplied when translating the sentence into English as *are*, *is*, or *am*, depending on the meaning, as in the examples above). Both parts of the nominal (verbless) sentence here take the nominative مَرْفوع case endings: with the ending ُ [u] for the definite part and ٌ [un] for the indefinite part, except for pronouns which have invariable endings.

4.2.1.3 Nominal/Verbless Sentences Containing a Definite Predicate
This type of sentence is used:

(a) when the predicate الخَبَر (i.e., the second part) occurs with a possessive pronoun suffix:

	الخَبَر	المُبْتَدَأ	
"This [is] her book."	كِتابُها .	هٰذا	20.
"The (male) teacher [is] his friend."	صَديقُهُ .	الأُسْتاذُ	21.
"My book [is] my friend."	صَديقي .	كِتابي	22.

(b) when the predicate is a prepositional or adverbial phrase (i.e., it consists of a preposition or adverb followed by a definite noun):

	الخَبَر	المُبْتَدَأ	
"The students [are] in the class."	في الصَّفِّ .	الطُّلّابُ	23.
"My book [is] on the table."	عَلىٰ الطّاوِلَةِ .	كِتابي	24.
"The bird [is] over the tree."	فَوْقَ الشَّجَرةِ .	العُصْفورُ	25.

(c) when the predicate occurs in the definite to express an intended definite meaning of the predicate, as in 26–30 below:

	الخَبَر	المُبْتَدَأ	
"My book [is] my friend."	صَديقي .	كِتابي	26.
"This [is] my (female) teacher."	أُسْتاذَتي .	هٰذِهِ	27.
"This [is] the (male) teacher."	الأُسْتاذُ .	هٰذا	28.
"This [is] the (male) teacher of Arabic."	أُسْتاذُ العَرَبِيَّةِ .	هٰذا	29.
"The engineers [are] the (ones) responsible."	المَسْؤولونَ .	المُهَنْدِسونَ	30.

In this case, a redundant independent personal pronoun may be inserted to separate the two parts of the sentence in order to clarify the structure (as a sentence vs. a phrase) or to emphasize the meaning, as in:

	الخَبَر		المُبْتَدَأ	
"My book [is] my friend."	صَديقي .	هُوَ	كِتابي	31.
"This [is] my (female) teacher."	أُسْتاذَتي .	هِيَ	هٰذِهِ	32.
"This [is] the (male) teacher."	الأُسْتاذُ .	هُوَ	هٰذا	33.
"This [is] the (male) teacher of Arabic."	أُسْتاذُ العَرَبِيَّةِ .	هُوَ	هٰذا	34.
"The engineers [are] the (ones) responsible."	المَسْؤولونَ	هُم	المُهَنْدِسونَ	35.

4.2.1.4 *Nominal Sentences Containing an Indefinite Subject*

Sometimes the subject المُبْتَدَأ of nominal sentences may be indefinite. In this case, the order of the subject المُبْتَدَأ and predicate الخَبَر must be reversed (thereby maintaining the beginning of the sentence with a definite meaning), as in the following (note that examples 23–25 above are given below as 36–38, with indefinite subjects):

	المُبْتَدَأ	الخَبَر	
"In the class [are] students/There are students in the class."	طُلّابٌ .	في الصَّفِّ	36.
"On the table [is] a book/There is a book on the table."	كِتابٌ .	عَلَى الطّاوِلَةِ	37.
"Over the tree [is] a bird/There is a bird over the tree."	عُصْفورٌ .	فَوْقَ الشَّجَرَةِ	38.
"For each student [is]/Each student has a specialization."	اِخْتِصاصٌ .	لِكُلِّ طالِبٍ	39.
"For me [is] a friend/I have a friend."	صَديقٌ .	لي	40.
"At him [is] a car/He has a car."	سَيّارَةٌ .	عِنْدَهُ	41.
"With her [is] a book/She has a book with her."	كِتابٌ .	مَعَها	42.

The order of the subject المُبْتَدَأ and predicate الخَبَر can be retained if a word with a definite meaning such as هُناكَ "there" is introduced as the predicate, as in:

	المُبْتَدَأ	الخَبَر	
"There [are] students in the class."	طُلَّابٌ في الصَّفِّ .	هُناكَ	43.
"There [is] a book on the table."	كِتابٌ عَلى الطّاوِلَةِ .	هُناكَ	44.
"There [is] a bird over the tree."	عُصفورٌ فَوْقَ الشَّجَرَةِ .	هُناكَ	45.

Note: In Arabic, an indefinite noun is treated as definite if it is modified by an indefinite adjective, an indefinite noun, or if it occurs within an إضافة *'iDaafa* phrase. Accordingly, a modified indefinite subject retains its initial position in the sentence, as in:

	الخَبَر	المُبْتَدَأ	
"A tall student [is] in the class."	في الصَّفِّ .	طالِبٌ طَويلٌ	46.
"A student of sciences [is] in the class."	في الصَّفِّ .	طالِبُ عُلومٍ	47.
"Every student reads in his book."	يَقْرَأُ في كِتابِهِ .	كُلُّ طالِبٍ	48.
"Older than you [is] more experience than you."	أَكْثَرُ مِنْكَ خِبْرَةً .	أَكْبَرُ مِنْكَ سِنّاً	49.

4.2.1.5 *Nominal Sentences Containing a Sentence Predicate*
In this case, a verbal sentence (50–51 below) or nominal sentence (52–53 below) can function as the predicate الخَبَر (i.e., second part) of a nominal sentence, as in:

	الخَبَر	المُبْتَدَأ	
"The friend is truthful with his friend."	يَصْدُقُ مَعَ صَديقِهِ .	الصَّديقُ	50.
"The students write their homework."	يَكْتُبونَ واجِبَهُم .	الطُّلَّابُ	51.
"The garden, its trees are high."	أَشْجارُها عالِيَةٌ .	الحَديقَةُ	52.
"The teachers, their offices are small."	مَكاتِبُهُم صَغيرَةٌ .	الأَساتِذَةُ	53.

Note: A verbal sentence functioning as a predicate is essentially the same as when the predicate is a verb (see 4.2.1.1 above).

4.2.1.6 *Nominal Sentences Containing a Clause Subject*

The subject الْمُبْتَدَأ of nominal sentences may comprise a clause, such as relative clause (i.e., preceded by a relative pronoun; see Chapter 5 on pronouns) or complementizer clause (i.e., preceded, in particular, by the complementizer أَنْ), as in:

	الْخَبَر	الْمُبْتَدَأ	
"The one who got out of the car [is] an old man."	رَجُلٌ عَجوزٌ .	الَّذي خَرَجَ مِنَ السَّيَّارَةِ	54.
"The one who exited the building [is] Mona."	مُنى .	الَّتي خَرَجَتْ مِنَ البِناءِ	55.
"To learn and graduate [is] better for you."	خَيْرٌ لَكَ .	أَنْ تَتَعَلَّمَ وتَتَخَرَّجَ	56.

4.2.2 Negation of Nominal Sentences

Nominal sentences which contain a verb or a verbal sentence as the predicate الْخَبَر are negated in the same way as any verbal sentence (see 4.1 above). Other types of nominal sentence are mostly negated by the negation word لَيْسَ "is not" (placed before the subject or after it), which conjugates as any verb and must agree with the subject and predicate in gender, number, and person, as in:

لَسْنَ "they all F are not"	لَيْسوا "they all M are not"	لَيْسَتا "they both F are not"	لَيْسا "they both M are not"	لَيْسَتْ "she is not"	لَيْسَ "he is not"
لَسْتُنَّ "you all F are not"	لَسْتُم "you all M are not"	لَسْتُما "you both are not"		لَسْتِ "you SF are not"	لَسْتَ "you SM are not"
لَسْنا "we are not"				لَسْتُ "I am not"	

	الخَبَر	لَيْسَ + المُبْتَدَأ	
"The students are not American."	أمريكيِّيَن .	لَيْسَ الطُّلَّابُ	57.
"They are not American."	أمريكيِّيَن .	لَيْسوا	58.
"She is not a student."	طالِبَةً .	لَيْسَتْ	59.
"I am not Arab (male)/Arab (female)."	عَرَبِيّاً / عَرَبِيَّةً .	لَسْتُ	60.
"Abdullah is not a (male) student."	طالِباً .	لَيْسَ عَبْدُ الله	61.
"My (female) teacher is not Syrian."	سوريَّةً .	لَيْسَتْ أُسْتاذَتي	62.
"This is not a (female) Syrian teacher."	أُسْتاذَةً سوريَّةً .	لَيْسَتْ هٰذِهِ	63.
"My book is not my friend."	صَديقي .	لَيْسَ كِتابي	64.

Note: With the use of the negation word لَيْسَ "is not," the predicate takes the accusative مَنْصوب case ending while the subject retains its nominative مَرْفوع case ending. This is also true when the order is reversed, where the second element (i.e., the subject المُبْتَدَأ) takes the nominative مَرْفوع case ending, as in:

	المُبْتَدَأ	الخَبَر	
"There is not a book on the table."	كِتابٌ .	لَيْسَ عَلَى الطّاوِلَةِ	65.
"For me there is not a friend/I do not have a friend."	صَديقٌ .	لَيْسَ لي	66.
"There are not students in the class."	طُلَّابٌ في الصَّفِّ .	لَيْسَ هُناكَ	67.

Finally, sentences such as 46–47 above are negated by the "genus negation" or "absolute negation" particle لا النافِيَة لِلْجِنْس , where the subject following it takes the accusative مَنْصوب case ending (without nunation) and its adjective (if modified by an adjective) takes the same case (with nunation), as in:

	الخَبَر	المُبْتَدَأ	
"There is no student in the class."	في الصَّفِّ .	لا طالِبَ	68.
"There is no tall student in the class."	في الصَّفِّ .	لا طالِبَ طَويلاً	69.
"There is no student of sciences in the class."	في الصَّفِّ .	لا طالِبَ عُلومٍ	70.

4.2.3 The Past Tense of the Nominal Sentence and its Negation

Nominal sentences containing a verb or verbal sentence as the predicate الْخَبَر are expressed in the past tense and negated in the past tense, just like any verbal sentence (see 4.1.3.4 above). Other types of verbless nominal sentences are expressed in the past by the verb to be كانَ "was" (placed before or after the subject), which must agree with the subject and predicate in gender, number, and person, as in:

كُنَّ "they all F were"	كانوا "they all M were"	كانَتا "they both F were"	كانا "they both M were"	كانَتْ "she was"	كانَ "he was"
كُنْتُنَّ "you all F were"	كُنْتُم "you all M were"	كُنْتُما "you both were"		كُنْتِ "you SF were"	كُنْتَ "you SM were"
كُنّا "we were"				كُنْتُ "I was"	

	الْخَبَر	كانَ + الْمُبْتَدَأ	
"The students were American."	أمريكيِّينَ .	كانَ الطُّلّابُ	.71
"They were American."	أمريكيِّينَ .	كانوا	.72
"She was Arab."	عَرَبيَّةً .	كانَتْ	.73
"I was a (male) student/(female) student."	طالِباً / طالِبَةً .	كُنْتُ	.74
"Abdullah was a (male) student."	طالِباً .	كانَ عَبْدُ الله	.75
"My (female) teacher was Syrian."	سوريَّةً .	كانَتْ أُسْتاذَتي	.76
"My book was my friend."	صَديقي .	كانَ كِتابي	.77

Note: With the use of the verb to be كانَ "was" the predicate (when it is not a verb) takes the accusative مَنْصوب case ending while the subject retains its nominative مَرْفوع case ending.

As for negating the past tense of nominal sentences, the rules of past-tense negation are followed (see 4.1.3.4 above), that is, by means of أَمْ "did not" or ما "did not" placed before the verb to be كانَ "was," as in:

	الخَبَر	لَمْ + يَكُنْ/ ما + كانَ + المُبْتَدَأ	
"The students were not American."	أمريكيّينَ .	لَمْ يَكُنْ الطُّلّابُ	78.
"The students were not American."	أمريكيّينَ .	ما كانَ الطُّلّابُ	79.
"They were not American."	أمريكيّينَ .	لَمْ يَكونوا	80.
"They were not American."	أمريكيّينَ .	ما كانوا	81.
"She was not Arab."	عَرَبيَّةً .	لَمْ تَكُنْ	82.
"She was not Arab."	عَرَبيَّةً .	ما كانَتْ	83.
"I was not a (male) student/(female) student."	طالِباً / طالِبَةً .	لَمْ أَكُنْ	84.
"I was not a (male) student/(female) student."	طالِباً / طالِبَةً .	ما كُنْتُ	85.
"My book was not my friend."	صَديقي .	لَمْ يَكُنْ كِتابي	86.
"My book was not my friend."	صَديقي .	ما كانَ كِتابي	87.

4.2.4 The Future Tense of the Nominal Sentence and its Negation

Nominal sentences which contain a verb or a verbal sentence as the predicate الخَبَر are expressed in the future and negated in the future in the same way as any verbal sentence (see 4.1.3.8 above). Other types of nominal (verbless) sentence are expressed in the future by means of the verb to be يَكونُ "is" preceded by the future particles سَـ or سَوْفَ "will," both of which are placed before or after the subject. The verb to be يَكونُ "is" agrees with the subject and predicate in gender, number, and person, as in:

	الخَبَر	سَـ/ سَوْفَ + يَكونُ + المُبْتَدَأ	
"I will be a (male)/(female) student."	طالِباً / طالِبَةً .	سَوْفَ أَكونُ	88.
"I will be a (male)/(female) student."	طالِباً / طالِبَةً .	سَأَكونُ	89.
"They will be students."	طُلّاباً .	سَوْفَ يَكونونَ	90.
"They will be students."	طُلّاباً .	سَيَكونونَ	91.
"My book will be my friend."	صَديقي .	سَوْفَ يَكونُ كِتابي	92.
"My book will be my friend."	صَديقي .	سَيَكونُ كِتابي	93.

As for negating the future tense of nominal sentences, the rules of future-tense negation are followed (see 4.1.3.8 above), that is, by dropping the future particles ‏ـس‎ or ‏سَوْفَ‎ "will," and placing the negation particle ‏لَنْ‎ "will not" before the verb ‏يَكونُ‎ "is," as in:

	الخَبَر	لَنْ + يَكونَ + المُبْتَدَأ	
"I will not be a (male)/(female) student."	طالِباً / طالِبَةً	لَنْ أكونَ	94.
"They will not be students."	طُلّاباً .	لَنْ يَكونوا	95.
"My book will not be my friend."	صَديقي .	لَنْ يَكونَ كِتابي	96.

4.2.5 *kaana* ‏كانَ‎ and its Sisters

As discussed above, ‏كانَ‎ "was" converts the nominal sentence into the past tense, while ‏لَيْسَ‎ "is not" negates it. Both belong to a class of 13 verbs called in Arabic ‏كانَ وأَخَواتُها‎ "*kaana* and its sisters," and are used with the nominal sentence, each according to its own meaning, although most of them have the general meaning of "became" and "remained." Below are the most common verbs of this class:

أَضْحىٰ	أَصْبَحَ	صارَ	لَيْسَ	كانَ
"became [at dawn]"	"became [in the morning]"	"became"	"is not"	"was"

ما دامَ	ما زالَ	ظَلَّ	باتَ	أَمْسىٰ
"is still"	"is still"	"remained"	"remained [at night]"	"became [in the evening]"

Like ‏كانَ‎ and ‏لَيْسَ‎ , when these verbs are used, the subject ‏المُبْتَدَأ‎ of the nominal sentence takes the nominative ‏مَرْفوع‎ case ending, whereas the predicate ‏الخَبَر‎ takes the accusative ‏مَنْصوب‎ case ending. Furthermore, the subject can be dropped, since the pronoun suffix attached to the verb serves as a subject, as in:

	الخَبَر	المُبْتَدَأ
"The weather became cold."	بارِداً .	صارَ الجَوُّ
"My sister is still sick."	مَريضَةً .	ما زالَتْ أُخْتي
"She is still sick."	مَريضَةً .	مازالَتْ
"The students became tired."	مُتْعَبينَ .	أَصْبَحَ الطُّلّابُ
"They became tired."	مُتْعَبينَ .	أَصْبَحوا

4.2.6 *'inna* إِنَّ and its Sisters

There is a small class of six particles and verbs called in Arabic إِنَّ وأَخَواتُها "*'inna* and its sisters" that are used with nominal sentences, each depending on its own meaning. The following are *'inna* and its sisters:

لٰكِنَّ	أَنَّ	إِنَّ
"but"	"that"	"indeed, that"

لَعَلَّ	لَيْتَ	كَأَنَّ
"hope that"	"wish that"	"seems that"

Unlike "*kaana* and its sisters" (see 4.2.5), when *'inna* and its sisters are used, the subject المُبْتَدَأ of the nominal sentence takes the accusative مَنْصوب case ending whereas the predicate الخَبَر takes the nominative مَرْفوع case ending, as in:

	الخَبَر	المُبْتَدَأ
"Indeed, the weather is cold."	بارِدٌ .	إِنَّ الجَوَّ
"I think that the weather is moderate."	مُعْتَدِلٌ .	أَظُنُّ أَنَّ الجَوَّ
"The teacher seems sick."	مَريضَةٌ .	كَأَنَّ الأُسْتاذَةَ
"But the students are tired."	مُتْعَبونَ .	لٰكِنَّ الطُّلّابَ
"[I] Wish that the place [were] near."	قَريبٌ .	لَيْتَ المَكانَ
"[I] Hope that our friend is happy."	سَعيدٌ .	لَعَلَّ صَديقَنا

The subject الْمُبْتَدَأ of the nominal sentence can be dropped if it is replaced by a pronoun suffix that refers to it, as in:

	الْخَبَر	الْمُبْتَدَأ
"You (female) seem sick."	مَريضَةٌ .	كَأَنَّكِ
"But they (male) are tired."	مُتْعَبونَ .	لٰكِنَّهُم
"[I] Hope that he is happy."	سَعيدٌ .	لَعَلَّهُ

Note: When the order of the subject الْمُبْتَدَأ of the nominal sentence is reversed, such as when it occurs indefinite (see 4.2.14), and the predicate الْخَبَر takes its position in the sentence, the subject still takes the accusative مَنْصوب case ending, as in:

	الْمُبْتَدَأ	الْخَبَر
"But there are students in the class."	طُلَّاباً .	لٰكِنَّ في الصَّفِّ
"There seems to be a bird in the tree."	عُصْفوراً .	كَأَنَّ فَوْقَ الشَّجَرةِ
"Indeed, I have a friend at the university."	صَديقاً في الجامِعةِ .	إنَّ لي

The particles *'inna* إِنَّ and *'anna* أَنَّ are mostly used as complementizers with the meaning of "that" following certain verbs that take *that*, in addition to a nominal sentence following them. In particular, the particle إِنَّ occurs after the verb قالَ – يَقولُ "to say" and *'anna* أَنَّ occurs after the rest, as in:

	الْخَبَر	الْمُبْتَدَأ
"He knows that the weather is moderate."	مُعْتَدِلٌ .	يَعْرِفُ أَنَّ الجَوَّ
"He thinks that the weather is moderate."	بارِدٌ .	يَظُنُّ أَنَّ الجَوَّ
"He believes that the plane will arrive at noon."	سَتَصِلُ ظُهْراً .	يَعْتَقِدُ أَنَّ الطّائِرةَ
"He said that he went home."	ذَهَبَ إلى البَيْتِ .	قالَ إنَّهُ
"He says that the weather is hot."	حارٌّ .	يَقولُ إنَّ الجَوَّ

In addition, the particle *'anna* أَنَّ has an idiomatic usage when combined with the preposition لِ "for" → لِأَنَّ having the meaning of "because," followed by a (nominal) sentence, whether by means of a noun subject and a predicate or a pronoun (suffix) subject and a predicate (note that, as discussed throughout 4.2, the predicate of the nominal sentence can be a noun, adjective, or verb), as in:

أَتَعَلَّمُ العَرَبِيَّةَ لِأَنَّ العَرَبِيَّةَ لُغَةٌ جميلةٌ .

"I learn Arabic, because Arabic is a beautiful language."

أَتَعَلَّمُ العَرَبِيَّةَ لِأَنَّها لُغَةٌ جميلةٌ .

"I learn Arabic, because it is a beautiful language."

أَتَعَلَّمُ العَرَبِيَّةَ لِأَنَّها جميلةٌ .

"I learn Arabic, because it is beautiful."

أَتَعَلَّمُ العَرَبِيَّةَ لِأَنِّي أُحِبُّ اللُّغاتَ .

"I learn the Arabic language, because I like languages."

4.3 Summary

This chapter discussed both types of sentences in Arabic. Remember:

- Arabic expresses three basic tenses: past, present, and future
- other tenses are not expressed by means of specialized grammatical forms, as in English, but simply by means of an appropriate adverb of time and words/particles
- each of the three basic tenses has a special negation particle with a specific mood ending on the verb following the particle, as follows:

Verb ending	Negated tense	Negation particle
المُضارِع المَرفوع "the indicative"	المُضارِع "the present"	لا "do not/does not"
المُضارِع المَجْزوم "the jussive"	الماضي "the past"	لَمْ "did not"
—	الماضي "the past"	ما "did not"
المُضارِع المَنْصوب "the subjunctive"	المُسْتَقْبَل "the future"	لَنْ "will not"

- nominal sentences are negated by a special negation word لَيْسَ "is not," which conjugates just like a verb and must agree with the subject and predicate in gender, number, and person
- the predicate of a nominal sentence occurring with the negation word لَيْسَ "is not" takes the accusative مَنْصوب case ending
- in a strict verbal sentence, where the verb precedes the subject, the verb agrees with the subject in gender only
- in a nominal sentence, the subject agrees with the predicate in gender and number; in those containing a verb as a predicate (i.e., following the subject), the verb (predicate) agrees with the subject in gender, number, and person
- a nominal/verbless sentence is always expressed in the present tense, where the verb "is/are/am" is inserted mentally between the subject and predicate, but it can also be expressed in the past and future by means of the verb كانَ "was" and يَكونُ "is" (together with a future particle), respectively
- the predicate of a nominal sentence occurring with the verb كانَ "was" and يَكونُ "is" takes the accusative مَنْصوب case ending
- *kaana* كانَ belongs to a small class of verbs that behave similarly and are used with the nominal sentence; following these verbs the subject takes the nominative مَرْفوع case ending while the predicate takes the accusative مَنْصوب case ending
- *'inna* إنَّ belongs to a small class of particles/verbs that behave similarly and are used with nominal sentences; following these particles/verbs the subject takes the accusative مَنْصوب case ending whereas the predicate takes the nominative مَرْفوع case ending.

5

Pronouns الضَّمَائِر

This chapter discusses Arabic pronouns, including personal pronouns, object pronouns, possessive pronouns, demonstrative pronouns, and relative pronouns. Like verbs, nouns, and adjectives covered in the previous chapter, pronouns are marked for features of gender and number. The chapter covers how:

- pronouns are generally marked for features of *person*, *gender*, and *number*
- demonstrative pronouns are marked additionally for features of *distance* and *humanness*
- demonstrative and relative pronouns are marked additionally for the feature *case*
- relative pronouns are sometimes dropped
- the particles ما *maa* and مَن *man* are used as relative pronouns
- sound changes are made to pronoun and word endings.

Modern Standard Arabic Grammar: A Learner's Guide, First Edition.
© 2011 Mohammad T. Alhawary. Published 2011 by Blackwell Publishing Ltd.

5.1 Personal Pronouns ضَمائِرُ الرَّفْع

Personal or subject pronouns ضَمائِر الرَّفْع *Damaa'ir 'ar-raf* "nominative pronouns" function as the subject of the sentence and are written independently (i.e., as separate words). Personal pronouns are marked for person (first, second, and third), gender (masculine and feminine), and number (singular, dual, and plural). Table 5.1 shows the personal pronouns available in MSA:

Table 5.1

Plural feminine	Plural masculine	Dual feminine	Dual masculine	Singular feminine	Singular masculine	Person
هُنَّ *hunna* "they all F"	هُم *hum* "they all M"	هُما *humaa* "they both M"		هِيَ *hiya* "she"	هُوَ *huwa* "he"	3rd
أَنْتُنَّ *'antunna* "you all F"	أَنْتُم *'antum* "you all M"	أَنْتُما *'antumaa* "you both"		أَنْتِ *'anti* "you F"	أَنْتَ *'anta* "you M"	2nd
نَحْنُ *naHnu* "we"				أَنا *'anaa* "I"		1st

5.2 Object Pronouns ضَمائِرُ النَّصْب

Object pronouns ضَمائِر النَّصْب *Damaa'ir 'an-naSb* "accusative pronouns" function as the object of the verb/action and are written as suffixes attached to the end of verbs. Like subject pronouns, object pronouns are marked for person (first, second, and third), gender (masculine and feminine), and number (singular, dual, and plural). Table 5.2 shows the object pronouns available in MSA and Table 5.3 gives an example of each:

Table 5.2

Plural feminine	*Plural masculine*	*Dual feminine*	*Dual masculine*	*Singular feminine*	*Singular masculine*	*Person*
ـهُنَّ -hunna "them all F"	ـهُم -hum "them all M"	ـهُمَا -humaa "them both"		ـها -haa "her"	ـهُ -hu "him"	3rd
ـكُنَّ -kunna "you all F"	ـكُم -kum "you all M"	ـكُمَا -kumaa "you both"		ـكِ -ki "you F"	ـكَ -ka "you M"	2nd
ـنا -naa "us"				ـني -nii "me"		1st

Table 5.3

Plural feminine	*Plural masculine*	*Dual feminine*	*Dual masculine*	*Singular feminine*	*Singular masculine*	*Person*
دَرَّسَهُنَّ darrasa-**hunna** "he taught them all F"	دَرَّسَهُم darrasa-**hum** "he taught them all M"	دَرَّسَهُمَا darrasa-**humaa** "he taught them both"		دَرَّسَها darrasa-**haa** "he taught her"	دَرَّسَهُ darrasa-**hu** "he taught him"	3rd
دَرَّسَكُنَّ darrasa-**kunna** "he taught you all F"	دَرَّسَكُم darrasa-**kum** "he taught you all M"	دَرَّسَكُمَا darrasa-**kumaa** "he taught you both"		دَرَّسَكِ darrasa-**ki** "he taught you F"	دَرَّسَكَ darrasa-**ka** "he taught you M"	2nd
دَرَّسَنا darrasa-**naa** "he taught us"				دَرَّسَني darrasa-**nii** "he taught me"		1st

Another type of object pronouns are written as independent words, consisting of the particle إِيَّا *'iyyaa* and the dependent object pronoun, with no change in spelling and pronunciation except in the case of the "me" pronoun, as in Table 5.4:

Table 5.4

Plural feminine	Plural masculine	Dual feminine	Dual masculine	Singular feminine	Singular masculine	Person
إِيَّاهُنَّ *'iyyaa-* **hunna** "them all F"	إِيَّاهُم *'iyyaa-* **hum** "them all M"	إِيَّاهُمَا *'iyyaa-* **humaa** "them both"		إِيَّاهَا *'iyyaa-* **haa** "her"	إِيَّاهُ *'iyyaa-* **hu** "him"	3rd
إِيَّاكُنَّ *'iyyaa-* **kunna** "you all F"	إِيَّاكُم *'iyyaa-* **kum** "you all M"	إِيَّاكُمَا *'iyyaa-* **kumaa** "you both"		إِيَّاكِ *'iyyaa-* **ki** "you F"	إِيَّاكَ *'iyyaa-* **ka** "you M"	2nd
إِيَّانا *'iyyaa-naa* "us"				إِيَّايَ *'iyyaa-ya* "me"		1st

These independent object pronouns are used in specific contexts, mostly as second objects of verbs that take two objects, such as ظَنَّ *Zanna* "he thought" and أَعْطَى *'aʿTaa* "he gave," as in:

ظَنَنْتُكَ إِيَّاهُ . ← . ظَنَنْتُكَ أَحْمَد .

"I thought you [were] him." ← "I thought you [were] Ahmad."

أَعْطَيْتُهُ إِيَّاهُ . ← . أَعْطَيْتُهُ الْقَلَم .

"I gave [him it M] it to him" ← "I gave him the pen."

5.3   Possessive Pronouns ضَمائِر الجَرّ

Possessive pronouns ضَمائِر الجَرّ *Damaa'ir 'al-jarr* "genitive pronouns" function as possessive particles and are written as suffixes attached at the
end of nouns. Like subject pronouns and object pronouns, possessive pronouns are marked for person (first, second, and third), gender
(masculine and feminine), and number (singular, dual, and plural).
Table 5.5 shows the possessive pronouns available in MSA and Table 5.6
gives an example of each. Except for the first-person singular, possessive
pronouns are identical in shape and pronunciation to object pronouns.

Table 5.5

Plural feminine	Plural masculine	Dual feminine	Dual masculine	Singular feminine	Singular masculine	Person
هُنَّ-‎ -*hunna* "their all F"	هُم-‎ -*hum* "their all M"	هُما-‎ -*humaa* "their both"		ها-‎ -*haa* "her"	هُ-‎ -*hu* "his"	3rd
كُنَّ-‎ -*kunna* "your all F"	كُم-‎ -*kum* "your all M"	كُما-‎ -*kumaa* "your both"		كِ-‎ -*ki* "your F"	كَ-‎ -*ka* "your M"	2nd
نا-‎ -*naa* "our"				ي-‎ -*ii* "my"		1st

Table 5.6

Plural feminine	Plural masculine	Dual feminine	Dual masculine	Singular feminine	Singular masculine	Person
فَضْلُهُنَّ *faSlu-hunna* "their all F class"	فَضْلُهُم *faSlu-hum* "their all M class"	فَضْلُهُما *faSlu-humaa* "their both class"		فَضْلُها *faSlu-haa* "her class"	فَضْلُهُ *faSlu-hu* "his class"	3rd
فَضْلُكُنَّ *faSlu-kunna* "your all F class"	فَضْلُكُم *faSlu-kum* "your all M class"	فَضْلُكُما *faSlu-kumaa* "your both class"		فَضْلُكِ *faSlu-ki* "your F class"	فَضْلُكَ *faSlu-ka* "your M class"	2nd
فَضْلُنا *faSlu-naa* "our class"				فَضْلي *faSl-ii* "my class"		1st

Note: The short vowel preceding the pronoun ـي "my" is always deleted for ease of pronunciation. This vowel is a grammatical ending on nouns and adjectives and it can be [u], [a], or [i] (see 22.2.2 on case endings).

5.4 Demonstrative Pronouns أَسْماء الإِشارَة

Demonstrative pronouns أَسْماء الإِشارَة *'asmaa' 'al-'ishaara* "nouns of referring" are written as independent words. Arabic demonstrative pronouns are marked for distance (near and far), gender (masculine and feminine), number (singular, dual, and plural), and humanness (human and non-human). Table 5.7 shows the demonstrative pronouns available in MSA and Table 5.8 gives an example of each. Demonstrative pronouns for the non-human plural (for both *near* and *far*) are identical to those of the singular feminine, just as verbs and adjectives are in the third-person singular feminine when referring to non-human plurals (see 3.1.1 and 4.1.2).

Table 5.7

Plural non-human	Plural human	Dual feminine	Dual masculine	Singular feminine	Singular masculine	Distance
هٰذِهِ *haadhihi* "these all non-H"	هٰؤُلاءِ *haa'ulaa'i* "these all H"	هاتانِ *haataani* "these two F"	هٰذانِ *haadhaani* "these two M"	هٰذِهِ *haadhihi* "this F"	هٰذا *haadhaa* "this M"	Near
تِلْكَ *tilka* "those all non-H"	أُولٰئِكَ *'ulaa'ika* "those all H"	تانِكَ *taanika* "those two F"	ذانِكَ *dhaanika* "those two M"	تِلْكَ *tilka* "that F"	ذٰلِكَ *dhaalika* "that M"	Far

Table 5.8

Plural (M/F) non-human	Plural (M/F) human	Dual feminine	Dual masculine	Singular feminine	Singular masculine	Dis-tance
هٰذِهِ الكَراسي "these all non-H chairs M P non-H"	هٰؤُلاءِ الطُّلّاب "these all H students M P H"	هاتانِ الطّالِبَتانِ "these two F students F D"	هٰذانِ الطّالِبانِ "these two M students MD"	هٰذِهِ الطّالِبَة "this F student F"	هٰذا الطّالِب "this M student M"	Near
هٰذِهِ الطّاوِلات "these all non-H tables FP non-H"	هٰؤُلاءِ الطّالِبات "these all H students FPH"	هاتانِ الطّاوِلَتانِ "these two F tables FD"	هٰذانِ الكُرْسِيّانِ "these two M chairs MD"	هٰذِهِ الطّاوِلَة "this F table F"	هٰذا الكُرْسِيّ "this M chair M"	
تِلْكَ الكَراسي "those all non-H chairs MP non-H"	أُولٰئِكَ الطُّلّاب "those all H students MPH"	تانِكَ الطّالِبَتانِ "those two F students FD"	ذانِكَ الطّالِبانِ "those two M students MD"	تِلْكَ الطّالِبَة "that F student F"	ذٰلِكَ الطّالِب "that M student M"	Far
تِلْكَ الطّاوِلات "those all non-H tables FP non-H"	أُولٰئِكَ الطّالِبات "those all H students FPH"	تانِكَ الطّاوِلَتانِ "those two F tables FD"	ذانِكَ الكُرْسِيّانِ "those two M chairs MD"	تِلْكَ الطّاوِلَة "that F table F"	ذٰلِكَ الكُرْسِيّ "that M chair M"	

Additionally, demonstrative pronouns are marked for case endings. However, only the dual demonstratives have distinct case endings. As explained in Chapter 2, the dual feature is marked by two case endings: {-aani} [اان] for the nominative and {-ayni} [يْن] for the accusative مَنْصوب and genitive مَجْرور (see also 22.2.2 on case endings). Accordingly, the two dual demonstrative pronouns are marked as follows (Table 5.9):

Table 5.9

Dual feminine accusative & genitive مَجْرور & مَنْصوب	Dual feminine nominative مَرْفوع	Dual masculine accusative & genitive مَجْرور & مَنْصوب	Dual masculine nominative مَرْفوع	Distance
هاتَيْنِ الطَّالِبَتَيْنِ "these two F students FD"	هاتانِ الطَّالِبَتانِ "these two F students FD"	هٰذَيْنِ الطَّالِبَيْنِ "these two M. students MD"	هٰذانِ الطَّالِبانِ "these two M students MD"	Near
هاتَيْنِ الطَّاوِلَتَيْنِ "these two F tables FD"	هاتانِ الطَّاوِلَتانِ "these two F tables FD"	هٰذَيْنِ الكُرْسِيَّيْنِ "these two M. chairs MD"	هٰذانِ الكُرْسِيّانِ "these two M chairs MD"	
تَيْنِكَ الطَّاوِلَتَيْنِ "those two F tables FD"	تانِكَ الطَّاوِلَتانِ "those two F tables FD"	ذَيْنِكَ الكُرْسِيَّيْنِ "those two M chairs MD"	ذانِكَ الكُرْسِيّانِ "those two M chairs MD"	Far

5.5 Relative Pronouns الأَسْماء المَوْصولَة and the Definite Relative Clause

Relative pronouns الأَسْماء المَوْصولَة 'al-'asmaa' 'al-mawSuula "connecting/relative nouns" function as pronouns introducing a clause called the "relative clause" or جُمْلَة صِلَة المَوْصول . A relative pronoun usually refers to a preceding noun and is written independently. The noun preceding the relative pronoun must be definite. Arabic relative pronouns are marked for gender (masculine and feminine) and number (singular, dual, and plural). Table 5.10 shows the relative pronouns available in MSA. Like demonstrative pronouns, relative pronouns are marked for case endings. The distinct accusative مَنْصوب and genitive مَجْرور case markings are similarly available only for the dual pronouns (see also 22.2.2 on case endings). All other pronouns remain identical.

Table 5.10

Plural feminine	Plural masculine	Dual feminine	Dual masculine	Singular feminine	Singular masculine	Case
اللَّاتي 'allaatii "who FP"	الَّذينَ 'alladhiina "who MP"	اللَّتانِ 'allataani "who FD"	اللَّذانِ 'alladhaani "who MD"	الَّتي 'allatii "who F"	الَّذي 'alladhii "who M"	Nominative مَرْفوع
اللَّاتي 'allaatii "who FP"	الَّذينَ 'alladhiina "who MP"	اللَّتَيْنِ 'allatayni "who FD"	اللَّذَيْنِ 'alladhayni "who MD"	الَّتي 'allatii "who F"	الَّذي 'alladhii "who M"	Accusative and genitive مَنْصوب & مَجْرور

The examples below illustrate relative pronoun use (note that the noun preceding the relative pronoun is definite):

الطّالِبُ الَّذي في الصَّفِّ مِنْ سوريَّة .
"The student (M) who (M) is in class is from Syria."

الطّالِبَةُ الَّتي في الصَّفِّ مِنْ سوريَّة .
"The student (F) who (F) is in class is from Syria."

الطّالِبانِ اللَّذانِ في الصَّفِّ مِنْ سوريَّة .
"The two students (M) who (MD) are in class are from Syria."

الطّالِبَتانِ اللَّتانِ في الصَّفِّ مِنْ سوريَّة .
"The two students (F) who (FD) are in class are from Syria."

الطُّلّابُ الَّذينَ في الصَّفِّ مِنْ سوريَّة .
"The students (M) who (MP) are in class are from Syria."

الطّالِباتُ اللّاتي في الصَّفِّ مِنْ سوريَّة .
"The students (F) who (FP) are in class are from Syria."

However, a relative pronoun need not refer to a preceding noun. It may also occur by itself (i.e., with the preceding noun dropped, as in the examples above when the noun is dropped) and can be used depending on its function within the sentence (e.g., as the subject/doer, object/doee, or following a preposition), as in:

جاءَ الَّذي يَتَكَلَّمُ كَثيراً .

"The one (M) who speaks a lot came."

جاءَتِ الَّتي تَتَكَلَّمُ كَثيراً .

"The one (F) who speaks a lot came."

قابَلْتُ الَّذي يَجْري خارِجَ الحَديقَةِ .

"I met the one (M) who jogs outside the park."

قابَلْتُ الَّتي تَجْري خارِجَ الحَديقَةِ .

"I met the one (F) who jogs outside the park."

سَلَّمْتُ علىٰ الَّذي يَجْري خارِجَ الحَديقَةِ .

"I greeted the one (M) who jogs outside the park."

سَلَّمْتُ علىٰ الَّتي تَجْري خارِجَ الحَديقَةِ .

"I greeted the one (F) who jogs outside the park."

5.6 Dropping of Relative Pronouns and the Indefinite Relative Clause

As mentioned above, relative pronouns are used to introduce "relative clauses" and are usually used when the preceding noun is definite. However, when the preceding noun is indefinite, the relative pronoun (whether introducing a verbal or nominal relative clause/sentence) must be dropped and its meaning is inferred from the context, as in:

لي صَديقٌ [Ø] يَقْرَأُ كَثيراً .

"I have a friend (M) [who] reads a lot."

لي صَديقَةٌ [Ø] تَقْرَأُ كَثيراً .

"I have a friend (F) [who] reads a lot."

لي صَديقٌ [Ø] اسْمُهُ سَليم .

"I have a friend [whose] name is Salim."

لي صَديقَةٌ [Ø] اسْمُها سَليمة .

"I have a friend [whose] name is Salima."

The best way to understand this (indefinite relative clause) structure and use is to think of the clause/sentence before which the relative pronoun is dropped as a run-on sentence in English – running into the previous clause/sentence. This is why such a clause/sentence is referred to as جُمْلَة الصِّفة "sentence adjective." In other words, the relative clause (or sentence) in this case functions just like an adjective, where nothing separates the adjective and the preceding noun, as in:

لي صَديقٌ [Ø] طَويلٌ .
"I have a tall friend (M)."

In addition, when it occurs with a verbal clause/sentence, the most accurate meaning of the dropped pronoun is "who," and when it occurs with a nominal sentence/clause, its most accurate meaning is "whose," as the glosses of the above examples show.

5.7 The Particles ما *maa* and مَنْ *man* Functioning as Relative Pronouns

The particles ما *maa* and مَنْ *man* are used as relative pronouns and are not preceded by a noun. Their use is characterized as more general or less specific than other relative pronouns. Hence, ما *maa* is used to denote "what/whatever" for non-human reference and مَنْ *man* is used to denote "who/whoever" for human reference. Both are typically used following a verb, after a preposition (as question words, see Chapter 7), or at the beginning of a sentence (for more on their use at the beginning of the sentence, see Chapter 17 on conditional sentences), as in:

كَتَبْتُ ما طَلَبَهُ الأُسْتاذُ .
"I wrote what/whatever the teacher requested."

ما تَزْرَعْ تَحْصِدْ .
"You reap what/whatever you sow."

قابَلْتُ مَنْ أَصْبَحَ مُديرَ المَدْرَسَةِ .
"I met who/whoever became the principal of the school."

مَنْ يَجْتَهِدْ يَنْجَحْ .
"Who/whoever works hard [he] shall succeed."

5.8   Sound Changes to Pronoun and Word Endings

When dependent pronouns are attached to certain words, for ease of pronunciation, slight changes occur to certain pronoun and word endings, including the following:

(A)   changing the vowel [u] of the third-person pronouns ـهُ "him," ـهُما "them both," ـهُم "them all M," and ـهُنَّ "them all F" into [i] when preceded by a short [i] or long [ii] vowel, as in:

Plural feminine	Plural masculine	Dual feminine	Dual masculine	Singular feminine	Singular masculine	Person
دَرَّسْتِهِنَّ darrasti-**hinna** "you F taught them all F"	دَرَّسْتِهِم darrasti-**him** "you F taught them all M"	دَرَّسْتِهِما darrasti-**himaa** "you F taught them both"		دَرَّسْتِها darrasti-**haa** "you F taught her"	دَرَّسْتِهِ darrasti-**hi** "you F taught him"	3rd

(B)   deleting the final [ni] of the dual انِ / ـيْنِ endings with all the dependent (possessive) pronouns; in addition, the pronoun ـي changes into ـيَ , as illustrated with the word فَصْلانِ *faSlaani* "two classes" below:

Plural feminine	Plural masculine	Dual feminine	Dual masculine	Singular feminine	Singular masculine	Person
فَصْلاهُنَّ faSlaa-**hunna** "their all F two classes"	فَصْلاهُم faSlaa-**hum** "their all M two classes"	فَصْلاهُما faSlaa-**humaa** "their both two classes"		فَصْلاها faSlaa-**haa** "her two classes"	فَصْلاهُ faSlaa-**hu** "his two classes"	3rd

فَصْلاكُنَّ faSlaa-kunna "your all F two classes"	فَصْلاكُم faSlaa-kum "your all M two classes"	فَصْلاكُما faSlaa-kumaa "your both two classes"	فَصْلاكِ faSlaa-ki "your F two classes"	فَصْلاكَ faSlaa-ka "your M two classes"	2nd
فَصْلانا faSlaa-naa "our two classes"			فَصْلايَ faSlaa-ya "my two classes"		1st

(C) deleting the [na] ending of the sound masculine plural ونَ / ـينَ with all the dependent pronouns. In addition, the pronoun ـِ changes into ـيَ [ya] and the long vowel [uu] of the sound plural ending (in the nominative مَرْفوع) changes into [y], so that the ending of the plural word and the pronoun ـِ become ـيّ and identical in both the nominative مَرْفوع and accusative مَنْصوب and genitive مَجْرور as illustrated with the word مُدَرِّسونَ *mudarris-uuna* "(male) teachers," below. Note that, with the accusative مَنْصوب and genitive مَجْرور plural ending [ii], the change to the vowel of the third-person pronoun as in (A) above also applies.

Plural feminine	*Plural masculine*	*Dual feminine*	*Dual masculine*	*Singular feminine*	*Singular masculine*	مَرْفوع
مُدَرِّسوهُنَّ mudarrisuu-hunna "their all F teachers"	مُدَرِّسوهُم mudarrisuu-hum "their all M teachers"	مُدَرِّسوهُما mudarrisuu-humaa "their both teachers"		ها مُدَرِّسو mudarrisuu-haa "her teachers"	مُدَرِّسوهُ mudarrisuu-hu "his teachers"	3rd
مُدَرِّسوكُنَّ mudarrisuu-kunna "your all F teachers"	مُدَرِّسوكُم mudarrisuu-kum "your all M teachers"	مُدَرِّسوكُما mudarrisuu-kumaa "your both teachers"		مُدَرِّسوكِ mudarrisuu-ki "your F teachers"	مُدَرِّسوكَ mudarrisuu-ka "your M teachers"	2nd
مُدَرِّسونا mudarrisuu-naa "our teachers"				مُدَرِّسيَّ mudarrisi-yya "my teachers"		1st

Plural feminine	Plural masculine	Dual feminine	Dual masculine	Singular feminine	Singular masculine	مَنْصوب و مَجْرور
مُدَرِّسيهِنَّ *mudarrisii-hinna* "their all F teachers"	مُدَرِّسيهِم *mudarrisii-him* "their all M. teachers"	مُدَرِّسيهِما *mudarrisii-himaa* "their both teachers"		مُدَرِّسيها *mudarrisii-haa* "her teachers"	مُدَرِّسيهِ *mudarrisii-hi* "his teachers"	3rd
مُدَرِّسيكُنَّ *mudarrisii-kunna* "your all F teachers"	مُدَرِّسيكُم *mudarrisii-kum* "your all M teachers"	مُدَرِّسيكُما *mudarrisii-kumaa* "your both teachers"		مُدَرِّسيكِ *mudarrisii-ki* "your F teachers"	مُدَرِّسيكَ *mudarrisii-ka* "your M teachers"	2nd
مُدَرِّسينا *mudarrisii-naa* "our teachers"				مُدَرِّسيَّ *mudarrisi-yya* "my teachers"		1st

(D) incorporating the *taa' marbuuTa* ة of a feminine word into a *taa' mabsuuTa* ت before attaching the pronoun to the word so as to retain the gender marking of the word, as illustrated with the word مُدَرِّسَة *mudarris-a* "(female) teacher" below.

Plural feminine	Plural masculine	Dual feminine	Dual masculine	Singular feminine	Singular masculine	
مُدَرِّسَتُهُنَّ *mudarrisatu-hunna* "their all F teacher F"	مُدَرِّسَتُهُم *mudarrisatu-hum* "their all M teacher F"	مُدَرِّسَتُهُما *mudarrisatu-humaa* "their both teacher F"		مُدَرِّسَتُها *mudarrisatu-haa* "her teacher F"	مُدَرِّسَتُهُ *mudarrisatu-hu* "his teacher F"	3rd
مُدَرِّسَتُكُنَّ *mudarrisatu-kunna* "your all F teacher F"	مُدَرِّسَتُكُم *mudarrisatu-kum* "your all M teacher F"	مُدَرِّسَتُكُما *mudarrisatu-kumaa* "your both teacher F"		مُدَرِّسَتُكِ *mudarrisatu-ki* "your F teacher F"	مُدَرِّسَتُكَ *mudarrisatu-ka* "your M teacher F"	2nd
مُدَرِّسَتُنا *mudarrisatu-naa* "our teacher F"				مُدَرِّسَتي *mudarrisat-ii* "my teacher F"		1st

5.9   Summary

This chapter discussed the basic aspects relevant to the different types of pronouns in Arabic. The pronouns discussed were personal pronouns, object pronouns, possessive pronouns, demonstrative pronouns, and relative pronouns. Remember:

- personal, object, and possessive pronouns are marked for person (first, second, and third), gender (masculine and feminine), and number (singular, dual, and plural)
- demonstrative pronouns are marked for distance (near and far), gender (masculine and feminine), number (singular, dual, and number), and humanness (human vs. non-human)
- relative pronouns are marked for gender (masculine and feminine) and number (singular, dual, and number)
- relative pronouns are used when the preceding noun is definite
- relative pronouns must be dropped when the preceding noun is indefinite, resulting in a run-on sentence/clause (as in English); in this case the meaning of the dropped pronoun is inferred from the context
- except for demonstrative and relative pronouns in the dual (which have different case endings for the nominative مَرْفوع vs. the accusative مَنْصوب and genitive مَجْرور), all pronouns have invariable endings (i.e., their ending does not change regardless of how they are used)
- pronouns following words with dual and sound plural endings result in certain sound changes to such word and pronoun endings, for ease of pronunciation.

6

Prepositions حُروف الجَرّ

This chapter discusses Arabic prepositions, which comprise a small set of particles. Prepositions are mainly followed by nouns (and to a lesser extent, pronouns and question words; see Chapter 7). Like most pronouns, prepositions have invariable endings; i.e., their endings do not change – except in certain contexts, for ease of pronunciation. Nouns following prepositions require the genitive مَجْرور case ending; hence they are called in Arabic حُروف الجَرّ "genitive particles" (see also 22.2.2 on case endings). This chapter covers:

- the basic meanings and use of each preposition
- idiomatic uses and expressions involving prepositions
- the occurrence of prepositions with pronoun suffixes and the resulting sound changes.

6.1 Basic Meanings and Use of Prepositions

The most common prepositions حُروف الجَرّ "genitive particles" in MSA include:

"from"	*min*	مِنْ
"to," "until"	*'ilaa*	إلى
"from," "off," "about," "instead of"	*ʿan*	عَنْ
"on," "about," "for"	*ʿalaa*	عَلى

Modern Standard Arabic Grammar: A Learner's Guide, First Edition.
© 2011 Mohammad T. Alhawary. Published 2011 by Blackwell Publishing Ltd.

"in," "at," "on"	fii	في
"up to," "until"	Hattaa	حَتّىٰ
"since," "for"	mundhu	مُنْذُ
"by," "in," "on," "for"	bi-	بِ
"for," "of," "to"	li-	لِ
"like," "such as"	ka-	كَ
"with," "at, " "with"	maʿa	مَعَ
"by [oath]," "with"	wa-	وَ

6.1.1 *min* مِنْ "from"

The most basic meanings of مِنْ *min* refer to direction and source, whether literally or figuratively, as in:

خَرَجْتُ مِنَ الْبَيْتِ .

"I left [from] the house."

خاتَمُها مِنْ فِضَّةٍ .

"Her ring is [made] from silver."

الوَقْتُ مِنْ ذَهَبٍ .

"Time is [made] from gold."

Note: As explained in Chapter 1 (1.9), since مِنْ ends with a *sukuun*, a helping vowel [a] is inserted when it is followed by a word with the definite article.

6.1.2 *'ilaa* إلىٰ "to," "until"

The most basic meanings of إلىٰ refer to destination of place and time, as in:

ذَهَبْتُ إلىٰ الْجامِعَةِ .

"I went to the university."

دَرَسْتُ إلىٰ الصَّباحِ .

"I studied until the morning."

6.1.3 ʿan عَنْ "from," "off," "about," "instead of"

The most basic meanings of عَنْ ʿan refer to distance from a location (equivalent to "from"), separation (equivalent to "from" or "off"), association (equivalent to "about," "concerning"), and substitution (equivalent to "instead of" or "on behalf of"), as in:

اِبْتَعَدْتُ عَنِ الـمَدينةِ .

"I got far away from the city."

وَقَعْتُ عَنِ الدَّرّاجةِ .

"I fell off the bike."

سَمِعْتُ خَبَراً عَنِ الجامِعَةِ .

"I heard a piece of news about/concerning the university."

قَامَ عَنْكَ بِهٰذا الْعَمَلِ .

"He did this work instead of you."

Note: In the above examples (as explained in Chapter 1, 1.9), since عَنْ is a word that ends with a *sukuun*, a helping vowel [i] is inserted instead of its *sukuun* when it is followed by a word containing the definite article.

6.1.4 ʿalaa عَلىٰ "on," "about," "for"

The most basic meanings of عَلىٰ ʿalaa refer to being above, whether referring to being above/on a surface either literally (equivalent to "on") or figuratively (equivalent to "about"), and to stating a reason (equivalent to "for"), as in:

جَلَسَتْ علىٰ الْكُرسِيِّ .

"She sat on the chair."

تَكَلَّمَ علىٰ الأُسْتاذِ .

"He spoke about the teacher."

شَكَرْتُها عَلىٰ الهَدِيَّةِ .

"I thanked her for the gift."

6.1.5 *fii* في "in," "at," "on"

The most basic meanings of في *fii* refer to location of place or time (whether literally or figuratively), as in:

أَسْكُنُ في شِقَّةٍ .

"I live in an apartment."

أَدْرُسُ في الْـمَكتَبَةِ .

"I study in/at the library."

لي في هذا هَدَفٌ .

"I have in this a goal."

أَدْرُسُ في السّاعةِ السّابِعَةِ .

"I study at seven o'clock."

في هذا الْيَوْمِ

"[in] on this day"

6.1.6 *hattaa* حَتَّىٰ "up to," "until"

Like the meanings of إلىٰ , the most basic meanings of حَتَّىٰ *Hattaa* refer to destination of place and time, as in:

مَشَيْتُ حَتَّىٰ الْبابِ .

"I walked up to the door."

دَرَسْتُ حَتَّىٰ الصَّباحِ .

"I studied until the morning."

The difference between إلىٰ and حَتَّىٰ is that حَتَّىٰ has a more strict use where reference is made only to the last part of the destination. Thus, whereas both of the following sentences are acceptable with إلىٰ :

سَهِرْتُ اللَّيْلَةَ إلىٰ آخِرِها .

"I stayed up the night until its end."

سَهِرْتُ اللَّيْلَةَ إلىٰ نِصْفِها .

"I stayed up the night until its middle."

only the first of the two following sentences is acceptable:

سَهِرْتُ اللَّيْلَةَ حَتَّىٰ آخِرِها .

"I stayed up the night until its end."

سَهِرْتُ اللَّيْلَةَ حَتَّىٰ نِصْفِها .

*"I stayed up the night until its middle."

6.1.7   *mundhu* مُنْذُ "for," "since"

The most basic meaning of مُنْذُ *mundhu* refers to the duration of a period, as in:

ما رَأَيْتُهُ مُنْذُ ثَلاثَةِ أَيَّام .

"I have not seen him for three days."

اِنْتَظَرْتُكَ مُنْذُ الصَّباح .

"I had been waiting for you since the morning."

6.1.8   *bi-* بِ "by," "in," "on," "for"

The most basic meanings of بِ *bi-* refer to contiguity or touching (whether literally or figuratively) and other related senses such as location of place and time (equivalent to *fii* "in"), instrument of the action (equivalent to "by," "by means of"), oath (equivalent to "in," "on"), and substitution (equivalent to "for"), as in:

أَمْسَكْتُ بِيَدِها .

"I held her by her hand."

مَرَرْتُ بِالْمَكْتَبَةِ .

"I passed by the library."

دَرَسْتُ في جامِعَةٍ بِواشنطن .

"I studied in a university in Washington."

زُرْتُهُ بِمُناسَبَةِ تَخَرُّجِهِ .

"I visited him [in] on the occasion of his graduation."

سافَرْتُ بِالسَّيَّارَةِ .

"I traveled by car."

أُقْسِمُ بِالله ما فَعَلْتُ هٰذا .

"I swear by God I did not do this."

اِشْتَرَيْتُ الْكِتابَ بِدولارٍ .

"I bought the book for a dollar."

6.1.9 *li-* لِ "for," "of," "to"

The most basic meanings of لِ *li-* refer to possession (equivalent to "for" or "of"), reporting (equivalent to "to"), and stating a reason or purpose (equivalent to "for"), as in:

الكِتابُ لِلْأُسْتاذِ .

"The book is for/belongs to the teacher."

النّائِبُ الأَوَّلُ لِلرَّئيسِ

"The first deputy of the president"

... قُلْتُ لَهُ

"I said to him . . ."

يَدْرُسُ لِلْحُصولِ على شهادةٍ .

"He studies for/toward obtaining a degree."

6.1.10 *ka-* كَ "like," "such as"

The basic meanings of كَ *ka-* include making a comparison or a simile (i.e., figuratively) and introducing a list (equivalent to "such as"). Unlike other prepositions, it cannot be followed by a pronoun, only by a noun, as in:

اللّاعِبُ طَويلٌ كالزَّرافةِ .

"The player is tall like a giraffe."

أُحِبُّ الفاكِهةَ كالْبُرْتُقالِ والْعِنَبِ والـمَوْزِ .

"I like fruits, such as oranges, grapes, and bananas."

Note: The meaning of كَ *ka-* "like," "such as" can be equally conveyed by the use of the noun مِثْل "like" (for the masculine and feminine) as in:

اللّاعِبُ طَويلٌ مِثْلُ الزَّرافةِ .

"The player (male) is tall like a giraffe."

اللّاعِبةُ طَويلةٌ مِثْلُ الزَّرافةِ .

"The player (female) is tall like a giraffe."

6.1.11 ma'a مَعَ "with," "at," "along"

Arabic grammar books treat ma'a مَعَ "with" as a noun functioning as an adverb (see also Chapter 8 on adverbs of time and place), not as a preposition particle. However, it can be used as a preposition (equivalent to "with" in English) to indicate accompaniment, either literally (equivalent to "with") or figuratively speaking, to indicate time (equivalent to "at"), as in:

أَكَلَ مَعَ الـمُديرِ .

"He ate with the manager/director."

سافَرْتُ مَعَ الْفَجْرِ .

"I traveled at dawn."

مَشَيْتُ مَعَ النَّهْرِ .

"I walked [with] along the river."

6.1.12 wa- وَ "by," "with," "at"

The basic use of وَ wa- as a preposition is when expressing an oath, as in:

وَاللهِ ما فَعَلْتُ هٰذا .

"By God, I did not do this."

Another use of وَ wa is equivalent to that of مَعَ ma'a "with," "at." In Arabic, this use is called المَفْعول مَعَهُ "the object with وَ wa," since the noun following وَ "with" has the accusative مَنْصوب rather than the genitive مَجْرور case ending, as in:

أَكَلَ وَ المُديرَ . = أَكَلَ مَعَ المُديرِ .

"He ate with the manager/director."

سافَرْتُ وَ الْفَجْرَ . = سافَرْتُ مَعَ الْفَجْرِ .

"I traveled at dawn."

6.2 Idiomatic Usage and Expressions Involving Prepositions

In addition to the above uses, and as in many languages including English, Arabic prepositions are used in other contexts subject to idiomatic usage. These include idiomatic expressions, such as:

بِالنِّسْبَةِ إِلَيَّ	عَلَىٰ فِكْرَةٍ	عَلَىٰ الْأَقَلِّ
"for me"	"by the way"	"at least"

لِي أَخٌ	مَعِي كِتَابٌ	عَلَيْنَا أَنْ نَذْهَبَ
"[I have] 'for me' a brother."	"[I have] 'with me' a book."	"We must go."

مِنَ اللَّازِمِ أَنْ	مِنَ الْمَعْروفِ أَنَّ	مِنَ غَيْرِ الْمَعْقولِ أَنْ
"It is necessary that"	"It is known that"	"It is illogical that"

and verb-preposition idioms (which may be confusing to English learners perhaps mainly because they are either used differently in English or not used at all), such as:

يَحْصُلُ علىٰ (عَمَل)	يُرَحِّبُ بِـ (ضَيْفٍ)	يُعَبِّرُ عَنْ (شُعورٍ)
"he obtains (a job)"	"he welcomes (a guest)"	"he expresses (a feeling)"

يَسْتَمْتِعُ بِـ (بَرْنامَجٍ)	يَصْفَحُ عَنْ (خَطَأٍ)	يَعْتَرِفُ بِـ (جَريمَةٍ)
"he enjoys (a program)"	"he forgives (a mistake)"	"he confesses (a crime)"

For such uses, prepositions are best learned individually as part of the complete expression or part of the verb with which they are used.

6.3 Occurrence with Pronoun Suffixes and the Resulting Sound Changes

As in nouns and verbs, pronoun suffixes can follow all prepositions except for حَتّىٰ , مُنْذُ , كَـ , and وَ . These are usually referred to as "object of preposition pronouns" which are identical to possessive pronouns (see Chapter 5) and, as in nouns and verbs, are attached to the end of prepositions. For ease of pronunciation, slight changes occur to preposition and pronoun endings, including the following:

(A) deleting the final [a] vowel of مَعَ with the pronoun ـي "me" (but retaining it with all other pronouns):

Plural feminine	Plural masculine	Dual feminine	Dual masculine	Singular feminine	Singular masculine	Person
مَعَهُنَّ ma'a-hunna "with you all F"	مَعَهُم ma'a-hum "with you all M"	مَعَهُما ma'a-humaa "with them both"		مَعَها ma'a-haa "with her"	مَعَهُ ma'a-hu "with him"	3rd
مَعَكُنَّ ma'a-kunna "with you all F"	مَعَكُم ma'a-kum "with you all M"	مَعَكُما ma'a-kumaa "with you both"		مَعَكِ ma'a-ki "with you F"	مَعَكَ ma'a-ka "with you M"	2nd
مَعَنا ma'a-naa "with us"				مَعـي ma'-ii "with me"		1st

(B) inserting an [n] consonant after مِنْ and عَنْ with the pronouns ـي "me" and نا "us," resulting in a *shadda* on the ending ـّـ, as illustrated with مِنْ :

Plural feminine	Plural masculine	Dual feminine	Dual masculine	Singular feminine	Singular masculine	Person
مِنْهُنَّ min-hunna "from you all F"	مِنْهُم min-hum "from you all M"	مِنْهُما min-humaa "from them both"		مِنها min-haa "from her"	مِنْهُ min-hu "from him"	3rd
مِنْكُنَّ min-kunna "from you all F"	مِنْكُم min-kum "from you all M"	مِنْكُما min-kumaa "from you both"		مِنْكِ min-ki "from you F"	مِنْكَ min-ka "from you M"	2nd
مِنّا minn-naa "from us"				مِنّي minn-ii "from me"		1st

(C)   inserting a *shadda* and a vowel [a] after في with the pronoun ـي "me," resulting from combining the identical long vowels [ii] of the pronoun and that of the preposition:

Plural feminine	Plural masculine	Dual feminine	Dual masculine	Singular feminine	Singular masculine	Person
فيهِنَّ *fii-hinna* "in you all F"	فيهِم *fii-him* "in you all M"	فيهِما *fii-himaa* "in them both"		فيها *fii-haa* "in her"	فيهِ *fii-hi* "in him"	3rd
فيـكُنَّ *fii-kunna* "in you all F"	فيـكُم *fii-kum* "in you all M"	فيكُما *fii-kumaa* "in you both"		فيكِ *fii-ki* "in you F"	فيكَ *fii-ka* "in you M"	2nd
فينا *fii-naa* "in us"				فيَّ *fiyya* "in me"		1st

Note: Additionally, when pronouns are attached to the preposition في, the vowel [u] occurring with the pronouns ـهُ "him," ـهُما "them both," ـهُمْ "them all M," and ـهُنَّ "them all F" changes into [i]; similarly, for ease of pronunciation, ـهِ , ـهِما , ـهِمْ , and ـهِنَّ , respectively (see also 5.7).

(D)   as in (C) above, changing the vowel [u] of the pronouns ـهُ "him," ـهُما "them both," ـهُمْ "them all M," and ـهُنَّ "them all F" into [i] when they occur with the preposition بِـ :

Plural feminine	Plural masculine	Dual feminine	Dual masculine	Singular feminine	Singular masculine	Person
بِهِنَّ bi-hinna "by you all F"	بِهِم bi-him "by you all M"	بِهِمَا bi-himaa "by them both"		بِهَا bi-haa "by her"	بِهِ bi-hi "by him"	3rd
بِكُنَّ bi-kunna "by you all F"	بِكُم bi-kum "by you all M"	بِكُمَا bi-kumaa "by you both"		بِكِ bi-ki "by you F"	بِكَ bi-ka "by you M"	2nd
بِنا bi-naa "by us"				بي b-ii "by me"		1st

(E)   changing the vowel [i] of the preposition لـ into the vowel [a], except when the preposition is attached to the pronoun ـي "me":

Plural feminine	Plural masculine	Dual feminine	Dual masculine	Singular feminine	Singular masculine	Person
لَهُنَّ la-hunna "for you all F"	لَهُم la-hum "for you all M"	لَهُمَا la-humaa "for them both"		لَهَا la-haa "for her"	لَهُ la-hu "for him"	3rd
لَكُنَّ la-kunna "for you all F"	لَكُم la-kum "for you all M"	لَكُمَا la-kumaa "for you both"		لَكِ la-ki "for you F"	لَكَ la-ka "for you M"	2nd
لَنا la-naa "for us"				لِي l-ii "for me"		1st

(F) changing the long vowel ـَى [aa] of the preposition عَلَى and إِلَى into the vowel sequence ـَيْ [ay], as illustrated with عَلَى below:

Plural feminine	Plural masculine	Dual feminine	Dual masculine	Singular feminine	Singular masculine	Person
عَلَيْهِنَّ	عَلَيْهِم	عَلَيْهِما		عَلَيْها	عَلَيْهِ	3rd
ⁿalay-hinna	ⁿalay-him	ⁿalay-himaa		ⁿalay-haa	ⁿalay-hi	
"on you all F"	"on you all M"	"on them both"		"on her"	"on him"	
عَلَيْكُنَّ	عَلَيْكُم	عَلَيْكُما		عَلَيْكِ	عَلَيْكَ	2nd
ⁿalay-kunna	ⁿalay-kum	ⁿalay-kumaa		ⁿalay-ki	ⁿalay-ka	
"on you all F"	"on you all M"	"on you both"		"on you F"	"on you M"	
عَلَيْنا				عَلَيَّ		1st
ⁿalay-naa				ⁿalayya		
"on us"				"on me"		

Note: Two additional sound changes occur due to the rules above: (1) the vowel [u] of the pronouns ـهُ "him," هُما "them both," هُم "them all M," and هُنَّ "them all F" changes into [i] and (2) a *shadda* and a vowel [a] are inserted at the end of عَلَى and إِلَى with the pronoun ـي "me."

6.4 Summary

This chapter discussed Arabic prepositions used in MSA belonging to a small class of 12 words, together with the basic meanings and usage of each. Remember:

- prepositions contribute to meaning by referring to direction, source, time, place, substitution, instrument, oath, etc., of the verb/action
- each preposition has its own basic meanings and usage
- as in English, prepositions have idiomatic uses, including idiomatic expressions and verb-preposition idioms
- as in English, prepositions occur before nouns

- a noun following a preposition has a grammatical (genitive مَجْرور) ending (see also 22.2.2 on case endings)
- as in English, Arabic prepositions (except حَتّى , مُنْذُ , كَ , and وَ) can occur before pronouns
- pronouns following prepositions are attached to the prepositions, resulting in certain sound changes to preposition and pronoun endings, for ease of pronunciation
- prepositions may also occur with other words, such as adverbs of time and place (Chapter 8) and question words (Chapter 7).

7

Question Words and Question Formation

This chapter discusses question words and how questions are formed in Arabic. Like pronouns and prepositions, all question words in Arabic (except one) have invariable endings, i.e., their endings do not change. All question words (except one) are written as independent words; hence in Arabic they are called أَدَوات الإسْتِفْهام "interrogative particles/words." The chapter covers:

- how questions are formed in Arabic
- the most commonly used question words
- the meaning and use of each question word
- the occurrence of question words with prepositions in order to generate additional questions.

7.1 Question Formation and Question Words
أَدَوات الإسْتِفْهام

Forming questions in Arabic is straightforward and easy, quite unlike English. In English, forming a question may involve many rules and sub-rules including, for example: (1) the use of the auxiliary verb *do*, (2) the use of *do* in the correct tense, (3) the use of the main verb in the infinitive form, and (4) reversing the order of the subject and that of the auxiliary verb *do* so that *do* precedes the main verb, etc. In Arabic, as explained in the sections below, forming questions involves one single rule: placing the question word at the beginning of the sentence. The basic question words in MSA are as follows:

Modern Standard Arabic Grammar: A Learner's Guide, First Edition.
© 2011 Mohammad T. Alhawary. Published 2011 by Blackwell Publishing Ltd.

for yes/no questions	*hal*	هَلْ
for yes/no questions	*'a-*	أ
"who"	*man*	مَنْ
"what"	*maa*	ما
"what"	*maadhaa*	ماذا
"why"	*limaadhaa*	لِماذا
"when"	*mataa*	مَتیٰ
"where"	*'ayna*	أَيْنَ
"how"	*kayfa*	كَيْفَ
"how many"	*kam*	كَمْ
"what/which"	*'ayy*	أَيّ

Note: Some of these question words can also function as conditional words/particles (see Chapter 17).

7.1.1 *hal* هَلْ "Yes/No" Question Word

As in English and many other languages, in Arabic yes/no questions can simply be formed by means of rising intonation (i.e., with the sentence not being preceded by a question word). However, more formally, the question word هَلْ *hal* is used to form yes/no questions (where the answer is either نَعَم *na'am* "yes" or لا *laa* "no") in verbal and nominal sentences, as in:

هَلْ كَتَبْتَ الْواجِب ؟

"Did you write the homework?"

هَلْ تَسْكُنُ في شِقَّة ؟

"Do you live in an apartment?"

هَلْ أَنْتِ طالِبَة ؟

"Are you a student?"

7.1.2 *'a* أ "Yes/No" Question Particle

The question particle أ *'a-* has three main uses. One of these, similar to that of هَلْ *hal*, is to form yes/no questions in verbal and nominal sentences, although أ *'a-* is used less frequently. As a particle, it is attached to the word that follows it, as in:

أَكَتَبْتَ الْواجِب ؟

"Did you write the homework?"

أَتَسْكُنُ في شِقَّة ؟

"Do you live in an apartment?"

أَهِيَ طالِبَة ؟

"Is she a student?"

The second (more common) use of the question particle أ *'a-* is to form negative interrogative sentences, where it is preceded by a negation particle/word, as in:

أَلَمْ تَكْتُبِ الْواجِب ؟

"Didn't you write the homework?"

أَلا تَسْكُنُ في شِقَّة ؟

"Don't you live in an apartment?"

أَ لَسْتِ طالِبَة ؟

"Aren't you a student?"

أَ لَنْ تُسافِرَ إلى الْجَزائِر ؟

"Won't you travel to Algeria?"

Note: To respond to negative interrogative questions in the affirmative, the answer word to be used is بَلَى (equivalent in this context to the English "yes"), while the answer word in the negative is نَعَم (equivalent in this contexts to the English "no").

The third use of the question particle أ *'a-* involves questions with two parts, where أَمْ (equivalent in English to "or") is used and where the answer required is no longer yes/no but an answer that affirms one of the two parts of the question, as in:

أَحَضَرَ خالِد أَمْ أَحْمَد ؟

"Did Khaled or Ahmad come?"

أَكَتَبْتَ الرِّسالةَ أم الْواجِب ؟

"Did you write the letter or the homework?"

أَهِيَ طالِبَةٌ أَمْ مُوَظَّفَة؟

"Is she a student or an employee?"

7.1.3 *man* مَنْ "Who" Question Word

The question word مَنْ *man* is equivalent to "who" (for humans) and is used in verbal and nominal sentences, as in:

مَنْ كَتَبَ الْواجِب ؟

"Who wrote the homework?"

مَنْ هذا ؟

"Who is this [person]?"

Prepositions may be combined and collapsed with مَنْ *man* "who" to generate additional question words, such as:

"from whom"	*mimman*	مِمَّنْ = مَنْ + مِنْ
"to whom"	*'ilaa man*	إِلَى مَنْ = مَنْ + إِلَى
"from whom"	*ᶜamman*	عَمَّنْ = مَنْ + عَنْ
"about/on whom"	*ᶜalaa man*	عَلَى مَنْ = مَنْ + عَلَى
"in whom"	*fiiman*	فِيمَنْ = مَنْ + فِي
"with whom"	*bi-man*	بِمَنْ = مَنْ + بِ
"for whom"	*li-man*	لِمَنْ = مَنْ + لِ
"with whom"	*maᶜa man*	مَعَ مَنْ = مَنْ + مَعَ

مِمَّنْ هٰذِهِ الرِّسالة ؟

"From whom is this letter?"

إِلَى مَنْ ذَهَبْتَ ؟

"To whom did you go?"

7.1.4 *maa* ما "What" Question Word

The question word ما *maa* is equivalent to "what" (for non-humans) and is used in verbal and nominal sentences, as in:

ما كَتَبْتَ ؟

"What did you write?"

ما هذا ؟

"What is this [thing]?"

Prepositions may be combined and collapsed with ما *maa* "what" to generate additional question words, where the long vowel [aa] of ما *maa* is shortened to [a], as in:

"from what"	*mimma*	مِمَّ =	ما +	مِنْ
"to what"	*'ilaama*	إلامَ =	ما +	إلى
"from what"	*ʿamma*	عَمَّ =	ما +	عَنْ
"about/on what"	*ʿalaama*	عَلا مَ =	ما +	عَلى
"in what"	*fiima*	فيمَ =	ما +	في
"until what"	*Hattaama*	حَتّامَ =	ما +	حَتّى
"with what"	*bi-ma*	بِمَ =	ما +	بِ
"for what/why"	*li-ma*	لِمَ =	ما +	لِ

مِمَّ يَتَأَلَّفُ التُّراب ؟

"What does earth consist of?"

لِمَ تَدْرُسُ في الْبَيْت ؟

"For what/why do you study at home?"

7.1.5   *maadhaa* ماذا "What" Question Word

The question word ماذا *maadhaa* is equivalent to "what" in English and is similar to ما *maa* "what," although ماذا *maadhaa* "what" is used primarily in verbal sentences, as in:

ماذا كَتَبْتَ ؟

"What did you write?"

ماذا تَفْعَلُ ؟

"What do you do/are doing?"

However, it can also be used in nominal sentences with the meaning equivalent to "what is that," as in:

ماذا مَعَكَ ؟

"What is that you have?"/["What do you have?"]

ماذا في السَّيَّارَة ؟

"What is that in the car?"/["What is in the car?"]

Note: ماذا *maadhaa* "what is that" cannot be used in a nominal sentence with هٰذا, since هٰذا is identical to ذا contained in ماذا.

7.1.6 *limaadhaa* لِماذا "Why" Question Word

The question word لِماذا *limaadhaa* "why" is used to enquire about *causes or reasons*, similar to the function of لِ ("for what," "why") resulting from combining ما *maa* "what" with the preposition لِ , as explained above), as in:

لِماذا تَدْرُسُ الْعَرَبِيَّة ؟

"Why do you study Arabic?"

7.1.7 *mataa* مَتىٰ "When" Question Word

The question word مَتىٰ *mataa* "when" is used to enquire about *time* in verbal and nominal sentences, as in:

مَتىٰ تُسافِرُ ؟

"When do you travel?"

مَتىٰ سَفَرُكَ ؟

"When is your travel?"

Prepositions may be combined with مَتىٰ *mataa* "when" to generate additional question words, such as:

"until when"	*'ilaa mataa*	إلىٰ مَتىٰ = مَتىٰ + إلىٰ
"until when"	*Hattaa mataa*	حَتىٰ مَتىٰ = مَتىٰ + حَتىٰ
"since when"	*mundhu mataa*	مُنْذُ مَتىٰ = مَتىٰ + مُنْذُ

إِلَىٰ مَتَىٰ تَسْتَمِعُ إِلَيْهِ ؟

"Until when do you listen to him?"

مُنْذُ مَتَىٰ تَقْرَأُ الرِّوايات ؟

"Since when have you been reading novels?"

7.1.8   'ayna أَيْنَ "Where" Question Word

The question word أَيْنَ *'ayna* "where" is used to enquire about *place or location* in verbal and nominal sentences, as in:

أَيْنَ تَسْكُنُ ؟

"Where do you live?"

أَيْنَ الْجامِعَةُ ؟

"Where is the university?"

Prepositions may be combined with أَيْنَ *'ayna* "where" to generate additional question words, such as:

| "where from" | *min 'ayna* | مِنْ أَيْنَ = أَيْنَ + مِنْ |
| "where to" | *'ilaa 'ayna* | إِلَى أَيْنَ = أَيْنَ + إِلَى |

مِنْ أَيْنَ أَنْتِ ؟

"Where are you (female) from?"

إِلَى أَيْنَ تَذْهَبُ ؟

"[To] where do you go/are you going?"

7.1.9   kayfa كَيْفَ "How" Question Word

The question word كَيْفَ *kayfa* "how" is used to enquire about the *condition, state, or verb/action* in nominal and verbal sentences, as in:

كَيْفَ حالُكَ ؟

"How is your condition?"/"How are you?"

كَيْفَ أَنْتَ ؟

"How are you?"

كَيْفَ سافَرْتَ ؟

"How did you travel?"

7.1.10   *kam* كَمْ "How Many" Question Word

The question word كَمْ *kam* "how many" is used to enquire about *quantity* in verbal and nominal sentences, as in:

كَمْ كِتاباً قَرَأْتَ ؟

"How many book[s] did you read?"

كَمْ طالِباً في الْفَصْلِ ؟

"How many student[s] are in the classroom?"

Note: As shown in the examples, the noun being enquired about following كَمْ *kam* "how many" is subject to three rules: (1) it is indefinite, (2) it is singular (not plural), and (3) it has the accusative مَنْصوب ending.

When it can be inferred from the context, the noun being enquired about is deleted and كَمْ *kam* would then be equivalent to "what," as in:

كَمْ عُمُرُكَ ؟	←	كَمْ (سَنَةً) عُمُرُكَ ؟
"What is your age?"		"How many (years) is your age?"
كَمْ ثَمَنُهُ ؟	←	كَمْ (دولاراً) ثَمَنُهُ ؟
"What is its price?"		"How many (dollars) is its price?"
كَمِ السّاعَةُ ؟	←	كَمْ (ساعَةً) السّاعَةُ ؟
"What is the time?"		"How many (hours) is the time?"

Note: As explained in Chapter 1 (1.9), since كَمْ is a word that ends with a *sukuun*, a helping vowel [i] is inserted instead of its *sukuun* when it is followed by a word containing the definite article.

When enquiring about non-count nouns, the preposition مِنْ *min* "from" is used and كَمْ *kam* would then be equivalent to "how much," as in:

كَمْ مِنَ الْحَليبِ عِنْدَكَ ؟

"How much milk do you have?"

كَمْ مِنَ المَطَرِ نَزَلَ ؟

"How much rain fell?"

Prepositions may be combined with كَمْ *kam* "how many" to generate additional question words. In this case, the noun following كَمْ can take the genitive مَجْرور case ending, as illustrated below:

"from how many"	*min kam*	مِنْ كَمْ = كَمْ + مِنْ
"to how many"	*'ilaa kam*	إلى كَمْ = كَمْ + إلى
"in how many"	*fii kam*	في كَمْ = كَمْ + في
"for how many"	*bi-kam*	بِكَمْ = كَمْ + بِ
"since how many"	*mundhu kam*	مُنْذُ كَمْ = كَمْ + مُنْذُ
"with how many"	*maʿa kam*	مَعَ كَمْ = كَمْ + مَعَ

مِنْ كَمْ فَصْلٍ يَتَأَلَّفُ هذا الْكِتاب ؟

"How many chapters does this book consist of?"

إلىٰ كَمْ ساعَةٍ تَحْتاجُ مِنَ النَّوْم ؟

"How many hours of sleep do you need?"

بِكَمْ دينارٍ اِشْتَرَيْتَ الْقَميص ؟

"For how many dinars did you buy the shirt?"

7.1.11 'ayy أَيّ "Which/Which One" Question Word

The question word أَيّ 'ayy is used to enquire about *identity*, equivalent to "which/which one." Unlike all other question words, أَيّ 'ayy takes (three) variable case endings depending on its function in the sentence: مَرْفوع nominative, مَنْصوب accusative, and مَجْرور genitive. However, the noun following أَيّ 'ayy, in all three cases, invariably takes the genitive ending, being treated as the second part of the إضافة 'iDaafa phrase (see Chapter 3, 3.3–4). The following examples illustrate the basic use of أَيّ 'ayy "which/which one" with (a) the nominative مَرْفوع ending functioning as the subject/doer of the action, (b) with the accusative مَنْصوب ending functioning as the object/doee of the action, and (c) with the genitive مَجْرور ending functioning as the object of/following a preposition (see (22.2.2 for more on case endings):

أَيُّ أُسْتاذٍ وَصَلَ ؟
"Which teacher arrived?"

أَيَّ فَرِيقٍ تُحِبُّ ؟

"Which team do you like?"

فِي أَيِّ ساعَةٍ رَجَعْتَ ؟

"At what time did you return?"

An equivalent feminine أَيَّة *'ayya* "which/which one" form that agrees in gender with a following noun is also used, although أَيّ *'ayy* "which/which one" can be used invariably with feminine and masculine nouns, as in:

أَيَّةُ / أَيُّ أُسْتاذَةٍ وَصَلَتْ ؟

"Which (female) teacher arrived?"

Prepositions may be combined with أَيّ *'ayy* "which/which one" to generate additional question words, such as:

"from which"	*min 'ayyi*	مِنْ أَيِّ =	أَيّ +	مِنْ
"to which"	*'ilaa 'ayyi*	إلى أَيِّ =	أَيّ +	إلى
"about which"	*ʿan 'ayyi*	عَنْ أَيِّ =	أَيّ +	عَنْ
"on which"	*ʿalaa 'ayyi*	عَلىٰ أَيِّ =	أَيّ +	عَلىٰ
"in which"	*fii 'ayyi*	فِي أَيِّ =	أَيّ +	فِي
"with which"	*bi-'ayyi*	بِأَيِّ =	أَيّ +	بِ
"for which"	*li-'ayyi*	لِأَيِّ =	أَيّ +	لِ
"with which"	*maʿa 'ayyi*	مَعَ أَيِّ =	أَيّ +	مَعَ

مِنْ أَيِّ بَلَدٍ الأُسْتاذُ ؟

"From which country is the teacher?"

إلىٰ أَيِّ بِلادٍ سافَرْتَ ؟

"To which countries did you travel?"

مَعَ أَيِّ صَديقٍ تَخاصَمْتَ ؟

"With which friend did you quarrel?"

Note: Since أَيّ *'ayy* is preceded by a preposition, it takes the genitive مَجْرور case ending (see 22.2.2 on case endings).

Finally, أيّ *'ayy* may occur with a pronoun, instead of a noun, as in:

أيُّكُم عُمَرَ ؟

"Which one of you is Omar?"

أيُّكُم يُجِيبُ عَلىٰ هٰذا السُّؤالِ ؟

"Which one of you answers this question?"

7.2   Summary

This chapter discussed Arabic question words used in MSA together with the basic meaning and usage of each. Remember:

*   forming questions in Arabic is extremely easy and involves merely placing the question word at the beginning of the sentence
*   as in English and other languages, question words in Arabic can be preceded by prepositions in order to generate additional question words
*   all question words are written independently, except for the particle أ which is attached to the word following it
*   all question words have invariable endings, except for أيّ *'ayy*, which has (three) variable case endings, depending on its function in the sentence: (1) مَرْفوع nominative, (2) مَنْصوب accusative, and (3) مَجْرور genitive (see 22.2.2 on case endings).

8

Adverbs of Time and Place
ظُروف الزَّمان والمَكان

This chapter discusses Arabic adverbs, or words used to refer to the time and place of the verb/action. Many words can function as adverbs. In Arabic such words are called ظُروف "envelopes" or "containers" within which a verb/action takes place with reference to *time*, called ظُروف زَمان "envelopes/ containers of time," and some with reference to *place*, called ظُروف مَكان "envelopes/containers of place." In other words, while adverbs of time concern the *when* of the verb/action, adverbs of place concern the *where* of the verb/ action. Adverbs usually take the accusative مَنْصوب case ending, although some have invariable endings (see 22.2.2 on case endings). Although such words are usually used as adverbs, they need not necessarily only function as such and, in fact, may function as any noun. The chapter covers:

- commonly used adverbs of time
- commonly used adverbs of place
- words used as adverbs of time or adverbs of place
- dropping adverbs while retaining adverbial meaning
- the occurrence of adverbs of place and time with prepositions
- expressing time and place of the verb/action by means of a preposition followed by a noun
- other uses of adverbs.

8.1 Adverbs of Time ظُروف الزَّمان

As their name suggests, adverbs of time ظُروف الزَّمان "envelopes/containers of time" refer to the time of the verb/action. Some adverbs of time take

Modern Standard Arabic Grammar: A Learner's Guide, First Edition.
© 2011 Mohammad T. Alhawary. Published 2011 by Blackwell Publishing Ltd.

the accusative مَنْصوب case ending اً [an] when used as single words (with feminine words requiring no 'alif seat), such as:

"in the morning"	SabaaH-an	صَباحاً
"at noon"	Zuhr-an	ظُهْراً
"after noon"	ʿaSr-an	عَصْراً
"in the evening"	masaa'-an	مَساءً
"at night"	layl-an	لَيْلاً
"tomorrow"	ghad-an	غَداً
"a minute"	daqiiqat-an	دَقيقَةً
"an hour"	saaʿat-an	ساعَةً
"a day"	yawm-an	يَوماً
"a week"	'usbuuʿ-an	أُسْبوعاً
"a month"	shahr-an	شَهْراً
"a year"	sanat-an	سَنَةً
"in the summer"	Sayf-an	صَيْفاً
"in the winter"	shitaa'-an	شِتاءً
"in the fall"	khariif-an	خَريفاً
"in the spring"	rabiiʿ-an	رَبيعاً
"a while"	waqt-an	وَقْتاً
"a while"	zaman-an	زَمَناً
"a while"	Hiin-an	حيناً

أَذْهَبُ إلى الجامِعَةِ صَباحاً وأَعودُ ظُهْراً .
"I go to the university in the morning and return at noon."

قَضَيْتُ في المَغْرِبِ أُسْبوعاً .
"I spent a week in Morocco."

تَسْقُطُ الثُّلوجُ هُنا شِتاءً .
"Snow falls here in winter."

Some adverbs of time have invariable endings, though they may have different meanings, including:

"yesterday"	'amsi	أَمْسِ
"now"	'al-'aana	الآنَ
"at"	maʿa	مَعَ
"since"	mundhu	مُنْذُ
"at," "with"	wa	وَ

as in:

غِبْتُ عَنِ الْجَامَعَةِ أَمْسِ وأنا فيها الآنَ.

"I was absent from the university yesterday and I am in it now."

مَشَيْتُ مَعَ النَّهْرِ.

"I walked along the river."

سافَرْتُ مَعَ الْفَجْرِ.

"I traveled at dawn."

سافَرْتُ وَ الْفَجْرَ.

"I traveled at dawn."

Note: The noun following وَ *wa* "at," "with" takes the accusative مَنْصوب case ending. This وَ *wa* "at," "with" is called in Arabic واو المَعِيَّة "*waaw* of company."

As in English, adverbs of time can also be used as part of an إضافة *'iDaafa* phrase (with the first part taking the accusative مَنْصوب case ending and the second part taking the genitive مَجْرور case ending) or as a definite demonstrative phrase (with the second part taking the accusative مَنْصوب case ending) (see also Chapter 3), including:

"this morning"	SabaaH-a l-yawm-i	صَباحَ الْيَوْمِ
"every morning"	SabaaH-a kulli yawm-in	صَباحَ كُلِّ يَوْمٍ
"last morning"	SabaaH-a 'amsi	صَباحَ أَمْسِ
"next morning"	SabaaH-a ghad-in	صَباحَ غَدٍ

"this morning"	haadhaa S-SabaaH-a	هٰذا الصَّباحَ
"this noon"	Zuhr-a l-yawm-i	ظُهْرَ الْيَوْمِ
"yesterday noon"	Zuhr-a 'amsi	ظُهْرَ أَمْسِ
"tomorrow noon"	Zuhr-a ghad-in	ظُهْرَ غَدٍ
"this afternoon"	ᶜaSr-a l-yawm-i	عَصْرَ الْيَوْمِ
"yesterday afternoon"	ᶜaSr-a 'amsi	عَصْرَ أَمْسِ
"tomorrow afternoon"	ᶜaSr-a ghad-in	عَصْرَ غَدٍ
"this evening"	masaa'-a l-yawm-i	مَساءَ الْيَوْمِ
"yesterday evening"	masaa'-a 'amsi	مَساءَ أَمْسِ
"tomorrow evening"	masaa'-a ghad-in	مَساءَ غَدٍ
"this evening"	haadha l-masaa'-a	هٰذا المَساءَ
"last night"	laylat-a 'amsi	لَيْلَةَ أَمْسِ
"tomorrow night"	laylat-a ghad-in	لَيْلَةَ غَدٍ
"the day of Friday"	yawm-a l-jumᶜat-i	يَوْمَ الْجُمْعةِ
"the day of the holiday"	yawm-a l-ᶜuTlat-i	يَوْمَ الْعُطْلَةِ
"today"	haadha l-yawm-a	هٰذا الْيَوْمَ
"every morning"	kull-a SabaaH-in	كُلَّ صَباحٍ
"every day"	kull-a yawm-in	كُلَّ يَوْمٍ
"every week"	kull-a 'usbuuᶜ-in	كُلَّ أُسْبوعٍ
"some time"	baᶜD-a l-waqt-i	بَعْضَ الْوَقْتِ
"half an hour"	niSf-a saaᶜat-in	نِصْفَ ساعَةٍ
"at sunrise"	waqt-a Tuluuᶜi sh-shams-i	وَقْتَ طُلوعِ الشَّمْسِ
"at noon time"	Hiin-a Z-Zuhr-i	حينَ الظُّهْرِ
"the year of 2009"	sanat-a 2009	سَنَةَ ٢٠٠٩
"the year of 2009"	ᶜaam-a 2009	عامَ ٢٠٠٩

as in:

دَرَسْتُ في الْمَكْتَبَةِ صَباحَ الْيَومِ كَما أَفْعَلُ كُلَّ صَباحٍ .

"I studied in the library this morning as I do every morning."

سَأَبْقىٰ في الْبَيْتِ هٰذا الصَّباحَ .

"I will stay at home this morning."

بَقيتُ في الْبَيْتِ يَوْمَ الْعُطْلَةِ .

"I stayed at home on the holiday."

دَرَسْتُ في الْفَصْلِ نِصْفَ ساعَةٍ .

"I studied in the classroom for half an hour."

8.2   Adverbs of Place ظُروف المَكان

As their name suggests, adverbs of place ظُروف المَكان "envelopes/containers of place" refer to the place where the verb/action takes place. Like adverbs of time, adverbs of place take the accusative مَنْصوب case ending ´ [a] / أَ [an] and include adverbs, such as:

"under"	taHt-a	تَحْتَ
"over"	fawq-a	فَوْقَ
"in front of"	'amaam-a	أمامَ
"in front of"	quddaam-a	قُدّامَ
"behind"	khalf-a	خَلْفَ
"behind"	waraa'-a	وَراءَ
"right of"	yamiin-a/an	يَمينَ / يَميناً
"left of"	shimaal-a/an	شِمالَ / شِمالاً
"left of"	yasaar-a/an	يَسارَ / يَساراً
"next to"	jaanib-a/an	جانِبَ / جانِباً
"between"	bayn-a	بَيْنَ
"north of"	shamaal-a/an	شَمالَ / شَمالاً
"south of"	januub-a/an	جَنوبَ / جَنوباً
"east of"	sharq-a/an	شَرْقَ / شَرْقاً
"west of"	gharb-a/an	غَرْبَ / غَرْباً

جَلَسَ تَحْتَ الشَّجَرَةِ .
"He sat under the tree."

طارَتْ فَوْقَ الجَبَلِ .
"It flew over the mountain."

يَقَعُ الأُرْدُنُّ جَنوبَ سوريَّة .
"Jordan is situated south of Syria."

Some adverbs of place have invariable endings, including:

"where"	*Haythu*	حَيْثُ
"here"	*hunaa*	هُنا
"there"	*hunaaka*	هُناكَ
"there"	*thamma/thammata*	ثَمَّ / ثَمَّةَ

as in

جَلَسْتُ حَيْثُ جَلَسوا .
"I sat where they sat."

أَسْكُنُ هُنا .
"I live here."

ثَمَّةَ مَنْ يَعْتَقِدُ ...
"There are those who believe . . ."

8.3   Words Used as Adverbs of Time or Place

A few words can be used as adverbs of time *or* adverbs of place, depending on the word following it. These adverbs include:

"before"	*qabl-a*	قَبْلَ
"after"	*ba'd-a*	بَعْدَ
"at"	*'ind-a*	عِنْدَ

as in:

ذَهَبْتُ إلى الجامِعَةِ قَبْلَ الظُّهرِ .

"I went to the university before noon."

أَسْكُنُ في بِنايَةٍ قَبْلَ الجامِعَةِ .

"I live in a building before the university."

8.4 Dropping of Adverbs while Retaining Adverbial Meaning

For brevity's sake, some adverbs can be dropped while the adverbial meaning is still retained, as in:

اِنْتَظَرْتُ طَويلاً . = اِنْتَظَرْتُ زَمَناً طَويلاً .

"I waited **long**."   "I waited a **long time**."

خَرَجْتُ طُلوعَ الشَّمْسِ . = خَرَجْتُ وَقْتَ طُلوعِ الشَّمْسِ .

"I went out **at sunrise**."   "I went out **at the time of sunrise**."

8.5 Occurrence of Adverbs of Time and Place with Prepositions

Adverbs of time and place may be preceded by prepositions, depending on the intended meaning. When preceded by a preposition, an adverb takes the genitive مَجْرور case ending [i]/[in] instead of the accusative مَنْصوب case ending, such as:

"from under"	min taHt-i	... مِنْ تَحْتِ
"from over"	min fawq-i	... مِنْ فَوْقِ
"from the front of"	min 'amaam-i	... مِنْ أمامِ
"to the front of"	'ilaa 'amaam-i	... إلى أمامِ
"to behind"	'ilaa waraa'-i	... إلى وَراءِ
"from behind"	min waraa'-i	... مِنْ وَراءِ
"to the right of"	'ilaa yamiin-i	... إلى يَمينِ
"from the right of"	ʿan yamiin-i	... عَنْ يَمينِ

"to the left of"	'ilaa shimaal-i	... إلى شِمالِ
"from the left of"	ʿan shimaal-i	... عَنْ شِمالِ
"from before"	min qabl-i	... مِنْ قَبْلِ
"from after"	min baʿd-i	... مِنْ بَعْدِ
"from at"	min ʿind-i	... مِنْ عِنْدِ

مَشَيْتُ مِنْ وَراءِ الشَّجَرةِ .
"I walked from behind the tree."

نَزَلْتُ مِنْ فَوْقِ الشَّجَرةِ .
"I descended from above the tree."

اِنْتَظَرْتُكَ مِنْ قَبْلِ الظُّهْرِ .
"I waited for you from/since before noon."

Note: When nothing follows the preposition and the adverb, in particular "from before" and "from after," the ending on the adverb is ضَمَّة [u], as in:

سافَرْتُ كَثيراً مِنْ قَبْلُ .
"I traveled a lot before."

As for adverbs with invariable endings, they retain their invariable endings when preceded by a preposition, such as:

"from now"	mina l-'aana	مِنَ الآنَ
"to now"	'ilaa l-'aana	إلى الآنَ
"until now"	Hattaa l-'aana	حَتّى الآنَ
"from here"	min hunaa	مِنْ هُنا
"to here"	'ilaa hunaa	إلى هُنا
"from where"	min Haythu	مِنْ حَيْثُ
"to where"	'ilaa Haythu	إلى حَيْثُ

سَأَكْتُبُ الْواجِبَ مِنَ الآنَ فَصاعِداً .
"I will write the homework from now on."

ذَهَبَ إلى حَيْثُ ذَهَبَتْ .
"He went to where she went."

8.6 Expressing Adverbial Meanings by a Preposition Followed by a Noun

As in English, adverbs of time and place can be expressed in Arabic by means of a preposition, particularly في *fii* "in," and a (definite) noun denoting time or place. In this case, the ending on the noun following the preposition is in the genitive مَجْرور (see also 22.2.2 on case endings), as in:

"in the morning"	*fi S-SabaaH-i*	في الصَّباح
"in the evening"	*fi l-masaa'-i*	في المَساءِ
"on Saturday"	*fii yawm-i s-sabt*	في يَوْم السَّبْتِ
"on the day of the holiday"	*fii yawm-i l-ᶜuTlat-i*	في يَوْم الْعُطْلَة
"on the holiday"	*fi l-ᶜuTlat-i*	في الْعُطْلَةِ
"in winter"	*fi sh-shitaa'-i*	في الشِّتاءِ
"in the summer"	*fi S-Sayf-i*	في الصَّيْفِ
"at home"	*fi l-bayt-i*	في الْبَيْتِ
"at the university"	*fi l-jaamiᶜat-i*	في الجَامِعَةِ
"at the market"	*fi s-suuq-i*	في السُّوقِ
"in the city"	*fi l-madiinat-i*	في الـمَدينَةِ
"in the sun"	*fi sh-shams-i*	في الشَّمْسِ

أَعْمَلُ في الصَّباحِ وأَدْرُسُ في المَساءِ .
"I work in the morning and study in the evening."

أَسْكُنُ في بَيْتٍ صَغيرٍ .
"I live in a small house"

Note: As discussed in Chapter 1 (1.9.3), if the preposition ends with a long vowel, the long vowel is shortened when it is followed by a word containing the definite article (e.g., في "in" *fii* ➔ *fi*).

Finally, there are three verbs (دَخَلَ *dakhala* "he entered," نَزَلَ *nazala* "he stayed," and سَكَنَ *sakana* "he lived") where use of the preposition في *fii* "in" (to indicate an adverb of place) is optional. In this case, when the preposition is not used, the ending on the noun is the accusative مَنْصوب case, as in:

دَخَلْتُ في الْبَيْتِ . = دَخَلْتُ الْبَيْتَ .
"I entered the house."

نَزَلْتُ في فُنْدُقٍ . = نَزَلْتُ فُنْدُقاً .
"I stayed at a hotel."

سَكَنْتُ في الْقاهِرَةِ . = سَكَنْتُ الْقاهِرَةَ .
"I lived in Cairo."

8.7   Other Uses of Adverbs

Like nouns, adverbs can have other functions, just as any other noun, including the subject/doer of the verb/action, the object/doee of the verb/action, and the subject of a nominal sentence, etc. (see 22.2.2 on case endings), as in:

مَضىٰ يَومُ الْجُمُعةِ .
"The day of Friday passed."

نُحِبُّ يَومَ الْجُمُعةِ .
"We like the day of Friday."

يَومُ الْجُمُعةِ قَصيرٌ .
"The day of Friday is short."

8.8   Summary

This chapter discussed the use of adverbs in Arabic. Remember:

- adverbs of time refer to the time of the verb/action or a (time) container within which the verb/action takes place
- adverbs of place refer to the place of the verb/action or as a (place) container within which the verb/action takes place
- certain words and expressions are used primarily as adverbs of time
- certain words and expressions are used primarily as adverbs of place
- certain words can be used as either adverbs of time or adverbs of place

- as in English and other languages, adverbs in Arabic can occur with prepositions preceding them
- for reasons of brevity, some adverbs can be dropped while the adverbial meaning is retained
- except for a small number of adverbs that have invariable endings, most adverbs take the accusative مَنْصوب case ending unless they are preceded by a preposition, in which case they take the genitive مَجْرور case ending
- adverbs (denoting time or place) that are clearly nouns can have other functions in the sentence (i.e., not just that of an adverb), just like any other noun (see 22.2.2 on case endings).

9

Adverbs of Manner الحال

This chapter discusses Arabic adverbs used to describe the manner حال
"condition" or the *how* of the verb/action or, more specifically, the person
of الحال. Adverbs of manner in Arabic are expressed by a word, phrase,
verbal sentence, or nominal sentence. Words that function as adverbs of
manner are usually derived words and take the accusative مَنْصوب case ending, much like adverbs of time and place which describe the *when* and *where*
of the verb/action, respectively (see Chapter 8). This chapter covers the
most common uses of adverbs of manner الحال, including the following:

- adverbs of manner occurring as a single word
- adverbs of manner occurring as a phrase
- adverbs of manner occurring as non-derived nouns
- adverbs of manner occurring as a verbal sentence
- adverbs of manner occurring as a nominal sentence
- dropping adverbs of manner with prepositional and adverbial phrases.

9.1 Adverbs of Manner Occurring as a Single Word

Adverbs of manner can be expressed by means of a single word (in the
indefinite) with the accusative مَنْصوب ending ً [an]. In the vast majority
of cases, such words are derived, which include adjectives, active participles, and passive participles (see Chapter 15), as in:

Modern Standard Arabic Grammar: A Learner's Guide, First Edition.
© 2011 Mohammad T. Alhawary. Published 2011 by Blackwell Publishing Ltd.

سافَرَ صَديقي حَزيناً .
"My friend traveled sadly."

حَضَرَ صَديقي مُبْتَسِماً .
"My friend came smiling."

تَراجَعَ العَدو مَهْزوماً .
"The enemy retreated in defeat."

Usually, adverbs of manner الحال pertain to the manner of the verb/action of the subject/doer or what is referred to as the person of الحال, as the above examples show. However, the person of الحال can also occur as any part of the sentence, such as the doee/object, a noun following a preposition, or following a question word, as in:

رَأَيْتُ الأُسْتاذ مُسْتَعْجِلاً .
"I saw the teacher (who was) in a hurry."

تُرَكِّزُ صَديقَتي على العَمَل وَحْدَهُ .
"My (female) friend focuses on work alone/by itself."

مالَكَ واقِفاً ؟
"What is the matter with you standing?"

An adverb of manner الحال may not pertain *directly* to the person of the الحال but only *partly* (i.e., referring to a noun following it, not the noun before it). In this case, the noun following the adverb takes the nominative مَرْفوع case ending and the adverb the accusative مَنْصوب case ending, as in (for a similar structure, the causative attributive adjective, see 3.1.2):

جاءَ الأُسْتاذ مُمَزَّقاً قَميصُهُ .
"The teacher came with his shirt torn."

رَأَيْتُ الأُسْتاذ مُمَزَّقاً قَميصُهُ .
"I saw the teacher with his shirt torn."

A basic aspect of adverb use is that the gender (i.e., masculine vs. feminine) and number (i.e., singular, dual, and plural) of the adverb match those of the noun/pronoun to which the adverb pertains directly, and the appropriate accusative مَنْصوب ending is used (see 22.2.2 on case ending), as in:

حَضَرَ الطَّالِبُ مُسْرِعاً .
"The (male) student came in a hurry."

حَضَرَتِ الطَّالِبَةُ مُسْرِعةً .
"The (female) student came in a hurry."

حَضَرَ الطَّالِبانِ مُسْرِعَيْنِ .
"The two (male) students came in a hurry."

حَضَرَتِ الطَّالِبَتانِ مُسْرِعَتَيْنِ .
"The two (female) students came in a hurry."

حَضَرَ الطُّلَّابُ مُسْرِعِينَ .
"The (male) students came in a hurry."

حَضَرَتِ الطَّالِباتُ مُسْرِعاتٍ .
"The (female) students came in a hurry."

Note: More than one adverb may be used together, as in:

حَضَرَ صَديقي مُبْتَسِماً مُسْرِعاً.
"My (male) friend came smiling (and) in a hurry."

سافَرَ صَديقي وَحْدَهُ حَزيناً .
"My (male) friend traveled alone sadly."

9.2 Adverbs of Manner Occurring as Non-derived Nouns

Although adverbs of manner الحال usually occur as derived nouns (i.e., derived adjectives, active and passive participles; see Chapter 15), they can occur as non-derived nouns, especially when they involve metaphoric use or are repeated to convey the meaning of order, as in:

إِنْطَلَقَ العَدَّاءُ في السِّباقِ سَهْماً .
"The sprinter dashed in the race [like] an arrow."

قَرَأْتُ الكِتابَ باباً باباً .
"I read the book chapter by chapter."

9.3   Adverbs of Manner Occurring as a Phrase

Adverbs of manner can also be expressed by means of a phrase. One such use involves the use of مِثْل *mithla* "like" as the first term of an إضافة *'iDaafa* phrase, as in:

اِنْطَلَقَ المُتَسابِقُ مِثْلَ السَّهْمِ .

"The sprinter dashed like the arrow."

يَكْتُبُ خالِدٌ مِثْلَ الأُسْتاذِ .

"Khaled writes like the teacher."

Another use of adverbs of manner occurring as a phrase involves phrases that denote a reciprocal meaning, as in:

سَلَّمْتُهُ الرِّسالَةَ يَداً بِيَدٍ .

"I handed him the letter hand to hand."

قابَلْتُهُ وَجْهاً لِوَجْهٍ .

"I met him face to face."

9.4   Adverbs of Manner Occurring as a Verbal Sentence

A verbal sentence, usually consisting of a single verb in the present tense, can be used as an adverb of manner, conveying the same meaning as that expressed by a word with the accusative مَنْصوب ending, as in:

حَضَرَ صَديقي مُبْتَسِماً .   =   حَضَرَ صَديقي يَبْتَسِمُ .

"My (male) friend came smiling."

خَرَجَ صَديقي حامِلاً حَقيبة .   =   خَرَجَ صَديقي يَحْمِلُ حَقيبة .

"My (male) friend came out carrying a bag."

جِئْتُ سائلاً عَنْهُ .   =   جِئْتُ أَسْأَلُ عَنْهُ .

"I came asking/to ask about him."

A verbal sentence, with the verb in the past tense, can also be used as an adverb of manner. In this case, the verb is usually preceded by the conjunction particle و *wa* "and" (and the قَدْ particle in the affirmative or and ما for negation), having the equivalent meaning in English of the past perfect tense, as in:

جاءَ صَديقي وقَدْ كَتَبَ الواجِب .

"My (male) friend came and he had written the homework."

جاءَ صَديقي ولَمْ يَكْتُبِ الواجِب   =   جاءَ صَديقي وما كَتَبَ الواجِب .

"My (male) friend came and he had not written the homework."

9.5   Adverbs of Manner Occurring as a Nominal Sentence

A nominal sentence, whether consisting of a pronoun as subject followed by a verb or other components (see 4.2 on the nominal sentence), can be used as an adverb of manner. In this case, the verb is usually preceded by the conjunction particle و *wa* "and," as in:

حَضَرَ صَديقي وهو يَبْتَسِمُ .

"My (male) friend came smiling."

دَخَلَ صَديقي والأُستاذُ في الصَّفِ .

"My (male) friend came in and the teacher [was] in class."

خَرَجَ مِنَ الْبَيْتِ والشَّمْسُ طالِعَةٌ .

"He went out of the house and the sun [was] rising."

Use of the conjunction particle و *wa* "and" is optional when the nominal sentence contains a pronoun referring back to the person of the الحال :

حَضَرَ صَديقي رِجْلُهُ مَكْسورةٌ .   =   حَضَرَ صَديقي ورِجْلُهُ مَكْسورةٌ .

"My (male) friend came with his leg broken."

حَضَرَ صَديقي بِيَدِهِ كِتابٌ .   =   حَضَرَ صَديقي وبِيَدِهِ كِتابٌ .

"My (male) friend came with a book in his hand."

9.6 Dropping Adverbs of Manner with Prepositional and Adverbial Phrases

Adverbs occurring before prepositional or adverbial phrases are usually dropped, as the meaning is implicitly understood, as in:

جاءَ بالسَّيّارةِ .   →   جاءَ (راكِباً) بالسَّيّارةِ .
"He came (riding) by car."

يُعجِبُني العُصفورُ فَوْقَ الشَّجَرةِ .   →   يُعجِبُني العُصفورُ (واقفاً) فَوْقَ الشَّجَرةِ .
"I like the bird (standing) on the tree."

أَنْتَ في المَلْعَبِ أَفْضَلُ مِنْكَ في الصَّفِ .   →   أَنْتَ (لاعِباً) في المَلْعَبِ أَفْضَلُ مِنْكَ (طالِباً) في الصَّفِّ .
"You are (as a player) in the playground better than (as a student) in class."

Note: Although there is more than one way of expressing the meaning of an adverb of manner, there are some subtle differences. On one hand, the adverbs of manner in the following two sentences give equal weight to both the act of "coming" and the manner of "smiling" (although the adverb occurring as a verb describes more the *manner of the action* than the *state* of the person of حال):

حَضَرَ صَديقي يَبْتَسِمُ .   =   حَضَرَ صَديقي مُبْتَسِماً .
"My (male) friend came smiling."   "My (male) friend came smiling."

On the other hand, an adverb of manner expressed through a nominal sentence, as in the following example, indicates that the act of "coming" is stated and then the manner of "smiling" is emphasized, amounting to two statements, as reflected by the conjunction particle و *wa* "and" connecting them (i.e., with the adverb of manner receiving a primary emphasis on its own):

حَضَرَ صَديقي وهو يَبْتَسِمُ .
"My (male) friend came and he was smiling."

9.7 Summary

This chapter discussed Arabic adverbs of manner. Remember:

- adverbs of manner usually describe the manner or "condition" of the subject/doer of the action; they can also describe the manner of the object/doee or any part of the sentence
- adverbs of manner in Arabic can be expressed by a word, phrase, verbal sentence, or nominal sentence
- words functioning as adverbs of manner are usually derived words (i.e., derived adjectives, active participles, and passive participles)
- words functioning as adverbs of manner take the accusative مَنْصوب case ending
- when an adverb of manner directly (i.e., not partly) pertains to the person of الحال (i.e., the one previously mentioned in the sentence), both agree in gender (i.e., masculine vs. feminine) and number (i.e., singular, dual, and plural)
- adverbs of manner are usually dropped when they occur before prepositional and adverbial phrases, as the meaning is usually implicitly understood.

10

Adverbs of Specification التَّمْيِيز

This chapter discusses Arabic adverbs of specification التَّمْيِيز used to specify or clarify the meaning of a word, verb, or nominal sentence which may otherwise remain ambiguous. Adverbs of specification in Arabic are expressed by a word in the indefinite singular. Unlike adverbs of manner الحال (see Chapter 9), words functioning as adverbs of specification التَّمْيِيز are usually non-derived words (as opposed to derived adjectives and active and passive participles), but they also take the accusative مَنْصوب case ending. The chapter covers the most common uses of adverbs of specification التَّمْيِيز including the following:

- adverbs of specification clarifying an ambiguous word
- adverbs of specification clarifying an ambiguous verb
- adverbs of specification clarifying an ambiguous (nominal) sentence.

10.1 Adverbs of Specification Clarifying an Ambiguous Word

Adverbs of specification are typically expressed by means of a non-derived word in the indefinite singular with the accusative مَنْصوب ending اً [an]. They are used primarily to clarify number, weight/measurement, or area (for other rules related to Arabic numbers, see Appendix E), as in:

Modern Standard Arabic Grammar: A Learner's Guide, First Edition.
© 2011 Mohammad T. Alhawary. Published 2011 by Blackwell Publishing Ltd.

جاءَ عِشْرونَ طالِباً.
"Twenty student[s] came."

حَضَرَ عِشْرونَ وَلَداً.
"Twenty boy[s] came."

شَرِبْتُ لِتْراً حَليباً.
"I drank a liter [of] milk."

شَرِبْتُ لِتْراً ماءً.
"I drank a liter [of] water."

عِنْدي كيسٌ خُبْزاً.
"I have a bag [of] bread."

عِنْدي كيسٌ سُكَّراً.
"I have a bag [of] sugar."

زَرَعَ هِكْتاراً قَمْحاً.
"He planted a hectare [worth of] wheat."

زَرَعَ هِكْتاراً ذُرَةً.
"He planted a hectare [worth of] corn."

Apart from adverbs specifying number where no alternative structure exists to express it differently, other structures can be (but are much more commonly) used to clarify weight/measurement and area by means of an إضافة *'iDaafa* phrase or prepositional phrase (with *min* مِنْ "from" as the preposition), as in:

شَرِبْتُ لِتْرَ حَليبٍ. = شَرِبْتُ لِتْراً مِنَ الحَليبِ. = شَرِبْتُ لِتْراً حَليباً.
"I drank a liter of milk."

عِنْدي كيسُ خُبْزٍ. = عِنْدي كيسٌ مِنَ الخُبْزِ. = عِنْدي كيسٌ خُبْزاً.
"I have a bag of bread."

زَرَعَ هِكْتارَ قَمْحٍ. = زَرَعَ هِكْتاراً مِنَ القَمْحِ. = زَرَعَ هِكْتاراً قَمْحاً.
"He planted a hectare of wheat."

10.2 Adverbs of Specification Clarifying an Ambiguous Verb

Adverbs of specification are also used to clarify the meaning of a verb that would otherwise be subject to many different meanings, as in:

اِمْتَلَأَ قَلْبِي سَعادَةً .
"My heart was filled [with] happiness."

اِمْتَلَأَ قَلْبِي حُزْناً .
"My heart was filled [with] sadness."

اِرْتَفَعَ خالِد رُتْبَةً .
"Khaled went up a rank."

اِرْتَفَعَ خالِد دَرَجَةً .
"Khaled went up a step."

10.3 Adverbs of Specification Clarifying an Ambiguous (Nominal) Sentence

Adverbs of specification are similarly used to clarify the meaning of a nominal sentence that would otherwise be subject to many different meanings, as in:

هُوَ أَكْثَرُ مِنِّي مالاً .
"He has more money than me."

هُوَ أَكْثَرُ مِنِّي عِلْماً .
"He has more knowledge than me."

هُوَ أَكْبَرُ مِنِّي سِنّاً .
"He is bigger in age than me."

هُوَ أَكْبَرُ مِنِّي حَجْماً .
"He is bigger in size than me."

10.4   Summary

This chapter discussed Arabic adverbs of specification. Remember:

- adverbs of specification clarify or disambiguate the meaning of a word, verb, or sentence
- adverbs of specification are typically non-derived words used in the indefinite singular
- like other types of Arabic adverbs, adverbs of specification take the accusative مَنْصوب case ending
- there are two alternative ways of clarifying ambiguous words such as those related to weight/measurement: the use of an إضافة *'iDaafa* phrase or a prepositional مِنْ "from" phrase.

11

Adverbs of Cause المَفْعول لِأَجْلِه

This chapter discusses Arabic adverbs of cause المَفْعول لِأَجْلِه used to describe
the cause or purpose of the verb/action. Adverbs of cause are expressed
by a verbal noun/gerund مَصْدَر and, like other adverbs, take the accusative
مَنْصوب case ending. The chapter discusses different ways of expressing
the meaning of adverbs of cause, including:

- adverbs of cause occurring as an indefinite singular verbal noun/
  gerund
- adverbs of cause occurring as an إضافة 'iDaafa phrase
- other ways of expressing the meaning of adverbs of cause.

11.1 Adverbs of Cause Occurring as an Indefinite Singular Verbal Noun/Gerund

Adverbs of cause are expressed by means of a verbal noun/gerund in the
indefinite singular. Typically, each verb in Arabic has a verbal noun/gerund
in addition to its conjugation in the perfect/past and imperfect/present;
e.g., رَغِبَ "he wished," يَرْغَبُ "he wishes," and رَغْبَة "wishing" (see Chapter 14
on the verbal noun/gerund). Thus, to express an adverb of cause, the verbal
noun/gerund form is used with the accusative مَنْصوب case ending اً [an],
as in:

Modern Standard Arabic Grammar: A Learner's Guide, First Edition.
© 2011 Mohammad T. Alhawary. Published 2011 by Blackwell Publishing Ltd.

يَدرُسُ رَغْبَةً في الحُصولِ عَلَىٰ شَهادَة .
"He studies out of the wish to obtain a degree."

وَقَفَ المُحامي احْتِراماً للقاضي .
"The lawyer stood out of respect for the judge."

أَهْدَيْتُها هَدِيَّةً حُبّاً لَها .
"I gave her a gift out of love for her."

11.2 Adverbs of Cause Occurring as an إضافة 'iDaafa Phrase

Adverbs of cause can also occur as an إضافة 'iDaafa phrase (see Chapter 3), the first part being the verbal noun/gerund. In this case, the first part takes the accusative مَنْصوب case ending ــَ [a], as in:

وَبَّخَ الأبُ ابْنَهُ رَغْبَةَ إشْعارِهِ بالمَسؤوليَّة .
"The father scolded his son out of the wish to make him feel responsibility."

تَعمَلُ الحُكومةُ بُغْيَةَ تَطْويرِ الإقْتِصادِ .
"The government works for the purpose of developing the economy."

11.3 Other Ways of Expressing Adverbs of Cause

Adverbs of cause can also be expressed by means of a preposition followed by a phrase or a sentence, as in:

يَدرُسُ للحُصولِ عَلَىٰ شَهادَة .	يَدرُسُ رَغْبَةً في الحُصولِ عَلَىٰ شَهادَة .
"He studies for obtaining a degree." =	"He studies out of the wish to obtain a degree."
يَدرُسُ لِيَحْصُلَ عَلَىٰ شَهادَة .	يَدرُسُ رَغْبَةً في الحُصولِ عَلَىٰ شَهادَة .
"He studies to obtain a degree." =	"He studies out of the wish to obtain a degree."

وَقَفَ المُحامي لِاحْتِرامِهِ القاضي .	=	وَقَفَ المُحامي اِحْتِراماً لِلقاضي .
"The lawyer stood for his respect for the judge."		"The lawyer stood out of respect for the judge."
وَقَفَ المُحامي بِسَبَبِ اِحْتِرامِهِ لِلقاضي .	=	وَقَفَ المُحامي اِحْتِراماً لِلقاضي .
"The lawyer stood for/because of his respect for the judge."		"The lawyer stood out of respect for the judge."
أَهْدَيْتُها هَدِيَّةً مِنْ حُبِّي لَها .	=	أَهْدَيْتُها هَدِيَّةً حُبّاً لَها .
"I gave her a gift out of my love for her."		"I gave her a gift out of love for her."
أَهْدَيْتُها هَدِيَّةً بِسَبَبِ حُبِّي لَها .	=	أَهْدَيْتُها هَدِيَّةً حُبّاً لَها .
"I gave her a gift because of my love for her."		"I gave her a gift out of love for her."
وَبَّخَ الأَبُ ابْنَهُ مِنْ أَجْلِ إشْعارِهِ بِالمَسؤولِيَّة .	=	وَبَّخَ الأَبُ ابْنَهُ رَغْبَةَ إشْعارِهِ بِالمَسؤولِيَّة .
"The father scolded his son for the sake of making him feel responsibility."	=	"The father scolded his son out of the wish to make him feel responsibility."
تَعمَلُ الحُكومةُ مِنْ أَجْلِ تَطْوير الاِقْتِصادِ .	=	تَعمَلُ الحُكومةُ بُغْيَةَ تَطْوير الاِقْتِصادِ .
"The government works for the sake of developing the economy."	=	"The government works for the purpose of developing the economy."

Note: An adverb of cause is used when it has the same time reference as the verb/action which it describes. Therefore, if a verb/action has a different tense (e.g., took place later) than the cause, alternative constructions are used (such as the use of a preposition followed by a sentence or a phrase), as in:

دَخَلَ السِّجْنَ لِأَنَّهُ اِرْتَكَبَ جَريمَة .

"He entered jail, for/because he committed a crime."

دَخَلَ السِّجْنَ لِارْتِكابِهِ جَريمَة .

"He entered jail for committing a crime."

دَخَلَ السِّجْنَ بِسَبَبِ اِرْتِكابِهِ جَريمَة .

"He entered jail for/because of his committing a crime."

Thus, since the verb/action of "going to jail" did not happen at the same time as the cause (i.e., committing a crime), expressing the cause by means of an adverb of cause is ungrammatical.

دَخَلَ السِّجْنَ ارْتِكابًا لِجَرِيمَة .

However, if the sentence is rephrased so that the cause of "going to jail" came as a "punishment," so that both action and cause reflect the same time reference, then the statement becomes grammatical, as in:

دَخَلَ السِّجْنَ عِقاباً لَه .

"He entered jail as a punishment for him."

11.4   Summary

This chapter discussed Arabic adverbs of cause. Remember:

- adverbs of cause describe the cause or purpose of a verb/action
- adverbs of cause are expressed by a verbal noun/gerund مَصْدَر
- like other types of Arabic adverbs, adverbs of cause take the accusative مَنْصوب case ending
- adverbs of cause are either expressed as an indefinite verbal noun/ gerund in the singular or as an إضافة *'iDaafa* phrase
- there are alternative ways of describing the cause of the verb/action, such as the use of a preposition followed by a sentence or a phrase.

12

Adverbs of Emphasis/ Cognate Accusative المَفْعُول المُطْلَق

This chapter discusses the Arabic adverbs called المَفْعُول المُطْلَق "cognate accusative" which are used to emphasize a verb/action, word, or sentence. Adverbs of emphasis in Arabic are expressed by means of a verbal noun/ gerund مَصْدَر (see Chapter 14) belonging to the same root consonants of the verb or word they are intended to emphasize, and take the accusative مَنْصُوب case ending, much like other adverbs. The chapter covers the most common uses of adverbs of emphasis المَفْعُول المُطْلَق, including the following:

- adverbs of emphasis emphasizing a verb/action or a word in a sentence
- other uses of adverbs of emphasis
- adverbs of emphasis emphasizing a sentence
- adverbs of emphasis occurring as an إضافة 'iDaafa phrase
- dropping adverbs of emphasis.

12.1 Adverbs of Emphasis Emphasizing a Verb/Action or a Word in a Sentence

Typically, adverbs of emphasis occur indefinite in the singular with the accusative مَنْصُوب case ending اً [an]. They are usually intended to empha- size a verb/action, as in:

ضَحِكَ ضَحِكاً.
"He laughed (quite) a laughing."

أَكَلَ أَكْلاً.
"He ate (quite) an eating."

Modern Standard Arabic Grammar: A Learner's Guide, First Edition.
© 2011 Mohammad T. Alhawary. Published 2011 by Blackwell Publishing Ltd.

However, adverbs of emphasis are often followed by an adjective adding to the emphasis, as in:

ضَحِكَ ضَحِكاً شَديداً .

"He laughed (quite) an intense laughing."

أَكَلَ أَكْلاً كَثيراً .

"He ate a lot (of eating)."

In addition to emphasizing the verb/action, adverbs of emphasis are used to emphasize an adjective, a derived noun such as an active or passive participle, and sometimes even another verbal noun, as in:

أراكَ سَعيداً سَعادَةً عَظيمَةً .

"I see you happy with (quite) great happiness."

جاءَ صَديقي ضاحِكاً ضَحِكاً عالِياً .

"My friend came laughing with (quite) a loud laughing."

جاؤوا بِهِ مُقَيَّداً تَقْييداً .

"They brought him (quite) chained."

لا بُدَّ مِن دِراسَةِ المَوْضوع دِراسَةً شامِلَةً .

"It is necessary to study the topic (quite) a comprehensive study/comprehensively."

12.2   Other Uses of Adverbs of Emphasis

Through use of a following adjective, adverbs of emphasis are also used to specify the type of emphasis intended, as in:

نامَتْ نَوْماً عَميقاً .

"She slept (quite) a deep sleep."

نامَتْ نَوْماً خَفيفاً .

"She slept (quite) a light sleep."

نامَتْ نَوْماً هادِئاً .

"She slept (quite) a quiet sleep."

سارَ سَيْراً سَريعاً .

"He walked (quite) a fast walking."

سارَ سَيْراً بَطيئاً .

"He walked (quite) a slow walking."

Adverbs of emphasis may also provide specific information about number, while providing emphasis, in which case the adverb can occur (in addition to the singular) in the dual or the plural, as in:

اِسْتَرَحْتُ اِسْتِراحَتَيْنِ .

"I had two breaks."

اِسْتَرَحْتُ اِسْتِراحاتٍ ثَلاثاً .   =   اِسْتَرَحْتُ ثَلاثَ اِسْتِراحاتٍ .   =   اِسْتَرَحْتُ ثَلاثاً .

"I had three breaks."

ضَرَبوهُ ضَرْبَتَيْنِ .

"They hit him twice."

ضَرَبوهُ ضَرَباتٍ ثَلاثاً .   =   ضَرَبوهُ ثَلاثَ ضَرَباتٍ .   =   ضَرَبوهُ ثَلاثاً .

"They hit him three times."

12.3   Adverbs of Emphasis Emphasizing a Sentence

The meaning of an entire sentence, whether verbal or nominal, can also be emphasized (when the listener has doubt) through many adverbs of emphasis, such as حَقّاً "truly," البَتَّةَ / بَتَّةً "definitely not," قَطْعاً "categorically," يَقيناً "for certain/sure," حَتْماً "definitely," etc., as in:

هو أخي حَقّاً .

"He is my brother truly."

هٰذا هُوَ مَوْقِفي قَطْعاً .

"This is my position categorically."

قابَلْتُهُ مِنْ قَبْلُ يَقيناً .

"I met him before for sure."

هٰذا سَيَحْدُثُ حَتْماً .

"This will happen definitely."

12.4   Adverbs of Emphasis Occurring as an إضافة 'iDaafa Phrase

Adverbs of emphasis may occur as the first term of an إضافة 'iDaafa phrase (i.e., followed by a noun), having the same function as that of adverbs of emphasis followed by an adjective, in order to specify the type of emphasis intended, as in:

هذه الخُدْعَةُ قديمَةٌ قِدَمَ التّاريخ .

"This trick is (as) old as old history/as old as history."

بَكَيْتُ بُكاءَ الأَطْفالِ .

"I cried the cry of babies."

مَشىٰ مَشْيَ المَغْرورِ .

"He walked the walk of the arrogant."

نَجَحَ بَعْضَ النَّجاحِ .

"He achieved some (of the) success."

نَجَحَ كُلَّ النَّجاحِ .

"I achieved all the success."

12.5   Dropping Adverbs of Emphasis

Adverbs of emphasis are dropped when the meaning of the dropped adverb can be inferred. This includes dropping them when they are followed by an adjective or when they occur as part of an إضافة 'iDaafa phrase. In this case, the adjective and the second term of the إضافة 'iDaafa phrase retain the accusative مَنْصوب case ending, as in:

أَكَلَ كثيراً .   ←   أَكَلَ أَكْلاً كثيراً .

"He ate a lot."

سارَ سَريعاً .   ←   سارَ سَيْراً سَريعاً .

"He walked fast."

قَعَدَ القُرْفُصاءَ .   ←   قَعَدَ قُعودَ القُرْفُصاءِ .

"He squatted."

Note: Unlike what is widely misunderstood about adverbs of emphasis المَفْعُول المُطْلَق , the verbal noun/gerund need not be the exact verbal noun of the verb or the word it is meant to emphasize, as long as it belongs to the same root consonants, as in:

<table>
<tr><td align="center">كَلَّمْتُكَ كَلاماً .</td><td align="center">=</td><td align="center">كَلَّمْتُكَ تَكْليماً .</td></tr>
<tr><td align="center">"I talked to you (quite) a talking."</td><td></td><td align="center">"I talked to you (quite) a talking."</td></tr>
<tr><td align="center">أَعْطى عَطاءً .</td><td align="center">=</td><td align="center">أَعْطى إعْطاءً .</td></tr>
<tr><td align="center">"He gave (quite) a giving."</td><td></td><td align="center">"He gave (quite) a giving."</td></tr>
<tr><td align="center">اِغْتَسَلْتُ غُسْلاً .</td><td align="center">=</td><td align="center">اِغْتَسَلْتُ اِغْتِسالاً .</td></tr>
<tr><td align="center">"I washed (quite) a washing."</td><td></td><td align="center">"I washed (quite) a washing."</td></tr>
</table>

Moreover, a synonym verbal noun/gerund (i.e., which has a similar meaning but does not belong to the same root consonants) can equally be used as adverb of emphasis, as in:

<table>
<tr><td align="center">بَكى نَحيباً .</td><td align="center">=</td><td align="center">بَكى بُكاءً .</td></tr>
<tr><td align="center">"He cried a sobbing."</td><td></td><td align="center">"He cried a sobbing."</td></tr>
<tr><td align="center">أَجْبَرْتُهُ قَسْراً .</td><td align="center">=</td><td align="center">أَجْبَرْتُهُ إجباراً .</td></tr>
<tr><td align="center">"I forced him with compulsion."</td><td></td><td align="center">"I forced him with compulsion."</td></tr>
</table>

12.6   Summary

This chapter discussed Arabic adverbs of emphasis. Remember:

• adverbs of emphasis are typically verbal nouns/gerunds
• adverbs of emphasis usually occur indefinite in the singular
• adverbs of emphasis take the accusative مَنْصوب case ending اً [an], like other adverbs
• adverbs of emphasis emphasize a verb/action, word in a sentence, or sentence
• in addition to providing emphasis, adverbs of emphasis may at the same time clarify or specify the meaning of a verb/action or word
• adverbs of emphasis may occur in the dual or plural
• adverbs of emphasis may occur as a phrase
• adverbs of emphasis may be dropped, as the meaning can be inferred from a retained modifying adjective or noun.

13

The Verb الفِعْل

This chapter discusses essential aspects of the *verb*, called in Arabic الفِعْل "the action," whether in the form of active voice, passive voice, the imperative, or the negative imperative, as well as common verb patterns/ forms. The chapter covers the following:

*   common triliteral verb forms and their meanings
*   common quadriliteral verb forms
*   verb categories and their conjugations
*   the imperative
*   the negative imperative
*   the passive voice.

13.1 Common Triliteral Verb Forms

Most commonly Arabic has ten verb patterns/forms of triliteral roots (see Chapter 2 for more on the notion of roots and patterns). While Form I exhibits somewhat unpredictable sound changes between the past and the present form, and vice versa, the rest (Forms II–X) exhibit predictable changes.

Modern Standard Arabic Grammar: A Learner's Guide, First Edition.
© 2011 Mohammad T. Alhawary. Published 2011 by Blackwell Publishing Ltd.

13.1.1   Form I

Form I exhibits a single slight sound change with respect to its past and present forms. The best way to understand this sound change is to consider the conjugation of English verbs in the present and past tenses (as well as the past participle), as shown in the examples below.

Present	Past	Past participle	Sound changes
travel	traveled	traveled	+ [d]
want	wanted	wanted	+ [id]
walk	walked	walked	+ [t]
buy	bought	bought	[ai] → [ɔt]
run	ran	run	[ʌ] → [æ] → [ʌ]
begin	began	begun	[i] → [æ] → [ʌ]
rise	rose	risen	[ai] → [oʊ] → [i] & [ən]
write	wrote	written	[ai] → [oʊ] → [i] & [ən]
stand	stood	stood	[æn] → [u]
go	went	gone	[goʊ] → [went] → [gɔn]
put	put	put	∅

In fact, the corresponding sound changes in English verbs are unpredictable and therefore irregular. The sound change irregularities are further compounded by additional irregularities in the spelling, as the list of the above examples shows. However, unlike English, Arabic Form I, which is the only verb pattern that can be characterized as irregular, exhibits a minimal sound change of one middle vowel, with six common subtypes of verbs, as follows:

	Present/المُضارع		*Past*/الماضي		*Form I*
"he reads"	يَقْرَأُ	—	قَرَأَ	"he read"	1.
"he writes"	يَكْتُبُ	—	كَتَبَ	"he wrote"	2.
"he sits"	يَجْلِسُ	—	جَلَسَ	"he sat"	3.
"he understands"	يَفْهَمُ	←	فَهِمَ	"he understood"	4.
"he thinks"	يَحْسِبُ	—	حَسِبَ	"he thought"	5.
"he becomes far"	يَبْعُدُ	←	بَعُدَ	"he became far"	6.

Note: The direction of the two arrows indicates that the present tense can be predicted from the form of the past tense.

However, while it is not possible to predict how the past-tense middle *fatHa* vowel would turn out in the present tense in subtypes 1–3, the past-tense middle *Damma* (in subtype 6 above) always surfaces as *Damma* in the present tense and the middle *kasra* in sub-type 4 almost always surfaces as a *fatHa*, as indicated by the arrows (with a few exceptions, as in subtype 5, although most of these exceptions are found in *mithaal* "assimilated" verbs; i.e., those starting with a long vowel, as in وَرِثَ → "he inherited" يَرِثُ "he inherits"). Hence, learning both past and present forms of Form I verbs at the same time, while noting the regularity in two of the subtypes (4 and 6), is necessary – just as it is necessary for the English learner to learn the conjugations of every single English verb in the past, present, and past participles. Perhaps the best way to learn the conjugations of Form I verbs is to learn both the past and present forms together.

The best way to capture the patterns of Form I is by means of the form فَعَلَ "he did" and يَفْعَلُ "he does," as a mnemonic device (see also Chapter 2), as follows:

Present/ المُضارع		*Past/* الماضي	*Form I*
يَفْعَلُ	–	فَعَلَ	1.
يَفْعُلُ	–	فَعَلَ	2.
يَفْعِلُ	–	فَعَلَ	3.
يَفْعَلُ	←	فَعِلَ	4.
يَفْعِلُ	–	فَعِلَ	5.
يَفْعُلُ	←	فَعُلَ	6.

Note: Arabic has no infinitive form equivalent to "to read," "to write," etc. Rather, the verb always occurs with a pronoun suffix attached to it. The verb with the third-person singular, as in قَرَأ "he read" and كَتَبَ "he wrote," is usually used (in dictionaries, textbooks, and elsewhere) instead when referring to any verb, since it is the shortest form.

13.1.2 Forms II–X

Unlike Form I, Forms II–X, which are derived from Form I (as will be explained below), are all regular and involve no irregular sound changes between the past and present forms, as shown below by means of the mnemonic-derived forms of فَعَلَ where knowing the past form entails the ability to predict the exact present form, and vice versa, as indicated in the bidirectional arrows.

*Present/*المُضارِع		*Past/*الماضي	Forms
يُفَعِّلُ	← →	فَعَّلَ	II
يُفاعِلُ	← →	فَاعَلَ	III
يُفْعِلُ	← →	أَفْعَلَ	IV
يَتَفَعَّلُ	← →	تَفَعَّلَ	V
يَتَفاعَلُ	← →	تَفاعَلَ	VI
يَنْفَعِلُ	← →	اِنْفَعَلَ	VII
يَفْتَعِلُ	← →	اِفْتَعَلَ	VIII
يَفْعَلُّ	← →	اِفْعَلَّ	IX
يَسْتَفْعِلُ	← →	اِسْتَفْعَلَ	X

13.2 Meanings of the Common Triliteral Verb Forms

The ten verb patterns differ from each other mainly in whether or not they are transitive (i.e., they require an object) or intransitive (they do not require an object), although some verb forms have additional subtle or specialized meanings according to their specific forms/patterns, all being derived from Form I.

13.2.1 Meanings of Form I Verbs

Like verbs in English, some Arabic Form I فَعَلَ verbs can be both intransitive (i.e., they do not require an object/doee of the action) or transitive,
although all verbs can take an adverb, a prepositional phrase (i.e., consisting of a preposition and a noun), or other parts of speech (written
below in parentheses), as in:

أَكَلَ الأُسْتاذُ (في الصَّباح) .

"The teacher ate (in the morning)."

أَكَلَ الأُسْتاذُ تُفَّاحَةً (في الصَّباح) .

"The teacher ate an apple (in the morning)."

Form I verbs with the pattern فَعَلَ ← يَفْعُلُ are always intransitive, since
their meaning is exclusively related to reflexive traits, as in:

قَصُرَ الثَّوْبُ .

"The dress got short."

سَهُلَ الأَمْرُ .

"The matter became easy."

Other Form I verbs can be either intransitive or transitive, but never both,
as in:

ذَهَبَ الأُسْتاذُ (إلى الجامِعَةِ في الصَّباح) .

"The teacher went (to the university in the morning)."

رَجَعَ الأُسْتاذُ (مِن الجامِعَةِ في الصَّباح) .

"The teacher returned (from the university in the morning)."

قَطَعَ الطُّلابُ الحَبْلَ (في الحَديقةِ) .

"The students cut the rope (in the garden)."

كَسَرَ الأُسْتاذُ القَلَمَ (في الصَّفِّ) .

"The teacher broke the pen (in class)."

قَتَلَ الفَلّاحُ الحَيَّةَ (في الحَديقةِ) .

"The farmer killed the snake (in the garden)."

Note: In all the above examples, other parts of speech (written in parentheses) can occur with any verb but are not required for the meaning of the sentence to be complete. While a complete sentence with an intransitive verb minimally requires a subject (i.e., a doer of the action) and a verb, a complete sentence with a transitive verb minimally requires a subject, a verb, and an object (i.e., doee of the action).

13.2.2   Meanings of Form II Verbs

Form II فَعَّلَ verbs have two specialized meanings: a causative meaning, which also requires the verb to be transitive, and a repetitive/intensive meaning (i.e., happening many times), as in:

دَرَّسَ الأُسْتاذُ الطُّلَّابَ .

(Literally: "The teacher caused the students to study.")
= "The teacher taught the students."

كَسَّرَ الأُسْتاذُ القَلَمَ .

(Literally: "The teacher broke the pen into pieces.")
= "The teacher shattered the pen."

13.2.3   Meanings of Form III Verbs

Form III فاعَلَ verbs have two specialized meanings: a transitive meaning (requiring an object) or a reciprocal meaning (denoting the sharing of the action with the object), as in:

شاهَدَ الطُّلَّابُ الفيلمَ .

"The students watched the movie."

ساعَدَ الأُسْتاذُ الطُّلَّابَ .

"The teacher helped the students."

قاتَلَ الجُنُودُ الأَعْداءَ .

"The soldiers fought (with) the enemies."

However, a few rare verbs of Form III may occur as intransitive, as in:

سافَرَ الأُسْتاذُ .

"The teacher traveled."

13.2.4 Meanings of Form IV Verbs

Form IV أَفْعَلَ verbs have a causative or transitive meaning, as in:

أَكْرَمَ الطُّلَّابُ الأُسْتاذَ .

(Literally: "The students caused the teacher to be honored.")
= "The students honored the teacher."

أَحْضَرَ الطُّلَّابُ كُتُبَهُم .

(Literally: "The students caused their books to attend.")
= "The students brought their books."

However, a small number of Form IV verbs are intransitive, as in:

أَقْبَلَ الطّالِبُ .

"The student came."

أَسْلَمَ مُعْظَمُ العَرَبِ .

"Most of the Arabs became Muslims."

13.2.5 Meanings of Form V Verbs

Form V تَفَعَّلَ verbs have a change of state or reflexive (i.e., a passive) meaning (not requiring an object) or a transitive meaning (requiring an object). In both cases, the verb has an additional intensive/repetitive meaning, as in:

تَكَسَّرَ القَلَمُ .

"The pen broke into pieces." = "The pen shattered."

يَتَكَلَّمُ الأُسْتاذُ العَرَبِيَّةَ .

"The teacher speaks Arabic."

13.2.6 Meanings of Form VI Verbs

Form VI تَفاعَلَ verbs have an intransitive (requiring no object) and a restricted reciprocal meaning (i.e., two people share the same action), with the subject occurring usually in the dual, as in:

تَقابَلَ الصَّديقانِ .

"The two friends met (each other)."

تَقاتَلَ الشَّعْبانِ .

"The two peoples fought (each other)."

However, some Form VI verbs may denote reciprocity rather loosely and may occur intransitively or transitively, as in:

تَمارَضَ العامِلُ .

"The worker pretended to be sick."

تَكاسَلَ الطّالِبُ .

"The student became lazy."

تَجاوَزَ السّائِقُ حُدودَ السُّرْعةِ .

"The driver went beyond the speed limit."

13.2.7 Meanings of Form VII Verbs

Form VII اِنْفَعَلَ verbs have a *change of state* or reflexive (i.e., passive) meaning, not requiring an object, as in:

اِنْكَسَرَ القَلَمُ .

"The pen broke."

اِنْقَطَعَ الحَبْلُ .

"The rope got cut."

13.2.8 Meanings of Form VIII Verbs

Most Form VIII اِفْتَعَلَ verbs have a *change of state* or reflexive (i.e., passive) meaning, not requiring an object, as in:

اِحْتَرَقَ البَيْتُ .

"The house burned."

اِقْتَرَبَ الوَقْتُ .

"The time drew near."

However, some Form VIII اِفْتَعَلَ verbs have a transitive meaning, requiring an object, as in:

اِكْتَسَبَ السِّياسِيُّ سُمْعَةً سَيِّئَةً .

"The politician gained a bad reputation."

اِحْتَسَبَ الأُسْتاذُ أَجْرَهُ عَلىٰ الله .

"The teacher assumed his reward (will be given) by God."

13.2.9   Meanings of Form IX Verbs

Like Forms VII and VIII, Form IX اِفْعَلَّ verbs have a change of state or reflexive (i.e., passive) meaning, not requiring an object, specific to colors or bodily and other defects/beauties, as in:

اِخْضَرَّ العُشْبُ .

"The grass turned green."

اِعْوَجَّ الطَّرِيقُ .

"The road became crooked."

13.2.10   Meanings of Form X Verbs

Form X اِسْتَفْعَلَ verbs have a transitive, synthetic meaning, as in:

اِسْتَخْدَمَ الأُسْتاذُ الكِتابَ .

(Literally: "The teacher sought the use of the book.")
= "The teacher used the book."

اِسْتَقْبَلَ الرَّئِيسُ الوَزِيرَ .

(Literally: "The president sought to be before the minister.")
= "The president met the minister."

اِسْتَغْفَرَ اللهَ مِنْ ذَنْبِهِ .

"He sought God for forgiveness for his sin/He sought God's forgiveness for his sin."

Some Form X اِسْتَفْعَلَ verbs have an intransitive meaning, although they would often require a prepositional phrase (a noun preceded by a preposition) in this case, as in:

اِسْتَغْفَرَ لِذَنْبِهِ .

"He sought forgiveness for his sin."

اِسْتَعْلَمَ السَّائِقُ عَنِ المَكانِ .

"The driver sought information/inquired about the place."

13.2.11 Deriving Forms II–X from Form I Verbs

While Forms II–X are all derived from Form I, not all the forms are available in the language. This all depends on the meaning of the verb (i.e., certain meanings are not possible for each form) and essentially what is already available in the language (i.e., learners cannot coin new verbs if these are not already available). Hence, the examples of the three verbs below show that only certain verbs are naturally available (depending on the meaning of each form described above) or simply what is already available in the language:

"to learn"	يَعْلَمُ	عَلِمَ	I
"to teach someone/something"	يُعَلِّمُ	عَلَّمَ	II
–	–	–	III
"to inform someone"	يُعْلِمُ	أَعْلَمَ	IV
"to learn"	يَتَعَلَّمُ	تَعَلَّمَ	V
"to pretend to be a scholar"	يَتَعالَمُ	تَعالَمَ	VI
–	–	–	VII
–	–	–	VIII
–	–	–	IX
"to inquire about something"	يَسْتَعْلِمُ	اِسْتَعْلَمَ	X

"to burn something"	يَحْرِقُ	حَرَقَ	I
"to burn something repeatedly"	يُحَرِّقُ	حَرَّقَ	II
–	–	–	III
"to make something burn"	يُحْرِقُ	أَحْرَقَ	IV
–	–	–	V
–	–	–	VI
–	–	–	VII
"to burn"	يَحْتَرِقُ	اِحْتَرَقَ	VIII
–	–	–	IX
–	–	–	X

"to cut something"	يَقْطَعُ	قَطَعَ	I
"to chop something"	يُقَطِّعُ	قَطَّعَ	II
"to interrupt someone"	يُقاطِعُ	قاطَعَ	III
"to carve someone something"	يُقْطِعُ	أَقْطَعَ	IV
"to get chopped"	يَتَقَطَّعُ	تَقَطَّعَ	V
"to intersect"	يَتَقاطَعُ	تَقاطَعَ	VI
"to get cut"	يَنْقَطِعُ	اِنْقَطَعَ	VII
"to cut/take part in something"	يَقْتَطِعُ	اِقْتَطَعَ	VIII
–	–	–	IX
"to request to be carved something"	يَسْتَقْطِعُ	اِسْتَقْطَعَ	X

Thus, one of the forms that is naturally missing in all of the three verbs above is Form IX, since its meaning is specific to change of color or bodily defects/beauties.

The practical benefits of learning such forms/patterns is that the learner is not only able to identify that the word is most likely to be a verb (vs. a noun or adjective) and how to pronounce it (including the placing of the *Damma* on the prefix of the present tense for Forms II–IV and the *fatHa* for the rest), but also may guess the meaning of the verb by reducing it to Form I or the root.

13.2.12   Triliteral Verb Form XI

One verb form/pattern that is not as common in MSA and usually not included in addition to the ten common verb forms of triliteral roots in most textbooks is Form XI. Like Forms II–X, Form XI is regular in both the past and present tenses (i.e., the middle vowels of one can be predictable from the other), as follows:

	*Present/*المُضارِع		*Past/*الماضي
	يَفْعَوْعِلُ	← →	اِفْعَوْعَلَ
"to grow grass"	يَعْشَوْشِبُ	← →	اِعْشَوْشَبَ
"to be humpbacked"	يَحْدَوْدِبُ	← →	اِحْدَوْدَبَ
"to turn green"	يَخْضَوْضِرُ	← →	اِخْضَوْضَرَ

The اِفْعَوْعَلَ Form XI carries a change of state or reflexive (i.e., passive) meaning, not requiring an object, specific to colors or bodily and other defects/beauties, like Form IX, as in:

اِعْشَوْشَبَ السَّهْلُ .
"The plateau grew grass."

اِحْدَوْدَبَ ظَهْرُ الأُستاذِ .
"The teacher's back humped."

13.3   Common Quadriliteral Verb Forms

In MSA there is, at least, one common verb pattern/form that has
a quadriliteral root (see Chapter 2 for more on roots and patterns).
The middle vowels in the past and present are quite regular, having
the same predictable patterns, like Forms II–X of triliteral roots, as
follows:

	Present/المُضارع		*Past*/الماضي
	يُفَعْلِلُ	← →	فَعْلَلَ
"to reassure"	يُطَمْئِنُ	← →	طَمْأَنَ
"to roll"	يُدَحْرِجُ	← →	دَحْرَجَ
"to shake"	يُزَلْزِلُ	← →	زَلْزَلَ
"to translate"	يُتَرْجِمُ	← →	تَرْجَمَ
"to camp"	يُعَسْكِرُ	← →	عَسْكَرَ

This form is usually transitive, requiring an object, as in:

دَحْرَجَ صَديقي كُرَةً مِنْ أَعْلَى الجَبَلِ .
"My friend rolled a ball from the top of the mountain."

طَمْأَنَ الرَّئيسُ شَعْبَهُ .
"The president reassured his people."

In addition, there are two common forms derived from فَعْلَلَ form that are also regular in the past and present tense, as follows:

	Present/المُضارِع		Past/الماضي
	يَتَفَعْلَلُ	← →	تَفَعْلَلَ
"to roll"	يَتَدَحْرَجُ	← →	تَدَحْرَجَ
"to pretend to be weak"	يَتَمَسْكَنُ	← →	تَمَسْكَنَ
"to pretend to be a jurist"	يَتَفَيْهَقُ	← →	تَفَيْهَقَ
"to be devilish"	يَتَشَيْطَنُ	← →	تَشَيْطَنَ

	Present/المُضارِع		Past/الماضي
	يَفْعَلِلُّ	← →	إفْعَلَلَّ
"to be reassured"	يَطْمَئِنُّ	← →	إطْمَأَنَّ
"one's hair stands on end"	يَقْشَعِرُّ	← →	إقْشَعَرَّ
"to dwindle"	يَضْمَحِلُّ	← →	إضْمَحَلَّ
"to feel nauseous"	يَشْمَئِزُّ	← →	إشْمَأَزَّ

Both of these forms carry an intransitive meaning, as in:

تَدَحْرَجَتْ كُرَةٌ مِنْ أَعْلَى الجَبَلِ .

"A ball rolled from the top of the mountain."

إطْمَأَنَّ شَعْبُهُ .

"His people were reassured."

13.4   Categories of Arabic Verbs and Conjugations

Arabic verbs belong to two major categories: (1) صَحيح "sound verbs" consisting of exclusively root consonants and (2) مُعْتَلّ "weak verbs" consisting of one or more long vowels in the root. In addition, sound verbs are divided into three subcategories: سالِم "sound/regular," مُضَعَّف "geminated" (with the second and third root consonants being identical), and مَهْموز "hamzated" (containing a *hamza* as any of the three root consonants). Weak verbs are divided into five subcategories: مِثال "assimilated" (containing يَ or وَ in initial position of the root), أَجْوَف "hollow" (containing ي , و , or ا as a middle vowel), ناقِص "defective" (containing ي , و , or ا as a root vowel in final position), لَفيف مَقْرون "non-separated, double weak" (containing two long vowels in second and third positions), and لَفيف مَفْروق "separated, double weak" (containing two long vowels in initial and final positions) verbs. While sound verbs undergo little or no sound changes in the different conjugations and derivation forms, weak verbs do. Hence, the Arabic terms given to them (by traditional Arab grammarians): "sound" and "weak." The following chart illustrates the different types of verbs available according to the sound–weak root type distinction:

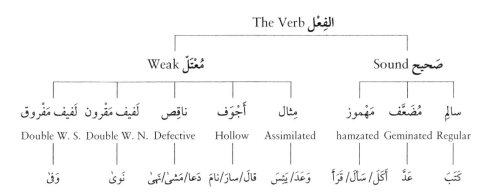

13.4.1   Conjugation of Sound Verbs سالِم

A sound/regular verb consists exclusively of root consonants none of which is a *hamza* or an identical consonant. Apart from a change in the middle vowel, as explained in 13.1 above, the conjugation of a sound verb with the different pronouns is regular and results in no additional changes, neither in the past nor present tense (except for the final endings of the subjunctive مَنْصوب and jussive مَجْزوم), as in the verb كَتَبَ – يَكْتُبُ "to write":

المُضارع المَجْزوم Jussive	المُضارع المَنْصوب Subjunctive	المُضارع المَرْفوع Present (indicative)	الماضي Past	الضمير Pronoun
يَكْتُبْ	يَكْتُبَ	يَكْتُبُ	كَتَبَ	هُوَ
يَكْتُبا	يَكْتُبا	يَكْتُبانِ	كَتَبا	هُما
يَكْتُبوا	يَكْتُبوا	يَكْتُبونَ	كَتَبوا	هُمْ
تَكْتُبْ	تَكْتُبَ	تَكْتُبُ	كَتَبَتْ	هِيَ
تَكْتُبا	تَكْتُبا	تَكْتُبانِ	كَتَبَتا	هُما
يَكْتُبْنَ	يَكْتُبْنَ	يَكْتُبْنَ	كَتَبْنَ	هُنَّ
تَكْتُبْ	تَكْتُبَ	تَكْتُبُ	كَتَبْتَ	أَنْتَ
تَكْتُبا	تَكْتُبا	تَكْتُبانِ	كَتَبْتُما	أَنْتُما
تَكْتُبوا	تَكْتُبوا	تَكْتُبونَ	كَتَبْتُم	أَنْتُمْ
تَكْتُبي	تَكْتُبي	تَكْتُبينَ	كَتَبْتِ	أَنْتِ
تَكْتُبا	تَكْتُبا	تَكْتُبانِ	كَتَبْتُما	أَنْتُما
تَكْتُبْنَ	تَكْتُبْنَ	تَكْتُبْنَ	كَتَبْتُنَّ	أَنْتُنَّ
أَكْتُبْ	أَكْتُبَ	أَكْتُبُ	كَتَبْتُ	أَنا
نَكْتُبْ	نَكْتُبَ	نَكْتُبُ	كَتَبْنا	نَحْنُ

Note: The subjunctive مَنْصوب mood ending is used after certain particles such as the future negation particle لَنْ "will not" (and أنْ "to," لِ "in order to," حَتّى "in order to," كَيْ "in order to," كَيْلا "in order not to" particles) and the jussive مَجْزوم mood ending is used after the past-tense negation particle لَمْ "did not" and the imperative and negative imperative forms (see also the sections on the use of imperative and negative imperative below, and 4.1 and 22.2.1 on the use of mood endings).

Note: Even though derived Forms III (ساعَدَ – يُساعِدُ "to help") and VI (يَتَنازَعُ – تَنازَعَ "to conflict") verbs contain a middle long vowel *'alif* [ا], they conjugate as sound/regular verbs (i.e., with no additional changes), as in the verb ساعَدَ – يُساعِدُ "to help":

المُضارِع المَجْزوم Present jussive	المُضارِع المَنْصوب Present subjunctive	المُضارِع المَرْفوع Present (indicative)	الماضي Past	الضمير Pronoun
يُساعِدْ	يُساعِدَ	يُساعِدُ	ساعَدَ	هُوَ
يُساعِدا	يُساعِدا	يُساعِدان	ساعَدا	هُما
يُساعِدوا	يُساعِدوا	يُساعِدونَ	ساعَدوا	هُمْ
تُساعِدْ	تُساعِدَ	تُساعِدُ	ساعَدَتْ	هِيَ
تُساعِدا	تُساعِدا	تُساعِدان	ساعَدَتا	هُما
يُساعِدْنَ	يُساعِدْنَ	يُساعِدْنَ	ساعَدْنَ	هُنَّ
تُساعِدْ	تُساعِدَ	تُساعِدُ	ساعَدْتَ	أنْتَ
تُساعِدا	تُساعِدا	تُساعِدان	ساعَدْتُما	أنْتُما
تُساعِدوا	تُساعِدوا	تُساعِدونَ	ساعَدْتُمْ	أنْتُمْ
تُساعِدي	تُساعِدي	تُساعِدينَ	ساعَدْتِ	أنْتِ
تُساعِدا	تُساعِدا	تُساعِدان	ساعَدْتُما	أنْتُما
تُساعِدْنَ	تُساعِدْنَ	تُساعِدْنَ	ساعَدْتُنَّ	أنْتُنَّ
أُساعِدْ	أُساعِدَ	أُساعِدُ	ساعَدْتُ	أنا
نُساعِدْ	نُساعِدَ	نُساعِدُ	ساعَدْنا	نَحْنُ

13.4.2 Conjugation of Geminated Verbs مُضَعَّف

A geminated مُضَعَّف verb is one whose second and third root consonants are identical. In this case, the following rules apply to Form I and derived Forms II–X: (1) the gemination/*shadda* is broken (i.e., the two identical consonants are separated) in the past tense in all first persons, all second persons, and third-person plural feminine; (2) the gemination is broken in the present form in second- and third-person plural feminine; and (3) the endings in the subjunctive مَنصوب and jussive مَجزوم are identical throughout, as in the verb عَدَّ – يَعُدُّ "to count":

المُضارع المَجزوم *Present jussive*	المُضارع المَنصوب *Present subjunctive*	المُضارع المَرفوع *Present (indicative)*	الماضي *Past*	الضمير *Pronoun*
يَعُدَّ	يَعُدَّ	يَعُدُّ	عَدَّ	هُوَ
يَعُدّا	يَعُدّا	يَعُدّانِ	عَدّا	هُما
يَعُدّوا	يَعُدّوا	يَعُدّونَ	عَدّوا	هُم
تَعُدَّ	تَعُدَّ	تَعُدُّ	عَدَّتْ	هِيَ
تَعُدّا	تَعُدّا	تَعُدّانِ	عَدّتا	هُما
يَعْدُدْنَ	يَعْدُدْنَ	يَعْدُدْنَ	عَدَدْنَ	هُنَّ
تَعُدَّ	تَعُدَّ	تَعُدُّ	عَدَدْتَ	أنتَ
تَعُدّا	تَعُدّا	تَعُدّانِ	عَدَدْتُما	أنتُما
تَعُدّوا	تَعُدّوا	تَعُدّونَ	عَدَدْتُم	أنتُم
تَعُدّي	تَعُدّي	تَعُدّينَ	عَدَدْتِ	أنتِ
تَعُدّا	تَعُدّا	تَعُدّانِ	عَدَدْتُما	أنتُما
تَعْدُدْنَ	تَعْدُدْنَ	تَعْدُدْنَ	عَدَدْتُنَّ	أنتُنَّ
أَعُدَّ	أَعُدَّ	أَعُدُّ	عَدَدْتُ	أنا
نَعُدَّ	نَعُدَّ	نَعُدُّ	عَدَدْنا	نَحنُ

Note: The ending of sound/regular verbs in the jussive مَجزوم – in the third-person singular, second-person singular masculine, and first-person – is a *sukuun.* However, the jussive مَجْزوم and subjunctive مَنْصوب ending of geminated verbs is a *fatHa* (which is usually the ending of the subjunctive مَنْصوب of sound verbs).

13.4.3 Conjugation of *hamzated* Verbs مَهْموز

A *hamzated* مَهْموز verb contains a *hamza* as any of the three root consonants. Of all *hamzated* verbs, only those containing a *hamza* in initial position undergo a slight change in the first-person singular: the initial *hamza* with *fatHa* أ is converted into *madda 'alif* آ (i.e., *hamza* followed by *'alif* [aa]) in the present, as in the verb أَخَذَ – يَأْخُذُ "to take":

المُضارع المَجْزوم Jussive	المُضارع المَنْصوب Subjunctive	المُضارع المَرْفوع Present (indicative)	الماضي Past	الضمير Pronoun
يَأْخُذْ	يَأْخُذَ	يَأْخُذُ	أَخَذَ	هُوَ
يَأْخُذا	يَأْخُذا	يَأْخُذانِ	أَخَذا	هُما
يَأْخُذوا	يَأْخُذوا	يَأْخُذونَ	أَخَذوا	هُمْ
تَأْخُذْ	تَأْخُذَ	تَأْخُذُ	أَخَذَتْ	هِيَ
تَأْخُذا	تَأْخُذا	تَأْخُذانِ	أَخَذَتا	هُما
يأْخُذْنَ	يأْخُذْنَ	يأْخُذْنَ	أَخَذْنَ	هُنَّ
تَأْخُذْ	تَأْخُذَ	تَأْخُذُ	أَخَذْتَ	أَنْتَ
تَأْخُذا	تَأْخُذا	تَأْخُذانِ	أَخَذْتُما	أَنْتُما
تَأْخُذوا	تَأْخُذوا	تَأْخُذونَ	أَخَذْتُمْ	أَنْتُمْ
تَأْخُذي	تَأْخُذي	تَأْخُذينَ	أَخَذْتِ	أَنْتِ
تَأْخُذا	تَأْخُذا	تَأْخُذانِ	أَخَذْتُما	أَنْتُما
تَأْخُذْنَ	تَأْخُذْنَ	تَأْخُذْنَ	أَخَذْتُنَّ	أَنْتُنَّ
آخُذْ	آخُذَ	آخُذُ	أَخَذْتُ	أنا
نَأْخُذْ	نَأْخُذَ	نَأْخُذُ	أَخَذْنا	نَحْنُ

While *hamzated* verbs containing a *hamza* in middle or final position do not undergo any additional changes, the verb رَأَىٰ – يَرىٰ "to see" conjugates irregularly (see also more on defective verbs below, 13.4.6), since the middle *hamza* is dropped in the present form, as in:

المُضارع المَجْزوم Jussive	المُضارع المَنْصوب Subjunctive	المُضارع المَرْفوع Present (indicative)	الماضي Past	الضمير Pronoun
يَرَ	يَرىٰ	يَرىٰ	رَأَىٰ	هُوَ
يَرَيا	يَرَيا	يَرَيانِ	رَأَيا	هُما
يَرَوْا	يَرَوْا	يَرَوْنَ	رَأَوْا	هُمْ
تَرَ	تَرىٰ	تَرىٰ	رَأَتْ	هِيَ
تَرَيا	تَرَيا	تَرَيانِ	رَأَتا	هُما
يَرَيْنَ	يَرَيْنَ	يَرَيْنَ	رَأَيْنَ	هُنَّ
تَرَ	تَرىٰ	تَرىٰ	رَأَيْتَ	أنْتَ
تَرَيا	تَرَيا	تَرَيانِ	رَأَيْتُما	أنْتُما
تَرَوْا	تَرَوْا	تَرَوْنَ	رَأَيْتُمْ	أنْتُمْ
تَرَيْ	تَرَيْ	تَرَيْنَ	رَأَيْتِ	أنْتِ
تَرَيا	تَرَيا	تَرَيانِ	رَأَيْتُما	أنْتُما
تَرَيْنَ	تَرَيْنَ	تَرَيْنَ	رَأَيْتُنَّ	أنْتُنَّ
أرَ	أرىٰ	أرىٰ	رَأَيْتُ	أنا
نَرَ	نَرىٰ	نَرىٰ	رَأَينا	نَحْنُ

13.4.4 Conjugation of Assimilated Verbs مِثال

An assimilated مِثال verb is one whose initial root consonant is a *waaw* وَ [wa] or *yaa'* ـيَ [ya]. In this case, the following rule applies to Form I only: the *waaw* وَ [wa] is dropped in the present tense, as in the verb وَضَعَ [wa] "to put": يَضَعُ –

المُضارع المَجْزوم Jussive	المُضارع المَنْصوب Subjunctive	المُضارع المَرْفوع Present (indicative)	الماضي Past	الضمير Pronoun
يَضَعْ	يَضَعَ	يَضَعُ	وَضَعَ	هُوَ
يَضَعا	يَضَعا	يَضَعانِ	وَضَعا	هُما
يَضَعوا	يَضَعوا	يَضَعونَ	وَضَعوا	هُمْ
تَضَعْ	تَضَعَ	تَضَعُ	وَضَعَتْ	هِيَ
تَضَعا	تَضَعا	تَضَعانِ	وَضَعَتا	هُما
يَضَعْنَ	يَضَعْنَ	يَضَعْنَ	وَضَعْنَ	هُنَّ
تَضَعْ	تَضَعَ	تَضَعُ	وَضَعْتَ	أَنْتَ
تَضَعا	تَضَعا	تَضَعانِ	وَضَعْتُما	أَنْتُما
تَضَعوا	تَضَعوا	تَضَعونَ	وَضَعْتُمْ	أَنْتُمْ
تَضَعي	تَضَعي	تَضَعينَ	وَضَعْتِ	أَنْتِ
تَضَعا	تَضَعا	تَضَعانِ	وَضَعْتُما	أَنْتُما
تَضَعْنَ	تَضَعْنَ	تَضَعْنَ	وَضَعْتُنَّ	أَنْتُنَّ
أَضَعْ	أَضَعَ	أَضَعُ	وَضَعْتُ	أَنا
نَضَعْ	نَضَعَ	نَضَعُ	وَضَعْنا	نَحْنُ

The above rule is applicable only to assimilated verbs with a *waaw* وَ [wa]. Therefore, the *yaa'* ـيـ [ya] in assimilated verbs is not dropped in the present tense conjugation, as in the verb يَئِسَ – يَيْأَسُ "to despair":

المُضارع المَجزوم *Jussive*	المُضارع المَنصوب *Subjunctive*	المُضارع المَرفوع *Present (indicative)*	الماضي *Past*	الضمير *Pronoun*
يَيْأَسْ	يَيْأَسَ	يَيْأَسُ	يَئِسَ	هُوَ
يَيْأَسا	يَيْأَسا	يَيْأَسانِ	يَئِسا	هُما
يَيْأَسوا	يَيْأَسوا	يَيْأَسونَ	يَئِسوا	هُمْ
تَيْأَسْ	تَيْأَسَ	تَيْأَسُ	يَئِسَتْ	هِيَ
تَيْأَسا	تَيْأَسا	تَيْأَسانِ	يَئِسَتا	هُما
يَيْأَسْنَ	يَيْأَسْنَ	يَيْأَسْنَ	يَئِسْنَ	هُنَّ
تَيْأَسْ	تَيْأَسَ	تَيْأَسُ	يَئِسْتَ	أَنْتَ
تَيْأَسا	تَيْأَسا	تَيْأَسانِ	يَئِسْتُما	أَنْتُما
تَيْأَسوا	تَيْأَسوا	تَيْأَسونَ	يَئِسْتُمْ	أَنْتُمْ
تَيْأَسي	تَيْأَسي	تَيْأَسينَ	يَئِسْتِ	أَنْتِ
تَيْأَسا	تَيْأَسا	تَيْأَسانِ	يَئِسْتُما	أَنْتُما
تَيْأَسْنَ	تَيْأَسْنَ	تَيْأَسْنَ	يَئِسْتُنَّ	أَنْتُنَّ
أَيْأَسْ	أَيْأَسَ	أَيْأَسُ	يَئِسْتُ	أَنا
نَيْأَسْ	نَيْأَسَ	نَيْأَسُ	يَئِسْنا	نَحْنُ

As for derived (Forms II–X) assimilated verbs, neither *waaw* وَ [wa] nor *yaa'* يَـ [ya] is dropped, as in the verb تَوَصَّلَ – يَتَوَصَّلُ "to reach":

المُضارِع المَجْزوم Jussive	المُضارِع المَنْصوب Subjunctive	المُضارِع المَرْفوع Present (indicative)	الماضي Past	الضمير Pronoun
يَتَوَصَّلْ	يَتَوَصَّلَ	يَتَوَصَّلُ	تَوَصَّلَ	هُوَ
يَتَوَصَّلا	يَتَوَصَّلا	يَتَوَصَّلانِ	تَوَصَّلا	هُما
يَتَوَصَّلوا	يَتَوَصَّلوا	يَتَوَصَّلونَ	تَوَصَّلوا	هُمْ
تَتَوَصَّلْ	تَتَوَصَّلَ	تَتَوَصَّلُ	تَوَصَّلَتْ	هِيَ
تَتَوَصَّلا	تَتَوَصَّلا	تَتَوَصَّلانِ	تَوَصَّلَتا	هُما
يَتَوَصَّلْنَ	يَتَوَصَّلْنَ	يَتَوَصَّلْنَ	تَوَصَّلْنَ	هُنَّ
تَتَوَصَّلْ	تَتَوَصَّلَ	تَتَوَصَّلُ	تَوَصَّلْتَ	أَنْتَ
تَتَوَصَّلا	تَتَوَصَّلا	تَتَوَصَّلانِ	تَوَصَّلْتُما	أَنْتُما
تَتَوَصَّلوا	تَتَوَصَّلوا	تَتَوَصَّلونَ	تَوَصَّلْتُمْ	أَنْتُمْ
تَتَوَصَّلي	تَتَوَصَّلي	تَتَوَصَّلينَ	تَوَصَّلْتِ	أَنْتِ
تَتَوَصَّلا	تَتَوَصَّلا	تَتَوَصَّلانِ	تَوَصَّلْتُما	أَنْتُما
تَتَوَصَّلْنَ	تَتَوَصَّلْنَ	تَتَوَصَّلْنَ	تَوَصَّلْتُنَّ	أَنْتُنَّ
أَتَوَصَّلْ	أَتَوَصَّلَ	أَتَوَصَّلُ	تَوَصَّلْتُ	أَنا
نَتَوَصَّلْ	نَتَوَصَّلَ	نَتَوَصَّلُ	تَوَصَّلْنا	نَحْنُ

13.4.5 Conjugation of Hollow Verbs أَجْوَف

A hollow أَجْوَف verb is one which contains a long middle vowel: *waaw* و [uu], *yaa'* يـ [ii], or *'alif* ا [aa]. In this case, the following rules apply to Form I and derived hollow Forms IV, VII–VIII, and X (note derived hollow Forms III and IV conjugate as a sound/regular verb; see 13.4.1): (1) the middle vowel is dropped in the present (indicative مَرْفوع and subjunctive مَنْصوب) in the third- and second-person plural feminine; (2) the middle vowel is dropped in the past tense in the third-person plural feminine and in all first and second persons; and (3) the middle vowel is dropped in the jussive مَجْزوم in the third-person singular masculine and feminine, the second-person singular masculine, the first person (singular and plural), and the second- and third-person plural feminine, as in the verbs نامَ – يَنامُ "to sleep":قالَ – يَقولُ "to say," سارَ – يَسيرُ "to walk," and

المُضارع المَجْزوم Jussive	المُضارع المَنْصوب Subjunctive	المُضارع المَرْفوع Present (indicative)	الماضي Past	الضمير Pronoun
يَقُلْ	يَقولَ	يَقولُ	قالَ	هُوَ
يَقولا	يَقولا	يَقولانِ	قالا	هُما
يَقولوا	يَقولوا	يَقولونَ	قالوا	هُمْ
تَقُلْ	تَقولَ	تَقولُ	قالَتْ	هِيَ
تَقولا	تَقولا	تَقولانِ	قالَتا	هُما
يَقُلْنَ	يَقُلْنَ	يَقُلْنَ	قُلْنَ	هُنَّ
تَقُلْ	تَقولَ	تَقولُ	قُلْتَ	أنْتَ
تَقولا	تَقولا	تَقولانِ	قُلْتُما	أنْتُما
تَقولوا	تَقولوا	تَقولونَ	قُلْتُمْ	أنْتُمْ
تَقولي	تَقولي	تَقولينَ	قُلْتِ	أنْتِ
تَقولا	تَقولا	تَقولانِ	قُلْتُما	أنْتُما
تَقُلْنَ	تَقُلْنَ	تَقُلْنَ	قُلْتُنَّ	أنْتُنَّ
أقُلْ	أقولَ	أقولُ	قُلْتُ	أنا
نَقُلْ	نَقولَ	نَقولُ	قُلْنا	نَحْنُ

المُضارع المَجْزوم Jussive	المُضارع المَنْصوب Subjunctive	المُضارع المَرْفوع Present (indicative)	الماضي Past	الضمير Pronoun
يَسِرْ	يَسِيرَ	يَسِيرُ	سارَ	هُوَ
يَسيرا	يَسيرا	يَسيرانِ	سارا	هُما
يَسيروا	يَسيروا	يَسيرونَ	ساروا	هُمْ
تَسِرْ	تَسِيرَ	تَسِيرُ	سارَتْ	هِيَ
تَسيرا	تَسيرا	تَسيرانِ	سارَتا	هُما
يَسِرْنَ	يَسِرْنَ	يَسِرْنَ	سِرْنَ	هُنَّ
تَسِرْ	تَسِيرَ	تَسِيرُ	سِرْتَ	أَنْتَ
تَسيرا	تَسيرا	تَسيرانِ	سِرْتُما	أَنْتُما
تَسيروا	تَسيروا	تَسيرونَ	سِرْتُمْ	أَنْتُمْ
تَسيري	تَسيري	تَسيرينَ	سِرْتِ	أَنْتِ
تَسيرا	تَسيرا	تَسيرانِ	سِرْتُما	أَنْتُما
تَسِرْنَ	تَسِرْنَ	تَسِرْنَ	سِرْتُنَّ	أَنْتُنَّ
أَسِرْ	أَسِيرَ	أَسِيرُ	سِرْتُ	أَنا
نَسِرْ	نَسِيرَ	نَسِيرُ	سِرْنا	نَحْنُ

المُضارع المَجْزوم Jussive	المُضارع المَنْصوب Subjunctive	المُضارع المَرْفوع Present (indicative)	الماضي Past	الضمير Pronoun
يَنَمْ	يَنَم	يَنامُ	نامَ	هُوَ
يَناما	يَناما	يَنامانِ	ناما	هُما
يَناموا	يَناموا	يَنامونَ	ناموا	هُمْ
تَنَمْ	تَنَم	تَنامُ	نامَتْ	هِيَ
تَناما	تَناما	تَنامانِ	نامَتا	هُما
يَنَمْنَ	يَنَمْنَ	يَنَمْنَ	نِمْنَ	هُنَّ
تَنَمْ	تَنَم	تَنامُ	نِمْتَ	أَنْتَ
تَناما	تَناما	تَنامانِ	نِمْتُما	أَنْتُما
تَناموا	تَناموا	تَنامونَ	نِمْتُمْ	أَنْتُمْ
تَنامي	تَنامي	تَنامينَ	نِمْتِ	أَنْتِ
تَناما	تَناما	تَنامانِ	نِمْتُما	أَنْتُما
تَنَمْنَ	تَنَمْنَ	تَنَمْنَ	نِمْتُنَّ	أَنْتُنَّ
أَنَمْ	أَنَم	أَنامُ	نِمْتُ	أَنا
نَنَمْ	نَنَم	نَنامُ	نِمْنا	نَحْنُ

As mentioned above, the rules similarly apply to derived Forms IV, VII–VIII, and X, as in اِسْتَفادَ – يَسْتَفيدُ "to benefit" (Form X):

المُضارِع المَجزوم Jussive	المُضارِع المَنصوب Subjunctive	المُضارِع المَرفوع Present (indicative)	الماضي Past	الضمير Pronoun
يَسْتَفِدْ	يَسْتَفيدَ	يَسْتَفيدُ	اِسْتَفادَ	هُوَ
يَسْتَفيدا	يَسْتَفيدا	يَسْتَفيدانِ	اِسْتَفادا	هُما
يَسْتَفيدوا	يَسْتَفيدوا	يَسْتَفيدونَ	اِسْتَفادوا	هُمْ
تَسْتَفِدْ	تَسْتَفيدَ	تَسْتَفيدُ	اِسْتَفادَتْ	هِيَ
تَسْتَفيدا	تَسْتَفيدا	تَسْتَفيدانِ	اِسْتَفادَتا	هُما
يَسْتَفِدْنَ	يَسْتَفِدْنَ	يَسْتَفِدْنَ	اِسْتَفَدْنَ	هُنَّ
تَسْتَفِدْ	تَسْتَفيدَ	تَسْتَفيدُ	اِسْتَفَدْتَ	أنْتَ
تَسْتَفيدا	تَسْتَفيدا	تَسْتَفيدانِ	اِسْتَفَدْتُما	أنْتُما
تَسْتَفيدوا	تَسْتَفيدوا	تَسْتَفيدونَ	اِسْتَفَدْتُمْ	أنْتُمْ
تَسْتَفيدي	تَسْتَفيدي	تَسْتَفيدينَ	اِسْتَفَدْتِ	أنْتِ
تَسْتَفيدا	تَسْتَفيدا	تَسْتَفيدانِ	اِسْتَفَدْتُما	أنْتُما
تَسْتَفِدْنَ	تَسْتَفِدْنَ	تَسْتَفِدْنَ	اِسْتَفَدْتُنَّ	أنْتُنَّ
أسْتَفِدْ	أسْتَفيدَ	أسْتَفيدُ	اِسْتَفَدْتُ	أنا
نَسْتَفِدْ	نَسْتَفيدَ	نَسْتَفيدُ	اِسْتَفَدْنا	نَحْنُ

As for the nature of the middle vowel of Forms I–X (in particular, III–IV, VI–VIII, and X, since there are no hollow verbs for Forms II, V, and IX), while the middle vowel is always *'alif* ا [aa] in the past, it varies in the present: from being irregular in Form I to being regular in the derived forms, as follows:

Middle vowel in the present		Present / المُضارع	Past / الماضي	
و	←	يَقولُ	قالَ	I
ي	←	يَسيرُ	سارَ	
ا	←	يَنامُ	نامَ	
ا	←	يُساعِدُ	ساعَدَ	III
ي	←	يُنيرُ	أنارَ	IV
ا	←	يَتَنازَعُ	تَنازَعَ	VI
ا	←	يَنْحازُ	اِنْحازَ	VII
ا	←	يَخْتارُ	اِخْتارَ	VIII
ي	←	يَسْتَفيدُ	اِسْتَفادَ	X

The middle vowels of hollow verbs belonging to Form I are best learned initially as part of the conjugation of the past and present forms together (until substantial knowledge of the root and verbal/noun has been attained). However, the middle vowels of the derived forms are predictable: *'alif* ا [aa] in Forms III, VI, VII–VIII, and *yaa'* ي [ii] in forms IV and X.

As for the short vowel following the initial consonant of hollow verbs in the past tense for the third-person feminine plural, all second persons, and all first persons, this, too, is predictable. It depends on the type of the middle long vowel in the present form: *Damma* [u] if the middle vowel is *waaw* و [uu] and *kasra* if the middle vowel is *yaa'* ي [ii] or *'alif* ا [aa], as follows:

قُلْتُ	←	ُ ـــ	←	يَقُولُ	قالَ
زُرْتُ	←	ُ ـــ	←	يَزُورُ	زارَ
عُدْتُ	←	ُ ـــ	←	يَعُودُ	عادَ
سِرْتُ	←	ـــ ِ	←	يَسِيرُ	سارَ
مِلْتُ	←	ـــ ِ	←	يَمِيلُ	مالَ
عِشْتُ	←	ـــ ِ	←	يَعِيشُ	عاشَ
نِمْتُ	←	ـــ ِ	←	يَنَامُ	نامَ
خِفْتُ	←	ـــ ِ	←	يَخَافُ	خافَ
هِبْتُ	←	ـــ ِ	←	يَهَابُ	هابَ

Table headers (right to left): الماضي / Past — المُضارع / Present — Short vowel in the past tense

13.4.6 Conjugation of Defective Verbs ناقِص

A defective ناقِص verb is one which contains a long final vowel: *waaw* و
[uu], *yaa'* ـي [ii], or *'alif* ا / ى [aa]. In this case, the following rules apply
to Form I and derived Forms II–X:

(A) In the present (indicative مَرْفوع and subjunctive مَنْصوب) form, (1) the
long vowel is dropped in the second- and third-person masculine plural
and second-person feminine singular; (2) if the final vowel is *'alif* (as in
يَنْهى "to forbid"), the *'alif* is converted into a *yaa'* [ii] in the second-
and third-person masculine and feminine dual; and (3) the *'alif* is
shortened into *fatHa* [a] resulting in (a) a *sukuun* on the *yaa'* ـيْ
following the *fatHa* (i.e., resulting in a diphthong [ay]) in the second
person singular feminine and second- and third-person feminine plural
and (b) a *sukuun* on the pronoun *waaw* of the second- and third-
person masculine plural (i.e., resulting in the [aw] diphthong).

(B)   In the past form, (1) *'alif* is retained in the third-person singular masculine and shortened in the rest; (2) in the rest *'alif* is converted into a *yaa'* (if *yaa'* is the original root vowel or if the verb is derived) or *waaw* (if *waaw* is the original root vowel), resulting in the diphthongs ـَيْ [ay] or ـَوْ [aw], respectively, except for the third-person masculine plural where the long vowel is dropped, with the resulting ending [aw] for all verbs; and (3) the final long vowel is shortened in the مَجْزوم jussive.

However, perhaps the most crucial rule to remember here is the diphthong rule, when the verb, whether in the past or present, ends with an *'alif* ا / ى [aa], as in the verbs دَعا – يَدْعو "to invite," مَشى – يَمْشي "to walk," and نَهى – يَنْهى "to forbid":

المُضارع المَجزوم *Jussive*	المُضارع المَنصوب *Subjunctive*	المُضارع المَرفوع *Present* *(indicative)*	الماضي *Past*	الضمير *Pronoun*
يَدْعُ	يَدْعُوَ	يَدْعُو	دَعا	هُوَ
يَدْعُوا	يَدْعُوا	يَدْعُوانِ	دَعَوا	هُما
يَدْعُوا	يَدْعُوا	يَدْعُونَ	دَعَوْا	هُمْ
تَدْعُ	تَدْعُوَ	تَدْعُو	دَعَت	هِيَ
تَدْعُوا	تَدْعُوا	تَدْعُوانِ	دَعَتا	هُما
يَدْعُونَ	يَدْعُونَ	يَدْعُونَ	دَعَوْنَ	هُنَّ
تَدْعُ	تَدْعُوَ	تَدْعُو	دَعَوْتَ	أنْتَ
تَدْعُوا	تَدْعُوا	تَدْعُوانِ	دَعَوْتُما	أنْتُما
تَدْعُوا	تَدْعُوا	تَدْعُونَ	دَعَوْتُمْ	أنْتُمْ
تَدْعِي	تَدْعِي	تَدْعِينَ	دَعَوْتِ	أنْتِ
تَدْعُوا	تَدْعُوا	تَدْعُوانِ	دَعَوْتُما	أنْتُما
تَدْعُونَ	تَدْعُونَ	تَدْعُونَ	دَعَوْتُنَّ	أنْتُنَّ
أدْعُ	أدْعُوَ	أدْعُو	دَعَوْتُ	أنا
نَدْعُ	نَدْعُوَ	نَدْعُو	دَعَوْنا	نَحْنُ

المُضارع المَجْزوم Jussive	المُضارع المَنْصوب Subjunctive	المُضارع المَرْفوع Present (indicative)	الماضي Past	الضمير Pronoun
يَمْشِ	يَمْشِيَ	يَمْشي	مَشىٰ	هُوَ
يَمْشِيا	يَمْشِيا	يَمْشِيانِ	مَشَيا	هُما
يَمْشُوا	يَمْشُوا	يَمْشُونَ	مَشَوْا	هُمْ
تَمْشِ	تَمْشِيَ	تَمْشي	مَشَتْ	هِيَ
تَمْشِيا	تَمْشِيا	تَمْشِيانِ	مَشَتا	هُما
يَمْشِينَ	يَمْشِينَ	يَمْشِينَ	مَشَيْنَ	هُنَّ
تَمْشِ	تَمْشِيَ	تَمْشي	مَشَيْتَ	أَنْتَ
تَمْشِيا	تَمْشِيا	تَمْشِيانِ	مَشَيْتُما	أَنْتُما
تَمْشُوا	تَمْشُوا	تَمْشُونَ	مَشَيْتُمْ	أَنْتُمْ
تَمْشِي	تَمْشِي	تَمْشِينَ	مَشَيْتِ	أَنْتِ
تَمْشِيا	تَمْشِيا	تَمْشِيانِ	مَشَيْتُما	أَنْتُما
تَمْشِينَ	تَمْشِينَ	تَمْشِينَ	مَشَيْتُنَّ	أَنْتُنَّ
أَمْشِ	أَمْشِيَ	أَمْشي	مَشَيْتُ	أَنا
نَمْشِ	نَمْشِيَ	نَمْشي	مَشَيْنا	نَحْنُ

المُضارع المَجْزوم Jussive	المُضارع المَنْصوب Subjunctive	المُضارع المَرْفوع Present (indicative)	الماضي Past	الضمير Pronoun
يَنْهَ	يَنْهَى	يَنْهَى	نَهَى	هُوَ
يَنْهَيا	يَنْهَيا	يَنْهَيانِ	نَهَيا	هُما
يَنْهَوْا	يَنْهَوْا	يَنْهَوْنَ	نَهَوْا	هُمْ
تَنْهَ	تَنْهَى	تَنْهَى	نَهَتْ	هِيَ
تَنْهَيا	تَنْهَيا	تَنْهَيانِ	نَهَتا	هُما
يَنْهَيْنَ	يَنْهَيْنَ	يَنْهَيْنَ	نَهَيْنَ	هُنَّ
تَنْهَ	تَنْهَى	تَنْهَى	نَهَيْتَ	أَنْتَ
تَنْهَيا	تَنْهَيا	تَنْهَيانِ	نَهَيْتُما	أَنْتُما
تَنْهَوْا	تَنْهَوْا	تَنْهَوْنَ	نَهَيْتُمْ	أَنْتُمْ
تَنْهَيْ	تَنْهَيْ	تَنْهَيْنَ	نَهَيْتِ	أَنْتِ
تَنْهَيا	تَنْهَيا	تَنْهَيانِ	نَهَيْتُما	أَنْتُما
تَنْهَيْنَ	تَنْهَيْنَ	تَنْهَيْنَ	نَهَيْتُنَّ	أَنْتُنَّ
أَنْهَ	أَنْهَى	أَنْهَى	نَهَيْتُ	أَنا
نَنْهَ	نَنْهَى	نَنْهَى	نَهَيْنا	نَحْنُ

The same above rules also apply to derived Forms II–X, as in سَمَّىٰ – يُسَمِّي "to name" (Form II):

المُضارع المَجْزوم Jussive	المُضارع المَنْصوب Subjunctive	المُضارع المَرْفوع Present (indicative)	الماضي Past	الضمير Pronoun
يُسَمِّ	يُسَمِّيَ	يُسَمِّي	سَمَّىٰ	هُوَ
يُسَمِّيا	يُسَمِّيا	يُسَمِّيانِ	سَمَّيا	هُما
يُسَمُّوا	يُسَمُّوا	يُسَمُّونَ	سَمَّوْا	هُمْ
تُسَمِّ	تُسَمِّيَ	تُسَمِّي	سَمَّتْ	هِيَ
تُسَمِّيا	تُسَمِّيا	تُسَمِّيانِ	سَمَّتا	هُما
يُسَمِّينَ	يُسَمِّينَ	يُسَمِّينَ	سَمَّيْنَ	هُنَّ
تُسَمِّ	تُسَمِّيَ	تُسَمِّي	سَمَّيْت	أَنْتَ
تُسَمِّيا	تُسَمِّيا	تُسَمِّيانِ	سَمَّيْتُما	أَنْتُما
تُسَمُّوا	تُسَمُّوا	تُسَمُّونَ	سَمَّيْتُمْ	أَنْتُمْ
تُسَمِّي	تُسَمِّي	تُسَمِّينَ	سَمَّيْت	أَنْتِ
تُسَمِّيا	تُسَمِّيا	تُسَمِّيانِ	سَمَّيْتُما	أَنْتُما
تُسَمِّينَ	تُسَمِّينَ	تُسَمِّينَ	سَمَّيْتُنَّ	أَنْتُنَّ
أُسَمِّ	أُسَمِّيَ	أُسَمِّي	سَمَّيْت	أَنا
نُسَمِّ	نُسَمِّي	نُسَمِّي	سَمَّيْنا	نَحْنُ

Note: The diphthong rules noted above (i.e., when the verb, whether in the past or present, ends with an 'alif ا / ى [aa], the middle and final vowel is either ـَيْ [ay] or ـَوْ [aw]) do not apply, for example, to the past form of a verb ending with يَ, as in the verb بَقِيَ – يَبْقى "to remain," but applies to the present form, since only the latter ends with an ى [aa]:

المُضارع المَجْزوم Jussive	المُضارع المَنْصوب Subjunctive	المُضارع المَرْفوع Present (indicative)	الماضي Past	الضَمير Pronoun
يَبْقَ	يَبْقى	يَبْقى	بَقِيَ	هُوَ
يَبْقَيا	يَبْقَيا	يَبْقَيان	بَقِيا	هُما
يَبْقَوا	يَبْقَوا	يَبْقَوْنَ	بَقُوا	هُمْ
تَبْقَ	تَبْقى	تَبْقى	بَقِيَت	هِيَ
تَبْقَيا	تَبْقَيا	تَبْقَيان	بَقِيَتا	هُما
يَبْقَيْنَ	يَبْقَيْنَ	يَبْقَيْنَ	بَقِينَ	هُنَّ
تَبْقَ	تَبْقى	تَبْقى	بَقِيتَ	أَنْتَ
تَبْقَيا	تَبْقَيا	تَبْقَيان	بَقِيتُما	أَنْتُما
تَبْقَوا	تَبْقَوا	تَبْقَوْنَ	بَقِيتُمْ	أَنْتُمْ
تَبْقَيْ	تَبْقَيْ	تَبْقَيْنَ	بَقِيتِ	أَنْتِ
تَبْقَيا	تَبْقَيا	تَبْقَيان	بَقِيتُما	أَنْتُما
تَبْقَيْنَ	تَبْقَيْنَ	تَبْقَيْنَ	بَقِيتُنَّ	أَنْتُنَّ
أَبْقَ	أَبْقى	أَبْقى	بَقِيتُ	أَنا
نَبْقَ	نَبْقى	نَبْقى	بَقِينا	نَحْنُ

As for the nature of the final vowel of Forms I–X (in particular, I–VIII and X, since there is no defective verb of Form IX), while the final vowel is always *'alif* ١ / ى [aa] in the past, it varies in the present: from being irregular in Form I to being regular in the derived forms, as follows:

Final vowel in the present		Present / المُضارِع	Past / الماضي	
و	←	يَدْعو	دَعا	I
ي	←	يَمْشي	مَشىٰ	
ا	←	يَنْهىٰ	نَهىٰ	
ي	←	يُسَمِّي	سَمّىٰ	II
ي	←	يُقاضي	قاضىٰ	III
ي	←	يُعْطي	أَعْطىٰ	IV
ا	←	يَتَمَنّىٰ	تَمَنّىٰ	V
ا	←	يَتَفادىٰ	تَفادىٰ	VI
ي	←	يَنْتَهي	اِنْتَهىٰ	VII
ي	←	يَعْتَدي	اِعْتَدىٰ	VIII
ي	←	يَسْتَثْني	اِسْتَثْنىٰ	X

The final vowels of defective verbs belonging to Form I are best learned initially as part of the conjugation of the past and present forms together (until substantial knowledge of the root and verbal/noun has been attained). However, the final vowels of the derived forms are predictable: *'alif* ١ [aa] in Forms V–VI and *yaa'* ي [ii] in the rest: II–IV, VII–VIII, and X.

13.4.7 Conjugation of Non-separated, Double Weak Verbs لَفيف مَقْرون

A non-separated, double weak لَفيف مَقْرون verb is one which contains two long vowels in second and third positions. The same rules of defective verbs apply here, especially the *sukuun* rule (i.e., when the verb, whether in the past or present, ends with an *'alif* ١ / ى [aa], the middle vowel is either ـَيْ [ay] or ـَوْ [aw]), as in the verb نَوَى – يَنْوي "to intend":

المُضارع المَجْزوم Jussive	المُضارع المَنْصوب Subjunctive	المُضارع المَرْفوع Present (indicative)	الماضي Past	الضمير Pronoun
يَنْوِ	يَنْوِيَ	يَنْوِي	نَوَى	هُوَ
يَنْوِيا	يَنْوِيا	يَنْوِيانِ	نَوَيا	هُما
يَنْوُوا	يَنْوُوا	يَنْوُونَ	نَوَوْا	هُمْ
تَنْوِ	تَنْوِيَ	تَنْوِي	نَوَتْ	هِيَ
تَنْوِيا	تَنْوِيا	تَنْوِيانِ	نَوَتا	هُما
يَنْوِينَ	يَنْوِينَ	يَنْوِينَ	نَوَيْنَ	هُنَّ
تَنْوِ	تَنْوِيَ	تَنْوِي	نَوَيْتَ	أَنْتَ
تَنْوِيا	تَنْوِيا	تَنْوِيانِ	نَوَيْتُما	أَنْتُما
تَنْوُوا	تَنْوُوا	تَنْوُونَ	نَوَيْتُمْ	أَنْتُمْ
تَنْوِي	تَنْوِي	تَنْوِينَ	نَوَيْتِ	أَنْتِ
تَنْوِيا	تَنْوِيا	تَنْوِيانِ	نَوَيْتُما	أَنْتُما
تَنْوِينَ	تَنْوِينَ	تَنْوِينَ	نَوَيْتُنَّ	أَنْتُنَّ
أَنْوِ	أَنْوِيَ	أَنْوِي	نَوَيْتُ	أَنا
نَنْوِ	نَنْوِيَ	نَنْوِي	نَوَيْنا	نَحْنُ

13.4.8 Conjugation of Separated, Double Weak Verbs لَفيف مَفْروق

A separated, double weak لَفيف مَفْروق verb is one which contains two long vowels in first and third positions. The same rules of defective verbs apply here, especially the *sukuun* rule (i.e., when the verb, whether in the past or present, ends with an *'alif* ا / ى [aa], the middle vowel is either ـَيْ [ay] or ـَوْ [aw]). The rule of *assimilated* verbs (containing *waaw* or *yaa'* in initial position) also applies by dropping the *waaw* in the present form, as in the verb وَفَى – يَفِي "to fulfill":

المُضارع المَجْزوم Jussive	المُضارع المَنْصوب Subjunctive	المُضارع المَرْفوع Present (indicative)	الماضي Past	الضمير Pronoun
يَفِ	يَفِيَ	يَفِي	وَفَى	هُوَ
يَفِيا	يَفِيا	يَفِيانِ	وَفَيا	هُما
يَفُوا	يَفُوا	يَفُونَ	وَفَوْا	هُمْ
تَفِ	تَفِيَ	تَفِي	وَفَتْ	هِيَ
تَفِيا	تَفِيا	تَفِيانِ	وَفَتا	هُما
يَفِينَ	يَفِينَ	يَفِينَ	وَفَيْنَ	هُنَّ
تَفِ	تَفِيَ	تَفِي	وَفَيْتَ	أَنْتَ
تَفِيا	تَفِيا	تَفِيانِ	وَفَيْتُما	أَنْتُما
تَفُوا	تَفُوا	تَفُونَ	وَفَيْتُمْ	أَنْتُمْ
تَفِي	تَفِي	تَفِينَ	وَفَيْتِ	أَنْتِ
تَفِيا	تَفِيا	تَفِيانِ	وَفَيْتُما	أَنْتُما
تَفِينَ	تَفِينَ	تَفِينَ	وَفَيْتُنَّ	أَنْتُنَّ
أَفِ	أَفِيَ	أَفِي	وَفَيْتُ	أَنا
نَفِ	نَفِيَ	نَفِي	وَفَيْنا	نَحْنُ

13.5   The Imperative فِعْل الأَمْر

The most common way of forming the imperative or verb command فِعْل الأَمْر is the one intended for fives types of addressees: the second-person singular masculine أَنتَ , second-person singular feminine أَنتِ , second-person dual (for both the masculine and feminine) أَنتُمَا , second-person masculine plural أَنتُم , and second-person feminine plural أَنتُنَّ . The imperative form is derived from the present form of the verb, slightly modified according to the pattern/form of the verb, and always receives the jussive مَجْزوم mood ending.

13.5.1   Imperative of Form I (Triliteral Verbs)

Form I of sound/regular verbs have three imperative patterns/forms افْعَل , افْعِل , and أُفْعُل .

(A)   The pattern افْعَل is used when the present-tense middle vowel is *fatHa*. It is formed by: (1) dropping the present-tense prefix, (2) inserting a light *hamza* with a *kasra* ا in initial position, (3) retaining the *fatHa* middle vowel, and (4) adding the jussive مَجْزوم mood ending, as in:

	افْعَل	←	يَفْعَل
"Go!"	اذْهَبْ	←	يَذْهَبُ
"Read!"	اقْرَأْ	←	يَقْرَأُ

(B)   The pattern افْعِل is used when the present-tense middle vowel is *kasra*. It is formed by: (1) dropping the present-tense prefix, (2) inserting a light *hamza* with a *kasra* ا in initial position, (3) retaining the *kasra* middle vowel, and (4) adding the jussive مَجْزوم mood ending, as in:

	افْعِل	←	يَفْعِل
"Sit!"	اجْلِسْ	←	يَجْلِسُ
"Come down!"	انْزِلْ	←	يَنْزِلُ

(C)   The pattern أُفْعُل is used when the present-tense middle vowel is *Damma*. It is formed by: (1) dropping the present-tense prefix, (2) inserting a light *hamza* with a *Damma* أ in initial position,

(3) retaining the *Damma* middle vowel, and (4) adding the jussive مَجْزوم mood ending, as in:

أُفْعُلْ	←	يَفْعُلُ
"Write!" أُكْتُبْ	←	يَكْتُبُ
"Study!" أُدْرُسْ	←	يَدْرُسُ

Accordingly, the following charts illustrate the three imperative forms with all five addresses as well as the jussive مَجْزوم endings (as opposed to the indicative مَرْفوع mood, which is the default ending of the present tense):

(Form I) "to go" ذَهَبَ – يَذْهَبُ

Imperative / الأَمْر (Jussive / المَجْزوم)		Present / المُضارِع (Indicative / المَرْفوع)	
اِذْهَبْ	←	تَذْهَبُ	أَنْتَ
اِذْهَبي	←	تَذْهَبينَ	أَنْتِ
اِذْهَبا	←	تَذْهَبانِ	أَنْتُما
اِذْهَبوا	←	تَذْهَبونَ	أَنْتُمْ
اِذْهَبْنَ	←	تَذْهَبْنَ	أَنْتُنَّ

(Form I) "to sit" جَلَسَ – يَجْلِسُ

Imperative / الأَمْر (Jussive / المَجْزوم)		Present / المُضارِع (Indicative / المَرْفوع)	
اِجْلِسْ	←	تَجْلِسُ	أَنْتَ
اِجْلِسي	←	تَجْلِسينَ	أَنْتِ
اِجْلِسا	←	تَجْلِسانِ	أَنْتُما
اِجْلِسوا	←	تَجْلِسونَ	أَنْتُمْ
اِجْلِسْنَ	←	تَجْلِسْنَ	أَنْتُنَّ

(Form I) "to write" كَتَبَ – يَكْتُبُ

Imperative / الأَمْر (Jussive / المَجْزوم)		Present / المُضارِع (Indicative / المَرْفوع)	
اُكْتُبْ	←	تَكْتُبُ	أَنْتَ
اُكْتُبي	←	تَكْتُبينَ	أَنْتِ
اُكْتُبا	←	تَكْتُبانِ	أَنْتُما
اُكْتُبوا	←	تَكْتُبونَ	أَنْتُمْ
اُكْتُبْنَ	←	تَكْتُبْنَ	أَنْتُنَّ

13.5.2   Imperative of Forms II–III (Triliteral Verbs)

The imperative of Forms II–III is formed by dropping the prefix of the present tense and retaining the *kasra*, as in:

(Form II) "to cut" قَطَّعَ – يُقَطِّعُ

Imperative / الأَمْر (Jussive / المَجْزوم)		Present / المُضارِع (Indicative / المَرْفوع)	
قَطِّعْ	←	تُقَطِّعُ	أَنْتَ
قَطِّعي	←	تُقَطِّعينَ	أَنْتِ
قَطِّعا	←	تُقَطِّعانِ	أَنْتُما
قَطِّعوا	←	تُقَطِّعونَ	أَنْتُمْ
قَطِّعْنَ	←	تُقَطِّعْنَ	أَنْتُنَّ

(Form III) "to watch" شاهَدَ – يُشاهِدُ

Imperative / الأَمْر (Jussive / المَجْزوم)		Present / المُضارِع (Indicative / المَرْفوع)	
شاهِدْ	←	تُشاهِدُ	أنْتَ
شاهِدي	←	تُشاهِدينَ	أنْتِ
شاهِدا	←	تُشاهِدانِ	أنْتُما
شاهِدوا	←	تُشاهِدونَ	أنْتُمْ
شاهِدْنَ	←	تُشاهِدْنَ	أنْتُنَّ

13.5.3 Imperative of Form IV (Triliteral Verbs)

The imperative of Form IV is formed by: (1) dropping the prefix of the present tense, (2) adding a *hamza* with a *fatHa* أ in initial position, and (3) retaining the *kasra* of the present-tense middle vowel, as in:

(Form IV) "to bring" أَحْضَرَ – يُحْضِرُ

Imperative / الأَمْر (Jussive / المَجْزوم)		Present / المُضارِع (Indicative / المَرْفوع)	
أَحْضِرْ	←	تُحْضِرُ	أنْتَ
أَحْضِري	←	تُحْضِرينَ	أنْتِ
أَحْضِرا	←	تُحْضِرانِ	أنْتُما
أَحْضِروا	←	تُحْضِرونَ	أنْتُمْ
أَحْضِرْنَ	←	تُحْضِرْنَ	أنْتُنَّ

13.5.4 Imperative of Forms V–VI (Triliteral Verbs)

The imperative of Forms V–VI is formed by (1) dropping the prefix of the present tense and (2) retaining the middle *fatHa* (Form V) or *'alif* (Form VI) of the present form, as in:

(Form V) "to speak" تَكَلَّمَ – يَتَكَلَّمُ

Imperative / الأَمْر (Jussive / المَجْزوم)		Present / المُضارع (Indicative / المَرْفوع)	
تَكَلَّمْ	←	تَتَكَلَّمُ	أَنْتَ
تَكَلَّمي	←	تَتَكَلَّمينَ	أَنْتِ
تَكَلَّمَا	←	تَتَكَلَّمانِ	أَنْتُمَا
تَكَلَّموا	←	تَتَكَلَّمونَ	أَنْتُمْ
تَكَلَّمْنَ	←	تَتَكَلَّمْنَ	أَنْتُنَّ

(Form VI) "to compete" تَنافَسَ – يَتَنافَسُ

Imperative / الأَمْر (Jussive / المَجْزوم)		Present / المُضارع (Indicative / المَرْفوع)	
تَنافَسْ	←	تَتَنافَسُ	أَنْتَ
تَنافَسي	←	تَتَنافَسينَ	أَنْتِ
تَنافَسا	←	تَتَنافَسانِ	أَنْتُمَا
تَنافَسوا	←	تَتَنافَسونَ	أَنْتُمْ
تَنافَسْنَ	←	تَتَنافَسْنَ	أَنْتُنَّ

13.5.5 Imperative of Forms VII–VIII and X (Triliteral Verbs)

The imperative of Forms VII–VIII and X is formed by: (1) dropping the present-tense prefix, (2) adding a light *hamza* with a *kasra* ا in initial position, and (3) retaining the *kasra* as the middle vowel of the verb, as in:

(Form VII) "to start/to depart" اِنْطَلَقَ – يَنْطَلِقُ

Imperative / الأَمْر (Jussive / المَجْزوم)		Present / المُضارِع (Indicative / المَرْفوع)	
اِنْطَلِقْ	←	تَنْطَلِقُ	أَنْتَ
اِنْطَلِقي	←	تَنْطَلِقينَ	أَنْتِ
اِنْطَلِقا	←	تَنْطَلِقانِ	أَنْتُما
اِنْطَلِقوا	←	تَنْطَلِقونَ	أَنْتُمْ
اِنْطَلِقْنَ	←	تَنْطَلِقْنَ	أَنْتُنَّ

(Form VIII) "to acquire" اِكْتَسَبَ – يَكْتَسِبُ

Imperative / الأَمْر (Jussive / المَجْزوم)		Present / المُضارِع (Indicative / المَرْفوع)	
اِكْتَسِبْ	←	تَكْتَسِبُ	أَنْتَ
اِكْتَسِبي	←	تَكْتَسِبينَ	أَنْتِ
اِكْتَسِبا	←	تَكْتَسِبانِ	أَنْتُما
اِكْتَسِبوا	←	تَكْتَسِبونَ	أَنْتُمْ
اِكْتَسِبْنَ	←	تَكْتَسِبْنَ	أَنْتُنَّ

(Form X) "to use" إِسْتَخْدَمَ – يَسْتَخْدِمُ

		Present / المُضارِع (المَرْفوع / Indicative)	
Imperative / الأَمْر (المَجْزوم / Jussive)			
إِسْتَخْدِمْ	←	تَسْتَخْدِمُ	أَنْتَ
إِسْتَخْدِمي	←	تَسْتَخْدِمينَ	أَنْتِ
إِسْتَخْدِما	←	تَسْتَخْدِمانِ	أَنْتُما
إِسْتَخْدِموا	←	تَسْتَخْدِمونَ	أَنْتُمْ
إِسْتَخْدِمْنَ	←	تَسْتَخْدِمْنَ	أَنْتُنَّ

Note: No imperative is used for form IX (or Form XI), since it has a passive meaning.

13.5.6   Imperative of Quadriliteral Verbs (Form فَعْلَلَ – يُفَعْلِلُ)

The imperative of the quadriliteral verb form of فَعْلَلَ – يُفَعْلِلُ is formed by: dropping the present-tense prefix and retaining the *kasra* as the middle vowel of the verb, as in:

"to translate" تَرْجَمَ – يُتَرْجِمُ

		Present / المُضارِع (المَرْفوع / Indicative)	
Imperative / الأَمْر (المَجْزوم / Jussive)			
تَرْجِمْ	←	تُتَرْجِمُ	أَنْتَ
تَرْجِمي	←	تُتَرْجِمينَ	أَنْتِ
تَرْجِما	←	تُتَرْجِمانِ	أَنْتُما
تَرْجِموا	←	تُتَرْجِمونَ	أَنْتُمْ
تَرْجِمْنَ	←	تُتَرْجِمْنَ	أَنْتُنَّ

13.5.7 Imperative of Derived Quadriliteral Verbs

The imperative of the derived quadriliteral verb form of تَفَعْلَلَ – يَتَفَعْلَلُ is formed by dropping the present-tense prefix and retaining the *fatHa* as the middle vowel of the verb, whereas the imperative of اِفْعَلَلَّ – يَفْعَلِلُّ is formed by dropping the present-tense prefix, adding a light *hamza* with a *kasra* اِ, and retaining the *kasra* as the middle vowel of the verb, as in:

تَمَسْكَنَ – يَتَمَسْكَنُ "to pretend to be weak"

Imperative / الأَمْر (Jussive / المَجْزوم)		Present / المُضارع (Indicative / المَرْفوع)	
تَمَسْكَنْ	←	تَتَمَسْكَنُ	أَنْتَ
تَمَسْكَني	←	تَتَمَسْكَنينَ	أَنْتِ
تَمَسْكَنا	←	تَتَمَسْكَنانِ	أَنْتُما
تَمَسْكَنوا	←	تَتَمَسْكَنونَ	أَنْتُمْ
تَمَسْكَنَّ	←	تَتَمَسْكَنَّ	أَنْتُنَّ

اِطْمَأَنَّ – يَطْمَئِنُّ "to be reassured"

Imperative / الأَمْر (Jussive / المَجْزوم)		Present / المُضارع (Indicative / المَرْفوع)	
اِطْمَئِنَّ / اِطْمَأْنِنْ	←	تَطْمَئِنُّ	أَنْتَ
اِطْمَئِنِّي	←	تَطْمَئِنِّينَ	أَنْتِ
اِطْمَئِنّا	←	تَطْمَئِنّانِ	أَنْتُما
اِطْمَئِنّوا	←	تَطْمَئِنّونَ	أَنْتُمْ
اِطْمَأْنِنَّ	←	تَطْمَأْنِنَّ	أَنْتُنَّ

13.5.8   Imperative of *hamzated* Verbs

The imperative of *hamzated* verbs, in particular those containing a *hamza* in initial position, is formed by dropping both the prefix of the present tense and the *hamza*, while retaining the middle vowel of the present tense, as in:

"to take" أَخَذَ – يَأْخُذُ

Imperative / الأَمْر (*Jussive* / المَجْزوم)		*Present* / المُضارِع (*Indicative* / المَرْفوع)	
خُذْ	←	تَأْخُذُ	أَنْتَ
خُذي	←	تَأْخُذينَ	أَنْتِ
خُذا	←	تَأْخُذانِ	أَنْتُما
خُذوا	←	تَأْخُذونَ	أَنْتُمْ
خُذْنَ	←	تَأْخُذْنَ	أَنْتُنَّ

13.5.9   Imperative of Geminated Verbs

The imperative of geminated verbs is formed by dropping the prefix of the present tense and retaining the middle vowel of the present tense, if the verbs belong to Form I; otherwise, the same rules of those beyond Form I are applied. However, here the gemination/*shadda* must be broken (i.e., the two identical consonants are separated) for the second-person plural feminine and is optionally broken for second-person singular masculine, as in:

(I) "to count" عَدَّ – يَعُدُّ

Imperative / الأَمْر (*Jussive* / المَجْزوم)		*Present* / المُضارِع (*Indicative* / المَرْفوع)	
عُدَّ / أُعْدُدْ	←	تَعُدُّ	أَنْتَ
عُدِّي	←	تَعُدّينَ	أَنْتِ

عُدّا	←	تَعُدّانِ	أَنْتُما
عُدّوا	←	تَعُدّونَ	أَنْتُمْ
اُعْدُدْنَ	←	تَعْدُدْنَ	أَنْتُنَّ

أَحَبَّ – يُحِبُّ "to love" (IV)

Imperative / الأَمْر (Jussive / المَجْزوم)		Present / المُضارع (Indicative / المَرْفوع)	
أَحِبَّ / أَحْبِبْ	←	تُحِبُّ	أَنْتَ
أَحِبّي	←	تُحِبّينَ	أَنْتِ
أَحِبّا	←	تُحِبّانِ	أَنْتُما
أَحِبّوا	←	تُحِبّونَ	أَنْتُمْ
أَحْبِبْنَ	←	تُحْبِبْنَ	أَنْتُنَّ

اِسْتَعَدَّ – يَسْتَعِدُّ "to get ready" (X)

Imperative / الأَمْر (Jussive / المَجْزوم)		Present / المُضارع (Indicative / المَرْفوع)	
اِسْتَعِدَّ / اِسْتَعْدِدْ	←	تَسْتَعِدُّ	أَنْتَ
اِسْتَعِدّي	←	تَسْتَعِدّينَ	أَنْتِ
اِسْتَعِدّا	←	تَسْتَعِدّانِ	أَنْتُما
اِسْتَعِدّوا	←	تَسْتَعِدّونَ	أَنْتُمْ
اِسْتَعْدِدْنَ	←	تَسْتَعْدِدْنَ	أَنْتُنَّ

13.5.10 Imperative of Assimilated Verbs

The imperative of assimilated verbs of Form I containing a *waaw* in initial position is formed by dropping the prefix of the present tense and retaining the middle vowel of the present tense, as in:

"to put" وَضَعَ – يَضَعُ

		Present / المُضارع (Indicative / المَرْفوع)	
Imperative / الأَمْر (Jussive / المَجْزوم)			
ضَعْ	←	تَضَعُ	أَنْتَ
ضَعِي	←	تَضَعِينَ	أَنْتِ
ضَعا	←	تَضَعانِ	أَنْتُما
ضَعوا	←	تَضَعونَ	أَنْتُمْ
ضَعْنَ	←	تَضَعْنَ	أَنْتُنَّ

"to stand" وَقَفَ – يَقِفُ

		Present / المُضارع (Indicative / المَرْفوع)	
Imperative / الأَمْر (Jussive / المَجْزوم)			
قِفْ	←	تَقِفُ	أَنْتَ
قِفِي	←	تَقِفِي	أَنْتِ
قِفا	←	تَقِفانِ	أَنْتُما
قِفوا	←	تَقِفونَ	أَنْتُمْ
قِفْنَ	←	تَقِفْنَ	أَنْتُنَّ

Assimilated verbs containing a *yaa'* in initial position retain the *yaa'* and follow the basic rules of sound/regular Form I verbs, as in:

"to despair" يَئِسَ – يَيْأَسُ

Imperative / الأَمْر (Jussive / المَجْزوم)		Present / المُضارِع (Indicative / المَرْفوع)	
اِيأَسْ	←	تَيْأَسُ	أَنْتَ
اِيْأَسي	←	تَيْأَسينَ	أَنْتِ
اِيأَسا	←	تَيْأَسانِ	أَنْتُما
اِيأَسوا	←	تَيْأَسونَ	أَنْتُمْ
اِيأَسْنَ	←	تَيْأَسْنَ	أَنْتُنَّ

13.5.11 Imperative of Hollow Verbs

The imperative of hollow verbs is formed by dropping the prefix of the present tense and, in singular masculine form, shortening the middle long vowel, as in:

"to say" قالَ – يَقولُ

Imperative / الأَمْر (Jussive / المَجْزوم)		Present / المُضارِع (Indicative / المَرْفوع)	
قُلْ	←	تَقولُ	أَنْتَ
قولي	←	تَقولينَ	أَنْتِ
قولا	←	تَقولانِ	أَنْتُما
قولوا	←	تَقولونَ	أَنْتُمْ
قُلْنَ	←	تَقُلْنَ	أَنْتُنَّ

سارَ – يَسيرُ "to walk"

Imperative / الأَمْر (Jussive / المَجْزوم)		Present / المُضارع (Indicative / المَرْفوع)	
سِرْ	←	تَسيرُ	أَنْتَ
سيري	←	تَسيرينَ	أَنْتِ
سيرا	←	تَسيرانِ	أَنْتُما
سيروا	←	تَسيرونَ	أَنْتُمْ
سِرْنَ	←	تَسِرْنَ	أَنْتُنَّ

نامَ – يَنامُ "to sleep"

Imperative / الأَمْر (Jussive / المَجْزوم)		Present / المُضارع (Indicative / المَرْفوع)	
نَمْ	←	تَنامُ	أَنْتَ
نامي	←	تَنامينَ	أَنْتِ
ناما	←	تَنامانِ	أَنْتُما
ناموا	←	تَنامونَ	أَنْتُمْ
نَمْنَ	←	تَنَمْنَ	أَنْتُنَّ

13.5.12   Imperative of Defective Verbs

The imperative of defective verbs is formed by: (1) dropping the prefix of the present tense, (2) inserting a light *hamza* أ or إ (following Form I rules above), and (3) shortening the final long vowel in the second-person singular masculine, as in:

دَعا – يَدْعو "to invite/call"

الأَمْر / Imperative (المَجْزوم / Jussive)		المُضارِع / Present (المَرْفوع / Indicative)	
اُدْعُ	←	تَدْعو	أَنْتَ
اُدْعي	←	تَدْعينَ	أَنْتِ
اُدْعُوَا	←	تَدْعُوَانِ	أَنْتُما
اُدْعوا	←	تَدْعونَ	أَنْتُمْ
اُدْعونَ	←	تَدْعونَ	أَنْتُنَّ

مَشىٰ – يَمْشي "to walk"

الأَمْر / Imperative (المَجْزوم / Jussive)		المُضارِع / Present (المَرْفوع / Indicative)	
اِمْشِ	←	تَمْشي	أَنْتَ
اِمْشي	←	تَمْشينَ	أَنْتِ
اِمْشِيا	←	تَمْشِيانِ	أَنْتُما
اِمْشوا	←	تَمْشونَ	أَنْتُمْ
اِمْشينَ	←	تَمْشينَ	أَنْتُنَّ

نَهىٰ – يَنْهىٰ "to forbid"

الأَمْر / Imperative (المَجْزوم / Jussive)		المُضارِع / Present (المَرْفوع / Indicative)	
اِنْهَ	←	تَنْهىٰ	أَنْتَ
اِنْهَيْ	←	تَنْهَيْنَ	أَنْتِ
اِنْهَيا	←	تَنْهَيانِ	أَنْتُما
اِنْهَوْا	←	تَنْهَوْنَ	أَنْتُمْ
اِنْهَيْنَ	←	تَنْهَيْنَ	أَنْتُنَّ

13.5.13   Imperative of Non-separated, Double Weak Verbs

The imperative of non-separated, double weak verbs is formed by the same rule as those of Form I sound/regular verbs and, in addition, (1) dropping the prefix of the present tense and (2) shortening the final long vowel in the second-person singular masculine, as in:

نَوٰى – يَنْوِي "to intend"

Imperative / الأَمْرُ (Jussive / المَجْزوم)		Present / المُضارِع (Indicative / المَرْفوع)	
اِنْوِ	←	تَنْوِي	أَنْتَ
اِنْوِي	←	تَنْوِينَ	أَنْتِ
اِنْوِيا	←	تَنْوِيانِ	أَنْتُما
اِنْوُوا	←	تَنْوُونَ	أَنْتُمْ
اِنْوِينَ	←	تَنْوِينَ	أَنْتُنَّ

13.5.14   Imperative of Separated, Double Weak Verbs

The imperative form of separated, double weak verbs is formed by dropping the prefix of the present tense and shortening the final long vowel in the second-person singular masculine, as in:

وَفٰى – يَفِي "to fulfill"

Imperative / الأَمْرُ (Jussive / المَجْزوم)		Present / المُضارِع (Indicative / المَرْفوع)	
فِ	←	تَفِي	أَنْتَ
فِي	←	تَفِينَ	أَنْتِ
فِيا	←	تَفِيا	أَنْتُما
فُوا	←	تَفُونَ	أَنْتُمْ
فِينَ	←	تَفِينَ	أَنْتُنَّ

An example of the imperative of separated, double weak verbs is given below:

$$فِ بِوَعْدِكَ .$$

"Fulfill your promise!"

13.5.15 Imperative of Two Common Irregular Verbs هاتِ ، تَعالَ

There are two irregular verbs that are quite common and used only as imperative verbs. These are:

	"give" هاتِ	
الأَمْر / *Imperative* (المَجْزوم / *Jussive*)		
هاتِ	أَنْتَ	
هاتي	أَنْتِ	
هاتِيا	أَنْتُما	
هاتُوا	أَنْتُمْ	
هاتِينَ	أَنْتُنَّ	

	"come" تَعالَ	
الأَمْر / *Imperative* (المَجْزوم / *Jussive*)		
تَعالَ	أَنْتَ	
تَعالَيْ	أَنْتِ	
تَعالَيا	أَنْتُما	
تَعالَوْا	أَنْتُمْ	
تَعالَيْنَ	أَنْتُنَّ	

13.6 The Negative Imperative النَّهْي

The negative imperative verb فِعْل النَّهْي is formed simply by using the present-tense form with the jussive مَجْزوم mood ending, preceded by the negative imperative particle لا referred to in Arabic as لا النّاهِيَة. No additional modifications or rules are involved, as in:

ذَهَبَ – يَذْهَبُ "to go"

الأمْر / Imperative (المَجْزوم / Jussive)		المُضارِع / Present (المَرْفوع / Indicative)	
لا تَذْهَبْ	←	تَذْهَبُ	أنْتَ
لا تَذْهَبي	←	تَذْهَبينَ	أنْتِ
لا تَذْهَبا	←	تَذْهَبانِ	أنْتُما
لا تَذْهَبوا	←	تَذْهَبونَ	أنْتُمْ
لا تَذْهَبْنَ	←	تَذْهَبْنَ	أنْتُنَّ

Except for the two irregular imperative verbs هاتِ and تَعالَ, all verbs can be used in the negative imperative in the same way, following the jussive مَجْزوم mood rules, including hollow and defective verbs, as in:

قالَ – يَقولُ "to say"

الأمْر / Imperative (المَجْزوم / Jussive)		المُضارِع / Present (المَرْفوع / Indicative)	
لا تَقُلْ	←	تَقولُ	أنْتَ
لا تَقولي	←	تَقولينَ	أنْتِ
لا تَقولا	←	تَقولانِ	أنْتُما
لا تَقولوا	←	تَقولونَ	أنْتُمْ
لا تَقُلْنَ	←	تَقُلْنَ	أنْتُنَّ

مَشیٰ – يَمْشِي "to walk"

Imperative / الأَمْر (Jussive / المَجْزوم)		Present / المُضارع (Indicative / المَرْفوع)	
لا تَمْشِ	←	تَمْشِي	أَنْتَ
لا تَمْشِي	←	تَمْشِينَ	أَنْتِ
لا تَمْشِيا	←	تَمْشِيانِ	أَنْتُما
لا تَمْشوا	←	تَمْشونَ	أَنْتُمْ
لا تَمْشينَ	←	تَمْشينَ	أَنْتُنَّ

13.7 The Passive Voice المَبْنِيّ لِلْمَجْهول

Unlike in English, where the passive voice is sometimes used for emphasis (e.g., "The book was written by John Smith" and "The door was broken by John Smith," where the subject/doer "John Smith" is emphasized or focused on), the passive voice in Arabic is used in the vast majority of cases only when the subject/doer of the action is unknown. Since some of the verb forms (I–X) already express a passive voice meaning, not all verb forms can be usually expressed in the passive voice, as explained below. There are two general rules that apply to all verbs in the past and present tense, respectively.

13.7.1 The Past-tense Passive Voice الماضي المَبْنِيّ لِلْمَجْهول

The past-tense passive voice الماضي المَبْنِيّ لِلْمَجْهول is marked by: (1) dropping the subject/doer of the verb/action, (2) making the verb agree with the new subject in gender (if the verb precedes the subject) and fully (if the verb follows the subject), (3) placing the nominative مَرْفوع case ending (which is the ending of the subject/doer) on the object/doee to replace its accusative مَنْصوب case ending (see also Chapter 22 on case endings), and (4) converting the middle vowel into a *kasra*. Because the object/doee here assumes the position of the subject/doer, it is called in Arabic نائِب الفاعِل "the vice or deputy subject/doer." In addition, the following rules apply:

(a) converting the (first) preceding vowel into a *Damma*, if the verb is Form I, as in:

كُسِرَ البابُ . ← كَسَرَ الطّالِبُ البابَ .

"The door was broken." "The student broke the door."

كُسِرَ البابانِ . ← كَسَرَ الطّالِبُ البابَيْنِ .

"The two doors were broken." "The student broke the two doors."

سُمِعَ المُهَنْدِسونَ . ← سَمِعَ الطّالِبُ المُهَنْدِسينَ .

"The (male) engineers were heard." "The student heard the (male) engineers."

سُمِعَتْ المُهَنْدِساتُ . ← سَمِعَ الطّالِبُ المُهَنْدِساتِ .

"The (female) engineers were heard." "The student heard the (female) engineers."

(b) converting the (two) preceding vowels into *Dammas*, if the verb is Form V, VIII, or X, as in:

تُعُلِّمَ هٰذا الفَنُّ . ← تَعَلَّمَ الطّالِبُ هٰذا الفَنَّ .

"This art was learned." "The student learned this art."

اُسْتُقْبِلَ الوَزيرُ . ← اِسْتَقْبَلَ الرَّئيسُ الوَزيرَ .

"The minister was received." "The president received the minister."

(c) additionally, if the verb is Form IV or X and is a hollow verb, the middle long vowel *'alif* [ا] is converted into a *yaa'* [ي], as in:

أُنيرَ الشّارِعُ . ← أنارَ المُحافِظُ الشّارِعَ .

"The street was lit." "The mayor lit the street."

"The oil was benefited from."   "The people benefited from the oil."

(d) if the verb is Form I and is a hollow verb, the middle long vowel *'alif* [ا] is converted into a *yaa'* [ي], as the only additional rule, as in:

"The house was sold."   "The real estate owner sold the house."

(e) if the verb is Form VIII and is a hollow verb, the middle long vowel *'alif* [ا] is converted into a *yaa'* [ي] and the preceding (first vowel) *kasra* of Form VIII is retained (for ease of pronunciation), as in:

"The teacher was chosen for the award."   "The student chose the teacher for the award."

(f) if the verb is Form III (which is essentially a hollow verb), the middle long vowel *'alif* [ا] is converted into a *waaw* [و] as the only additional rule, as in:

"The criminal was seen."   "The student saw the criminal."

(g) if the verb is a defective verb (i.e., ending with a final long vowel *'alif* [ا] / [ى] in the past tense), then additionally the final long vowel *'alif* [ا] / [ى] is converted into a [يَ], as in:

دُعِيَ الأُسْتاذُ إلى الحَفْلَةِ . ← دَعا الطُّلابُ الأُسْتاذَ إلى الحَفْلَةِ .

"The teacher was invited to the party."   "The students invited the teacher to the party."

سُمِّيَ ← الشَّارِعُ بِاسْمِ الرَّئِيسِ .   المُحافِظُ الشَّارِعَ بِاسْمِ الرَّئِيسِ . ← سَمَّىٰ

"The street was named after the
president."

"The mayor named the street
after the president."

Accordingly, the following chart of verb patterns summarizes the different forms of passive voice in the past tense in the different verb forms:

الفِعْل النّاقِص *Defective verb*	الفِعْل الأَجْوَف *Hollow verb*	الفِعْل السّالِم *Sound verb*	الماضي المَجْهول *Past passive*	الماضي المَعْلوم *Past active*	*Forms*
قَضىٰ ← قُضِيَ دَعا ← دُعِيَ نَهىٰ ← نُهِيَ	باعَ ← بِيعَ قالَ ← قِيلَ نالَ ← نِيلَ	كَسَرَ ← كُسِرَ	فُعِلَ	فَعَلَ / فَعِلَ	I
سَمَّىٰ ← سُمِّيَ	—	كَسَّرَ ← كُسِّرَ	فُعِّلَ	فَعَّلَ	II
نادىٰ ← نودِيَ	شاهَدَ ← شوهِدَ	—	فوعِلَ	فاعَلَ	III
أَعْطىٰ ← أُعْطِيَ	أنارَ ← أنِيرَ	أَكْرَمَ ← أُكْرِمَ	أُفْعِلَ	أَفْعَلَ	IV
تَمَّىٰ ← تُمِّيَ	—	تَعَلَّمَ ← تُعُلِّمَ	تُفُعِّلَ	تَفَعَّلَ	V
تَفادىٰ ← تُفودِيَ	تَنازَعَ ← تُنوزِعَ	—	تُفوعِلَ	تَفاعَلَ	VI
—	—	—	—	إِنْفَعَلَ	VII
اِعْتَدىٰ ← اُعْتُدِيَ	اِختارَ ← اِختِيرَ	اِحْتَفَظَ ← اُحْتُفِظَ	اُفْتُعِلَ	اِفْتَعَلَ	VIII
—	—	—	—	اِفْعَلَّ	IX
اِسْتَثْنىٰ ← اُسْتُثْنِيَ	اِسْتَفادَ ← اُسْتُفِيدَ	اِسْتَقْبَلَ ← اُسْتُقْبِلَ	اُسْتُفْعِلَ	اِسْتَفْعَلَ	X

Note: The past-tense passive form of quadriliteral verbs, in particular فَعْلَلَ – يُفَعْلِلُ, is formed in the same way as Form I of triliteral verbs; i.e., by converting the middle vowel into a *kasra* and the (first) preceding vowel into a *Damma*, as in:

تُرْجِمَ ← الكِتابُ إِلى العَرَبِيَّةِ .   الأُستاذُ الكِتابَ إِلى العَرَبِيَّةِ . ← تَرْجَمَ

"The book was translated into
Arabic."

"The teacher translated the book into
Arabic."

13.7.2   The Present-tense Passive Voice
المُضارع المَبْنيّ لِلْمَجْهول

The present-tense passive voice المُضارع المَبْنيّ لِلْمَجْهول is marked by: (1) dropping the subject/doer of the verb/action, (2) making the verb agree with
the new subject in gender (if the verb precedes the subject) and fully (if
the verb follows the subject), (3) placing the nominative مَرْفوع case ending
(which is the ending of the subject/doer) on the object/doee to replace its
accusative مَنْصوب case ending (see also Chapter 22 on case endings), and
(4) converting the first vowel into a *Damma*. Because the object/doee here
assumes the position of the subject/doer, it is called in Arabic نائب الفاعل
"the vice or deputy subject/doer." Additionally, the following rules apply:

(a)   converting the middle vowel into a *fatHa* if the verb is a sound verb,
      as in:

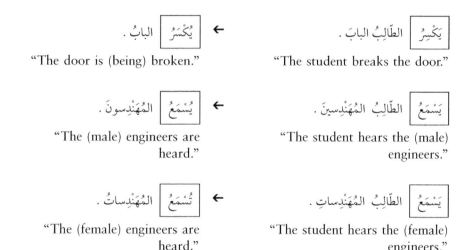

يُكْسَرُ البابُ . ←	يَكْسِرُ الطّالِبُ البابَ .
"The door is (being) broken."	"The student breaks the door."
يُسْمَعُ المُهَنْدِسونَ . ←	يَسْمَعُ الطّالِبُ المُهَنْدِسينَ .
"The (male) engineers are heard."	"The student hears the (male) engineers."
تُسْمَعُ المُهَنْدِساتُ . ←	يَسْمَعُ الطّالِبُ المُهَنْدِساتِ .
"The (female) engineers are heard."	"The student hears the (female) engineers."
يُتَعَلَّمُ هٰذا الفَنُّ . ←	يَتَعَلَّمُ الطّالِبُ هٰذا الفَنَّ .
"This art is (being) learned."	"The student learns this art."
يُسْتَقْبَلُ الوَزيرُ . ←	يَسْتَقْبِلُ الرَّئيسُ الوَزيرَ .
"The minister is (being) received."	"The president receives the minister."

(b)   if the verb is a hollow verb, then additionally the long middle vowel, whether it is a *yaa'* [ي], a *waaw* [و] or an *'alif* [١], is converted into an *'alif* [١], as in:

يُباعُ البَيْتُ .   ←   يَبيعُ مالِكُ العَقاراتِ البَيْتَ .

"The house is (being) sold."   "The real estate owner sells the
                                      house."

يُقالُ هٰذا المَثَلُ كَثيراً .   ←   يَقولُ الأُسْتاذُ هٰذا المَثَلَ كَثيراً .

"This proverb is said a lot."   "The teacher says this proverb a
                                      lot."

يُخْتارُ الأُسْتاذُ لِلْجائِزَةِ دائِماً .   ←   يَخْتارُ الطُّلّابُ الأُسْتاذَ لِلْجائِزَةِ .

"The teacher is chosen for the   "The students choose the teacher
award always."   for the award."

(c)   if the verb is a defective verb (i.e., ending with a final long vowel), then additionally the final long vowel, whether it is a *yaa'* [ي], a *waaw* [و], or an *'alif* [١], is converted into an *'alif* [ى], as in:

يُشْتَرىٰ البَيْتُ .   ←   يَشْتَري مالِكُ العَقاراتِ البَيْتَ .

"The house is (being) bought."   "The real estate owner buys the
                                      house."

يُدْعىٰ الأُسْتاذُ إِلىٰ الحَفْلَةِ دائِماً .   ←   يَدْعو الطُّلّابُ الأُسْتاذَ إِلىٰ الحَفْلَةِ .

"The teacher is invited to the party "The students invite the teacher
always."   to the party."

يُتَمَنّىٰ النَّجاحُ دائِماً .   ←   يَتَمَنّىٰ الطُّلّابُ النَّجاحَ دائِماً .

"Success is always hoped for."   "The students hope for success
                                      always."

Accordingly, the following chart of verb patterns summarizes the different forms of passive voice in the present tense in the different verb forms:

الفِعْل النّاقِص Defective verb	الفِعْل الأَجْوَف Hollow verb	الفِعْل السّالِم Sound verb	المُضارع المَجْهول Present passive	المُضارع المَعْلوم Present active	Forms
يَقْضي ← يُقْضىٰ يَدْعو ← يُدْعىٰ يَنْهىٰ ← يُنْهىٰ	يَبيعُ ← يُباعُ يَقولُ ← يُقالُ يَنالُ ← يُنالُ	يَكْسِرُ ← يُكْسَرُ	يُفْعَلُ	يَفْعَلُ / يَفْعِلُ	I
يُسَمّي ← يُسَمّىٰ	–	يُكَسِّرُ ← يُكَسَّرُ	يُفَعَّلُ	يُفَعِّلُ	II
–	يُشاهِدُ ← يُشاهَدُ	–	يُفاعَلُ	يُفاعِلُ	III
يُعْطي ← يُعْطىٰ	يُنيرُ ← يُنارُ	يُكْرِمُ ← يُكْرَمُ	يُفْعَلُ	يُفْعِلُ	IV
يَتَمَنّىٰ ← يَتَمَنّىٰ	–	يَتَعَلَّمُ ← يُتَعَلَّمُ	يُتَفَعَّلُ	يَتَفَعَّلُ	V
يَتَفادىٰ ← يُتَفادىٰ	يَتَنازَعُ ← يُتَنازَعُ	–	يُتَفاعَلُ	يَتَفاعَلُ	VI
–	–	–	–	يَنْفَعِلُ	VII
يَعْتَدي ← يُعْتَدىٰ	يَخْتارُ ← يُخْتارُ	يَحْتَفِظُ ← يُحْتَفَظُ	يُفْتَعَلُ	يَفْتَعِلُ	VIII
–	–	–	–	يَفْعَلُّ	IX
يَسْتَثْني ← يُسْتَثْنىٰ	يَسْتَفيدُ ← يُسْتَفادُ	يَسْتَقْبِلُ ← يُسْتَقْبَلُ	يُسْتَفْعَلُ	يَسْتَفْعِلُ	X

Note: The present-tense passive form of quadriliteral verbs, in particular فَعْلَلَ – يُفَعْلِلُ , is formed by simply converting the middle vowel into a *fatHa*, as in:

يُتَرْجَمُ الكِتابُ إلى العَرَبِيَّةِ . ← يُتَرْجِمُ الأُسْتاذُ الكِتابَ إلى العَرَبِيَّةِ .

"The book is (being) translated into Arabic." | "The teacher translates the book into Arabic."

Additionally, although the *waaw* in *assimilated* verbs is retained in the past but dropped in the present (see 13.4.4 on *assimilated* verbs), in the passive voice the *waaw* is retained in both tenses, as in:

وُضِعَ البَرِيدُ هُنا . ← وَضَعَ السّائِقُ البَرِيدَ هُنا .

"The mail was placed here."   "The driver placed the mail here."

يُوضَعُ البَرِيدُ هُنا . ← يَضَعُ السّائِقُ البَرِيدَ هُنا .

"The mail is placed here."   "The driver places the mail here."

13.8   Summary

This chapter discussed the essentials of the Arabic verb, its patterns/forms as well as its active voice, passive voice, the imperative, and the negative imperative forms. Remember:

- while Form I verbs involve an irregular change in the middle vowel in the past and present tense (of four of the six sub-types), the remaining Forms II–X involve regular changes
- Arabic has two main categories of verbs: sound verbs that fit into three sub-categories (sound/regular, *hamzated*, and geminated) and weak verbs that fit into five sub-categories (assimilated; hollow; defective; non-separated, double weak; and separated, double weak)
- although seven of the eight subcategories involve certain changes with respect to conjugation, the imperative, and passive voice, the changes are regular in that any verb that belongs to any of the categories/sub-categories is subject to the same changes and rules
- the overarching rule of the past passive form is maintaining *kasra* as the middle vowel and *Damma* as the preceding vowel/s, whereas the rule of the present passive is maintaining *fatHa* as the middle vowel and *Damma* as the preceding vowel/s
- the imperative forms follow regular patterns each according to the verb form
- the negative imperative for all verbs is formed by using the present form of the verb (with the jussive مَجْزوم ending) preceded by the negative imperative particle لا.

14

The Noun الإِسْم

This chapter discusses the main categories or classes of the Arabic *noun*, called in Arabic الإِسْم "the name," although generally speaking all nouns in Arabic fall into one of two categories: non-derived or derived nouns. Other words that behave as nouns include relative/nisba adjectives and quantifiers (for more on these two subclasses, see Chapters 15–16, respectively).

The chapter covers the following:

- the non-derived noun
- the verbal noun
- the active participle
- the passive participle
- the noun of time and place
- the noun of instrument
- the noun of once
- the derived abstract noun
- the diminutive
- the five nouns.

14.1   The Non-derived Noun

Typically, a noun referring to an entity, thing, or object is a non-derived noun. That is, it is derived directly from its respective (triliteral, quadriliteral, and quinqueliteral) core root consonants but, unlike a derived noun, is not derived secondarily from other words. Non-derived nouns include both concrete and abstract entities or things. Below are examples of non-derived nouns (see also Chapter 2 for a detailed description of word structure):

"a man"	*rajul*	رَجُل	r-j-l	ر – ج – ل	الثُّلاثي triliteral
"a reason"	*sabab*	سَبَب	s-b-b	س – ب– ب	الثُّلاثي triliteral
"a penny"	*dirham*	دِرْهَم	d-r-h-m	د – ر – هـ– م	الرُّباعي quadriliteral
"quince"	*safarjal*	سَفَرْجَل	s-f-r-j-l	س – ف – ر– ج – ل	الخُماسي quinqueliteral

14.2 The Verbal Noun المَصْدَر

As the name suggests, the verbal noun مَصْدَر (also referred to in English as the *gerund*) is a noun derived from a verb whereby the meaning of the verb is converted into a noun (setting the traditional controversy related to it aside). Therefore, each verb has a verbal noun. Unlike in English, where a verb is converted into a verbal noun/gerund by adding the {-ing} suffix, verbal nouns in Arabic have different forms, depending on the verb form.

14.2.1 Verbal Nouns of Form I Verbs

Verbal nouns of Form I verbs have several different forms and therefore such words are perhaps best learned initially on a word-by-word basis.

	Verbal noun / المَصْدَر		*Present* / المُضارع	*Past* / الماضي
"reading"	القِراءَة	←	يَقْرَأُ	قَرَأَ
"writing"	الكِتابَة	←	يَكْتُبُ	كَتَبَ
"sitting"	الجُلوس	←	يَجْلِسُ	جَلَسَ
"understanding"	الفَهْم	←	يَفْهَمُ	فَهِمَ
"reckoning"	الحِسْبان	←	يَحْسِبُ	حَسِبَ
"getting far"	البُعْد	←	يَبْعُدُ	بَعُدَ

14.2.2 Verbal Nouns of Forms II–X Verbs

Verbal nouns of Forms II–X verbs are predictable, just like the conjugations of the past and present tenses in those forms. Hence, such forms are best learned as part of their derivation patterns, as listed below:

Verbal noun / المَصْدَر	←	Present / المُضارِع	Past / الماضي	form
التَّفْعيل	←	يُفَعِّلُ	فَعَّلَ	II
المُفاعَلَة	←	يُفاعِلُ	فاعَلَ	III
الإفْعال	←	يُفْعِلُ	أَفْعَلَ	IV
التَّفَعُّل	←	يَتَفَعَّلُ	تَفَعَّلَ	V
التَّفاعُل	←	يَتَفاعَلُ	تَفاعَلَ	VI
الإنْفِعال	←	يَنْفَعِلُ	إنْفَعَلَ	VII
الإفْتِعال	←	يَفْتَعِلُ	إفْتَعَلَ	VIII
الإفْعِلال	←	يَفْعَلُّ	إفْعَلَّ	IX
الإسْتِفْعال	←	يَسْتَفْعِلُ	إسْتَفْعَلَ	X

Below are specific examples of verbal nouns of Forms II–X verbs, including those belonging to sound verbs, hollow verbs, and defective verbs:

مَصْدَر الفِعْل النّاقِص VN of defective verb	مَصْدَر الفِعْل الأَجْوَف VN of hollow verb	مَصْدَر الفِعْل السّالِم VN of sound verb	المَصْدَر Verbal noun	المُضارِع Present	الماضي Past	Forms
سَمّى ← التَّسْمِيَة	–	كَسَّرَ ← التَّكْسير	التَّفْعيل	يُفَعِّلُ	فَعَّلَ	II
نادى ← المُناداة	شاهَدَ ← المُشاهَدَة	–	المُفاعَلَة	يُفاعِلُ	فاعَلَ	III
أَعْطى ← الإعْطاء	أنارَ ← الإنارة	أَكْرَمَ ← الإكْرام	الإفْعال	يُفْعِلُ	أَفْعَلَ	IV
تَمَّنى ← التَّمَنّي	–	تَعَلَّمَ ← التَّعَلُّم	التَّفَعُّل	يَتَفَعَّلُ	تَفَعَّلَ	V
تَفادى ← التَّفادي	تَنازَعَ ← التَّنازُع	–	التَّفاعُل	يَتَفاعَلُ	تَفاعَلَ	VI
إنْتَهى ← الإنْتِهاء	إنْحازَ ← الإنْحِياز	إنْقَطَعَ ← الإنْقِطاع	الإنْفِعال	يَنْفَعِلُ	إنْفَعَلَ	VII
إعْتَدى ← الإعْتِداء	إخْتارَ ← الإخْتِيار	إحْتَفَظَ ← الإحْتِفاظ	الإفْتِعال	يَفْتَعِلُ	إفْتَعَلَ	VIII
–	–	إخْضَرَّ ← الإخْضِرار	الإفْعِلال	يَفْعَلُّ	إفْعَلَّ	IX
إسْتَثْنى ← الإسْتِثْناء	إسْتَفادَ ← الإسْتِفادة	إسْتَقْبَلَ ← الإسْتِقْبال	الإسْتِفْعال	يَسْتَفْعِلُ	إسْتَفْعَلَ	X

14.2.3   Verbal Noun Use

A verbal noun is used just like any other noun. In addition, it occurs definite, unless it occurs within an إضافة *'iDaafa* phrase, in which case it follows the إضافة *'iDaafa* phrase rule of definiteness (see Chapter 3), or when it occurs as an adverb of emphasis/cognate accusative (see Chapter 12), as in:

أُحِبُّ السِّباحَةَ .

"I like [the act of] swimming."

يُحِبُّونَ السِّباحَةَ .

"They like [the act of] swimming."

أُحِبُّ قِراءَةَ الصُّحُفِ .

"I like [the act of] reading newspapers."

يَدْرُسُ لِلسَّفَرِ إلَى الخارِجِ .

"He studies for [the act of] traveling abroad."

An equivalent structure is the use of the particle أَنْ "to" or لِ "in order to" followed by a verb (with the subjunctive مَنْصوب ending). This use is called in Arabic مَصْدَر مُؤَوَّل "interpreted/rephrased verbal noun," as in:

أُحِبُّ أَنْ أَسْبَحَ .	=	أُحِبُّ السِّباحَةَ .
"I like to swim."		"I like swimming."
يُحِبُّونَ أَنْ يَسْبَحوا .	=	يُحِبُّونَ السِّباحَةَ .
"They like to swim."		"They like swimming."
أُحِبُّ أَنْ أَقْرَأَ الصُّحُفَ .	=	أُحِبُّ قِراءَةَ الصُّحُفِ .
"I like to read newspapers."		"I like [the act of] reading newspapers."
يَدْرُسُ لِيُسافِرَ إلَى الخارِجِ .	=	يَدْرُسُ لِلسَّفَرِ إلَى الخارِجِ .
"He studies in order to travel abroad."		"He studies for traveling abroad."

Note: While there is a subtle semantic difference between the two structures in English, in Arabic the two structures are identical in meaning.

14.3 The Active Participle إِسْم الفاعِل

As the name suggests, the active participle إِسْم الفاعِل is derived to form the *doer* meaning of a given verb/action. This is similar to deriving the active participle *writer* from the verb *write* in English. However, this type of derivation in English involves predictable as well as unpredictable sound and spelling changes and so can be characterized as irregular, as the examples in the table below illustrate:

Verb		Active participle	Sound changes
write	→	writer	+ [ər]
kill	→	killer	+ [ər]
rob	→	robber	+ [bər]
travel	→	traveler	+ [ər]
falsify	→	falsifier	+ [ai ər]
apply	→	applicant	+[ikənt]
study	→	student	+[udənt]
act	→	actor	+ [ər]
register	→	registrar/registrant	+ [ar]/[ənt]
inhabit	→	inhabitant	+[ənt]
tour	→	tourist	+[ist]
anesthetize	→	anesthetic/anesthetist	+[ik]/[ist]
practice	→	practitioner	+[ʃnər]
massage	→	masseur/masseuse	+[ur]/[us]
gra'duate	→	'graduate	(stress shift)
pilot	→	pilot	+[ø]

Unlike in English, deriving the active participle in Arabic follows predict-able sound changes with a specific pattern for each of the ten verb forms, as shown in the table below:

اِسْم الفاعِل / Active participle		المُضارِع / Present	الماضي / Past	Form
فاعِل	←	يَفعَل / يَفعِل / يَفعُل	فَعَل / فَعِل	I
مُفَعِّل	←	يُفَعِّل	فَعَّل	II
مُفاعِل	←	يُفاعِل	فاعَل	III
مُفعِل	←	يُفعِل	أَفعَل	IV
مُتَفَعِّل	←	يَتَفَعَّل	تَفَعَّل	V
مُتَفاعِل	←	يَتَفاعَل	تَفاعَل	VI
مُنفَعِل	←	يَنفَعِل	اِنفَعَل	VII
مُفتَعِل	←	يَفتَعِل	اِفتَعَل	VIII
مُفعَّل	←	يَفعَّل	اِفعَلَّ	IX
مُستَفعِل	←	يَستَفعِل	اِستَفعَل	X

The table below gives specific examples of active participles of Forms I–X verbs, including those belonging to sound verbs, hollow verbs, and defective verbs:

الفِعْل النّاقِص AP of defective verb	الفِعْل الأَجْوَف AP of hollow verb	الفِعْل السّالِم AP of sound verb	اِسْم الفاعِل Active participle	المُضارِع Present	الماضي Past	Forms
قَضىٰ ← قاضٍ / القاضي دَعا ← داعٍ / الدّاعي نَهىٰ ← ناهٍ / النّاهي	باعَ ← بائِع قالَ ← قائِل نالَ ← نائِل	كَتَبَ ← كاتِب	فاعِل	يَفعُل	فَعَل	I
سَمّىٰ ← مُسَمٍّ / المُسَمّي	–	كَسَّرَ ← مُكَسِّر	مُفَعِّل	يُفَعِّل	فَعَّل	II
نادىٰ ← مُنادٍ / المُنادي	شاهَدَ ← مُشاهِد	–	مُفاعِل	يُفاعِل	فاعَل	III
أَعطىٰ ← مُعطٍ / المُعطي	أَنارَ ← مُنير	أَكرَمَ ← مُكرِم	مُفعِل	يُفعِل	أَفعَل	IV
تَمَنّىٰ ← مُتَمَنٍّ / المُتَمَنّي	–	تَعَلَّمَ ← مُتَعَلِّم	مُتَفَعِّل	يَتَفَعَّل	تَفَعَّل	V
تَفادىٰ ← مُتَفادٍ / المُتَفادي	تَنازَعَ ← مُتَنازِع	–	مُتَفاعِل	يَتَفاعَل	تَفاعَل	VI
اِنقَضىٰ ← مُنقَضٍ / المُنقَضي	اِنحازَ ← مُنحاز	اِنقَطَعَ ← مُنقَطِع	مُنفَعِل	يَنفَعِل	اِنفَعَل	VII
اِعتَدىٰ ← مُعتَدٍ / المُعتَدي	اِختارَ ← مُختار	اِحتَفَظَ ← مُحتَفِظ	مُفتَعِل	يَفتَعِل	اِفتَعَل	VIII
–	–	اِخضَرَّ ← مُخضَرّ	مُفعَلّ	يَفعَلّ	اِفعَلَّ	IX
اِستَثنىٰ ← مُستَثنٍ / المُستَثني	اِستَفادَ ← مُستَفيد	اِستَقبَلَ ← مُستَقبِل	مُستَفعِل	يَستَفعِل	اِستَفعَل	X

As shown above, the active participle of Form I hollow verbs always has a medial *hamza*, as in:

$$\text{بَاعَ} \quad \text{يَبِيعُ} \quad \leftarrow \quad \text{بائِع}$$

$$\text{قَالَ} \quad \text{يَقولُ} \quad \leftarrow \quad \text{قائِل}$$

$$\text{نامَ} \quad \text{يَنامُ} \quad \leftarrow \quad \text{نائِم}$$

As for active participles of *hamzated* verbs, these follow the same rule and retain the *hamza* whether in initial, medial, or final position, as in:

$$\text{أَخَذَ} \quad \text{يَأْخُذُ} \quad \leftarrow \quad \text{آخِذ}$$

$$\text{أَكَلَ} \quad \text{يَأْكُلُ} \quad \leftarrow \quad \text{آكِل}$$

$$\text{سَأَلَ} \quad \text{يَسْأَلُ} \quad \leftarrow \quad \text{سائِل}$$

$$\text{ثَأَرَ} \quad \text{يَثْأَرُ} \quad \leftarrow \quad \text{ثائِر}$$

$$\text{قَرَأَ} \quad \text{يَقْرَأُ} \quad \leftarrow \quad \text{قارِئ}$$

$$\text{بَرِئَ} \quad \text{يَبْرَأُ} \quad \leftarrow \quad \text{بارِئ}$$

14.3.1 Active Participle Use

Active participles in Arabic are used in the same way as any nouns (and also as adjectives and verbs; see Chapter 15) and therefore can be used either by themselves or modified/followed by an adjective, and can occur in the dual and plural, as in:

وَالِدي كاتِبٌ .
"My father is a writer."

وَالِدي كاتِبٌ مَشْهورٌ .
"My father is a famous writer."

قابَلْتُ كاتِبَيْنِ مَشْهورَيْنِ .
"I met two famous writers."

قابَلْتُ كاتِبينَ مَشْهورينَ .
"I met famous writers."

The *yaa'* ي of the active participles derived from defective verbs is dropped when the noun occurs indefinite with the nominative مَرْفوع and genitive مَجْرور case, but retained in the مَنْصوب accusative, as in (see 22.2.2 on case endings):

حَضَرَ قاضٍ .

"A judge came."

قابَلْتُ قاضِياً .

"I met a judge."

ذَهَبْتُ إلىٰ قاضٍ .

"I went to a judge."

However, the *yaa'* ي is retained in all cases when the active participle occurs definite, as in:

حَضَرَ القاضي .

"The judge came."

قابَلْتُ القاضيَ .

"I met the judge"

ذَهَبْتُ إلىٰ القاضي .

"I went to the judge."

14.4   The Passive Participle إِسْم المَفْعول

As the name suggests, the passive participle إِسْم المَفْعول is derived to form the *doee* or *object* meaning of a given verb/action. This is similar to deriving the passive participle *written* from the verb *write* in English. However, this type of derivation in English involves predictable as well as unpredictable sound and spelling changes, and so can be characterized as irregular (for examples, see 13.1.1). However, unlike in English, deriving the passive participle in Arabic follows predictable sound changes with a specific pattern for each of the ten verb forms, as can be seen in the table below:

Passive participle / اِسْم المَفعول	←	Present / المُضارع	Past / الماضي	Form
مَفعول	←	يَفعَل/ يَفعِل/ يَفعُل	فَعَل/ فَعِل	I
مُفَعَّل	←	يُفَعِّل	فَعَّل	II
مُفاعَل	←	يُفاعِل	فاعَل	III
مُفعَل	←	يُفعِل	أَفعَل	IV
مُتَفَعَّل	←	يَتَفَعَّل	تَفَعَّل	V
مُتَفاعَل	←	يَتَفاعَل	تَفاعَل	VI
مُنفَعِل / مُنفَعَل	←	يَنفَعِل	اِنفَعَل	VII
مُفتَعِل / مُفتَعَل	←	يَفتَعِل	اِفتَعَل	VIII
مُفعَلّ	←	يَفعَلّ	اِفعَلّ	IX
مُستَفعَل	←	يَستَفعِل	اِستَفعَل	X

The table below gives specific examples of passive participles of Forms I–X verbs, including those belonging to sound verbs, hollow verbs, and defective verbs:

الفِعْل النّاقِص PP of defective verb	الفِعْل الأَجْوَف PP of hollow verb	الفِعْل السّالِم PP of sound verb	اِسْم المَفعول Passive participle	المُضارع Present	الماضي Past	Forms
قَضىٰ ← مَقضِيٌّ/ المَقضِيّ دَعا ← مَدعُوٌّ/ المَدعُوّ نَهىٰ ← مَنهِيٌّ/ المَنهِيّ	باعَ ← مَبيع قالَ ← مَقول نالَ ← مَنول	كَتَبَ ← مَكتوب	مَفعول	يَفعُل	فَعَل	I
سَمّىٰ ← مُسَمّىً/ المُسَمّىٰ	–	كَسَّر ← مُكَسَّر	مُفَعَّل	يُفَعِّل	فَعَّل	II
نادىٰ ← مُنادىً/ المُنادىٰ	شاهَدَ ← مُشاهَد	–	مُفاعَل	يُفاعِل	فاعَل	III
أَعطىٰ ← مُعطىً/ المُعطىٰ	أَنارَ ← مُنار	أَكرَم ← مُكرَم	مُفعَل	يُفعِل	أَفعَل	IV
تَمَنّىٰ ← مُتَمَنّىً/ المُتَمَنّىٰ	–	تَعَلَّم ← مُتَعَلَّم	مُتَفَعَّل	يَتَفَعَّل	تَفَعَّل	V
تَفادىٰ ← مُتَفادىً/ المُتَفادىٰ	تَنازَع ← مُتَنازَع	–	مُتَفاعَل	يَتَفاعَل	تَفاعَل	VI
اِنقَضىٰ ← مُنقَضٍ/ المُنقَضِي	اِنحازَ ← مُنحاز	اِنقَطَع ← مُنقَطِع	مُنفَعِل	يَنفَعِل	اِنفَعَل	VII
اِعتَدىٰ ← مُعتَدىً/ المُعتَدىٰ	اِختارَ ← مُختار	اِحتَرَق ← مُحتَرَق	مُفتَعِل	يَفتَعِل	اِفتَعَل	VIII
–	–	اِخضَرَّ → مُخضَرّ	مُفعَلّ	يَفعَلّ	اِفعَلّ	IX
اِستَثنىٰ ← مُستَثنىً/ المُستَثنىٰ	اِستَفاد ← مُستَفاد اِستَقبَل ← مُستَقبَل	اِستَفعَل ← مُستَفعَل	مُستَفعَل	يَستَفعِل	اِستَفعَل	X

14.4.1 Passive Participle Use

Passive participles in Arabic are used in the same way as any nouns (although they are mostly used as adjectives; see Chapter 15) and therefore can be used either by themselves or modified/followed by an adjective, as in:

جاءَ المَدْعُوونَ إلى الحَفْلةِ .

"The invitees came to the party."

رَأَيْتُ المَقْتولَ قَبْلَ الحادِثِ .

"I saw the murdered one before the incident."

دَخَلَ المُتَّهَمُ المِسْكينُ إلى المَحْكَمةِ .

"The poor accused one entered the court."

14.5 Nouns of Time and Place أَسْماء الزَّمان والمَكان

Nouns of time and place are usually derived from a verb to indicate the time or place of the verb/action, although the derived form is mostly used as a noun of place. A noun of time and place is derived according to a certain pattern, depending on whether the verb is Form I, any of the Forms II–X, or whether it is derived from a noun rather than a verb.

14.5.1 Nouns of Time and Place Derived from Form I Verbs

When derived from a Form I verb, the noun of time and place has the following patterns:

(a) مَفْعِل if the medial vowel of the present tense is *kasra*, as in:

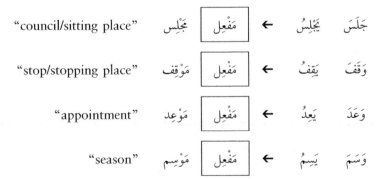

(b) مَفْعِل with a medial *yaa'* if the verb is hollow with a *yaa'* vowel, as in:

"sleeping place"	مَبِيت	مَفْعِل	←	يَبِيتُ بَاتَ
"walking place"	مَسِير	مَفْعِل	←	يَسِيرُ سَارَ
"summer place"	مَصِيف	مَفْعِل	←	يَصِيفُ صَافَ

(c) مَفْعَل if the medial vowel of the present tense is *fatHa* or *Damma*, or if the verb is defective, as in:

"playground/playing place"	مَلْعَب	مَفْعَل	←	يَلْعَبُ لَعِبَ
"swimming pool/place"	مَسْبَح	مَفْعَل	←	يَسْبَحُ سَبَحَ
"shelter"	مَلْجَأ	مَفْعَل	←	يَلْجَأُ لَجَأَ
"office desk/writing place"	مَكْتَب	مَفْعَل	←	يَكْتُبُ كَتَبَ
"entrance"	مَدْخَل	مَفْعَل	←	يَدْخُلُ دَخَلَ
"exit"	مَخْرَج	مَفْعَل	←	يَخْرُجُ خَرَجَ
"crossing"	مَعْبَر	مَفْعَل	←	يَعْبُرُ عَبَرَ
"amusement place"	مَلْهىٰ	مَفْعَل	←	يَلْهو لَها
"Winter place"	مَشْتىٰ	مَفْعَل	←	يَشْتو شَتا
"throwing range/place"	مَرْمىٰ	مَفْعَل	←	يَرْمي رَمىٰ
"pasture/grazing place"	مَرْعىٰ	مَفْعَل	←	يَرْعىٰ رَعىٰ

(d) مَفْعَل with a medial *'alif* if the verb is hollow with a root *waaw* vowel, as in:

"place"	مَكَان	مَفْعَل	←	كَانَ يَكونُ
"visiting place"	مَزَار	مَفْعَل	←	زَارَ يَزورُ
"sleeping place"	مَنَام	مَفْعَل	←	نَامَ يَنامُ

However, a few irregular nouns have the pattern مَفْعِل rather than مَفْعَل, as in:

"mosque/prostrating place"	مَسْجِد	مَفْعِل	←	سَجَدَ يَسْجُدُ
"morning/place of sunrise"	مَطْلِع الشَّمْس	مَفْعِل	←	طَلَعَ يَطْلُعُ
"west/place of sunset"	مَغْرِب	مَفْعِل	←	غَرَبَ يَغْرُبُ
"growing place"	مَنْبِت	مَفْعِل	←	نَبَتَ يَنْبُتُ

In addition, some (irregular) nouns of time and place have a *taa' marbuuTa* ة , as in:

"farm/farming place"	مَزْرَعَة	مَفْعَلَة	←	زَرَعَ يَزْرَعُ
"publishing place"	مَطْبَعَة	مَفْعَلَة	←	طَبَعَ يَطْبَعُ
"burial place/cemetery"	مَقْبَرَة	مَفْعَلَة	←	قَبَرَ يَقْبُرُ
"school/studying place"	مَدْرَسَة	مَفْعَلَة	←	دَرَسَ يَدْرُسُ
"library"	مَكْتَبَة	مَفْعَلَة	←	كَتَبَ يَكْتُبُ

14.5.2 Nouns of Time and Place Derived from Forms II–X Verbs

When derived from any of Forms II–X verbs, the noun of time and place has the identical pattern of the passive participle (see 14.4 above), as in:

"mosque/praying place"	مُصَلًّى	مُفَعَّل	←	يُصَلِّي	صَلَّى	II
"park/excursion place"	مُتَنَزَّه	مُتَفَعَّل	←	يَتَنَزَّهُ	تَنَزَّهَ	V
"turning place"	مُنْعَطَف	مُنْفَعَل	←	يَنْعَطِفُ	اِنْعَطَفَ	VII
"parting place"	مُفْتَرَق	مُفْتَعَل	←	يَفْتَرِقُ	اِفْتَرَقَ	VIII
"hospital/healing place"	مُسْتَشْفًى	مُسْتَفْعَل	←	يَسْتَشْفِي	اِسْتَشْفَى	X

14.5.3 Nouns of Time and Place Derived from Nouns

A noun of time and place can be derived from a noun with the pattern of مَفْعَلَة to indicate the place where the noun is found in quantity, as in:

"cow farm"	مَبْقَرَة	مَفْعَلَة	←	بَقَر
"fish place"	مَسْمَكَة	مَفْعَلَة	←	سَمَك
"meat place"	مَلْحَمَة	مَفْعَلَة	←	لَحْم
"lion land"	مَأْسَدَة	مَفْعَلَة	←	أَسَد

14.6　Nouns of Instrument إسْم الآلَة

As the name suggests, nouns of instrument إسْم الآلَة are nouns derived from the verb whereby the meaning of the verb/action is converted into a noun to indicate the name of the instrument of that verb/action. Nouns of instrument fit into one of seven patterns, as follows:

مِقْوَد	مِشْرَط	مِبْرَد	مِثْقَب	مِلْقَط	مِفْعَل
"steering wheel"	"cutter"	"rasp"	"drill"	"pincers"	
مِرْوَحَة	مِلْعَقَة	مِطْبَعَة	مِكْنَسَة	مِطْرَقَة	مِفْعَلَة
"fan"	"spoon"	"printer"	"sweeper"	"hammer"	
ميزان	مِسْمار	مِجْداف	مِفْتاح	مِنْشار	مِفْعال
"scale"	"nail"	"oar"	"key"	"seesaw"	
سَيّارَة	ثَلّاجَة	دَرّاجَة	عَبّارَة	غَسّالَة	فَعّالَة
"car"	"refrigerator"	"bicycle"	"ferry"	"washer"	
حِجاب	رِباط	حِزام	لِجام	شِراع	فِعال
"scarf"	"lace"	"belt"	"bridle"	"sail"	
حاسِبَة	ناقِلَة	سارِيَة	رافِعة	باخِرَة	فاعِلَة
"calculator"	"carrier"	"flagpole"	"crane"	"steamboat"	
حاسوب	ساطور	خازوق	ماعون	تابوت	فاعول
"computer"	"cleaver"	"stake/pole"	"pot"	"coffin"	

Note: There are many nouns of instrument that are irregular and do not fit any of the above patterns, as in:

شَوْكَة	سِكّين	حَبْل	مُنْخُل	سَيْف	فَأْس
"fork"	"knife"	"rope"	"strainer"	"sword"	"axe"

دَلْو	مِشْط	بَكَرَة	ساعَة	إِبْرَة	قَلَم
"bucket"	"comb"	"pulley"	"watch/clock"	"needle"	"pen"

14.7 Nouns of Once اِسْم المَرَّة

As the name suggests, nouns of once اِسْم المَرَّة are nouns derived from the verb/action to indicate that the verb/action takes place only once. This is a subtype of المَفْعول المُطْلَق (see Chapter 12). The derivation of these nouns are subject to one of three rules:

14.7.1 Nouns of Once Derived from Form I Verbs

Nouns of once of Form I verbs are derived on the pattern of فَعْلَة , as in:

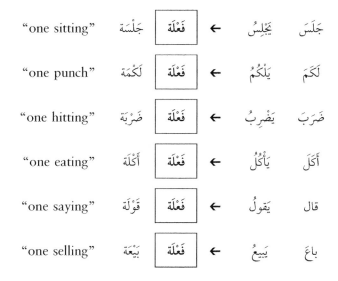

"one sitting"	جَلْسَة	فَعْلَة	←	جَلَسَ يَجْلِسُ
"one punch"	لَكْمَة	فَعْلَة	←	لَكَمَ يَلْكُمُ
"one hitting"	ضَرْبَة	فَعْلَة	←	ضَرَبَ يَضرِبُ
"one eating"	أَكْلَة	فَعْلَة	←	أَكَلَ يَأْكُلُ
"one saying"	قَوْلَة	فَعْلَة	←	قال يَقولُ
"one selling"	بَيْعَة	فَعْلَة	←	باعَ يَبيعُ

جَلَسْتُ مَعَهُ جَلْسَةً .

"I sat with him one sitting."

لَكَمَهُ لَكْمَةً .

"He punched him a punch."

14.7.2 Nouns of Once Derived from Forms II–X Verbs

Nouns of once of any of Forms II–X verbs are almost identical to verbal nouns مَصْدَر of the verb, subject to two rules:

(a) *taa' marbuuTa* ــة is added to the verbal noun (if it does not have it), as in:

II حَرَّكَ يُحَرِّكُ ← تَفْعِيل تَحْرِيك + ـة = تَحْرِيكَة "one moving"

VII انْطَلَقَ يَنْطَلِق ← انْفِعَال انْطِلاق + ـة = انْطِلاقَة "one darting"

VIII الْتَفَتَ يَلْتَفِتُ ← افْتِعَال الْتِفات + ـة = الْتِفاتَة "one turning"

انْطَلَقَ المُتَسابِقونَ انْطِلاقَةً .
"The sprinters darted a darting."

(b) the word واحِدَة "once/one time" is added if the verbal noun already ends with *taa' marbuuTa* ــة so that the noun of once is distinguished from the verbal noun, as in:

III شاهَدَ يُشاهِدُ ← مُشاهَدَة مُشاهَدَة + واحِدَة = مُشاهَدَة واحِدَة "one viewing"

X اسْتَراحَ يَسْتَريحُ ← اسْتِراحَة اسْتِراحَة + واحِدَة = اسْتِراحَة واحِدَة "one resting/break"

اسْتَرَحْنا بَعْدَ التَّمْرِينِ اسْتِراحَةً واحِدَةً .
"We rested after the exercise one resting."

شاهَدْنا الفيلمَ مُشاهَدَةً واحِدَةً .
"We viewed the film one viewing."

Note: A noun of once اسْم المَرَّة differs from اسْم الهَيْئَة "a noun of manner" (another subtype of المَفْعول المُطْلَق) which is derived from Form I verbs on the pattern of فِعْلَة and rarely from derived verbs. The noun of manner is always modified by a noun or adjective to indicate the manner of the verb (see also Chapter 12 on adverb of emphasis/cognate accusative as another way that conveys the same meaning), as in:

جَلَسَ   يَجْلِسُ   ←   فِعْلَة   جِلْسَة   "a sitting"

قَتَل   يَقْتُل   ←   فِعْلَة   قِتْلَة   "a killing"

وَقَفَ   يَقِفُ   ←   فِعْلَة   وِقْفَة   "a standing"

جَلَسَ جِلْسَةَ المُتَواضِعِ .
"He sat a humble sitting."

وَقَفَ نُجاهَ القَضِيَّةِ وِقْفَةً مُشَرَّفَةً .
"He stood/took towards the case an honorable stance."

اِلْتَفَتَ اِلْتِفاتَةَ المُتَكَبِّرِ .
"He turned his head the turning of the arrogant."

Note: Finally, even though a noun of once indicates one time, nouns of once can occur in the dual and the plural, as in:

جَلَسَ يَجْلِسُ   ←   فَعْلَة   جَلْسَة   "2 sittings" جَلْسَتانِ   جَلَسات "sittings"

لَكَمَ يَلْكُمُ   ←   فَعْلَة   لَكْمَة   "2 punches" لَكْمَتانِ   لَكَمات "punches"

أَكَلَ يَأْكُلُ   ←   فَعْلَة   أَكْلَة   "2 meals" أَكْلَتانِ   أَكَلات "meals"

شاهَدَ يُشاهِدُ   ←   مُفاعَلَة   مُشاهَدَة   "2 viewings" مُشاهَدَتانِ   مُشاهَدات "viewings"

وَجَّهَ المُلاكِمُ إلىٰ خَصْمِهِ ثلاثَ لَكَماتٍ قَوِيَّةٍ .
"The boxer handed his opponents three strong punches."

يَأْكُلُ الطُّلّابُ أَكْلَتينِ في الجامِعَةِ يَوْمِيّاً .
"The students eat two meals at the university every day."

14.8 Derived Abstract Nouns المَصْدَر الصَّناعيّ

Derived abstract nouns المَصْدَر الصَّناعيّ are derived from other (non-derived) nouns. They are derived by adding a geminate يّ [yy] and a *taa' marbuuTa* ـة to (1) un-derived nouns, (2) proper nouns, and derived nouns, including (3) active participles, (4) passive participles, (5) verbal nouns, and (6) the comparative form أَفْعَل, as below (for more on the comparative forms, see Chapter 15):

إِنْسانِيَّة = ـة + يّ + إِنْسان		non-derived noun
"humanity"　　　　　　　"a human being"		
عَبّاسِيَّة = ـة + يّ + عَبّاس		proper noun
"Abbasid"　　　　　　　"Abbas"		
جاهِلِيَّة = ـة + يّ + جاهِل		active participle
"ignorance"　　　　　　"ignorant"		
مَسْؤولِيَّة = ـة + يّ + مَسْؤول		passive participle
"responsibility"　　　　"responsible"		
اِشْتِراكِيَّة = ـة + يّ + اِشْتِراك		verbal noun
"socialism"　　　　　　"participation"		
أَكْثَرِيَّة = ـة + يّ + أَكْثَر		comparative form
"majority"　　　　　　　"more"		

14.9   The Diminutive Noun الإسْم المُصَغَّر

A diminutive noun الإسْم المُصَغَّر is derived (from a noun) through a process referred to as التَّصْغير "making smaller." Arabic has three main patterns for the diminutive: one pattern is specialized for triliteral root-based words, another for quadriliteral root-based words, and a third for quadriliteral root-based words with a medial long vowel, as follows:

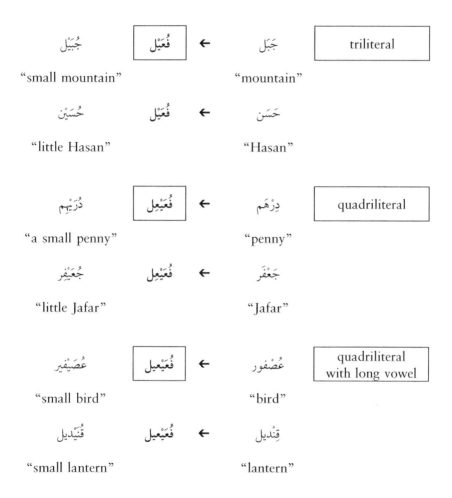

جُبَيْل   فُعَيْل ←   جَبَل   triliteral

"small mountain"   "mountain"

حُسَيْن   فُعَيْل ←   حَسَن

"little Hasan"   "Hasan"

دُرَيْهِم   فُعَيْعِل ←   دِرْهَم   quadriliteral

"a small penny"   "penny"

جُعَيْفِر   فُعَيْعِل ←   جَعْفَر

"little Jafar"   "Jafar"

عُصَيْفِير   فُعَيْعِيل ←   عُصْفور   quadriliteral with long vowel

"small bird"   "bird"

قُنَيْديل   فُعَيْعِيل ←   قِنْديل

"small lantern"   "lantern"

In addition, certain sub-rules are followed when deriving the diminutive, the most important of which are the following:

(a)   endings such as the feminine and number suffixes are preserved when deriving the diminutive:

لُقَيْمَة	لُقْمَة
"small bite"	"a bite"
حُمَيْراء	حَمْراء
"small red F"	"red F"
كُتَيِّبانِ	كِتابانِ
"two small books"	"two books"
عُثَيْمان	عُثْمان
"little Uthman M"	"Uthman M"

(b)   triliteral root-based words that are feminine and do not contain a feminine suffix receive a *taa' marbuuTa* ـة after the diminutive form is derived:

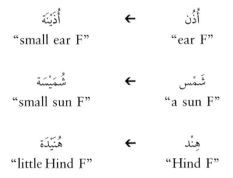

أُذَيْنَة	أُذُن
"small ear F"	"ear F"
شُمَيْسَة	شَمْس
"small sun F"	"a sun F"
هُنَيْدَة	هِنْد
"little Hind F"	"Hind F"

(c)   the last consonant of a quinqueliteral root-based word is dropped:

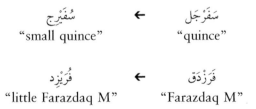

سُفَيْرِج	سَفَرْجَل
"small quince"	"quince"
فُرَيْزِد	فَرَزْدَق
"little Farazdaq M"	"Farazdaq M"

(d) if a word contains an extra 'alif in second position, such as that belonging to the active participle of فاعِل , or the 'alif's underlying root vowel is a *waaw*, then the 'alif is converted into a *waaw*:

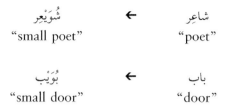

شُوَيْعِر	←	شاعِر
"small poet"		"poet"

بُوَيْب	←	باب
"small door"		"door"

(e) if a word contains an 'alif in second position whose underlying root vowel is a *yaa'*, then the 'alif is converted into a *yaa'*:

نُيَيْب	←	ناب
"small canine tooth"		"canine tooth"

(f) if a word contains a *yaa'* in second position, then the *yaa'* is retained:

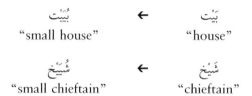

بُيَيْت	←	بَيْت
"small house"		"house"

شُيَيْخ	←	شَيْخ
"small chieftain"		"chieftain"

(g) except for a few rare words, diminutive words receive the sound feminine (in feminine or non-human nouns) and sound masculine plural endings, even though their non-diminutive plural forms are irregular/broken:

كُوَيْتِبون	←	كُوَيْتِب	كُتّاب / كاتِبون ←	كاتِب
"lesser writers M"		"lesser writer"	"writers"	"writer"

كُوَيْتِبات	←	كُوَيْتِبَة	كاتِبات ←	كاتِبة
"lesser writers F"		"lesser writer F"	"writers F"	"write F"

شُوَيْعِرون	←	شُوَيْعِر	شُعَراء ←	شاعِر
"lesser poets M"		"lesser poet"	"poets"	"poet"

لُقَيْمات	←	لُقَيْمَة	لُقَم ←	لُقْمَة
"few small bites"		"small bite"	"bites"	"bite"

14.9.1   Use of the Diminutive

The diminutive is used to express many meanings, including (1) scorn, as in شُوَيْعِر "lesser poet"; (2) endearment, as in هُنَيْدَة "little/young Hind"; (3) small size, as in كُتَيِّب "a small book"; (4), lesser quantity, as in بِضْع لُقَيْمات "few small bites"; and (5) short duration, as in قُبَيْلَ الظُّهْر "a short time before Noon" or بُعَيْدَ الظُّهْر "a short time after Noon."

Note: ambiguity may result from use of the diminutive whether for scorn or endearment, but the context clarifies the intended meaning.

14.10   The Five Nouns الأَسْماء الخَمْسَة

Arabic has five words referred to as الأَسْماء الخَمْسَة "the five nouns." Unlike other nouns in the singular (see also Chapter 2), they have distinct مَرْفوع nominative, مَنْصوب accusative, and مَجْرور genitive endings when they occur within an إضافة 'iDaafa phrase – whether they are followed by a noun or a possessive pronoun suffix, except for the first-person possessive pronoun, as in:

	Genitive	Accusative	Nominative
"father"	أَبي	أَبا	أَبو
"brother"	أَخي	أَخا	أَخو
"father-in-law"	حَمي	حَما	حَمو
"owner of"	ذي	ذا	ذو
"mouth"	في	فا	فو

حَضَرَ أَبوكَ / أَخوكَ / حَموكَ .
"Your father/brother/father-in-law came."

قابَلْتُ أَباكَ / أَخاكَ / حَماكَ .
"I met your father/brother/father-in-law."

سَلَّمْتُ عَلىٰ أَبيكَ / أَخيكَ / حَميكَ .
"I shook hands with your father/brother/father-in-law."

هٰذا أَخو صَديقي .
"This is my friend's brother."

قابَلْتُ أَخا صَديقي .
"I met my friend's brother."

سَلَّمْتُ عَلىٰ أَخي صَديقي .
"I shook hands with my friend's brother."

Note: When the five nouns do not occur within an إضافة *'iDaafa* phrase or when they occur with the first-person possessive pronoun ي "my," they are treated as any singular noun, as in:

هٰذا أَبي .
"This is my father."

لي أَخٌ واحِدٌ .
"I have one brother."

Note: Additionally the three nouns exemplified above are the most commonly used of the five nouns. The other two are rarely used and occur mostly in CA. Below are examples of ذو "owner" and فو "mouth."

هٰذا ذو مالٍ كَثيرٍ .
"This is an owner of a lot of money."

قابَلْتُ ذا مالٍ كَثيرٍ .
"I met an owner of a lot of money."

سَلَّمْتُ عَلىٰ ذي مالٍ كَثيرٍ .
"I shook hands with an owner of a lot of money."

فوكَ كَبيرٌ .
"Your mouth is big."

لِماذا تُغَطّي فاكَ ؟
"Why are you covering your mouth?"

ماذا حَدَثَ لِفيكَ ؟
"What happened to your mouth?"

14.11   Summary

This chapter discussed the main classes and patterns of Arabic nouns. Remember:

- Arabic nouns belong to two main classes: non-derived and derived
- non-derived nouns refer to names of entities, things, or objects, whether abstract or concrete
- every verb in Arabic has a verbal noun or *gerund*, making the verb a noun
- while verbal nouns of Form I verbs are irregular and therefore learned as individual words (together with the past- and present-tense forms of the verb), verbal nouns of all other verbs are regular, and patterns can be learned instead as mnemonic devices
- unlike in English, active and passive participles of all verb forms in Arabic are regular, and follow specific patterns that can be learned to make it easier to remember the correct form or identify the word
- nouns of time or place are derived from a verb which indicates the time or place of the verb/action and have regular patterns/forms that can be learned to make it easier to remember the correct form or identify the word
- while many nouns of instrument do not follow a regular pattern, many others follow one of seven patterns that make it easier to learn and/ or identify such words
- derived abstract nouns are a special class of nouns derived from non-derived nouns to form abstract nouns
- Arabic employs diminutive nouns following three main patterns to express additional meanings, such as scorn, endearment, small size, less quantity, and short duration
- Arabic has a class of five nouns that behave like any other nouns when used by themselves, but which have three distinct endings (مَرْفوع nominative, مَنْصوب accusative, and مَجْرور genitive) when used in an إضافة *’iDaafa* phrase (i.e., when followed by a noun or any possessive pronoun except for the first-person singular possessive pronoun).

15

The Adjective الصِّفَة

This chapter discusses the main categories or classes of Arabic adjective, called in Arabic الصِّفَة "the description." Adjectives in Arabic are derived from verbs according to certain patterns, some of which are regular and some irregular. Certain patterns have specific meanings. The chapter covers the following:

- main adjective patterns, their meanings, and use
- color adjectives
- the comparative and superlative forms of adjectives
- active participles
- passive participles
- relative adjectives.

15.1   Main Adjective Patterns

Adjective patterns are derived from Form I verbs فَعَلَ , فَعِلَ , and فَعُلَ (for more on verb forms, see Chapter 13). These patterns are all irregular (with irregular plural forms as most plural forms in Arabic), and each may be derived from more than one form (i.e., from فَعَلَ , فَعِلَ , or فَعُلَ). At least 14 forms/patterns can be derived. Knowing or just being familiar with these patterns may be useful for learning the adjectives or understanding how they are derived, as well as their meanings.

Modern Standard Arabic Grammar: A Learner's Guide, First Edition.
© 2011 Mohammad T. Alhawary. Published 2011 by Blackwell Publishing Ltd.

The following are 14 available adjective patterns with examples and
the types of verbs from which they are derived (adjective patterns appear
in boxes):

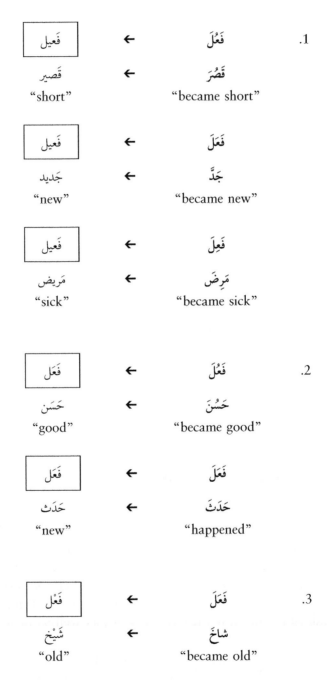

فَعيل ←	فَعُلَ	.1
قَصير ←	قَصُرَ	
"short"	"became short"	

فَعيل ←	فَعَلَ
جَديد ←	جَدَّ
"new"	"became new"

فَعيل ←	فَعِلَ
مَريض ←	مَرِضَ
"sick"	"became sick"

فَعَل ←	فَعُلَ	.2
حَسَن ←	حَسُنَ	
"good"	"became good"	

فَعَل ←	فَعَلَ
حَدَث ←	حَدَثَ
"new"	"happened"

فَعْل ←	فَعَلَ	.3
شَيْخ ←	شاخَ	
"old"	"became old"	

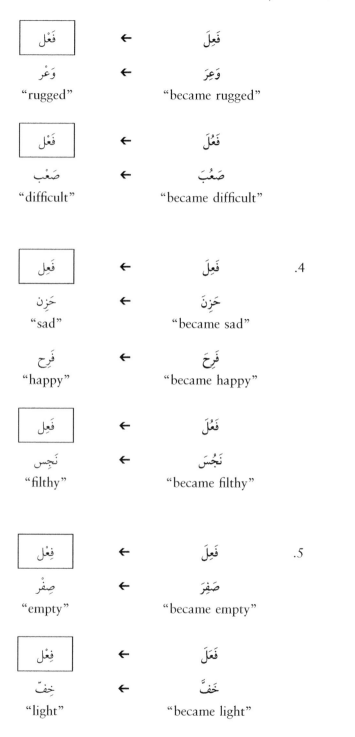

فَعْل ← فَعِلَ

وَعْر ← وَعِرَ
"rugged"   "became rugged"

فَعْل ← فَعُلَ

صَعْب ← صَعُبَ
"difficult"   "became difficult"

فَعِل ← فَعِلَ   4.

حَزِن ← حَزِنَ
"sad"   "became sad"

فَرِح ← فَرِحَ
"happy"   "became happy"

فَعِل ← فَعُلَ

نَجِس ← نَجُسَ
"filthy"   "became filthy"

فِعْل ← فَعِلَ   5.

صِفْر ← صَفِرَ
"empty"   "became empty"

فِعْل ← فَعَلَ

خِفّ ← خَفَّ
"light"   "became light"

6.

$$\boxed{\text{فُعْل}} \leftarrow \text{فَعُلَ}$$

صُلْب ← صَلُبَ
"hard"   "became hard"

$$\boxed{\text{فُعْل}} \leftarrow \text{فَعَلَ}$$

سُخْن ← سَخَنَ
"hot"   "became hot"

7.

$$\boxed{\text{فُعُل}} \leftarrow \text{فَعُلَ}$$

جُنُب ← جَنُبَ
"impure"   "became impure"

8.

$$\boxed{\text{فاعِل}} \leftarrow \text{فَعَلَ}$$

عارِف ← عَرَفَ
"knowledgeable"   "knew"

$$\boxed{\text{فاعِل}} \leftarrow \text{فَعِلَ}$$

ناشِط ← نَشِطَ
"active"   "became active"

$$\boxed{\text{فاعِل}} \leftarrow \text{فَعُلَ}$$

كامِل ← كَمُلَ
"perfect"   "became perfect"

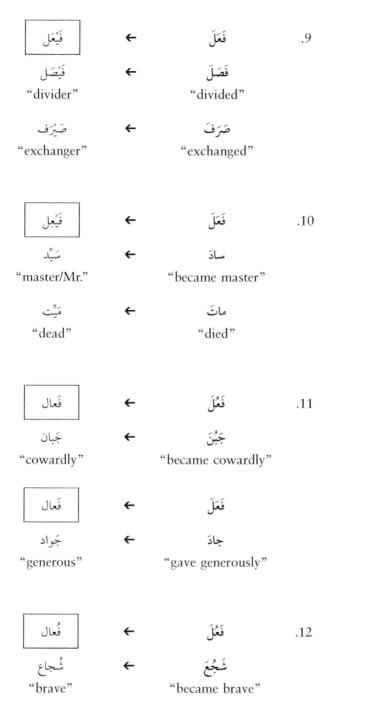

9. فَعَلَ ← فَيْعَل

فَصَلَ ← فَيْصَل
"divided"   "divider"

ضَرَفَ ← صَيْرَف
"exchanged"   "exchanger"

10. فَعَلَ ← فَيْعِل

سادَ ← سَيِّد
"became master"   "master/Mr."

ماتَ ← مَيِّت
"died"   "dead"

11. فَعُلَ ← فَعال

جَبُنَ ← جَبان
"became cowardly"   "cowardly"

فَعَلَ ← فَعال

جادَ ← جَواد
"gave generously"   "generous"

12. فَعُلَ ← فُعال

شَجُعَ ← شُجاع
"became brave"   "brave"

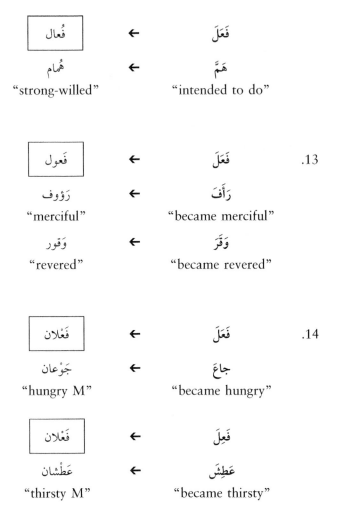

فُعَال   ←   فَعَلَ

هُمَام   ←   هَمَّ
"strong-willed"   "intended to do"

.13   فَعَلَ   ←   فَعُول

رَأَفَ   ←   رَؤُوف
"became merciful"   "merciful"

وَقَرَ   ←   وَقُور
"became revered"   "revered"

.14   فَعَلَ   ←   فَعْلان

جاعَ   ←   جَوْعان
"became hungry"   "hungry M"

فَعِلَ   ←   فَعْلان

عَطِشَ   ←   عَطْشان
"became thirsty"   "thirsty M"

The last form فَعْلان is specialized for the masculine. The feminine form is either فَعْلى or فَعْلانَة, as follows:

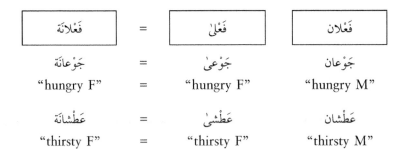

فَعْلان   فَعْلى   =   فَعْلانَة

جَوْعان   جَوْعى   =   جَوْعانَة
"hungry M"   "hungry F"   =   "hungry F"

عَطْشان   عَطْشى   =   عَطْشانَة
"thirsty M"   "thirsty F"   =   "thirsty F"

In other words, the latter form (which is the more common of the two in MSA) has the *taa' marbuuTa*, which is the feminine ending for all 14 adjective forms listed above and most adjective forms in general (see also Chapter 2 and the sections immediately below).

15.1.1 Meanings of Adjective Patterns

Adjective patterns have two main distinctions – permanent adjectives and temporary adjectives. The latter is conveyed through the pattern فَعْلان (masculine) → فَعْلانَة / فَعْلى (feminine) as opposed to the former, for example, the pattern فَعِيل (masculine) → فَعِيلَة (feminine) as in:

Permanent	فَعِيل:	Temporary	فَعْلان:
"tall"	طَويل	"hungry"	جَوْعان
"short"	قَصير	"tired"	تَعْبان
"old"	قَديم	"drunk"	سَكْران

However, apart from the pattern فَعْلان (see also the pattern for color and bodily defect/beauty adjectives in the section immediately below), the distinction between temporary and permanent meanings ultimately depends on the meaning of the root from which verbs and adjectives are derived. Therefore, while the pattern فَعِيل may convey a permanent adjectival meaning, as in the above examples, other words conforming to the same pattern may have a temporary meaning, such as مَريض "sick" and سَريع "fast."

15.2 Color and Bodily Defect/Beauty Adjective Patterns

Adjectives for colors, complexions, and bodily defects/beauties follow a specific pattern: أَفْعَل for (singular) masculine and فَعْلاء for (singular) feminine. In addition, the masculine form has a regular plural pattern فُعْل, whereas the dual (for both the feminine and masculine) and plural feminine follow the regular rules (see also Chapter 2 on the dual and plural, especially words ending with the feminine suffix اء [aa']). Below are common color, complexion, and bodily defect/beauty adjectives in the singular, dual, and plural, and in both the masculine and feminine.

أَفْعَل	أَفْعَلان DM	فُعْل PM	فَعْلاء	فَعْلاوانِ DF	فَعْلاوات PF	
أَخْضَر	أَخْضَرانِ	خُضْر	خَضْراء	خَضْراوانِ	خَضْراوات	"green"
أَزْرَق	أَزْرَقانِ	زُرْق	زَرْقاء	زَرْقاوانِ	زَرْقاوات	"blue"
أَصْفَر	أَصْفَرانِ	صُفْر	صَفْراء	صَفْراوانِ	صَفْراوات	"yellow"
أَحْمَر	أَحْمَرانِ	حُمْر	حَمْراء	حَمْراوانِ	حَمْراوات	"red"
أَسْوَد	أَسْوَدانِ	سُود	سَوْداء	سَوْداوانِ	سَوْداوات	"black"
أَبْيَض	أَبْيَضانِ	بِيض	بَيْضاء	بَيْضاوانِ	بَيْضاوات	"white"

أَفْعَل	أَفْعَلان DM	فُعْل PM	فَعْلاء	فَعْلاوانِ DF	فَعْلاوات PF	
أَشْقَر	أَشْقَرانِ	شُقْر	شَقْراء	شَقْراوانِ	شَقْراوات	"blonde"
أَسْمَر	أَسْمَرانِ	سُمْر	سَمْراء	سَمْراوانِ	سَمْراوات	"brunette"
أَبْرَص	أَبْرَصانِ	بُرْص	بَرْصاء	بَرْصاوانِ	بَرْصاوات	"leprous"
أَغْبَر	أَغْبَرانِ	غُبْر	غَبْراء	غَبْراوانِ	غَبْراوات	"dusty"

أَفْعَل	أَفْعَلان DM	فُعْل PM	فَعْلاء	فَعْلاوانِ DF	فَعْلاوات PF	
أَطْرَش	أَطْرَشانِ	طُرْش	طَرْشاء	طَرْشاوانِ	طَرْشاوات	"deaf"
أَصَمّ	أَصَمّانِ	صُمّ	صَمّاء	صَمّاوانِ	صَمّاوات	"deaf"
أَبْكَم	أَبْكَمانِ	بُكْم	بَكْماء	بَكْماوانِ	بَكْماوات	"mute"
أَعْمىٰ	أَعْمَيانِ	عُمِيّ	عَمْياء	عَمْياوانِ	عَمْياوات	"blind"
أَصْلَع	أَصْلَعانِ	صُلْع	صَلْعاء	صَلْعاوانِ	صَلْعاوات	"bald"
أَكْحَل	أَكْحَلانِ	كُحْل	كَحْلاء	كَحْلاوانِ	كَحْلاوات	"black-eyed"
أَحْوَر	أَحْوَرانِ	حُور	حَوْراء	حَوْراوانِ	حَوْراوات	"intensely white and black-eyed"
أَهْيَف	أَهْيَفانِ	هِيف	هَيْفاء	هَيْفاوانِ	هَيْفاوات	"slender/slim"

Note: Adjectives that do not belong to basic colors do not follow the أَفْعَل (for singular masculine) and فَعْلاء (for singular feminine) patterns. Rather, they follow rules of الإِسْم المَنْسوب relative adjective where the يّ [yy] suffix is added to the noun to which the color is attributed (see 15.7 below on relative adjectives). Below are examples of common (non-basic) color adjectives.

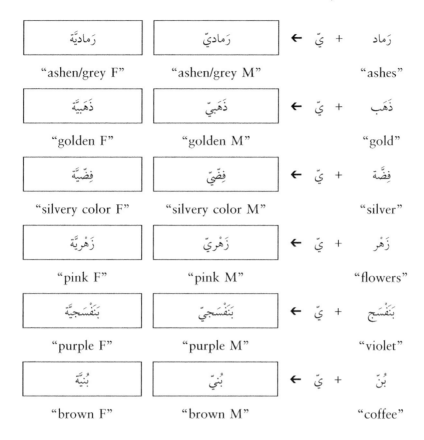

رَمادِيَّة	رَمادِيّ	← يّ +	رَماد
"ashen/grey F"	"ashen/grey M"		"ashes"
ذَهَبِيَّة	ذَهَبِيّ	← يّ +	ذَهَب
"golden F"	"golden M"		"gold"
فِضِّيَّة	فِضِّيّ	← يّ +	فِضَّة
"silvery color F"	"silvery color M"		"silver"
زَهْرِيَّة	زَهْرِيّ	← يّ +	زَهْر
"pink F"	"pink M"		"flowers"
بَنَفْسَجِيَّة	بَنَفْسَجِيّ	← يّ +	بَنَفْسَج
"purple F"	"purple M"		"violet"
بُنِّيَّة	بُنِّيّ	← يّ +	بُنّ
"brown F"	"brown M"		"coffee"

15.3 Adjective Use

In addition to the attributive use of adjectives within the different noun–adjective and إضافة ’iDaafa adjective phrases (see Chapter 3), as well as adjective predicate use within the nominal sentence (see Chapter 4), adjectives can be used as nouns if they occur definite and without being modified/followed by an adjective, as in:

الجَديدُ لَيْسَ دائماً أحْسَنَ مِنَ القَديمِ .
"The new (thing) is not always better than the old (thing)."

هذا الفيلمُ لَيْسَ مُناسِباً للصِّغارِ .
"This movie is not suitable for the young (children)."

هذا الفيلمُ لِلْكِبارِ فَقَط .
"This movie is for the grown-ups only."

15.4   The Comparative and Superlative اِسْم التَّفْضيل

15.4.1   The Comparative Form أَفْعَل

To express a comparison between two things, the comparative form أَفْعَل
of the adjective is used. That is, the adjective is modified to fit the pattern
أَفْعَل , as in the examples below (see also Chapter 2 on the notion of root
and pattern).

"shorter"	أَقْصَر	أَفْعَل	←	"short"	قَصير
"taller"	أَطْوَل	أَفْعَل	←	"tall"	طَويل
"older"	أَقْدَم	أَفْعَل	←	"old"	قَديم
"newer"	أَجَدّ	أَفْعَل	←	"new"	جَديد
"bigger"	أَكْبَر	أَفْعَل	←	"big"	كَبير
"smaller"	أَصْغَر	أَفْعَل	←	"small"	صَغير
"more beautiful"	أَجْمَل	أَفْعَل	←	"beautiful"	جَميل
"uglier"	أَقْبَح	أَفْعَل	←	"ugly"	قَبيح
"colder"	أَبْرَد	أَفْعَل	←	"cold"	بارِد
"hotter"	أَحَرّ	أَفْعَل	←	"hot"	حارّ
"braver"	أَشْجَع	أَفْعَل	←	"brave"	شُجاع
"more cowardly"	أَجْبَن	أَفْعَل	←	"cowardly"	جَبان
"more difficult"	أَصْعَب	أَفْعَل	←	"difficult"	صَعْب

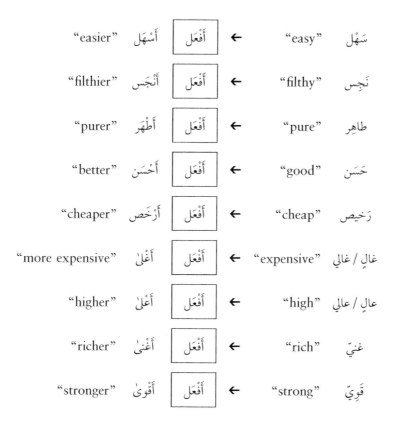

"easier" أَسْهَل	أَفْعَل	←	"easy" سَهْل
"filthier" أَنْجَس	أَفْعَل	←	"filthy" نَجِس
"purer" أَطْهَر	أَفْعَل	←	"pure" طاهِر
"better" أَحْسَن	أَفْعَل	←	"good" حَسَن
"cheaper" أَرْخَص	أَفْعَل	←	"cheap" رَخيص
"more expensive" أَغْلىٰ	أَفْعَل	←	"expensive" غالٍ / غالي
"higher" أَعْلىٰ	أَفْعَل	←	"high" عالٍ / عالي
"richer" أَغْنىٰ	أَفْعَل	←	"rich" غَنيّ
"stronger" أَقْوىٰ	أَفْعَل	←	"strong" قَويّ

Note: As shown above, in adjectives, including defective adjectives (see also 14.3), ending with the long vowel ي [ii] or the geminate يّ [yy], these change into ىٰ [aa] in the comparative form.

In addition, the comparative adjectival structure requires the use of the preposition مِنْ "from/than," with the pattern أَفْعَل used for both masculine and feminine, as in:

أَحْمَد أَقْصَرُ مِنْ سالِمٍ .
"Ahmad is shorter than Salem."

جامِعَةُ ميشغان أَكْبَرُ مِنْ جامِعَةِ جورجتاون .
"The University of Michigan is bigger than Georgetown University."

فَصْلي أَصْغَرُ مِنْ فَصْلِك .
"My classroom is smaller than your classroom."

سَميرَة أَجْمَلُ مِنْ لَيْلىٰ .
"Samira is more beautiful than Layla."

15.4.2 The Superlative Forms أَفْعَل and فُعْلى

Superlative comparisons can be expressed in one of two ways. First, the superlative form is used indefinite, where both the superlative form and the noun following it are used as an إضافة *'iDaafa* phrase (see also Chapter 3). In this case, the pattern أَفْعَل is used irrespective of gender and number agreement, but the noun following it can be either indefinite (in the singular, dual, or plural) or definite (in the plural), as in:

هُوَ أَصْغَرُ الطُّلَّابِ .	=	هُوَ أَصْغَرُ طالِبٍ .
"He is the youngest of the students."		"He is the youngest student."
هُما أَصْغَرُ الطُّلَّابِ .	=	هُما أَصْغَرُ طالِبَيْنِ .
"They both (M) are the youngest of the students."		"They both (M) are the youngest students."
هُم أَصْغَرُ الطُّلَّابِ .	=	هُم أَصْغَرُ طُلَّابٍ .
"They (M) are the youngest of the students."		"They (M) are the youngest students."
هِيَ أَصْغَرُ الطَّالِباتِ .	=	هِيَ أَصْغَرُ طالِبَةٍ .
"She is the youngest of the students."		"She is the youngest student."
هُما أَصْغَرُ الطَّالِباتِ .	=	هُما أَصْغَرُ طالِبَتَيْنِ .
"They both (F) are the youngest of the students."		"They both (F) are the youngest students."
هُنَّ أَصْغَرُ الطَّالِباتِ .	=	هُنَّ أَصْغَرُ طالِباتٍ .
"They (F) are the youngest of the students."		"They (F) are the youngest students."

Second, although not as common as the first use, the superlative form can be used definite, where both the superlative form and the noun following it are used as a noun-adjective phrase (see also Chapter 3). In this case, the pattern أَفْعَل is used for the masculine and must agree in number with the noun preceding it, and the pattern فُعْلى is used for the feminine and must agree in number with the noun preceding it, as in:

هُوَ الطّالِبُ الأَصْغَرُ .

"He is the youngest student."

هُما الطّالِبانِ الأَصْغَرانِ .

"They both (M) are the two youngest students."

هُم الطُّلَّابُ الأَصْغَرونَ .

"They (M) are the youngest students."

هِيَ الطّالِبَةُ الصُّغْرىٰ .

"She is the youngest student."

هُما الطّالِبَتانِ الصُّغْريانِ .

"They both (F) are the two youngest students."

هُنَّ الطّالِباتُ الصُّغْرياتُ .

"They (F) are the youngest students."

Note: There are two notable exceptions of the comparative/superlative form أَفْعَل . These are خَيْر "better/more righteous" and شَرّ "worse/more evil," which should have been أَخْيَر and أَشَرّ , respectively. However, the two words have also two synonymous words that follow the pattern, as in:

العِلْمُ أفضَلُ مِنَ الجَهْل .	=	العِلْمُ خَيْرٌ مِنَ الجَهْل .
"Knowledge is better than ignorance."	=	"Knowledge is better than ignorance."
الظُّلْمُ أَسْوَأُ مِنَ الجَهْل .	=	الظُّلْمُ شَرٌّ مِنَ الجَهْل .
"Injustice is worse than ignorance."	=	"Injustice is worse than ignorance."

15.4.3   The Comparative and Superlative of Derived Words

Adjectives of derived verbs, such as the active participles of the derived verb Forms II–X (see also Chapters 13–14 on derived verbs and active participles), and other derived words, such as derived abstract nouns (see Chapter 14), do not follow the أَفْعَل pattern rule. Rather, a comparative word such as أَعْظَم "more," أَقَلّ "less," أَشَدّ "more intense," أَكْثَر "greater," or أَصْغَر "smaller" is used, followed by the verbal noun of the derived verb (see Chapter 14 on verbal nouns of derived verbs) or derived word, with the accusative مَنْصوب case ending. The distinction between comparative and superlative structure follows the same rules, as in the examples of adjectives/active participles of derived Forms II–X below:

العِراقُ أَكْثَرُ تَدْريساً لِلُغَةِ العَرَبِيَّةِ مِنْ تونُس .	تَدْريساً	← مُدَرِّس	II

"Iraq teaches Arabic more than Tunisia."

سوريَّةُ أَكْثَرُ البِلادِ تَدْريساً لِلُغَةِ العَرَبِيَّةِ .	تَدْريساً	← مُدَرِّس	II

"Syria is the country that teaches Arabic the most."

الكُوَيْتُ أَكْثَرُ إِنْتاجاً لِلنِّفْطِ مِن قَطَر .	إِنْتاجاً	← مُنْتِج	IV

"Kuwait produces more oil than Qatar."

السُّعودِيَّةُ أَكْثَرُ البِلادِ إِنْتاجاً لِلنِّفْط .	إِنْتاجاً	← مُنْتِج	IV

"Saudi Arabia is the country that produces oil the most."

بَريطانيا أَكْثَرُ تَقَدُّماً مِن رومانيا .	تَقَدُّماً	← مُتَقَدِّم	V

"Britain is more progressive than Romania"

الوِلاياتُ المُتَّحِدةُ أَكْثَرُ البِلادِ تَقَدُّماً .	تَقَدُّماً	← مُتَقَدِّم	V

"The USA is the most progressive country."

المازوتُ أَقَلُّ اشْتِعالاً مِنَ البِنْزين.	اِشْتِعالاً	← مُشْتَعِل	VIII

"Diesel is less flammable than gas."

المَعْدِنُ أَقَلُّ الأَشْياءِ اِشْتِعالاً .	اِشْتِعالاً	← مُشْتَعِل	VIII

"Metal is the least flammable thing."

لُبْنانُ أَقَلُّ اِسْتِخْدِاماً لِلطَّاقَةِ مِنْ كَنَدا .	اِسْتِخْداماً	← مُسْتَخْدِم	X

"Lebanon uses less energy than Canada."

جيبوتي أَقَلُّ البِلادِ اِسْتِخداماً لِلطَّاقَة .	اِسْتِخْداماً	← مُسْتَخْدِم	X

"Djibouti is the country that uses energy the least."

The comparative and superlative forms of other derived words, such as feminine abstract nouns (see Chapter 14), are expressed in the same way, as in:

والِدي أَكْثَرُ إِنْسانِيَّةً مِنْ عَمّي .

"My father is more humane than my uncle."

جَدّي أَكْثَرُ النّاسِ إِنْسانِيَّةً .
"My grandfather is the most humane (person) of all people."

أُخْتي أَكْثَرُ مَسْؤولِيَّةً مِنْ أَخي .
"My sister is more responsible than my brother."

أُسْتاذي أَكْثَرُ النّاسِ مَسْؤولِيَّةً .
"My teacher is the most responsible (person) of all people."

Note: It is similarly possible to express (by means of the verbal noun with the accusative مَنْصوب case ending) the comparative and superlative of adjectives derived from Form I verbs that are usually expressed by means of the pattern أَفْعَل , as in:

خالِد أَكْثَرُ كَرَماً مِنْ سَمير .   =   خالِد أَكْرَمُ مِنْ سَمير .
"Khalid is more generous than   =   "Khalid is more generous than
Samir."   Samir."

أَحْمَد أَكْثَرُ صَديقٍ كَرَماً .   =   أَحْمَد أَكْرَمُ صَديقٍ .
"Ahmad is the most generous   =   "Ahmad is the most generous
friend."   friend."

15.5   The Active Participle اِسْم الفاعِل

A passive participle اِسْم الفاعِل is derived to form the *doer* meaning of a given verb/action. This is similar to deriving the active participle *writer* from the verb *write* in English (see Chapter 14 on how active participles are derived). Active participles in Arabic are used in the same way as any adjective, noun (see Chapter 14), and (not as commonly in MSA) verb, such as:

(a)   an attributive adjective within a noun–adjective phrase (see also Chapter 3), as in:

الطّالِبَةُ الجالِسَةُ هُناكَ هِيَ صَديقَتي .
"The (female) student sitting there is my friend."

خَرَجَ الضّابِطُ المُناوِبُ قَبْلَ قَليل .
"The on-duty officer went out a short while ago."

(b)   a predicate adjective within a nominal/verbless sentence (see Chapter 4), as in:

والِدي واقِفٌ خارِجَ الحَديقَة .

"My father [is] standing outside the park."

والِدَتي مُسافِرَةٌ إلى المَغرِبِ غَداً .

"My mother [is] traveling to Amman."

(c)   a verb (used restrictively in the present or future tense and never in the past tense) where the noun following it functions as an object with the accusative مَنْصوب case ending (see Chapter 4), as in:

أنا شاكِرٌ فَضْلَكَ .

"I am thankful for your favor."

Note: When the active participle functions as a verb, it appears with *nunation* تَنْوين and accordingly it is distinct from its function as a noun (such as when it occurs within an إضافة *'iDaafa* phrase), and where the difference in meaning between the two is restrictively futuristic in its verbal function, as in:

هُوَ مُعَلِّمٌ الفَصْلَ غَداً .

"He is teaching the class tomorrow."

هُوَ مُعَلِّمُ الفَصْلِ .

"He is the teacher of the class."

15.6   The Passive Participle اِسْم المَفْعول

A passive participle اِسْم المَفْعول is derived to form the *doee* or *object* meaning of a given verb. This is similar to deriving the passive participle *written* from the verb *write* in English (see Chapter 14 on how passive participles are derived). Passive participles in Arabic are used as any adjective (and also as nouns, see Chapter 14), such as:

(a)   an attributive adjective within a noun–adjective phrase (see also Chapter 3), as in:

الرِّسالَةُ المَكْتوبَةُ بالإنْجليزيَّةِ مِنْ صَديقي جون .

"The letter written in English is from my friend, John."

العُمْلَةُ المُسْتَخْدَمَةُ في الأُرْدُنِّ هِيَ الدّينار .

"The currency used in Jordan is the dinar."

(b)   a predicate adjective within a nominal/verbless sentence (see Chapter 4), as in:

هٰذا البابُ مَصْنوعٌ مِنَ الحَديد .

"This door [is] made of iron."

هٰذِهِ الشِّقَّةُ مُؤَجَّرةٌ لِطالِبٍ سودانيّ .

"This apartment [is] rented to a Sudanese student."

15.7   The Relative/*nisba* Adjective الإِسْم المَنْسوب

A relative/*nisba* adjective الإِسْم المَنْسوب is formed when the adjective suffix
يّ [yy] *yaa'* with shadda is added to a noun to form an adjective attributed
or related in meaning to the noun, as in:

"Lebanese"	لُبْنانيّ	←	يّ	+	"Lebanon"	لُبْنان
"Tunisian"	تونِسيّ	←	يّ	+	"Tunisia"	تونِس
"national"	وَطَنيّ	←	يّ	+	"nation"	وَطَن
"scientific"	عِلْميّ	←	يّ	+	"knowledge"	عِلْم
"Islamic"	إِسْلاميّ	←	يّ	+	"Islam"	إِسْلام
"international"	دُوَليّ	←	يّ	+	"countries"	دُوَل
"legal"	حُقوقيّ	←	يّ	+	"rights"	حُقوق

The above is the general rule. However, there are additional rules that
apply, most important of which are:

(a)   the feminine *taa' marbuuTa* ـة [a] suffix is dropped if the noun ends
with it, as in:

"political"	سِياسيّ	←	يّ	+	"politics"	سِياسَة
"academic"	جامِعيّ	←	يّ	+	"university"	جامِعَة
"Fatimid"	فاطِميّ	←	يّ	+	"Fatima"	فاطِمَة

(b)   the final *hamza* of the feminine ـاء [*aa'*] suffix is converted into a *waaw* [w] if the noun ends with the feminine suffix, as in:

"desert-like"	صَحْراوِيّ	←	يّ	+	"desert"	صَحْراء
"blackish"	سَوْداوِيّ	←	يّ	+	"black"	سَوْداء
"blondish"	شَقْراوِيّ	←	يّ	+	"blonde"	شَقْراء

Note: Accordingly, the final *hamza* is retained if it is not part of the feminine suffix ـاء [*aa'*] (i.e., if the *hamza* is a root consonant of the word), as in:

"related to water"	مائِيّ	←	يّ	+	"water"	ماء
"medicinal"	دَوائِيّ	←	يّ	+	"medicine"	دَواء
"elementary"	اِبْتِدائِيّ	←	يّ	+	"beginning"	اِبْتِداء

(c)   a final *'alif* [aa] is converted into the sequence [a–w] if the *'alif* is preceded by two consonants within the word, as in:

"related to usury"	رِبَوِيّ	←	يّ	+	"usury"	رِبا
"stick-like"	عَصَوِيّ	←	يّ	+	"stick"	عَصا
"young"	فَتَوِيّ	←	يّ	+	"young man"	فَتىٰ

(d)   a final *'alif* [aa] is dropped if the *'alif* is preceded by more than two consonants within the word, as in:

"related to entertainment"	مَلْهِيّ	←	يّ	+	"entertainment place"	مَلْهىٰ
"Canadian"	كَنَدِيّ	←	يّ	+	"Canada"	كَنَدا
"French"	فَرَنْسِيّ	←	يّ	+	"France"	فَرَنْسا
"related to Mustafa"	مُصْطَفِيّ	←	يّ	+	"Mustafa"	مُصْطَفىٰ
"American"	أَمْرِيكِيّ	←	يّ	+	"America"	أَمْرِيكا

(e)   a final *yaa'* and *'alif* sequence يا [yaa] is dropped, as in:

"Libyan"	لِيبِيّ	←	يّ	+	"Libya"	لِيبيا
"Spanish"	إِسْبانِيّ	←	يّ	+	"Spain"	إِسْبانيا
"Nigerian"	نَيْجِيرِيّ	←	يّ	+	"Nigeria"	نَيْجِيريا

(f)   if a word consists of one consonant followed by a final *yaa' with a shadda* [yy] (i.e., followed by a double *yaa'*), the first *yaa'* is converted into the original root vowel *waaw* [w] or *yaa'* [y] with a *fatHa* in each case (i.e., [wa] and [ya], respectively) and the second *yaa'* [y] is converted into *waaw* [w], as in:

"lively"	حَيَوِيّ	←	يّ	+	"live"	حَيّ
"related to folding"	طَوَوِيّ	←	يّ	+	"folding"	طَيّ

(g)   if a word consists of two consonants followed by a final *yaa' with a shadda* [yy] (i.e., followed by a double *yaa'*), the first *yaa'* is dropped and the second *yaa'* [y] is converted into the sequence [a–w]; otherwise if the word consists of more than three consonants, the *yaa'* is retained and no additional يّ is added, as in:

"prophet-like"	نَبَوِيّ	←	يّ	+	"prophet"	نَبِيّ
"related to Ali"	عَلَوِيّ	←	يّ	+	"Ali"	عَلِيّ
"related to Shafi'i"	شافِعِيّ	←	يّ	+	"Shafi'i"	شافِعِيّ

(h)   if a word contains a dropped root consonant in initial position, then the root consonant is reinserted, as in (the two common words below):

"descriptive"	وَصْفِيّ	←	يّ	+	"description"	صِفَة / وَصْف
"related to weight"	وَزْنِيّ	←	يّ	+	"weight"	زِنَة / وَزْن

(i)   if a word contains a dropped root consonant in final position, then the root consonant is reinserted, as in (the common words below):

"fatherly"	أَبَوِيّ	←	يّ	+	"father"	أَب
"brotherly"	أَخَوِيّ	←	يّ	+	"brother"	أَخ
"yearly"	سَنَوِيّ	←	يّ	+	"year"	سَنَة
"linguistic"	لُغَوِيّ	←	يّ	+	"language"	لُغَة
"manual"	يَدَوِيّ	←	يّ	+	"hand"	يَد
"anal"	فَمَوِيّ	←	يّ	+	"mouth"	فَم
"related to blood"	دَمَوِيّ	←	يّ	+	"blood"	دَم

(j)   finally, while most words that have a long medial *yaa'* vowel [ii] retain the vowel when a relative noun is derived, the medial *yaa'* vowel [ii] is dropped (in a few common words, some of which end with a *taa' marbuuTa*), as in:

"princely"	أَميريّ	←	يّ	+	"prince"	أَمير
"clinical"	سَريريّ	←	يّ	+	"bed"	سَرير
"related to Husayn"	حُسَيْنيّ	←	يّ	+	"Husayn"	حُسَيْن
"natural"	طَبيعيّ	←	يّ	+	"nature"	طَبيعَة
"vanguard-like"	طَليعيّ	←	يّ	+	"vanguard"	طَليعة
"related to Hanifa"	حَنَفيّ	←	يّ	+	"Hanifa"	حَنيفَة
"journalist"	صَحَفيّ	←	يّ	+	"newspaper"	صَحيفَة
"tribal"	قَبَليّ	←	يّ	+	"tribe"	قَبيلة

15.8   Summary

This chapter discussed the main classes and patterns of Arabic adjectives. Remember:

*   Arabic adjectives are basically derived from verbs and the derivation is mostly irregular, but knowing the patterns is useful for knowing how adjectives are derived, as well as their meanings
*   some patterns have specific (temporary vs. permanent) meanings, such as the patterns فَعْلان and فَعيل
*   adjectives for colors and bodily defects/beauties are quite regular, with specific patterns for the singular (masculine and feminine), the dual, and the plural
*   the comparative and superlative forms of adjectives are also regular, with specific patterns and structures (for adjectives derived from verbs vs. adjectives derived from derived verbs or derived words)
*   active and passive participles can be used as adjectives (see also Chapter 14 on their use as nouns)
*   not all adjectives are derived from verbs; relative/*nisba* adjectives are derived from nouns by means of the suffix يّ [yy] *yaa' with shadda* (with certain additional sub-rules), where the adjectival meaning is related or attributed to that of the noun.

16

Quantifiers and Emphasis

Certain words in Arabic function as quantifiers. Quantifiers are used primarily to specify quantity, and some, in addition, are used to emphasize quantity at the same time. Arabic also uses other specialized emphasis words and structures for purposes of emphasis. The chapter covers the following:

- common quantifiers
- common emphasis words
- other ways or structures used for the purposes of emphasis.

16.1 Quantifiers

In Arabic, there are certain words that express the range of quantities from zero to all, including: no one/none or nothing, any, some, a number of, many, a few, most, every, all, and both. Some of these can also be used to emphasize quantity.

16.1.1 لا أَحَدَ "No one" and لا شَيْءَ "Nothing"

As in English, one way of expressing zero quantity is by means of expressions such as لا أَحَدَ "no one" and لا شَيْءَ "nothing", that is, by using the "genus" or absolute negation particle لا النّافِيَة لِلْجِنس followed by the word denoting the genus/thing in the (indefinite) singular. The noun following لا is used with the accusative مَنْصوب *fatHa* [a] case ending without nunation (see

Modern Standard Arabic Grammar: A Learner's Guide, First Edition.
© 2011 Mohammad T. Alhawary. Published 2011 by Blackwell Publishing Ltd.

Chapter 4 on the use of the absolute negation particle لا). The verb or predicate following such expressions is similarly in the singular, as in:

لا أَحَدَ مِنَ الطُّلّابِ هُنا يُحِبُّ الواجِباتِ .

"None of the students here likes homework."

لا شَيْءَ أَحَبُّ إلَيْهِ مِنَ النَوْمِ .

"Nothing is dearer to him than sleeping."

Zero quantity can also be expressed by the absolute negation particle لا النافِيَة لِلْجِنس followed by (indefinite) nouns in the singular, dual, or plural (with the accusative مَنْصوب case ending). If followed by a verb, the verb agrees with the preceding noun in number and gender, as in:

لا طالِبَ هُنا يُحِبُّ الواجِباتِ .

"No student here likes homework."

لا طالِبَيْنِ هُنا يُحِبّانِ الواجِباتِ .

"No two students here like homework."

لا طُلّابَ هُنا يُحِبّونَ الواجِباتِ .

"No students here like homework."

16.1.2   أَيّ "Any"

The word أَيّ can be used to express the meaning of "any" (see also Chapter 7 for أَيّ functioning as a question word). The word أَيّ "any" and the noun following it form an إضافة *'iDaafa* phrase, with أَيّ taking the مَرْفوع nominative, مَنْصوب accusative, or مَجْرور genitive case ending and the (indefinite) noun following it taking the genitive case ending مَجْرور (see Chapter 3), as in:

هَلْ مَعَكَ أَيُّ كِتابٍ ؟

"Do you have any book?"

يُريدُ أَنْ يَشْتَرِيَ أَيَّ كِتابٍ .

"He wants to buy any book."

تُريدُ أَنْ تَذْهَبَ إلى أَيِّ طَبيبٍ .

"She wants to go to any doctor."

When occurring with feminine nouns, the feminine suffix *taa' marbuuTa* ـَة is optionally used with أيّ , as in:

<table>
<tr><td>لَيْسَ لَهَا أَيَّةٌ قَرِيبَةٍ .</td><td>=</td><td>لَيْسَ لَهَا أَيُّ قَرِيبَةٍ .</td></tr>
<tr><td>"She does not have any (female) relative."</td><td></td><td>"She does not have any (female) relative."</td></tr>
<tr><td>يُرِيدُ أَنْ يَشْتَرِيَ أَيَّةَ سَيَّارَةٍ .</td><td>=</td><td>يُرِيدُ أَنْ يَشْتَرِيَ أَيَّ سَيَّارَةٍ .</td></tr>
<tr><td>"He wants to buy any car."</td><td></td><td>"He wants to buy any car."</td></tr>
<tr><td>تُرِيدُ أَنْ تَسْكُنَ فِي أَيَّةِ مَدِينَةٍ .</td><td>=</td><td>تُرِيدُ أَنْ تَسْكُنَ فِي أَيِّ مَدِينَةٍ .</td></tr>
<tr><td>"She wants to live in any city."</td><td></td><td>"She wants to live in any city."</td></tr>
</table>

16.1.3 بَعْض "Some"

The word بَعْض is used to express the quantity "some." The word بَعْض "some" and the noun following it form an إضافة *'iDaafa* phrase, with بَعْض taking the مَرْفوع nominative, مَنْصوب accusative, or مَجْرور genitive case ending and the (definite) noun following it with the genitive مَجْرور (see Chapter 3), as in:

حَضَرَ بَعْضُ الطُّلَّابِ .
"Some (male) students came."

قَابَلْتُ بَعْضَ الطُّلَّابِ .
"I met some (male) students."

سَلَّمْتُ عَلَى بَعْضِ الطُّلَّابِ .
"I shook hands with some (male) students."

The word بَعْض "some" is treated as a *singular masculine noun*, as are most quantifiers. Accordingly, when بَعْض is followed by (human) plural masculine or feminine nouns, the verb preceding it occurs in the singular masculine while the verb (or predicate) following it can occur in the plural; similarly, when used with a non-human plural (masculine or feminine) the verb following it can be used in the singular feminine. Thus, in the former, the verb (or predicate) agrees with the word بَعْض and in the latter it may agree with the quantified noun (or it may remain in the singular masculine to agree with the singular masculine word بَعْض), as in:

بَعْضُ الطُّلَّابِ دَرَسوا / دَرَسَ .	=	دَرَسَ بَعْضُ الطُّلَّابِ .
"Some (male) students studied."		"Some (male) students studied."

بَعْضُ الطّالِباتِ دَرَسْنَ / دَرَسَ .	=	دَرَسَ بَعْضُ الطّالِباتِ .
"Some (female) students studied."		"Some (female) students studied."

بَعْضُ السّيّاراتِ مَرَّتْ / مَرَّ .	=	مَرَّ بَعْضُ السّيّاراتِ .
"Some cars passed by."		"Some cars passed by."

The word بَعْض "some" may also occur definite (with or without a pronoun), as in:

يَظُنُّ بَعْضُ النّاسِ أَنَّ الأَزْمَةَ الإِقْتِصادِيَّةَ مُؤَقَّتَةٌ .	=	يَظُنُّ البَعْضُ أَنَّ الأَزْمَةَ الإِقْتِصادِيَّةَ مُؤَقَّتَةٌ .
"Some people believe that the economic crisis is temporary."		"Some believe that the economic crisis is temporary."

يَظُنُّ بَعْضُ النّاسِ أَنَّ الأَزْمَةَ الإِقْتِصادِيَّةَ مُؤَقَّتَةٌ .	=	يَظُنُّ بَعْضُهُم أَنَّ الأَزْمَةَ الإِقْتِصادِيَّةَ مُؤَقَّتَةٌ .
"Some people believe that the economic crisis is temporary."		"Some of them believe that the economic crisis is temporary."

16.1.4   عَدَد مِنْ and عِدَّة مِنْ "A Number of"

The phrases عَدَد مِنْ and عِدَّة مِنْ are used to specify the quantity "a number of" for masculine and feminine nouns and take the مَرْفوع nominative, مَنْصوب accusative, or مَجْرور genitive case ending, as in:

حَضَرَ عِدَّةٌ مِنَ الطُّلَّابِ .	=	حَضَرَ عَدَدٌ مِنَ الطُّلَّابِ .
"A number of (male) students came."		"A number of (male) students came."

قابَلْتُ عِدَّةً مِنَ الطّالِباتِ .	=	قابَلْتُ عَدَداً مِنَ الطّالِباتِ .
"I met a number of (female) students."		"I met a number of (female) students."

سَلَّمْتُ عَلى عِدَّةٍ مِنَ الطُّلَّابِ .	=	سَلَّمْتُ عَلى عَدَدٍ مِنَ الطُّلَّابِ .
"I greeted a number of (male) students."		"I greeted a number of (male) students."

Like بَعْض "some," the quantifier عَدَد "a number of" is treated as a *singular masculine noun* where it agrees with a preceding verb, and a verb following it may agree with the quantified noun, as in:

عَدَدٌ مِنَ الطُّلَّابِ دَرَسوا .	=	دَرَسَ عَدَدٌ مِنَ الطُّلَّابِ .
"A number of (male) students studied."		"A number of (male) students studied."
عَدَدٌ مِنَ الطَّالِباتِ دَرَسْنَ .	=	دَرَسَ عَدَدٌ مِنَ الطَّالِباتِ .
"A number of (female) students studied."		"A number of (female) students studied."
عَدَدٌ مِنَ السَّيّاراتِ مَرَّتْ .	=	مَرَّ عَدَدٌ مِنَ السَّيّاراتِ .
"A number of cars passed by."		"A number of cars passed by."

The word عِدَّة "a number of" can be used without the preposition مِنْ and, together with the (indefinite) noun following it, both form an إضافة *'iDaafa* phrase, as in:

حَضَرَ عِدَّةُ طُلَّابٍ .

"A number of (male) students came."

حَضَرَتْ عِدَّةُ طالِباتٍ .

"A number of (female) students came."

قابَلْتُ عِدَّةَ طالِباتٍ .

"I met a number of (female) students."

سَلَّمْتُ عَلىٰ عِدَّةِ طُلَّابٍ .

"I greeted a number of (male) students."

In addition, the word عِدَّة can be used as an adjective (without the preposition مِنْ) following the noun in order to emphasize the meaning of "many," where the word عِدَّة agrees with the preceding noun in case, as in:

حَضَرَ الطُّلَّابُ مِنْ وِلاياتٍ عِدَّةٍ .

"The (male) students came from many states."

حَضَرَتِ الطَّالِباتُ مِنْ وِلاياتٍ عِدَّةٍ .

"The (female) students came from many states."

في مَدينَتي أَسواقٌ عِدَّةٌ .

"In my city there are many markets."

16.1.5 عَديد مِنْ and كَثير مِنْ "Many of," كَثير "Many," and عَديد "Many"

The phrases كَثير مِنْ and عَديد مِنْ are used (as singular masculine) to express the quantity of "many of" for masculine and feminine nouns and take the مَرْفوع nominative, مَنْصوب accusative, or مَجْرور genitive case ending, as in:

حَضَرَ عَديدٌ مِنَ الطُّلّابِ .	=	حَضَرَ كَثيرٌ مِنَ الطُّلّابِ .
"Many (male) students came."		"Many (male) students came."
حَضَرَ عَديدٌ مِنَ الطّالِباتِ .	=	حَضَرَ كَثيرٌ مِنَ الطّالِباتِ .
"Many (female) students came."		"Many (female) students came."
قابَلْتُ عَديداً مِنَ الطّالِباتِ .	=	قابَلْتُ كَثيراً مِنَ الطّالِباتِ .
"I met many (female) students."		"I met many (female) students."
سَلَّمْتُ عَلىٰ عَديدٍ مِنَ الطُّلّابِ .	=	سَلَّمْتُ عَلىٰ كَثيرٍ مِنَ الطُّلّابِ .
"I shook hands with many (male) students."		"I shook hands with many (male) students."

In addition, the word كَثيرَة "many" or عَديدَة "many" can be used by itself as an adjective following the noun in order to emphasize the meaning of "many," in which case كَثيرَة "many" and عَديدَة "many" are used for the non-human plural and كَثيرات / كَثيرونَ "many" and عَديدات / عَديدونَ "many" are used for the human plural (masculine and feminine). In this case, the quantifier agrees with the preceding noun in case, as in:

سافَروا إلىٰ دُوَلٍ عَديدَةٍ .	=	سافَروا إلىٰ دُوَلٍ كَثيرَةٍ .
"They traveled to many countries."		"They traveled to many countries."
عِنْدَهُ كُتُبٌ عَديدَةٌ .	=	عِنْدَهُ كُتُبٌ كَثيرَةٌ .
"He has many books."		"He has many books."
اِجْتَمَعوا مَعَ أُناسٍ عَديدينَ .	=	اِجْتَمَعوا مَعَ أُناسٍ كَثيرينَ .
"They met with many people."		"They met with many people."
لَهُ أَصْدِقاءُ عَديدونَ .	=	لَهُ أَصْدِقاءُ كَثيرونَ .
"He has many (male) friends."		"He has many (male) friends."
لَها صَديقاتٌ عَديداتٌ .	=	لَها صَديقاتٌ كَثيراتٌ .
"She has many (female) friends."		"She has many (female) friends."

The quantifiers كَثير "many" and عَديد "many" can also be used definite and for both masculine and feminine nouns, as in:

لَهُ العَديدُ مِنَ الأَصْدِقاءِ .	=	لَهُ الكَثيرُ مِنَ الأَصْدِقاءِ .
"He has many (male) friends."		"He has many (male) friends."
لَها العَديدُ مِنَ الصَّديقاتِ .	=	لَها الكَثيرُ مِنَ الصَّديقاتِ .
"She has many (female) friends."		"She has many (female) friends."
زارَ العَديدَ مِنَ الجامِعاتِ	=	زارَ الكَثيرَ مِنَ الجامِعاتِ .
"He visited many universities."		"He visited many universities."
سافَرَ إلى العَديدِ مِنَ الدُّوَلِ .	=	سافَرَ إلى الكَثيرِ مِنَ الدُّوَلِ .
"He traveled to many countries."		"He traveled to many countries."

16.1.6 قَليل مِنْ "A Few," "A Little"

The phrase قَليل مِنْ is used (as singular masculine) to express the quantity of "a few" or "a little" for masculine and feminine nouns and may take the مَرْفوع nominative, مَنْصوب accusative, or مَجْرور genitive case ending, as in:

حَضَرَ قَليلٌ مِنَ الرِّجالِ .
"A few men attended."

حَضَرَ قَليلٌ مِنَ النِّساءِ .
"A few women attended."

يَبْذُلُ قَليلاً مِنَ الجُهْدِ .
"He exerts a little effort."

يَعيشُ عَلى قَليل مِنَ المالِ .
"He lives on a little money."

The quantifier قَليل "a few" or "a little" can also be used in the definite, as in:

ذَهَبَ الكَثيرُ ولَمْ يَبْقَ إلّا القَليلُ .
"A lot went away and nothing remained except a little bit."

16.1.7 مُعْظَم and أَكْثَر "Most of"

The words مُعْظَم and أَكْثَر are used (as singular masculine words) to express the quantity of "most of." Together with the noun following them, they form an إضافة 'iDaafa phrase, with مُعْظَم and أَكْثَر taking the مَرْفوع nominative, مَنْصوب accusative, or مَجْرور genitive case ending and the (definite) noun following it taking the genitive مَجْرور case ending (see Chapter 3), as in:

دَرَسَ أَكْثَرُ الطُّلّابِ .	=	دَرَسَ مُعْظَمُ الطُّلّابِ .
"Most of the (male) students studied."		"Most of the (male) students studied."
دَرَسَ أَكْثَرُ الطَّالِباتِ .	=	دَرَسَ مُعْظَمُ الطَّالِباتِ .
"Most of the (female) students studied."		"Most of the (female) students studied."
قابَلْتُ أَكْثَرَ الطُّلّابِ .	=	قابَلْتُ مُعْظَمَ الطُّلّابِ .
"I met most of the students."		"I met most of the students."
سَلَّمْتُ عَلىٰ أَكْثَرِ الطُّلّابِ .	=	سَلَّمْتُ عَلىٰ مُعْظَمِ الطُّلّابِ .
"I shook hands with most of the students."		"I shook hands with most of the students."

16.1.8 كُلّ "Every," "All"

When كُلّ is followed by an indefinite, singular noun, it expresses the meaning of "every," and when followed by a definite (singular or plural) noun, it expresses the meaning of "every." In both cases, كُلّ and the noun following it form an إضافة 'iDaafa phrase, with كُلّ taking the مَرْفوع nominative, مَنْصوب accusative, or مَجْرور genitive case ending (see Chapter 3), as in:

كُلُّ طالِبٍ هُنا يَكْتُبُ الواجِبَ .
"Every student here writes the homework."

كُلُّ الطُّلّابِ هُنا يَكْتُبونَ الواجِبَ .
"All the students here write the homework."

يَكْتُبونَ الواجِبَ كُلَّ يَوْمٍ .
"They write the homework every day."

يَدْرُسونَ كُلَّ الْيَوْمِ .

"They study all day."

يُسَلِّمُ عَلىٰ كُلِّ رَجُلٍ .

"He shakes hands with every man."

يُسَلِّمُ عَلىٰ كُلِّ الرِّجالِ .

"He shakes hands with all men."

The quantified noun can be dropped, in which case كُلّ here "all" is usually used definite; that is, with the definite article or a possessive pronoun. It can also be used indefinite (with nunation). In addition, كُلّ can be treated as a singular noun; therefore, the verb (or predicate) occurring with it can be in the singular (agreeing with كُلّ) or plural (agreeing with the quantified noun), as in:

كُلٌّ / الكُلُّ نَجَحوا / نَجَحَ .

"All males passed."

=

نَجَحَ كُلُّ الطُّلَّابِ / كُلُّ الطُّلَّابِ نَجَحوا .

"All the (male) students passed."

كُلٌّ / كُلُّهُمْ نَجَحوا / نَجَحَ .

"All males passed."

=

نَجَحَ كُلُّ الطُّلَّابِ / كُلُّ الطُّلَّابِ نَجَحوا .

"All the (male) students passed."

كُلٌّ / كُلُّهُنَّ نَجَحْنَ / نَجَحَتْ .

"All females passed."

=

نَجَحَتْ كُلُّ الطَّالِباتِ / كُلُّ الطَّالِباتِ نَجَحْنَ .

"All the (female) students passed."

Note: As the above examples show, and unlike other quantifiers (especially بَعض "some"), when كُلّ is used in the singular, it can be used as singular *feminine* or singular *masculine*, depending on the gender of the quantified noun following it.

In addition, the quantifier كُلّ "all" can be used (with a pronoun suffix) as an adjective following the noun in order to emphasize the meaning of "all," in which case the word كُلّ agrees with the preceding noun in case, as in:

نَجَحَ الطُّلَّابُ كُلُّهُمْ .

"The (male) students passed, all of them."

نَجَحَتِ الطَّالِباتُ كُلُّهُنَّ .

"The (female) students passed, all of them."

قابَلْتُ الطُّلَّابَ كُلَّهُمْ .

"I met the (male) students, all of them."

قابَلْتُ الطّالِباتِ كُلَّهُنَّ .

"I met the (female) students, all of them."

سَلَّمْتُ عَلَى الطُّلّابِ كُلِّهِم .

"I shook hands with the (male) students, all of them."

سَلَّمْتُ عَلَى الطّالِباتِ كُلِّهِنَّ .

"I shook hands with the (female) students, all of them."

16.1.9   جَمِيع and عامَّة "All"

Like كُلّ "all," the words جَمِيع and عامَّة can be used as quantifiers expressing the meaning of "all," as in:

نَجَحَ عامَّةُ الطُّلّابِ .   =   نَجَحَ جَمِيعُ الطُّلّابِ .

"All the students passed."   "All the students passed."

قابَلْتُ عامَّةَ الطُّلّابِ .   =   قابَلْتُ جَمِيعَ الطُّلّابِ .

"I met all the students."   "I met all the students."

سَلَّمْتُ عَلَى عامَّةِ الطُّلّابِ .   =   سَلَّمْتُ عَلَى جَمِيعِ الطُّلّابِ .

"I shook hands with all the   "I shook hands with all the
students."   students."

Additionally, and similar to كُلّ "all," جَمِيع and عامَّة can be used to emphasize the quantified meaning of "all." In this function, they are similarly used (with a pronoun suffix) as adjectives following a noun, in which case the words جَمِيع and عامَّة agree with the preceding noun in case, as in:

نَجَحَ الطُّلّابُ عامَّتُهُم .   =   نَجَحَ الطُّلّابُ جَمِيعُهُم .

"The students passed, all of them."   "The students passed, all of them."

قابَلْتُ الطُّلّابَ عامَّتَهُم .   =   قابَلْتُ الطُّلّابَ جَمِيعَهُم .

"I met the students, all of them."   "I met the students, all of them."

سَلَّمْتُ عَلَى الطُّلّابِ عامَّتِهِم .   =   سَلَّمْتُ عَلَى الطُّلّابِ جَمِيعِهِم .

"I shook hands with the students,   "I shook hands with the students,
all of them."   all of them."

16.1.10 كِلا "Both M" and كِلتا "Both F"

The words كِلا and كِلتا express the quantity for the dual masculine and dual feminine, respectively. Together with the noun following كِلا or كِلتا, both form an إضافة *'iDaafa* phrase (i.e., with the quantified noun having the genitive مَجْرور case ending), but neither كِلا nor كِلتا show any case ending, as in:

حَضَرَ كِلا الطَّالِبَيْنِ .
"Both (male) students came."

حَضَرَتْ كِلتا الطَّالِبَتَيْنِ .
"Both (female) students came."

قابَلْتُ كِلا الطَّالِبَيْنِ .
"I met both (male) students."

قابَلْتُ كِلتا الطَّالِبَتَيْنِ .
"I met both (female) students."

سَلَّمْتُ عَلىٰ كِلا الطَّالِبَيْنِ .
"I shook hands with both (male) students."

سَلَّمْتُ عَلىٰ كِلتا الطَّالِبَتَيْنِ .
"I shook hands with both (female) students."

In addition, كِلا and كِلتا are treated as singular nouns; therefore, the verb (or predicate) occurring with them can be either singular (agreeing with the كِلا and كِلتا) or dual (agreeing with the quantified noun), as in:

كِلا الطَّالِبَيْنِ حَضَرا .	=	كِلا الطَّالِبَيْنِ حَضَرَ .
"Both (male) students came."		"Both (male) students came."
كِلتا الطَّالِبَتَيْنِ حَضَرَتا .	=	كِلتا الطَّالِبَتَيْنِ حَضَرَتْ .
"Both (female) students came."		"Both (female) students came."

Finally, the quantifier كِلا and كِلتا can be used (with the dual pronoun suffix) as an adjective following the quantified noun in order to emphasize the meaning of "both," where كِلا and كِلتا agree with the preceding noun in case and accordingly may take the مَرْفوع nominative, مَنْصوب accusative, and مَجْرُور genitive (dual) case ending, according to the function of the preceding noun in the sentence, as in:

حَضَرَ الطَّالِبانِ كِلاهُما .

"The two (male) students came, both of them."

حَضَرَتِ الطَّالِبَتانِ كِلْتاهُما .

"The two (female) students came, both of them."

قابَلْتُ الطَّالِبَيْنِ كِلَيْهِما .

"I met the two (male) students, both of them."

قابَلْتُ الطَّالِبَتَيْنِ كِلْتَيْهِما .

"I met the two (female) students, both of them."

سَلَّمْتُ عَلَىٰ الطَّالِبَيْنِ كِلَيْهِما .

"I shook hands with the two (male) students, both of them."

سَلَّمْتُ عَلَىٰ الطَّالِبَتَيْنِ كِلْتَيْهِما .

"I shook hands with the two (female) students, both of them."

Note: The quantified nouns preceding كِلا and كِلْتا can be dropped, as in:

حَضَرَ كِلاهُما .

"Both of them (males) came."

حَضَرَتْ كِلْتاهُما .

"Both of them (females) came."

قابَلْتُ كِلَيْهِما .

"I met both of them (males)."

قابَلْتُ كِلْتَيْهِما .

"I met both of them (females)."

سَلَّمْتُ عَلَىٰ كِلَيْهِما .

"I shook hands with both of them (males)."

سَلَّمْتُ عَلَىٰ كِلْتَيْهِما .

"I shook hands with both of them (females)."

16.2 Emphasis Words نَفْس ، عَيْن

The words نَفْس and عَيْن are used to emphasize the literal meaning when the exact or self-same person or thing is intended, although the former is more commonly used than the latter. These words are used as adjectives agreeing in case (مَرْفوع nominative, مَنْصوب accusative, and مَجْرور genitive) with the preceding noun and usually occur with a pronoun suffix, as in:

حَضَرَ المُديرُ عَيْنُهُ .	=	حَضَرَ المُديرُ نَفْسُهُ .
"The manager himself came."		"The manager himself came."
قابَلْتُ المُديرَ عَيْنَهُ .	=	قابَلْتُ المُديرَ نَفْسَهُ .
"I met the manager himself."		"I met the manager himself."
اِتَّصَلْتُ بالمُديرة عَيْنِها .	=	اِتَّصَلْتُ بالمُديرة نَفْسِها .
"I called the manager herself."		"I called the manager herself."

The emphasis words نَفْس and عَيْن can be preceded by the preposition بِ , in which case, accordingly, they take the genitive مَجْرور case, as in:

حَضَرَ المُديرُ بِعَيْنِهِ .	=	حَضَرَ المُديرُ بِنَفْسِهِ .
"The manager himself came."		"The manager himself came."
قابَلْتُ المُديرَ بِعَيْنِهِ .	=	قابَلْتُ المُديرَ بِنَفْسِهِ .
"I met the manager himself."		"I met the manager himself."
اِتَّصَلْتُ بالمُديرة بِعَيْنِها .	=	اِتَّصَلْتُ بالمُديرة بِنَفْسِها .
"I called the manager herself."		"I called the manager herself."

In addition, when referring to the plural of نَفْس and عَيْن the plural أَنْفُس and أَعْيُن (followed by the plural suffix) are used, respectively. However, when referring to the dual, three variations are allowed: use of the singular (i.e., نَفْس and عَيْن followed by the dual suffix), use of the dual (i.e., نَفْسان and عَيْنان followed by the dual suffix), or use of the plural (i.e., أَنْفُس and أَعْيُن followed by the dual suffix), as in the following (here too, نَفْس is more commonly used than عَيْن):

حَضَرَ الطُّلَّابُ أَعْيُنُهُمْ .	=	حَضَرَ الطُّلَّابُ أَنْفُسُهُمْ .
"The students themselves came."		"The students themselves came."

قابَلْتُ الطُّلَّابَ أَعْيُنَهُم .   =   قابَلْتُ الطُّلَّابَ أَنْفُسَهُم .
"I met the students themselves."   "I met the students themselves."

اِتَّصَلْتُ بِالطُّلَّابِ أَعْيُنِهِم .   =   اِتَّصَلْتُ بِالطُّلَّابِ أَنْفُسِهِم .
"I called the students themselves."   "I called the students themselves."

حَضَرَ الطَّالِبانِ عَيْنُهُما / عَيْناهُما / أَعْيُنُهُما   =   حَضَرَ الطَّالِبانِ نَفْسُهُما / نَفْساهُما / أَنْفُسُهُما
"The two students themselves   "The two students themselves
came."   came."

قابَلْتُ الطَّالِبَيْنِ عَيْنَهُما / عَيْنَيْهِما / أَعْيُنَهُما   =   قابَلْتُ الطَّالِبَيْنِ نَفْسَهُما / نَفْسَيْهِما / أَنْفُسَهُما
"I met the two students themselves."   "I met the two students themselves."

اِتَّصَلْتُ بِالطَّالِبَيْنِ عَيْنِهِما / عَيْنَيْهِما / أَعْيُنِهِما   =   اِتَّصَلْتُ بِالطَّالِبَيْنِ نَفْسِهِما / نَفْسَيْهِما / أَنْفُسِهِما
"I called the two students   "I called the two students
themselves."   themselves."

Note: The emphasis words نَفْس and عَيْن do not follow a verb unless preceded by a noun which they emphasize or an object pronoun suffix (attached to the verb). Otherwise, they must be preceded by an independent (personal) pronoun, as in:

قابَلْتُكَ نَفْسَكَ .   ←   قابَلْتُكَ .
"I met you yourself."   "I met you."

قابَلْتُها نَفْسَها .   ←   قابَلْتُها .
"I met her herself."   "I met her."

حَضَرْتَ أَنْتَ نَفْسُكَ .   ←   حَضَرْتَ .
"You yourself came."   "You came."

حَضَرَتْ هِيَ نَفْسُها .   ←   حَضَرَتْ .
"You yourself came."   "You came."

حَضَرَ خَالِدٌ نَفْسُهُ .   ←   حَضَرَ خَالِدٌ .
"Khaled himself came."   "Khaled came."

حَضَرَ المُدِيرُ نَفْسُهُ .   ←   حَضَرَ المُدِيرُ .
"The manager himself came."   "The manager came."

16.3   Other Ways of Expressing Emphasis

Other ways of expressing emphasis are more explicit and consist of literally repeating the part of speech intended to be emphasized, such as a particle, pronoun, noun, preposition and pronoun, preposition and noun, verb, phrase, or sentence, etc., as in:

لا لا .	←	لا .
"No, no."		"No."
حَضَرْتَ أَنْتَ .	←	حَضَرْتَ .
"You, you came."		"You came."
سافَرَ سَليمٌ سَليمٌ .	←	سافَرَ سَليمٌ .
"Salim Salim traveled."		"Salim traveled."
تَكَلَّمْتُ مَعَكَ مَعَكَ .	←	تَكَلَّمْتُ مَعَكَ .
"I talked to you to you."		"I talked to you."
الأُسْتاذُ في الفَصْلِ في الفَصْلِ .	←	الأُسْتاذُ في الفَصْلِ .
"The teacher is in class in class."		"The teacher is in class."
سافَرَ سافَرَ سَليمٌ .	←	سافَرَ سَليمٌ .
"Salim traveled traveled."		"Salim traveled."
أَهْلاً وَسَهْلاً أَهْلاً وَسَهْلاً .	←	أَهْلاً وَسَهْلاً .
"Welcome, welcome."		"Welcome."
سافَرَ سَليمٌ سافَرَ سَليمٌ .	←	سافَرَ سَليمٌ .
"Salim traveled Salim traveled."		"Salim traveled."

Note: Other structures used for emphasis and covered in previous chapters include the use of *'inna* إِنَّ in the nominal sentence (see 4.2.6) and adverbs of emphasis/cognate accusative (see Chapter 12).

16.4 Summary

This chapter discussed common quantifiers and ways of expressing emphasis in Arabic. Remember:

- Like English, Arabic has words called *quantifiers* that express the different meanings of no one/none/nothing, any, some, a number of, many, a few, most, every, all, and both
- Some quantifiers can additionally be used for emphasis when used as adjectives following nouns which they quantify
- the words نَفْس and عَيْن emphasize literally the meaning of the "self-same" person or thing and agree with the preceding nouns which they emphasize in number (though not gender)
- as a general rule, emphasis in Arabic follows a basic intuitive rule which consists of repeating any part of speech intended for emphasis
- other emphasis structures covered in previous chapters include the use of إنَّ for the nominal sentence (4.2.6) and adverbs of emphasis/cognate accusative (Chapter 12).

17

Conditional Sentences الجُمَل الشَّرْطِيَّة

Arabic has three main types of conditional sentence الجُمَل الشَّرْطِيَّة which are similarly expressed in English: the possible/probable, the improbable, and the impossible. As in English, a conditional sentence in Arabic consists of two clauses or parts: (1) the *condition* clause/part, called in Arabic جُمْلَة فِعْل الشَّرْط "the sentence stating the condition" and (2) the *result* clause/part, called in Arabic جُمْلَة جَواب الشَّرْط "the sentence stating the result of the condition." Each part has a certain structure or tense to express the type of condition and result intended. However, in Arabic there are many different *if* or *conditional* particles, called أَدَوات الشَّرْط "tools of the condition," which additionally serve to signal the type of conditional structure intended. This chapter covers the following:

- the structure of the three main types of conditional sentence
- the specialized particles expressing conditional sentences
- the different components of each of the two parts of conditional sentences
- optional ways of expressing a given conditional structure, especially the possible/improbable conditional sentence.

17.1 The Possible/Probable Conditional Sentence

This type of conditional sentence expresses a possible or probable condition; that is, the condition is likely to be met, since it has to do with

Modern Standard Arabic Grammar: A Learner's Guide, First Edition.
© 2011 Mohammad T. Alhawary. Published 2011 by Blackwell Publishing Ltd.

realistic situations that are likely to happen in the present or future. At least ten conditional particles or words are used to express the possible/probable conditional sentence. Below are examples of the conditional particles, with the two parts of each of conditional sentences underlined separately (note that some of these words also function as question words; see Chapter 7):

إِنْ تَجْتَهِدْ تَنْجَحْ .

"If you exert effort, you (will) succeed."

إِنْ
"if"

مَنْ يَجْتَهِدْ يَنْجَحْ .

"Whoever exerts effort, he (will) succeed."

مَنْ
"whoever"

ما تَبْذُلْ مِنْ جُهْدٍ تَحْصُدْه .

"Whatever effort you exert, you (will) reap (it)."

ما
"whatever"

مَهْما تَبْذُلْ مِنْ جُهْدٍ تَحْصُدْه .

"No matter the effort you exert, you (will) reap (it)."

مَهْما
"no matter"

مَتىٰ تَجْتَهِدْ تَنْجَحْ .

"Whenever you exert effort, you (will) succeed."

مَتىٰ / مَتىٰ ما
"whenever"

أَيْنَ تَجْتَهِدْ تَنْجَحْ .

"Wherever you exert effort, you (will) succeed."

أَيْنَ / أَيْنَا
"wherever"

حَيْثُما تَجْتَهِدْ تَنْجَحْ .

"Wherever you exert effort, you (will) succeed."

حَيْثُ / حَيْثُما
"wherever"

كَيْفَ تَجْتَهِدْ أَجْتَهِدْ .

"However you exert effort, I (will) exert effort."

كَيْفَ / كَيْفَما
"however"

أَيُّ إِنْسَانٍ يَجْتَهِدْ يَنْجَحْ .	أَيُّ
"Any man who exerts effort, he (will) succeed."	"any"
أَيَّ جُهْدٍ تَبْذُلْهُ تَحْصُدْهُ .	أَيَّ
"Any effort which you exert, you (will) reap (it)."	"any"
لِأَيِّ هَدَفٍ تَجْتَهِدْ تَنْجَحْ .	أَيِّ
"For any goal that you exert effort, you (will) succeed."	"any"
إِذَا تَجْتَهِدُ تَنْجَحُ .	إِذَا
"If you exert effort, you (will) succeed."	"if"

Note: Except for the last conditional sentence with the particle إِذَا "if," where the two parts of the sentence occur in the present tense and where the two verbs occur with the indicative مَرْفوع mood ending, the two verbs in all the other sentences with the other conditional particles occur in the (present) jussive مَجْزوم mood (see Chapter 4 on mood endings). However, this use of a conditional sentence with the particle إِذَا (where both parts in the present) is less commonly used. More commonly used conditional sentences with إِذَا include those where the first part is in the past and the second part in the present or future (see 17.1.2 below), or where both parts are in the past, as in:

إِذَا اجْتَهَدْتَ نَجَحْتَ .	إِذَا
"If you exert effort, you (will) succeed."	"if"

Note: Additionally, the conditional particle أَيّ has three different case endings (i.e., the مَرْفوع nominative, مَنْصوب accusative, and مَجْرور genitive), depending on its function, such as the subject/doer of the verb/action, object/doee of the verb/action, and following a preposition (see 22.2.2 on case endings). The particle أَيّ also functions as a question word (see 7.1.11) and as a quantifier (see 16.1.2).

17.1.1   Use of Other Structures and Tenses

The possible/probable conditional sentence allows other types of tenses and structures to be used, not just the present tense in both parts of the conditional sentence. Below are three additional variations exemplified with the particle إِنْ "if," where:

(a)   both parts of the possible/probable conditional sentence are in the past tense:

إِنِ اجْتَهَدْتَ نَجَحْتَ .

"If you exert effort, you (will) succeed."

(b)   the *conditional* part is in the present jussive مَجْزوم and the *result* part in the past tense:

إِنْ تَجْتَهِدْ نَجَحْتَ .

"If you exert effort, you (will) succeed."

(c)   the *conditional* part is in the past tense and the *result* part in the present jussive مَجْزوم or present indicative مَرْفوع:

إِنِ اجْتَهَدْتَ تَنْجَحْ / تَنْجَحُ .

"If you exert effort, you (will) succeed."

17.1.2   Use of the Particle فَـ

The possible/probable conditional sentence involves the use of the particle فَـ introducing the *result* clause/part of the sentence. The English equivalent is the word "then." In particular, the particle فَـ is required when at least seven other types of structures are used in the *result* clause/part – but only when the *condition* clause/part precedes the *result* clause/part – containing (but optional when the condition part is in the past tense and the result part is a nominal sentence or in the imperative):

(1)   a nominal sentence:

إِنْ تَقْرَأْ فَأَنْتَ الْمُسْتَفيدُ .   ←   إِنْ تَقْرَأْ أَنْتَ الْمُسْتَفيدُ .

"If you read, then you [are] the
(one) benefiting."

(2)   a verb in the imperative or negative imperative:

إِذا انْتَهَيْتَ فاذْهَبْ إِلَى البَيْتِ .   ←   إِذا انْتَهَيْتَ اِذْهَبْ إِلَى البَيْتِ .
"If you finish, then go home."

إِذا انْتَهَيْتَ فَلا تَذْهَبْ إِلَى البَيْتِ .   ←   إِذا انْتَهَيْتَ لا تَذْهَبْ إِلَى البَيْتِ .
"If you finish, then do not go
home."

(3)   the negation particle لَيْسَ "is not" or a few verbs which have a past
form only, such as عَسَى "may be," لَعَلَّ "hope that," لَيْتَ "wish that,"
كَأَنَّ "look like," are used:

إِذا أَرَدْتَ أَنْ تَزورَني الآنَ فَلَيْسَ الوَقْتُ مُناسِباً .   ←   إِذا أَرَدْتَ أَنْ تَزورَني الآنَ لَيْسَ الوَقْتُ مُناسِباً .
"If you want to visit me now,
then the time is not suitable."

(4)   the negation particle ما "not":

مَنْ طَلَبَ مُساعَدَتي فَما أَرْفُضُ طَلَبَهُ .   ←   مَنْ طَلَبَ مُساعَدَتي ما أَرْفُضُ طَلَبَهُ .
"Whoever seeks my help, then
I don't refuse his request."

(5)   the negation particle لَنْ "will not":

مَنْ طَلَبَ مُساعَدَتي فَلَنْ أَرْفُضَ طَلَبَهُ .   ←   مَنْ طَلَبَ مُساعَدَتي لَنْ أَرْفُضَ طَلَبَهُ .
"Whoever seeks my help, then
I won't refuse his request."

(6)   the particle قَدْ "may/perhaps" or رُبَّما "may/perhaps":

إِذا اجْتَهَدْتَ الآنَ فَقَدْ تَنْجَحُ .   ←   إِذا اجْتَهَدْتَ الآنَ قَدْ تَنْجَحُ .
"If you exert effort now, then
you may succeed."

إِذا اجْتَهَدْتَ الآنَ فَرُبَّما تَنْجَحُ .   ←   إِذا اجْتَهَدْتَ الآنَ رُبَّما تَنْجَحُ .
"If you exert effort now, then
you may succeed."

(7) the future particle ـَسَ or سَوْفَ "will":

إذا اجْتَهَدْتَ الآنَ سَتَنْجَحُ .   ←   إذا اجْتَهَدْتَ الآنَ فَسَتَنْجَحُ .

"If you exert effort now, then
you will succeed."

إذا اجْتَهَدْتَ الآنَ سَوْفَ تَنْجَحُ .   ←   إذا اجْتَهَدْتَ الآنَ فَسَوْفَ تَنْجَحُ .

"If you exert effort now, then
you will succeed."

Note: The particle فَ is not needed when the *result* clause/part precedes the *condition* clause/part, as in:

سَوْفَ تَنْجَحُ إذا اجْتَهَدْتَ .

"You will succeed, if you exert effort."

Note: Additionally, whereas both the particles إذا "if" and إنْ "if" are used in the possible/probable conditional sentence, they do not convey the same meaning. The particle إذا "if" conveys a *possible* condition (i.e., without any doubt), while the particle إنْ "if" conveys a *probable* condition (i.e., with some doubt about its possibility).

17.2   The Improbable Conditional Sentence

This type of conditional sentence expresses an improbable condition; that is, the condition is not likely to be met, since it has to do with hypothetical situations or wishful thinking unlikely to happen. Two conditional particles are used for expressing the improbable conditional sentence: لَوْ "if" and لَوْلا "were it not for." In addition, the particle لَ "then" is usually used to introduce the *result* clause/part of the sentence in the affirmative.

17.2.1   لَوْ "if"

The particle لَوْ "if" is used to express an improbable conditional sentence. It introduces the *condition* clause/part of the conditional sentence which can be either a verb (past or present) or a nominal sentence, whereas the verb occurring in the *result* clause/part is always in the past tense, as in:

لَوْ أَمْلِكُ طائِرَةً لَسافَرْتُ حَوْلَ العالَمِ .

"If I had a plane, then I would travel around the world."

لَوْ مَلَكْتُ طائِرَةً لَسافَرْتُ حَوْلَ العالَمِ .

"If I had a plane, then I would travel around the world."

لَوْ كُنْتُ أَمْلِكُ طائِرَةً لَسافَرْتُ حَوْلَ العالَمِ .

"If I had a plane, then I would travel around the world."

لَوْ أَنا غَنِيٌّ لَساعَدْتُ الفُقَراءَ .

"If I were rich, then I would help the poor."

لَوْ كُنْتُ غَنِيّاً لَساعَدْتُ الفُقَراءَ .

"If I were rich, then I would help the poor."

لَوْ أَنا في واشِنطُن الآنَ لَزُرْتُ المَتاحِفَ هُناكَ .

"If I were in Washington now, then I would visit the museums there."

لَوْ كُنْتُ في واشِنطُن الآنَ لَزُرْتُ المَتاحِفَ هُناكَ .

"If I were in Washington now, then I would visit the museums there."

Note: When both parts are in the past tense, the improbable conditional sentence may be identical to the impossible sentence (see 17.3 below), but meaning and context set the two uses apart, such as the time and place of speaking or words such as الآنَ "now" in the sentence.

17.2.2   لَوْلا "were it not for"

The particle لَوْلا "were it not for" is used to express an improbable conditional sentence. It introduces the *condition* clause/part of the conditional sentence, containing a pronoun, a noun, a phrase, or a clause (such as that introduced by the particle أَنْ), whereas the *result* clause/part contains a verb in the past tense only, as in:

لَوْلا هُم لَتَرَكْتُ العَمَلَ .

"Were it not for them, then I would quit work."

لَوْلا الدِّراسَةُ لَسافَرْتُ .

"Were it not for studying, then I would travel."

لَوْلا دِراسَةُ العَرَبِيَّةِ لَالْتَحَقْتُ بِجامِعَةٍ أُخْرىٰ .

"Were it not for studying Arabic, then I would join another university."

لَوْلا أَنْ يُقالَ انْهَزَمَ لَانْسَحَبْتُ مِنَ المُباراةِ .

"Were it not that it would be said he was defeated, then I would withdraw from the match."

17.3 The Impossible Conditional Sentence

This type of conditional sentence expresses an impossible condition; that is, the condition is not likely to be met, since it has to do with the past and is too late. One conditional particle لَوْ "if" is used to express the impossible conditional sentence where both clauses/parts of the sentence contain verbs in the past tense only. Like the improbable conditional sentence, the particle لَ "then" is usually used here to introduce the *result* clause/part of the sentence in the affirmative, as in:

لَوْ دَرَسْتَ لَنَجَحْتَ .

"If you had studied, then you would have succeeded."

لَوْ عَلِمْتُ أَنَّ الاِقْتِصادَ صَعْبٌ لَدَرَسْتُهُ في الصَّيْفِ .

"If I had known that economics is hard, then I would have studied it in the summer."

لَوْ سافَرْتُ إلىٰ القاهِرَةِ في الشَّهْرِ الماضي لَكُنْتُ هُناكَ الآنَ .

"If I had traveled to Cairo last month, then I would be there now."

Note: When the result clause/part of the improbable and impossible sentences occurs in the negative, it is not usually introduced by the particle لَ "then" and is never introduced with the negation particle لَمْ "did not," as in:

لَوْ دَرَسْتَ ما رَسَبْتَ .

"If you had studied, you would not have failed."

لَوْ دَرَسْتَ لَمْ تَرْسُبْ .

"If you had studied, you would not have failed."

17.4 Summary

This chapter discussed the three types of conditional sentence available in Arabic. Remember:

- each conditional sentence consists of two clauses or parts: a *condition* clause/part and a *result* clause/part
- possible/probable conditional sentences use at least ten conditional particles
- possible/probable conditional sentences allow for four main structural variations of the two parts: (1) both can be in the present jussive مَجْزوم , (2) both can be in the past tense, (3) the *condition* part can be in the present jussive مَجْزوم and the *result* part can be in the past, and (4) the *condition* part can be in the past tense and the *result* part can be in the present
- the particle فَ is required to introduce the *result* part (of the possible/probable conditional sentence) when the *result* part contains one of the following: a nominal sentence, an imperative verb, the negation particle لَيْسَ "is not" or a few verbs that occur in the past tense (such as عَسى "may be," لَعَلَّ "hope that," لَيْتَ "wish that," كَأَنَّ "look like"), the particles قَدْ and رُبَّا , the negation particles ما and لَنْ , or the future particles سَـ and سَوْفَ
- improbable conditional sentences use two conditional particles لَوْ and لَوْلَا , whereas (in the improbable conditional sentence) the *condition* part introduced by لَوْ may contain a verb in the past or present tense and its *result* part contains a verb in the past tense only, the *condition* part introduced by لَوْلَا may contain a pronoun, a noun, a phrase, or a (nominal) sentence
- impossible conditional sentences use one conditional particle لَوْ
- both parts of the impossible conditional sentence are in the past tense
- the particle لَ "then" is usually used to introduce the *result* part of improbable and impossible conditional sentences in the affirmative but not in the negative.

18

Exceptive Sentences الإِسْتِثْناء

Unlike in English, where the exceptive structure is conveyed more generally through words and phrases such as "except," "except for," and "apart from," etc., Arabic has a specific grammatical structure called الإِسْتِثْناء "the exception." In addition to the use of exceptive particles or words called in Arabic أَدَوات الإِسْتِثْناء "the tools of exception," certain words have certain case endings as a result of the exceptive structure. This chapter covers the following:

- common exceptive particles and words, their meanings, and use
- variations in the use of exceptive sentence structure
- the different case endings involved in the use of different exceptive particles/words and their different structures.

18.1 Exceptive Words and Their Use

There are at least seven exceptive particles or words used in MSA to express the exceptive sentence structure. Some are treated as particles, some as nouns, and some as verbs. An exceptive sentence structure usually consists of three parts: (1) a noun preceding the exceptive particle/word, called in Arabic الْمُسْتَثْنى مِنْهُ "the excepted-from noun"; (2) the exceptive particle/word itself; and (3) a noun following the exceptive word, called in Arabic الْمُسْتَثْنى "the excepted noun."

Modern Standard Arabic Grammar: A Learner's Guide, First Edition.
© 2011 Mohammad T. Alhawary. Published 2011 by Blackwell Publishing Ltd.

18.1.1 إِلّا "Except for"

Of all the exceptive particles/words, the particle إِلّا is the most commonly used for expressing exceptive sentences. The *excepted* noun المُسْتَثْنىٰ following إِلّا occurs always with the accusative case ending, as long as the *excepted-from noun* المُسْتَثْنىٰ مِنْهُ is not dropped, as in:

حَضَرَ الطُّلّابُ إِلّا واحِداً .

"The students came except for one."

حَضَرَ الطُّلّابُ إِلّا سَليماً .

"The students came except for Salim."

حَضَرَ الطُّلّابُ إِلّا أُسْتاذَهُم .

"The students came except for their teacher."

In the sentences above, the *excepted-from* noun المُسْتَثْنىٰ مِنْهُ preceding إِلّا occurs as the subject/doer of the verb/action. The *excepted-from* noun can also occur as the object/doee of the verb/action or following a preposition, as in:

قابَلْتُ الطُّلّابَ إِلّا واحِداً .

"I met the students except for one."

اِسْتَمَعْتُ إِلىٰ الطُّلّابِ إِلّا واحِداً .

"I listened to the students except for one."

18.1.2 غَيْر and سِوىٰ "Except for"

The words غَيْر and سِوىٰ follow the same rule as that of إِلّا . However, unlike إِلّا , they are treated as nouns and receive the accusative مَنْصوب case ending themselves rather than the noun following them, although the accusative *fatHa* case ending does not appear on سِوىٰ since the latter ends with the *'alif* [aa] long vowel. As for the *excepted* noun المُسْتَثْنىٰ following غَيْر and سِوىٰ , it receives the genitive مَجْرور case ending (since together with the exceptive word it forms an إِضافة *'iDaafa* phrase), as in:

حَضَرَ الطُّلّابُ سِوىٰ واحِدٍ .   =   حَضَرَ الطُّلّابُ غَيْرَ واحِدٍ .

"The students came except for one."   "The students came except for one."

قابَلْتُ الطُّلَّابَ سِوىٰ واحِدٍ .	=	قابَلْتُ الطُّلَّابَ غَيْرَ واحِدٍ .
"I met the students except for one."		"I met the students except for one."
اِسْتَمَعْتُ إِلَى الطُّلَّابِ سِوىٰ واحِدٍ .	=	اِسْتَمَعْتُ إِلَى الطُّلَّابِ غَيْرَ واحِدٍ .
"I listened to the students except for one."		"I listened to the students except for one."

18.1.3   خَلا , عَدا , and حاشا "Except for"

The exceptive words خَلا , عَدا , and حاشا "except for" are subject to two optional rules: (1) they can be treated as verbs where the *excepted* noun المُسْتَثْنىٰ following them occurs with the accusative مَنْصوب case ending or (2) as particles (or prepositions) where the *excepted* noun المُسْتَثْنىٰ following them occurs with the genitive مَجْرور case ending, as in:

حَضَرَ الطُّلَّابُ عَدا واحِدٍ .	=	حَضَرَ الطُّلَّابُ عَدا واحِداً .
"The students came except for one."		"The students came except for one."
قابَلْتُ الطُّلَّابَ عَدا واحِدٍ .	=	قابَلْتُ الطُّلَّابَ عَدا واحِداً .
"I met the students except for one."		"I met the students except for one."
اِسْتَمَعْتُ إِلَى الطُّلَّابِ عَدا واحِدٍ .	=	اِسْتَمَعْتُ إِلَى الطُّلَّابِ عَدا واحِداً .
"I listened to the students except for one."		"I listened to the students except for one."

18.1.4   ماخَلا and ماعَدا "Except for"

Both عَدا and خَلا can be preceded by the particle ما in which case they are treated as verbs where the *excepted* noun المُسْتَثْنىٰ following them occurs with the accusative مَنْصوب case ending only, as in:

حَضَرَ الطُّلَّابُ ماخَلا واحِداً .	=	حَضَرَ الطُّلَّابُ ماعَدا واحِداً .
"The students came except for one."		"The students came except for one."
قابَلْتُ الطُّلَّابَ ماخَلا واحِداً .	=	قابَلْتُ الطُّلَّابَ ماعَدا واحِداً .
"I met the students except for one."		"I met the students except for one."
اِسْتَمَعْتُ إِلَى الطُّلَّابِ ماخَلا واحِداً .	=	اِسْتَمَعْتُ إِلَى الطُّلَّابِ ماعَدا واحِداً .
"I listened to the students except for one."		"I listened to the students except for one."

18.2   Variations in the Exceptive Structure

18.2.1   Use of Negation Preceding إِلّا

If negation is used with the exceptive structure involving إِلّا , then one of two optional rules may apply: (1) the *excepted* noun المُسْتَثْنى following إِلّا may occur always with the accusative مَنْصوب case ending or (2) the *excepted* noun may occur with the مَرْفوع nominative, مَنْصوب accusative, or مَجْرور genitive case ending, according to the function in the sentence of the *excepted-from* noun المُسْتَثْنى مِنْه (that precedes إِلّا), as in:

<table>
<tr><td align="center">ما حَضَرَ الطُّلّابُ إِلّا واحِدٌ .</td><td align="center">=</td><td align="center">ما حَضَرَ الطُّلّابُ إِلّا واحِداً .</td></tr>
<tr><td align="center">"The students did not come except
for one."</td><td></td><td align="center">"The students did not come except
for one."</td></tr>
<tr><td align="center">ما قابَلْتُ الطُّلّابَ إِلّا واحِداً .</td><td align="center">=</td><td align="center">ما قابَلْتُ الطُّلّابَ إِلّا واحِداً .</td></tr>
<tr><td align="center">"I did not meet the students except
for one."</td><td></td><td align="center">"I did not meet the students except
for one."</td></tr>
<tr><td align="center">ما اِسْتَمَعْتُ إِلى الطُّلّابِ إِلّا واحِدٍ .</td><td align="center">=</td><td align="center">ما اِسْتَمَعْتُ إِلى الطُّلّابِ إِلّا واحِداً .</td></tr>
<tr><td align="center">"I did not listen to the students
except for one."</td><td></td><td align="center">"I did not listen to the students
except for one."</td></tr>
</table>

18.2.2   Use of Negation Preceding غَيْر and سِوى

If negation is used with the exceptive structure involving غَيْر or سِوى , then one of two optional rules may apply: (1) غَيْر and سِوى may occur always with the accusative مَنْصوب case ending (although no case ending appears on سِوى since it ends with an *'alif* [aa] long vowel) or (2) غَيْر and سِوى may occur with the مَرْفوع nominative, مَنْصوب accusative, or مَجْرور genitive case ending, depending on the function in the sentence of the *excepted-from* noun المُسْتَثْنى مِنْه (that precedes غَيْر and سِوى). In either case, the *excepted* noun المُسْتَثْنى following غَيْر and سِوى receives the genitive مَجْرور case ending (since it forms with the exceptive word an إِضافة *'iDaafa* phrase), as in:

<table>
<tr><td align="center">ما حَضَرَ الطُّلّابُ غَيْرُ واحِدٍ .</td><td align="center">=</td><td align="center">ما حَضَرَ الطُّلّابَ غَيْرَ واحِدٍ .</td></tr>
<tr><td align="center">"The students did not come except
for one."</td><td></td><td align="center">"The students did not come except
for one."</td></tr>
<tr><td align="center">ما قابَلْتُ الطُّلّابَ غَيْرَ واحِدٍ .</td><td align="center">=</td><td align="center">ما قابَلْتُ الطُّلّابَ غَيْرَ واحِدٍ .</td></tr>
<tr><td align="center">"I did not meet the students except
for one."</td><td></td><td align="center">"I did not meet the students except
for one."</td></tr>
</table>

ما اِسْتَمَعْتُ إلى الطُّلَّابِ غَيْرِ واحِدٍ .	=	ما اِسْتَمَعْتُ إلى الطُّلَّابِ غَيْرَ واحِدٍ .
"I did not listen to the students except for one."		"I did not listen to the students except for one."
ما حَضَرَ الطُّلَّابُ سِوىٰ واحِدٍ .	=	ما حَضَرَ الطُّلَّابُ سِوىٰ واحِدٍ .
"The students did not come except for one."		"The students did not come except for one."
ما قابَلْتُ الطُّلَّابِ سِوىٰ واحِدٍ .	=	ما قابَلْتُ الطُّلَّابَ سِوىٰ واحِدٍ .
"I did not meet the students except for one."		"I did not meet the students except for one."
ما اِسْتَمَعْتُ إلى الطُّلَّابِ سِوىٰ واحِدٍ .	=	ما اِسْتَمَعْتُ إلى الطُّلَّابِ سِوىٰ واحِدٍ .
"I did not listen to the students except for one."		"I did not listen to the students except for one."

18.2.3 Use of Negation and Dropping the Noun Preceding إلّا

If the *excepted-from* noun المُسْتَثْنىٰ مِنْه preceding the exceptive particle إلّا is dropped, then one rule applies: the *excepted* noun occurs with the مَرْفوع nominative, مَنْصوب accusative, or مَجْرور genitive case ending, depending on its own function in the sentence (i.e., irrespective of the presence of إلّا in the sentence), as in:

ما حَضَرَ إلّا طالِبٌ .
"Only one student came."

ما قابَلْتُ إلّا طالِباً .
"I met only one student."

ما اِسْتَمَعْتُ إلّا إلى طالِبٍ .
"I listened to only one student."

18.2.4 Use of Negation and Dropping the Noun Preceding سِوىٰ and غَيْر

If the *excepted-from* noun المُسْتَثْنىٰ مِنْه preceding the exceptive particle غَيْر or سِوىٰ is dropped, then one rule applies: غَيْر and سِوىٰ occur with the مَرْفوع nominative, مَنْصوب accusative, or مَجْرور genitive case ending, depending on its function in the sentence (although no case ending appears on سِوىٰ since it ends with an *'alif* [aa] long vowel). In this case, the *excepted* noun المُسْتَثْنىٰ following غَيْر and سِوىٰ receives the genitive مَجْرور case ending (since together with the exceptive word it forms an إضافة *'iDaafa* phrase), as in:

ما حَضَرَ سِوىٰ طالِبٍ .	=	ما حَضَرَ غَيْرُ طالِبٍ .
"Only one student came."		"Only one student came."
ما قابَلْتُ سِوىٰ طالِبٍ .	=	ما قابَلْتُ غَيْرَ طالِبٍ .
"I met only one student."		"I met only one student."
ما اسْتَمَعْتُ إِلىٰ سِوىٰ طالِبٍ .	=	ما اسْتَمَعْتُ إِلىٰ غَيْرِ طالِبٍ .
"I listened to only one student."		"I listened to only one student."

18.3   The Structure of لا سِيَّا "Especially"

In addition to the above exceptive particles/words, لا سِيَّا "especially" is usually listed among exceptive words, although its meaning is the opposite of *except for*. It is usually used with the conjunction وَ "and." As for the case ending on the noun following لا سِيَّا "especially," it depends on whether it is indefinite or definite. If indefinite, the word can occur with any of the case endings (i.e., مَرْفوع nominative, مَنْصوب accusative, or genitive مَجْرور), although most usually with the genitive مَجْرور case, and if definite, it (most) usually occurs with the genitive مَجْرور and less so with the nominative مَرْفوع case, as in:

يُعْجِبُني كُلُّ تِلْميذٍ وَلا سِيَّا تِلْميذٍ مُجْتَهِدٍ / تِلْميذاً مُجْتَهِداً / تِلْميذٌ مُجْتَهِدٌ .
"Every student impresses me, especially a hard-working student."

يُعْجِبُني كُلُّ تِلْميذٍ وَلا سِيَّا التِّلْميذِ المُجْتَهِدِ / التِّلْميذُ المُجْتَهِدُ .
"Every student impresses me, especially the hard-working student."

حَضَرَ المُوَظَّفونَ الحَفْلَ وَلا سِيَّا مُديرِهِم / مُديرُهُم .
"The employees attended the party/celebration, especially their manager."

نَجَحَ الطُّلَّابُ وَلا سِيَّا سَليمٍ / سَليمٌ .
"The students passed, especially Salim."

18.4 Summary

This chapter discussed the exceptive structure in Arabic. Remember:

- the structure of the exceptive sentence consists of three components: (1) the "excepted-from noun" المُسْتَثْنَى مِنْهُ preceding the exceptive particle/word, (2) the exceptive particle/word itself, and (3) the "excepted noun" المُسْتَثْنَى following the exceptive particle/word
- there are at least seven exceptive particles/words, some of which function as particles, some as nouns, and some as verbs
- when the exceptive structure is not missing any of its three parts and is in the affirmative (i.e., not used with negation), the ending on the *excepted noun* المُسْتَثْنَى following إلّا is the accusative مَنْصوب case; the other exceptive words themselves exhibit the accusative مَنْصوب case ending, with the noun following them having the genitive مَجْرور case ending
- when negation is used with the exceptive structure, the case ending on the *excepted noun* المُسْتَثْنَى following إلّا is (a) either the accusative مَنْصوب or (b) any of the three case endings (مَرْفوع nominative, مَنْصوب accusative, or مَجْرور genitive), depending on the function of the *excepted-from* noun المُسْتَثْنَى مِنْهُ preceding إلّا in the sentence; the other exceptive words themselves exhibit (a) the accusative مَنْصوب case ending or (b) any of the three case endings, depending on the function of the *excepted-from* noun in the sentence, with the noun following the exceptive words having the genitive مَجْرور case ending
- when negation is used with the exceptive structure and the *excepted-from* noun المُسْتَثْنَى مِنْه is dropped, the case ending on the *excepted noun* المُسْتَثْنَى following إلّا is any of the three case endings, depending on the function of the *excepted* noun in the sentence; the other exceptive words themselves exhibit any of the three case endings, depending on the function of the *excepted* noun in the sentence, with the noun following the exceptive words having the genitive مَجْرور case ending.

19

The Vocative النِّداء

The vocative structure, known in Arabic as النِّداء "the calling," is unique to Arabic, and has no exact equivalent in English. It consists of two components: the vocative particle, known in Arabic as أداة النِّداء "the tool of calling," and the vocative noun, known in Arabic as المُنادىٰ "the one being called," occurring after the vocative particle. The chapter covers the following:

- the most common vocative particles and their meanings and use
- the different types of vocative nouns used
- the different case endings occurring with vocative nouns
- the dropping of the vocative particle.

19.1 The Vocative Particle يا

The most common vocative particle is يا , used to call someone or attract someone's attention. The closest English equivalent is "Oh, you," and it is usually not translated, since it does not have an exact English equivalent. (There are three other vocative particles, but these are not commonly used.) As for the vocative المُنادىٰ noun or phrase (i.e., the one being called or the one whose attention is being attracted) following the vocative particle يا , this requires the nominative مَرْفوع or accusative مَنْصوب case ending, depending on the type of noun or phrase used, including whether it is a proper name, an indefinite noun with reference, an indefinite noun without reference, or an إضافة 'iDaafa phrase.

Modern Standard Arabic Grammar: A Learner's Guide, First Edition.
© 2011 Mohammad T. Alhawary. Published 2011 by Blackwell Publishing Ltd.

19.1.1 The Vocative Noun المُنادى as a Proper Name

When the vocative noun المُنادى following the vocative particle يا is a proper name, then it occurs with the nominative مَرْفوع *Damma* case ending (without nunation), unless the name ends with a long *'alif* vowel (in which case no *Damma* is required), as in:

... ، يا عَلِيُّ	... ، يا سَعيدُ
"Ali, ..."	"Said, ..."
... ، يا زَيْنَبُ	... ، يا فاطِمَةُ
"Zaynab, ..."	"Fatima, ..."
... ، يا اللهُ	... ، يا مُصْطَفى
"Oh, God ..."	"Mustafa, ..."

19.1.2 The Vocative Noun المُنادى as an Indefinite Noun with Reference

A vocative مُنادى noun following the vocative particle يا usually occurs indefinite (i.e., without the definite article الـ "the") when the caller/speaker is addressing a specific person/persons in front of him/her. In this case, the noun occurs with the nominative مَرْفوع case ending (without nunation), as in:

... ، يا طُلّابُ	... ، يا طالِبُ
"Students, ..."	"Student, ..."
... ، يا طالِبَتانِ	... ، يا طالِبانِ
"Students (DF), ..."	"Students (DM), ..."
... ، يا رِجالُ	... ، يا رَجُلُ
"Men, ..."	"Man, ..."

19.1.3 The Vocative Noun المُنادى as an Indefinite Noun without Reference

A vocative مُنادى noun following the vocative particle يا can occur indefinite and without referring to anyone in particular, such as when it is used proverbially. In this case, the noun occurs with the accusative مَنْصوب case ending (with nunation), as in:

يا مُقامِراً اِحْذَرْ .

"Oh you gambler, be careful."

يا مُسافِراً هَنيئاً لَكَ .

"Oh you traveler, lucky you."

19.1.4 The Vocative Noun المُنادىٰ as an إضافة 'iDaafa phrase

A vocative مُنادىٰ following the vocative particle يا may occur as an إضافة 'iDaafa phrase whether it consists of a compound proper name (i.e., consisting of two names) or a regular (definite) 'iDaafa phrase (i.e., consisting of two nouns or a noun and a pronoun). In this case, the first noun of the إضافة 'iDaafa phrase occurs with the accusative مَنصوب case ending and the second noun with the genitive مَجْرور case ending, following the 'iDaafa phrase rules (see 3.3–4), as in:

يا عَبْدَ اللَّطيفِ ، ...

"Abdallatif, ..."

يا عَبْدَ الله ، ...

"Abdallah, ..."

يا مُجيبَ الدُّعاءِ ، ...

"Oh, You [God] who responds to prayers, ..."

يا صَديقَ العُمُرِ ، ...

"Oh, lifelong friend, ..."

يا أبا سَعيدٍ ، ...

"Abu Said, ..."

يا ابْنَ الكِرامِ ، ...

"Son of the generous ones, ..."

19.1.5 Use of More than One Vocative مُنادىٰ Noun

More than one type of vocative مُنادىٰ noun, such as a proper name and an إضافة 'iDaafa phrase, may occur together following the vocative particle يا , in which case each one follows its own case-ending rule (as explained above), regardless of the order in which it occurs after يا , as in:

يا صَديقَنا سَعيدُ ، ...

"Our friend, Said, ..."

=

يا سَعيدُ صَديقَنا ، ...

"Said, our friend, ..."

يا أبا عَليٍّ سَعيدُ ، ...

"Abu Ali, Said, ..."

=

يا سَعيدُ أبا عَليٍّ ، ...

"Said, Abu Ali, ..."

يا صَديقَنا عَبْدَ الله ، ...

"Our friend, Abdallah, ..."

=

يا عَبْدَ الله صَديقَنا ، ...

"Abdallah, our friend, ..."

19.1.6 Use of an Adjective Following the Vocative
مُنادَى Noun

An adjective can be used after the vocative مُنادَى noun, agreeing with it in definiteness and case ending (i.e., it occurs definite and either with the accusative مَنْصوب or nominative مَرْفوع case ending, depending on the type of vocative noun used), as in:

يا اللهُ الرَّحيمُ ، ...	يا سَعيدُ الفاضِلُ ، ...
"Oh, God the Merciful, ..."	"Said, the gracious, ..."
يا أُسْتاذَنا المُحْتَرَمَ ، ...	يا عَبْدَ الله الفاضِلَ ، ...
"Our, respected teacher, ..."	"Abdallah, the gracious, ..."

When the vocative noun ends with the first-person possessive pronoun ـي "my" (i.e., when it occurs within an إضافة *'iDaafa* phrase), the possessive suffix is subject to two rules:

(1) if the vocative noun is defective (i.e., ends with a long vowel), then the suffix consists of a *yaa'* with a *fatHa* [ya] or of a *shadda* with a *fatHa* [yya] if the long vowel is a *yaa'*, as in:

يا فَتايَ	←	فَتايَ	←	فَتىً
"My young man, ..."		"My young man"		"A young man"

يا مُحامِيَّ	←	مُحامِيَّ	←	مُحامي
"My lawyer, ..."		"My lawyer"		"A lawyer"

(2) if the vocative noun is non-defective (i.e., does not end with a vowel before adding the possessive first-person suffix ـي "my"), then the possessive pronoun may: (a) stay unchanged, (b) be followed by a *fatHa*, or (c) be shortened into a *kasra*, as in:

يا أُسْتاذِ، ...	=	يا أُستاذِيَ ، ...	=	يا أُستاذي ، ...
"My teacher, ..."		"My teacher, ..."		"My teacher, ..."

19.2   Dropping the Vocative Particle يا

The vocative particle يا is optional, except when it is used with an indefinite noun, and it can be dropped when it is used with a proper name or a (definite) إضافة *'iDaafa* phrase, as in:

سَعيدٌ ، ...	=	يا سَعيدٌ ، ...
"Said, ..."		"Said, ..."
أُستاذي ، ...	=	يا أُسْتاذي ، ...
"My teacher, ..."		"My teacher, ..."
أُسْتاذَنا المُحْتَرَمَ ، ...	=	يا أُسْتاذَنا المُحْتَرَمَ ، ...
"Our respected teacher, ..."		"Our respected teacher, ..."

19.3   Optative Use of the Vocative Particle يا

Instead of being followed by a noun, the vocative particle يا may be followed by لَيْتَ "wish" (followed by a pronoun), in which case it would have an optative meaning (i.e., to express a wish). In this case, the use of the vocative particle يا itself is optional, as in:

لَيْتَني كُنْتُ هُناكَ .	=	يا لَيْتَني كُنْتُ هُناكَ .
"I wish I were there."		"Oh, I wish I were there."
لَيْتَني ماحَضَرْتُ .	=	يا لَيْتَني ماحَضَرْتُ .
"I wish I had not attended."		"Oh, I wish I had not attended."

19.4   Derogatory Use of the Vocative Particle يا

The vocative particle يا may have a derogatory meaning, especially when followed by a demonstrative pronoun, as in:

يا هٰذِهِ .	يا هٰذا .
"You this F"	"You this M"

19.5 The Vocative Particles أيُّها and أيَّتُها

If the vocative مُنادًى noun occurs with the definite article, then the particles أيُّها (for masculine and feminine nouns) and أيَّتُها (for feminine nouns) are used optionally with or without the vocative particle يا , although the latter is more generally used. As for the definite noun following the vocative particles أيُّها and أيَّتُها , it occurs with the nominative مَرْفوع case ending (without nunation), as in:

... ، أيُّها الطّالِبُ	=	... ، يا أيُّها الطّالِبُ
"Student (M), . . ."		"Student (M), . . ."
... ، أيُّها الطّلّابُ	=	... ، يا أيُّها الطّلّابُ
"Students (M), . . ."		"Students (M), . . ."
... ، أيَّتُها الطّالِبَةُ	=	... ، يا أيَّتُها الطّالِبَةُ
"Student (F), . . ."		"Student (F), . . ."
... ، أيَّتُها الطّالِباتُ	=	... ، يا أيَّتُها الطّالِباتُ
"Students (F), . . ."		"Students (F), . . ."
... ، أيُّها السّادَةُ والسَّيِّداتُ	=	... ، يا أيُّها السّادَةُ والسَّيِّداتُ
"Gentlemen and ladies, . . ."		"Gentlemen and ladies, . . ."
... ، أيُّها السَّيِّداتُ والسّادَةُ	=	... ، يا أيُّها السَّيِّداتُ والسّادَة
"Ladies and gentlemen, . . ."		"Ladies and gentlemen, . . ."

19.6 Summary

This chapter discussed the structure of the vocative in Arabic. Remember:

- the most commonly used vocative particle to call someone or attract someone's attention is يا
- the vocative مُنادًى noun following the vocative particle يا may be a proper name, an indefinite noun with reference, an indefinite noun without reference, or an إضافة *'iDaafa* phrase, with each having a specific case ending: a proper name and an indefinite noun with specific reference occur with the nominative مَرْفوع case ending, whereas an

indefinite noun (without reference) and the first noun of an إضافة 'iDaafa phrase occur with the accusative مَنْصوب case ending

- the vocative particle يا is optional except when used with an indefinite noun; i.e., it can be dropped when used with a proper name or a definite إضافة 'iDaafa phrase
- the vocative particle يا can additionally have an optative meaning (i.e., expressing a wish) or a derogatory meaning when addressing someone
- the vocative particles أَيُّها (for masculine and feminine nouns) and أَيَّتُها (for feminine nouns) are used with (definite) nouns; the vocative particle يا may optionally be used with them.

20

Exclamation التَّعَجُّب

The exclamation structure, called in Arabic التَّعَجُّب "expressing wonder," can be conveyed in many different ways. It can be expressed by means of two regular patterns, certain particles, question words, and certain phrases. The chapter covers the following:

- use of regular expressions based on two main regular patterns to express an exclamation sentence
- use of certain particles to express exclamation
- use of question words and certain phrases to express exclamation.

20.1 Two Regular Expressions ما أَفْعَلَ and بِ أَفْعِلْ

There are at least two regular expressions used to express exclamation. These expressions are based on two main patterns أَفْعَلَ and أَفْعِلْ, derived from Form I verbs. In MSA, the former pattern is more commonly used than the latter. Derived verbs and words follow a similar regular rule where certain words having the same patterns of أَفْعَلَ and أَفْعِلْ (followed by the derived verbal noun/gerund or derived word) are used.

20.1.1 Exclamation of Form I Verbs

For triliteral Form I verbs فَعَلَ , فَعِلَ, and فَعُلَ and adjectives derived from them (for more on verb forms, see Chapter 13), two patterns أَفْعَلَ and أَفْعِلْ

Modern Standard Arabic Grammar: A Learner's Guide, First Edition.
© 2011 Mohammad T. Alhawary. Published 2011 by Blackwell Publishing Ltd.

are used, with the former pattern being identical to the comparative/ superlative form of adjectives (see Chapter 15), but here أَفْعَلَ has the subjunctive مَنْصوب *fatHa* mood ending and أفْعِلْ has the jussive مَجْزوم *sukuun* mood ending, as though it were an imperative verb. In addition, the pattern أَفْعَلَ is preceded by the exclamation particle ما ← ما أَفْعَلَ (for use of ما as a question particle, see 7.1.4, and as a conditional particle, see 17.1), and the pattern أَفْعِلْ is followed by the preposition بِـ ← أَفْعِلْ بِـ as part of the rule, as in:

ما + أَجْمَلَ = ما أَجْمَلَ	أَفْعَلَ	← "to become beautiful"	جَمُلَ – يَجْمُلُ – جَميل
أَجْمِلْ + بِـ = أَجْمِلْ بِـ	أَفْعِلْ	←	
ما + أَطْوَلَ = ما أَطْوَلَ	أَفْعَلَ	← "to become tall/long"	طالَ – يَطولُ – طَويل
أَطْوِلْ + بِـ = أَطْوِلْ بِـ	أَفْعِلْ	←	
ما + أَعَزَّ = ما أَعَزَّ	أَفْعَلَ	← "to become proud"	عَزَّ – يَعِزُّ – عَزيز
أَعْزِزْ + بِـ = أَعْزِزْ بِـ	أَفْعِلْ	←	

As for the noun following أَفْعَلَ called in Arabic المُتَعَجَّب مِنْه "the exclaimed from noun," it occurs with the accusative مَنْصوب *fatHa* case ending, while the exclaimed from noun following أَفْعِلْ بِـ occurs with the genitive مَجْرور case ending. In either case, the exclaimed from noun following the two patterns must be definite, as in:

أَجْمِلْ بِالحَديقَةِ !	=	ما أَجْمَلَ الحَديقَةَ !
"How beautiful the garden is!"		"How beautiful the garden is!"
أَطْوِلْ بِالسَّفَرِ !	=	ما أَطْوَلَ السَّفَرَ !
"How long travel is!"		"How long travel is!"

The exclaimed from noun following أَفْعَلَ and أَفْعِلْ can also be in the dual, or plural as well as the singular, as in:

أَجْمِلْ بِالحَديقَتَيْنِ !	=	ما أَجْمَلَ الحَديقَتَيْنِ !
"How beautiful the two gardens are!"		"How beautiful the two gardens are!"

أَجْمِلْ بِالحَدائِقِ !	=	ما أَجْمَلَ الحَدائِقَ !
"How beautiful the gardens are!"		"How beautiful the gardens are!"

Note: The exclaimed from noun following ما أَفْعَلَ occurs with the accusative case مَنْصوب ending, rather than the nominative مَرْفوع case ending, for example, so that the exclamation structure is distinguished from the interrogative structure, as in:

ما أَجْمَلُ الحَديقَةِ ؟	≠	ما أَجْمَلَ الحَديقَةَ !
"What is the most beautiful thing in the garden?"	≠	"How beautiful the garden is!"

The exclaimed from noun following ما أَفْعَلَ and بِ أَفْعِلْ can occur with the nominative case ending, but only if it occurs at the beginning of the sentence, and a pronoun suffix referring to it takes its position following ما أَفْعَلَ and بِ أَفْعِلْ (although this is not as common as the above structure), as in:

الحَديقَةُ أَجْمِلْ بِها !	=	الحَديقَةُ ما أَجْمَلَها !
"The garden, how beautiful it is!"		"The garden, how beautiful it is!"

السَّفَرُ أَطْوِلْ بِهِ !	=	السَّفَرُ ما أَطْوَلَهُ !
"Travel, how long it is!"		"Travel, how long it is!"

Note: As mentioned above, the exclamation pattern ما أَفْعَلَ is more common than بِ أَفْعِلْ . However, the pattern أَفْعِلْ بِ is used in very common expressions, as in:

أَنْعِمْ بِهِذِهِ العائلة !
"How excellent this family is!"

أَكْرِمْ بِهِذِهِ العائلة !
"How generous this family is!"

أَكْرِمْ وأَنْعِمْ بِكُم !
"How excellent and generous you are!"

20.1.2 Exclamation of Derived Verbs and Words

The exclamation of derived verbs of Forms II–X or other non-derived quadriliteral verbs (see 13.1–3) does not follow the ما أَفْعَلَ and بِ أَفْعِلْ rule directly. Rather, a comparative word having either of the two patterns, such as أَكْثَر "more," أَقَلّ "less," أَشَدّ "more intense," أَعْظَم "greater," or أَصْغَر "smaller," is used and followed by the verbal noun of the derived verb (see 14.2). In addition, the word with the pattern أَفْعَل is to be preceded by the particle ما (otherwise the preposition بِ is used following أَفْعِل if the pattern أَفْعِل is used), as in:

II دَرَّسَ ← تَدْريسَ   ما أَعْظَمَ تَدْريسَهُ لِلُّغَةِ العَرَبِيَّة ! / أَعْظِمْ بِتَدْريسِهِ لِلُّغَةِ العَرَبِيَّة !
"How great is his teaching of the Arabic language!"

IV أَنْتَجَ ← إِنْتاج   ما أَكْثَرَ إِنْتاجَ السُّعوديَّةِ لِلنِّفْط !
"How plentiful is the oil production of Saudi Arabia!"

VIII اِشْتَعَلَ ← اِشْتِعال   ما أَشَدَّ اشْتِعالَ البِنْزينِ !
"How intense is the burning of gas!"

X اِسْتَقْبَلَ ← اِسْتِقْبالَ   ما أَكْرَمَ اسْتِقْبالَ العَرَبِيِّ !
"How generous is the reception of the Arab!"

Exclamation of nouns, whether derived – such as derived abstract nouns (see 14.8) – or non-derived, are expressed in the same way, as in:

ما أَعْظَمَ إِنْسانِيَّةَ جَدّي !
"How great the humanity of my grandfather is!"

ما أَصْغَرَ مَسْؤوليَّةَ هٰذا المُوَظَّفِ !
"How small the responsibility of this employee is!"

ما أَعْظَمَ صَوْتَ هٰذا المُغَنّي !
"How great the voice of this singer is!"

20.1.3   Use of the Particles ما and أَنْ with ما أَفْعَل and أَفْعِل بِ

When the verb is in the passive voice, preceded by a negation particle, or happens to be كانَ or any of its sisters (see 4.2.5), a comparative word having the pattern of أَفْعَل (or أَفْعِل), such as أَكْثَر "more," أَقَلّ "less," أَشَدّ "more intense," أَعْظَم "greater," or أَصْغَر "smaller," can be used (preceded by the exclamation particle ما for the pattern أَفْعَل) followed by the particle أَنْ or ما , as in:

يُظْلَمُ النَّاسُ أَثْنَاءَ الْحُروب . ← ما أَكْثَرَ ما يُظْلَمُ النَّاسُ أَثْنَاءَ الْحُروب !

"People are wronged during wars."   "How many people are wronged during wars!"

لا يَنْجَحُ سَليمٌ في الإِمْتِحان . ← ما أَصْعَبَ أَلَّا (=أَنْ+لا) يَنْجَحَ سَليمٌ في الإِمْتِحان !

"Salim does not pass the test."   "How difficult it is that Salim does not pass the test!"

يَكونُ الأَقارِبُ بَيْنَنا . ← ما أَسْعَدَ أَنْ يَكونَ الأَقارِبُ بَيْنَنا !

"The relatives are among us."   "How happy it is for the relatives to be among us!"

20.2 Use of the Vocative Particle يا and the Exclamation Particle لَـ

Another way of expressing exclamation in Arabic is by means of the vocative particle يا (for more on the vocative, see Chapter 19) and the exclamation particle لَـ , where:

(a) the vocative particle يا is used by itself, in which case it can be followed by an indefinite noun with the nominative مَرْفوع or accusative مَنْصوب case ending (without nunation), such as:

يا عَجَبُ !   يا عَجَبَا !

"What a wonder!"   "What a wonder!"

يا سَماءُ !   يا سَماءَا !

"What a sky!"   "What a sky!"

(b) the vocative particle يا is used together with the exclamation particle لَـ , where the definite noun following the exclamation particle لَـ occurs with the genitive مَجْرور case ending, as in:

يا لَجَمالِ البَحْرِ !   يا لَزُرْقَةِ السَّماءِ !

"How beautiful the sea is!"   "How blue the sky is!"

يا لَلْعَجَبِ !   يا لَلسَّماءِ !

"What a wonder!"   "What a sky!"

يا لَلْهَوْلِ !
"What a horror!"

يا لَلْمُصِيبَةِ !
"What a catastrophe!"

يا لَلْعارِ !
"What a shame!"

يا لَلْفَضِيحَةِ !
"What a scandal!"

(c) the vocative particle يا is used together with the exclamation particle لَ , followed by a pronoun suffix as well as the preposition مِنْ (and an indefinite noun), as in:

يا لَكَ مِنْ رَجُلٍ !
"What a man you are!"

يا لَكِ مِنِ امْرَأَةٍ !
"What a woman you are!"

يا لَهُ مِنْ شابٍّ جَبان !
"How cowardly a young man he is!"

يا لَها مِنْ شابَّةٍ شُجاعَة !
"How brave a young woman she is!"

20.3 Use of Certain Question Words and Phrases

Question words, such as كَيْفَ "how" and ماذا "what," can be used to express exclamation just as they are used to form questions (Chapter 7), but with falling intonation when expressing exclamation. In addition, there are certain phrases, such as اللهُ أَكْبَرُ "God is the greatest," and سُبْحانَ الله "God is glorified," which can be used by themselves or in combination with sentences to express exclamation, as in:

كَيْفَ يَفْعَلُ هٰذا !
"How does he do this!"

كَيْفَ يَفْعَلُ هٰذا وَهُوَ صَدِيقِي !
"How does he do this yet he is my friend!"

اللهُ أَكْبَرُ !
"God is the greatest!"

اللهُ أَكْبَرُ ماذا أَرىٰ !
"God is the greatest; what do I see!"

سُبْحانَ الله !
"God is glorified!"

سُبْحانَ الله الجَوُّ جَمِيلٌ اليَوْم !
"God is glorified; the weather is nice today!"

20.4 Summary

This chapter discussed the exclamation structures in Arabic. Remember:

- the most regular and common way of expressing exclamation is by means of the expressions ما أَفْعَلَ and بِ أَفْعِلْ applicable to triliteral Form I verbs
- the expression ما أَفْعَلَ is followed by a definite noun with the accusative مَنْصوب case ending, whereas بِ أَفْعِلْ is followed by a definite noun with the genitive مَجْرور case ending
- ما أَفْعَلَ is a more common structure than بِ أَفْعِلْ
- for verbs that do not belong to Form I (such as the derived verbs of Forms II–X, or quadriliteral verbs), their verbal nouns are used instead, preceded by a comparative word with the pattern أَفْعِلْ or أَفْعَلَ (e.g., أَعْظَمَ "greater" and أَصْغَرَ "smaller") to fit the phrase ما أَفْعَلَ or بِ أَفْعِلْ (e.g., ما أَعْظَمَ "how great" and ما أَصْغَرَ "how small")
- for nouns (derived or non-derived), exclamation is expressed by resorting to the same rule of using a comparative word preceding the noun
- for verbs in the passive voice, preceded by a negation particle, or which happen to be كانَ or any of its sisters, exclamation is expressed by resorting to the same rule of using a comparative word in addition to using the particles ما or أَنْ before the verb
- the vocative particle يا can be used to express exclamation when used before indefinite nouns with the nominative مَرْفوع or accusative مَنْصوب case ending (without nunation)
- the vocative particle يا can be used with the exclamation particle لَ to express exclamation when used before definite nouns with the genitive مَجْرور case ending
- certain question words and certain (religious) phrases can be used to express exclamation.

21

Apposition البَدَل

The apposition structure, called in Arabic البَدَل "substitution," refers to the use of a noun following another noun, not separated from it by any conjunction, where either of the two nouns can be dropped without affecting the grammaticality of the sentence, hence the term *substitution* in Arabic. The use of a second noun here is for the purpose of further clarifying or defining the meaning of the first noun. The noun–noun apposition structure is distinct from the إضافة *'iDaafa* phrase structure where, although two nouns are used together, neither can be dropped without affecting the grammaticality or the meaning of the sentence (see Chapter 3). The apposition structure consists mainly of two nouns, the first of which is called in Arabic المُبْدَل مِنْهُ "the noun being substituted," and the second called البَدَل "the substituting noun," or *apposition* noun. An apposition بَدَل noun belongs to one of four main types, each of which may occur in different positions in a sentence. The chapter covers the following:

- the main types of apposition structures and their uses
- the case endings occurring with the two nouns of the apposition structure
- definiteness agreement between the two nouns of the apposition structure
- the use of compound nouns consisting of the word اِبْن "son" followed by a noun as an additional type of apposition structure.

Modern Standard Arabic Grammar: A Learner's Guide, First Edition.
© 2011 Mohammad T. Alhawary. Published 2011 by Blackwell Publishing Ltd.

21.1 Types of Apposition Nouns

There are four main types of apposition بَدَل nouns, depending on the degree of how the apposition noun relates to a preceding noun, whether (a) wholly, (b) partly, (c) indirectly, or (d) by mistake.

21.1.1 Whole Noun–Noun Apposition بَدَل الكُلّ مِنَ الكُلّ

In this type of apposition structure, the apposition noun and the noun preceding it refer equally to the same thing (although the apposition noun serves to further clarify or define the preceding noun) to the extent that one of them can be dropped without affecting the grammaticality or the meaning of the sentence. Hence, this type is called in Arabic بَدَل الكُلّ مِنَ الكُلّ "whole noun-noun apposition." The apposition noun occurs with the same case ending as that of the preceding noun, which can be any of the three case endings (i.e., مَرْفوع nominative, مَنْصوب accusative, or مَجْرور genitive), depending on the function of the word in the sentence (see 22.2.2 on case endings), as in:

حَضَرَ صَديقُكَ .	=	حَضَرَ سَليمٌ .	=	حَضَرَ سَليمٌ صَديقُكَ .
"Your friend came."		"Salim came."		"Your friend Salim came."

قابَلْتُ صَديقَكَ .	=	قابَلْتُ سَليماً .	=	قابَلْتُ سَليماً صَديقَكَ .
"I met your friend."		"I met Salim."		"I met your friend Salim."

قَرَأْتُ عَن عَليٍّ .	=	قَرَأْتُ عَنِ الإِمام .	=	قَرَأْتُ عَنِ الإِمام عَليٍّ .
"I read about Ali."		"I read about the Imam."		"I read about the Imam Ali."

21.1.2 Partial Noun–Noun Apposition بَدَل البَعْض مِنَ الكُلّ

This type of apposition structure consists of an apposition noun referring to a part of the noun preceding it and may occur with a possessive pronoun referring to it. Hence, this type is called in Arabic بَدَل البَعْض مِنَ الكُلّ "partial noun–noun apposition." Although the apposition noun here serves to further clarify or define the preceding noun, either noun can be dropped, although some difference in meaning may result, especially when the apposition noun is dropped (and the preceding noun is retained). The apposition noun occurs with the same case ending as that of the preceding noun, which can be any of the three case endings (i.e., مَرْفوع nominative, مَنْصوب accusative, or مَجْرور genitive), depending on the function of the word in the sentence (see 22.2.2 on case endings), as in:

أَعْجَبَني البَيْتُ .	≠	أَعْجَبَني سَقْفُهُ .	=	أَعْجَبَني البَيْتُ سَقْفُهُ .
"The house impressed me."		"Its ceiling impressed me."		"The house's ceiling impressed me."

قَرَأْتُ القِصَّةَ .	≠	قَرَأْتُ نِصْفَها .	=	قَرَأْتُ القِصَّةَ نِصْفَها .
"I read the story."		"I read half of it."		"I read half of the story."

بَحَثْتُ عَنْ كِتابَيْنِ : كِتابٍ في اللُّغَةِ و كِتابٍ في الخَطِّ .
"I looked for two books: a book on language and a book on calligraphy."

بَحَثْتُ عَنْ كِتابَيْنِ .
"I looked for two books."

بَحَثْتُ عَنْ كِتابٍ في اللُّغَةِ وكِتابٍ في الخَطِّ .
"I looked for a book on language and a book on calligraphy."

21.1.3   Inclusive Noun–Noun Apposition بَدَل الإشْتِمال

This type of apposition structure is similar to the *partial noun–noun apposition*. It consists of an apposition noun referring to one of the features or attributes of the noun preceding it in a rather indirect way. Hence, this type is called in Arabic بَدَل الإشْتِمال "inclusive noun–noun apposition." Although the apposition noun here serves to further clarify or define the preceding noun, either noun can be dropped, although some difference in meaning may result when the apposition noun is dropped. The apposition noun occurs with the same case ending as that of the preceding noun, which can be any of the three case endings (i.e., مَرْفوع nominative, مَنْصوب accusative, or مَجْرور genitive), depending on the function of the word in the sentence (see 22.2.2 on case endings), as in:

سَرَّني الأُسْتاذُ .	≠	سَرَّني تَدْريسُهُ .	=	سَرَّني الأُسْتاذُ تَدْريسُهُ .
"The teacher pleased me."		"His teaching pleased me."		"The teacher's teaching pleased me."

سَمِعْتُ الرَّئيسَ .	≠	سَمِعْتُ خِطابَهُ .	=	سَمِعْتُ الرَّئيسَ خِطابَهُ .
"I heard the president."		"I heard his speech."		"I heard the president's speech."

اِسْتَمَعْتُ إلَى الأُسْتاذِ .	≠	اِسْتَمَعْتُ إلَى رَأْيِهِ .	=	اِسْتَمَعْتُ إلَى الأُسْتاذِ رَأْيِهِ .
"I listened to the teacher."		"I listened to his opinion."		"I listened to the teacher's opinion."

Note: بَدَل الإِشْتِمال "inclusive noun–noun apposition" is less commonly used in MSA than the other types.

21.1.4 Mistaken Noun–Noun Apposition بَدَل الغَلَط

This is not a real type of apposition structure, but is one used when the noun preceding the apposition noun is said by mistake as a result of misspeaking or a false start and, therefore, the apposition noun is used to indicate the correct intended noun instead. Hence, this type is called in Arabic بَدَل الغَلَط "mistaken noun–noun apposition." The apposition noun occurs with the same case ending as that of the preceding noun, which can be any of the three case endings (i.e., مَرْفوع nominative, مَنْصوب accusative, or مَجْرور genitive), depending on function of the word in the sentence (see 22.2.2 on case endings), as in:

حَضَرَ الأُسْتاذُ ، المُديرُ .
"The teacher came, (rather) the principal."

تَفَضَّلِ القَلَمَ ، الدَّفْتَرَ .
"Please take the pen, (rather) the notebook."

بَحَثْتُ عَنِ الدَّفْتَرِ ، القَلَمِ .
"I looked for the notebook, (rather) the pen."

Note: As mentioned above, the use of the two nouns within a noun–noun apposition structure is different than that within an إضافة *'iDaafa* phrase: (a) the order of the two nouns in an *'iDaafa* phrase is the reverse of that in an apposition phrase, (b) the case endings in both nouns are not necessarily the same in an *'iDaafa* phrase, and (c) neither of the two nouns in an *'iDaafa* phrase can be dropped (see 3.3–4). Nevertheless, the second and third types of noun–noun apposition explained above (21.1.2–3) can be expressed by means of إضافة *'iDaafa* phrases, as in:

قَرَأْتُ نِصْفَ القِصَّةِ .

"I read half of the story."

سَرَّني تَدْريسُ الأُسْتاذِ .

"The teacher's teaching pleased me."

21.2 Definiteness Agreement within Noun–Noun Apposition

The apposition noun is not required to agree with the preceding noun in definiteness (although it agrees with it in case ending). Therefore, an apposition noun can be either indefinite or definite, regardless of the preceding noun, as in:

الطّالِبُ نَوْعانِ : مُجْتَهِدٌ وكَسولٌ .	=	الطّالِبُ نَوْعانِ : المُجْتَهِدُ والكَسولُ .
"The student is one of two types: a hardworking and a lazy one."		"The student is one of two types: the hardworking and the lazy one."

قابَلْتُ سَليماً ، طالِباً مُجْتَهِداً .	=	قابَلْتُ سَليماً ، الطالِبَ المُجْتَهِدَ .
"I met Salim: a hardworking student."		"I met Salim: the hardworking student."

21.3 Use of اِبْن "Son" and the Noun Following it as an Apposition Noun

In Arabic grammar, the word اِبْن "son" is treated as an adjective of the preceding noun, having the same case ending as that of the noun preceding it (although the noun following it has the genitive مَجْرور case ending). The word اِبْن "son," together with the noun following it, further clarifies and defines the noun preceding it and either noun can be dropped without affecting the meaning or the grammaticality of the sentence. Accordingly, the use of the compound structure consisting of the word اِبْن "son" and the noun following it resembles and functions as an apposition noun, as in:

كانَ اِبْنُ الوَليدِ شُجاعاً .	=	كانَ خالِدٌ شُجاعاً .	=	كانَ خالِدُ بْنُ الوَليدِ شُجاعاً .
"Ibn Al-Walid was brave."		"Khalid was brave."		"Khalid Ibn Al-Walid was brave."

إِنَّ ابْنَ الوَلِيدِ شُجَاعٌ.	=	إِنَّ خَالِداً شُجَاعٌ.	=	إِنَّ خَالِدَ بْنَ الوَلِيدِ شُجَاعٌ.
"Indeed, Ibn Al-Walid is brave."		"Indeed, Khalid is brave."		"Indeed, Khalid Ibn Al-Walid is brave."
قَرَأْتُ عَنِ ابْنِ الوَلِيدِ.	=	قَرَأْتُ عَنْ خَالِدٍ.	=	قَرَأْتُ عَنْ خَالِدِ بْنِ الوَلِيدِ.
"I read about Ibn Al-Walid."		"I read about Khalid."		"I read about Khalid Ibn Al-Walid."

Furthermore, the word اِبْن "son," together with the noun following it, may clarify and define a preceding noun that is itself an apposition noun for a preceding noun which also may be dropped without affecting the grammaticality or meaning of the sentence. In other words, اِبْن "son," together with the noun following it, can function as a second apposition noun, as in:

كانَ القائِدُ خالِدُ بْنُ الوَلِيدِ شُجاعاً.
"The leader Khalid Ibn Al-Walid was brave."

إِنَّ القائِدَ خالِدَ بْنَ الوَلِيدِ شُجاعٌ.
"Indeed, the leader Khalid Ibn Al-Walid is brave."

قَرَأْتُ عَنِ القائِدِ خالِدِ بْنِ الوَلِيدِ.
"I read about the leader Khalid Ibn Al-Walid."

Note: As the examples above show, three rules apply when using the word اِبْن "son" as an apposition noun (or as an adjective): (a) the case ending of the noun preceding it is pronounced without nunation; (b) the light *hamza* with *'alif* ا is dropped both in speech and writing; and (c) when the noun preceding it is dropped, the light *hamza* with *'alif* ا is retained in writing but dropped in speech. Otherwise, if the word اِبْن "son" and the noun following it occur as any other part of speech (i.e., other than that of an adjective/apposition noun), or if the word اِبْن "son" is followed by a pronoun (even though it is used as an apposition noun), then nunation of the case ending on the noun preceding it is retained and the light *hamza* with *'alif* ا is retained in writing but dropped in speech (with a helping vowel *kasra* following the nunation of the preceding noun added), as in:

سَعيدٌ ابْنُ سَعْدٍ.
"Said (is) Sad's son."

إِنَّ سَعيداً ابْنُ سَعْدٍ .
"Indeed, Said (is) Sad's son."

حَضَرَ سَعيدٌ ابْنُ عَمِّكَ .
"Said, your (paternal) cousin, came."

Note: In addition, when the noun preceding اِبْن "son" is also a compound noun (referring to the same person) consisting of أَبو "father" or أُمّ "mother" and a noun following it (which always occurs with the genitive مَجْرور case ending), the word اِبْن "son" agrees with the first part of the compound noun (i.e., with أَبو "father" or أُمّ "mother") in case ending, not with the noun immediately preceding it, as in (see 14.10 on the five nouns):

زارَني أَبو سَعيدٍ ابْنُ طَلالٍ .
"Abu Said Ibn Talal visited me."

قابَلْتُ أَبا سَعيدٍ ابْنَ طَلالٍ .
"I met Abu Said Ibn Talal."

سَلَّمْتُ عَلىٰ أَبي سَعيدٍ ابْنِ طَلالٍ .
"I shook hands with Abu Said Ibn Talal."

21.4   Summary

This chapter discussed the structure of noun–noun apposition. Remember:

- the noun–noun apposition structure البَدَل is used when the apposition noun (i.e., the second noun) serves to further clarify or modify a preceding noun
- both nouns within noun–noun apposition agree in case endings but do not necessarily agree in definiteness
- there are four main types of noun–noun apposition, depending on how the apposition بَدَل noun relates to a preceding noun whether (a) wholly, (b) partly, (c) indirectly, or (d) by mistake or as a false start
- the two nouns used in an إضافة *'iDaafa* phrase may resemble a noun–noun apposition superficially (by means of having two nouns used without being separated by any conjunction); the comparison stops here, since in an إضافة *'iDaafa* phrase (a) the two nouns do not agree

in case endings, (b) the word order of the two nouns is reversed, and (3) neither part of the two nouns can be deleted without affecting the grammaticality and the meaning of the sentence

- a fifth type of noun–noun apposition structure is compound names consisting of the word اِبْن "son" and a noun following it (which always occurs with the genitive مَجْرور case ending), where the word اِبْن "son" agrees with a preceding noun which it further clarifies and defines; it can also be dropped without affecting the grammaticality or the meaning of the sentence.

22

Triptote, Diptote, and Indeclinable/Invariable
المُعْرَب والمَبْنيّ

Most Arabic words have variable grammatical or vowel endings, depending on their function in the sentence. In Arabic this feature is called الإعْراب "declinability" (or exhibiting the grammatical endings of case or mood), and the word that exhibits these features is termed مُعْرَبَة "declinable." Certain other words have invariable vowel endings, regardless of their function in the sentence. This feature is called البِناء "indeclinability" (or not exhibiting grammatical endings due to the structure of the word), and the word that exhibits this feature is called مَبْنِيَّة "indeclinable" or "invariable." Declinable words belong to two categories: (1) those allowing three different endings in addition to nunation, called مُنَصَرِفَة "triptote" and (2) those allowing only two different endings and no nunation, called مَمْنوعَة مِنَ الصَّرْف "diptote." Declinable and indeclinable words (except for diptotes) have occurred throughout the previous chapters. This chapter focuses on all these formal aspects of the language in a holistic fashion, and covers the following:

- distinguishing between declinable and indeclinable words in Arabic
- mood endings (on verbs in the present/imperfect form)
- case endings (on nouns and adjectives)
- the diptote المَمْنوع مِنَ الصَّرْف .

22.1 The Indeclinable/Invariable المَبْنيّ

Indeclinable مَبْنِيَّة words have invariable endings (i.e., do not change), regardless of their function or position in the sentence. These include

Modern Standard Arabic Grammar: A Learner's Guide, First Edition.
© 2011 Mohammad T. Alhawary. Published 2011 by Blackwell Publishing Ltd.

336 *Triptote, Diptote, and Indeclinable/Invariable* المُعْرَب والمَبْنيّ

all past-tense verbs (2.2.1, 4.1.3.4, and 13.4.1); pronouns (Chapter 5); prepositions (Chapter 6); question words (Chapter 7); conditional particles (Chapter 17); all other particles, including the vocative particles (Chapter 20); a few adverbs of time and place (Chapter 8); some nouns and adjectives; and compound numbers 11 and 13–19 (Appendix E), as illustrated below:

المَبْنيّ
The Indeclinable/Invariable

الأعداد ١١، ١٣-١٩ / Numbers 11, 13–19	أسماء وصفات / Nouns & Adj. (some)	ظروف / Adverbs (a few)	أدوات الشَّرط / Conditional Particles	أسماء الاستفهام / Question Words	حروف الجرّ / Prepositions	الضمائر / Pronouns	الفعل الماضي / Past Tense
أَحَدَ عَشَرَ	هَدايا	أَمْسِ	إذا	هَلْ	مِنْ	هُوَ، ـهُ	دَرَسَ
إحْدى عَشْرَةَ	قَضايا	الآنَ	إنْ	أ	إلى	هُما، ـهُما	دَرَسا
ثَلاثَةَ عَشَرَ	شَظايا	مُنْذُ	ما	ما	عَنْ	هُمْ، ـهُمْ	دَرَسوا
ثَلاثَ عَشْرَةَ	كُبرى	حَيْثُ	مَنْ	مَنْ	عَلى	هِيَ، ـها	دَرَسَتْ
أَرْبَعَةَ عَشَرَ	صُغرى	هُنا	مَهْما	ماذا	في	هُما، ـهُما	دَرَسَتا
أَرْبَعَ عَشْرَةَ	عُظمى	هُناكَ	حَيْثُ/حَيْثُما	لِماذا	حَتّى	هُنَّ، ـهُنَّ	دَرَسْنَ
خَمْسَةَ عَشَرَ	لَيْلى		مَتى/مَتى ما	مَتى	مُنْذُ	أَنْتَ، ـكَ	دَرَسْتَ
خَمْسَ عَشْرَةَ	مُنى		أَيْنَ/أَيْنَما	أَيْنَ	بِ	أَنْتُما، ـكُما	دَرَسْتُما
سِتَّةَ عَشَرَ	مَها		كَيْفَ/كَيْفَما	كَيْفَ	لِ	أَنْتُمْ، ـكُمْ	دَرَسْتُم
سِتَّ عَشْرَةَ	القُرى/قُرىً			كَمْ	كَ	أَنْتِ، ـكِ	دَرَسْتِ
سَبْعَةَ عَشَرَ	الهُدى/هُدىً				مَعَ	أَنْتُما، ـكُما	دَرَسْتُما
سَبْعَ عَشْرَةَ	العَصا/عَصاً				وَ	أَنْتُنَّ، ـكُنَّ	دَرَسْتُنَّ
ثَمانِيَةَ عَشَرَ	الفَتى/فَتىً					أنا، ـي	دَرَسْتُ
ثَماني عَشْرَةَ						نَحْنُ، ـنا	دَرَسْنا
تِسْعَةَ عَشَرَ						هٰذا، ذٰلِكَ	
تِسْعَ عَشْرَةَ						هٰذِهِ، تِلْكَ	
						هٰؤُلاءِ، أُولٰئِكَ	
						الَّذي، الَّتي	
						الَّذينَ، اللّاتي	

As explained in the previous chapters, there are a few exceptions. These include: the demonstrative pronouns for the dual (هٰذَيْنِ ، هٰذانِ and ، هاتانِ

هائَيْنِ), the relative pronouns for the dual (اللَّتانِ ، اللَّتَيْنِ and اللَّذانِ ، اللَّذَيْنِ),
the question and conditional particle (أَيُّ , أَيَّ and أَيِّ), and the compound
number 12 (اِثْنَيْ عَشَرَ ، اِثْنا عَشَرَ and اِثْنَتا عَشْرَةَ ، اِثْنَتَيْ عَشْرَةَ) (for a specific explanation of these, see 5.4, 5.5, 7.11, 17.11, and Appendix E, respectively).

In addition, a distinction is sometimes made between pure invariable
words which have one ending (including proper names ending with a
long vowel) and indeclinable words, where some nouns and adjectives,
examples of which are listed above, have a *nunation* تَنْوين ending [an]
when used indefinite (i.e., مَقْهىً "a coffee house") and a long vowel ending
[aa] when used definite (i.e., المَقْهى "the coffee house"). Below are examples
of indeclinable/invariable مَبْنيَّة words and compound numbers 11 and 13–19
(for more on number rules, see Appendix E), which have different positions/
functions in the sentence; yet which appear with one ending:

هٰذِهِ هَدايا جَميلَةٌ .
"These are beautiful presents."

اِشْتَرَيْتُ هَدايا ثَمينَةً .
"I bought pricey presents."

أَرْسَلْتُ إِلَيْها بِهَدايا كَثيرَةٍ .
"I sent her many presents."

حَضَرَ أَرْبَعَةَ عَشَرَ طالِباً .
"Fourteen (male) students came."

قابَلْتُ أَرْبَعَةَ عَشَرَ طالِباً .
"I met fourteen (male) students."

سَلَّمْتُ عَلىٰ أَرْبَعَةَ عَشَرَ طالِباً .
"I shook hands with fourteen (male) students."

Note: For ease of pronunciation, certain sound changes to the endings of
the indeclinable words and particles occur due to: (1) the *sukuun* at the
end of such words/particles when they are followed by a word whose initial
sound is a light *hamza* (as part of the definite article or the word itself),
necessitating the insertion of one of three helping vowels (see 1.9); (2) the
presence of the *kasra* [i] or *yaa'* [ii] vowel preceding the object and possessive pronouns هـ , هُما , هُمْ , and هُنَّ (see 5.7); and (3) the final long vowel at
the end of prepositions when they are combined with pronouns (see 6.3).

22.2 The Declinable المُعْرَب

Unlike indeclinable مَبْنِيَّة words, declinable مُعْرَبَة words have variable endings (i.e., their ending changes) depending on their function or position with respect to other words or particles in the sentence. These constitute the majority of Arabic words, including verbs in the present/imperfect form, nouns, and adjectives, as illustrated below.

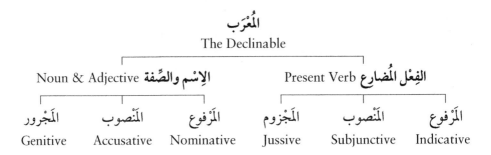

The two main categories of declinable words in Arabic (i.e., verbs vs. nouns and adjectives) have completely different names in English, although the terms are identical in Arabic apart from the jussive مَجْزوم (ending of verbs) and the genitive مَجْرور (ending of nouns and adjectives). In English, the verb endings are called *mood* endings (مَرْفوع indicative, مَنْصوب subjunctive, and مَجْزوم jussive), and the noun and adjective endings are called *case* endings (مَرْفوع nominative, مَنْصوب accusative, and مَجْرور genitive), as explained in the sections below.

22.2.1 Mood Endings on Present/Imperfect Verbs

Unlike past/perfect verbs, which have invariable endings, present/imperfect verbs have different grammatical endings, called mood endings, depending on the function or position of the verbs with respect to other words or particles in the sentence, as explained in the previous chapters (see 4.1.3 and 13.4–13.6). Thus, verbs in the present/imperfect are considered مُعْرَبَة triptotes. Table 22.1 summarizes the different mood endings of present/imperfect verbs in Arabic with a sound verb يَدْرُسُ "he studies" (for endings of weak verbs, see 13.4–13.6) and the main reasons for the use of mood endings (for use of the jussive mood in some conditional sentences, see also Chapter 17).

Table 22.1

Ending: 2SF, 2D, 2PM, 3D, 3PM	Ending: 3SM, 3S F, 2SM, 1S, 1P	Verb and mood type	Use (used with)
، تَدْرُسينَ ، تَدْرُسانِ ، تَدْرُسونَ يَدْرُسانِ ، يَدْرُسونَ	، تَدْرُسُ ، تَدْرُسُ ، يَدْرُسُ أَدْرُسُ ، نَدْرُسُ ←	المُضارع المَرْفوع Indicative	+ default use/ لا
، تَدْرُسي ، تَدْرُسا ، تَدْرُسوا يَدْرُسا ، يَدْرُسوا	، تَدْرُسَ ، تَدْرُسَ ، يَدْرُسَ أَدْرُسَ ، نَدْرُسَ ←	المُضارع المَنْصوب Subjunctive	+ لَنْ/أَنْ / لِـ / حَتّى
، تَدْرُسي ، تَدْرُسا ، تَدْرُسوا يَدْرُسا ، يَدْرُسوا	، تَدْرُسْ ، تَدْرُسْ ، يَدْرُسْ أَدْرُسْ ، نَدْرُسْ ←	المُضارع المَجْزوم Jussive	+ imperative/ لَم

The subjunctive and jussive mood endings for the second-person singular feminine (2SF), second- and third-person dual (2D and 3D), second-person masculine plural (2PM), and third-person masculine plural (3PM) are identical.

22.2.2 Case Endings on Nouns and Adjectives

Like present/imperfect verbs, the majority of Arabic nouns and adjectives have *three* different grammatical endings, called *case* endings, depending on their function or position in the sentence. Thus, such words are declinable مُعْرَبة , in Arabic also called مُنْصَرِفَة *triptotes*. Moreover, nouns and adjectives (in the singular, broken/irregular plural, and sound feminine plural) are used with nunation when they occur indefinite (ٌ [un], ً [an], and ٍ [in]), but are used without nunation when they occur definite (ُ [u], َ [a], and ِ [i]). Table 22.2 summarizes the different case endings and the main reasons for the use of case-endings (see also Chapters 16 and 18–21 for other reasons of case ending use).

Thus, in the singular and broken/irregular plural, nouns and adjectives have three distinct case endings for the مَرْفوع nominative, مَنْصوب accusative, and مَجْرور genitive: ٌ [un], ً [an], and ٍ [in], respectively. The dual, sound masculine plural, and sound feminine plural each have two endings: one distinct case ending for the nominative مَرْفوع (انِ [aani], ونَ [uuna], and ٌ [un], respectively), and an identical ending for both the accusative مَنْصوب and the genitive مَجْرور (يْنِ [ayni], ينَ [iina], and ٍ [in], respectively). Below are examples of the three main categories of use: (A), (C), and (J) listed in Table 22.2.

Table 22.2

Case type	Use (or used with)		Ending: singular	Ending: dual	Ending: broken P	Ending: sound P.M.	Ending: sound P.F.
الرَّفْع Nom	(A) subject/doer of verb/action (B) both parts of nominal sentence	↓	ـُ / ـٌ	انِ	ـُ / ـٌ	ونَ	ـُ / ـٌ
النَّصْب Acc	(C) object/doee of verb/action (D) subject of إِنَّ and its sisters (E) predicate of كَانَ and its sisters (F) adverb of manner	↓	ـَ / ـً	يْنِ	ـَ / ـً	ينَ	ـِ / ـٍ
	(G) all other adverbs (H) following كَمْ (I) following 11–99	↓	ـَ / ـً	—	—	—	—
الجَرّ Gen	(J) following a preposition (K) 2/3/4th noun of 'iDaafa	↓	ـِ / ـٍ	يْنِ	ـِ / ـٍ	ينَ	ـِ / ـٍ
	(L) following 3–10, 100, 1000 & other rounded numbers	↓	ـِ / ـٍ	—	—	—	—

(A)   The following are examples for the use of the مَرْفوع nominative case ending with the noun functioning as the subject/doer of the verb/action and the adjective following it having the same case, since the adjective agrees with the noun it modifies/describes in all respects including case:

<table>
<tr><td>حَضَرَ الطّالِبُ الجَديدُ .</td><td>حَضَرَ طالِبٌ جَديدٌ .</td></tr>
<tr><td>"The new (male) student came."</td><td>"A new (male) student came."</td></tr>
<tr><td>حَضَرَتِ الطّالِبَةُ الجَديدَةُ .</td><td>حَضَرَتْ طالِبَةٌ جَديدَةٌ .</td></tr>
<tr><td>"The new (female) student came."</td><td>"A new (female) student came."</td></tr>
<tr><td>حَضَرَ الطّالِبانِ الجَديدانِ .</td><td>حَضَرَ طالِبانِ جَديدانِ .</td></tr>
<tr><td>"The two new (male) students came."</td><td>"Two new (male) students came."</td></tr>
<tr><td>حَضَرَتِ الطّالِبَتانِ الجَديدَتانِ .</td><td>حَضَرَتْ طالِبَتانِ جَديدَتانِ .</td></tr>
<tr><td>"The two new (female) students came."</td><td>"Two new (female) students came."</td></tr>
<tr><td>حَضَرَ الطُّلّابُ الجُدُدُ .</td><td>حَضَرَ طُلّابٌ جُدُدٌ .</td></tr>
<tr><td>"The new (male) students came."</td><td>"New (male) students came."</td></tr>
<tr><td>حَضَرَ المُهَنْدِسونَ الجُدُدُ .</td><td>حَضَرَ مُهَنْدِسونَ جُدُدٌ .</td></tr>
<tr><td>"The new (male) engineers came."</td><td>"New (male) engineers came."</td></tr>
<tr><td>حَضَرَتِ المُهَنْدِساتُ الجَديداتُ .</td><td>حَضَرَتْ مُهَنْدِساتٌ جَديداتٌ .</td></tr>
<tr><td>"The new (female) engineers came."</td><td>"New (female) engineers came."</td></tr>
</table>

(C)   The following are examples for the use of the مَنْصوب accusative case ending with the noun functioning as the object/doee of the verb/action and the adjective following it having the same case, since the adjective agrees with the noun it modifies/describes in all respects including case:

<table>
<tr><td>قَابَلْتُ الطّالِبَ الجَديدَ .</td><td>قَابَلْتُ طالِباً جَديداً .</td></tr>
<tr><td>"I met the new (male) student."</td><td>"I met a new (male) student."</td></tr>
<tr><td>قَابَلْتُ الطّالِبَةَ الجَديدَةَ .</td><td>قَابَلْتُ طالِبَةً جَديدَةً .</td></tr>
<tr><td>"I met the new (female) student."</td><td>"I met a new (female) student."</td></tr>
<tr><td>قَابَلْتُ الطّالِبَيْنِ الجَديدَيْنِ .</td><td>قَابَلْتُ طالِبَيْنِ جَديدَيْنِ .</td></tr>
<tr><td>"I met the two new (male) students."</td><td>"I met two new (male) students."</td></tr>
</table>

قابَلْتُ طالِبَتَيْنِ جَديدَتَيْنِ .
"I met two new (female) students."

قابَلْتُ الطّالِبَتَيْنِ الجَديدَتَيْنِ .
"I met the two new (female) students."

قابَلْتُ طُلّاباً جُدُداً .
"I met new (male) students."

قابَلْتُ الطُّلّابَ الجُدُدَ .
"I met the new (male) students."

قابَلْتُ مُهَنْدِسينَ جُدُداً .
"I met new (male) engineers."

قابَلْتُ المُهَنْدِسينَ الجُدُدَ .
"I met the new (male) engineers."

قابَلْتُ مُهَنْدِساتٍ جَديداتٍ .
"I met new (female) engineers."

قابَلْتُ المُهَنْدِساتِ الجَديداتِ .
"I met the new (female) engineers."

(J)   The following are examples for the use of the مَجْرور genitive case ending with the noun occurring after a preposition and the adjective following it having the same case, since the adjective agrees with the noun it modifies/describes in all respects including case:

سَلَّمْتُ عَلى طالِبٍ جَديدٍ .
"I greeted a new (male) student."

سَلَّمْتُ عَلى الطّالِبِ الجَديدِ .
"I greeted the new (male) student."

سَلَّمْتُ عَلى طالِبَةٍ جَديدَةٍ .
"I greeted a new (female) student."

سَلَّمْتُ عَلى الطّالِبَةِ الجَديدَةِ .
"I greeted the new (female) student."

سَلَّمْتُ عَلى طالِبَيْنِ جَديدَيْنِ .
"I greeted two new (male) students."

سَلَّمْتُ عَلى الطّالِبَيْنِ الجَديدَيْنِ .
"I greeted the two new (male) students."

سَلَّمْتُ عَلى طالِبَتَيْنِ جَديدَتَيْنِ .
"I greeted two new (female) students."

سَلَّمْتُ عَلى الطّالِبَتَيْنِ الجَديدَتَيْنِ .
"I greeted the two new (female) students."

سَلَّمْتُ عَلى طُلّابٍ جُدُدٍ .
"I greeted new (male) students."

سَلَّمْتُ عَلى الطُّلّابِ الجُدُدِ .
"I greeted the new (male) students."

سَلَّمْتُ عَلى مُهَنْدِسينَ جُدُدٍ .
"I greeted new (male) engineers."

سَلَّمْتُ عَلى المُهَنْدِسينَ الجُدُدِ .
"I greeted the new (male) engineers."

سَلَّمْتُ عَلى مُهَنْدِساتٍ جَديداتٍ .
"I greeted new (female) engineers."

سَلَّمْتُ عَلى المُهَنْدِساتِ الجَديداتِ .
"I greeted the new (female) engineers."

Note: Adjectives with irregular/broken plural and occurring after a noun with a regular/sound feminine ending ات [aat] need not take an identical accusative case ending, since in this case the adjective has a singular feminine ending (see also 3.1). Thus, when functioning as an object, the adjective with irregular/broken plural takes the accusative case ending ً [an] and the noun takes the accusative case ending ٍ [in] , following the regular/sound feminine plural case-ending rule. Below are examples with a (regular/sound plural feminine) noun and adjective in the nominative مَرْفوع (as the subject/doer of the verb/action), in the accusative مَنْصوب (as the object/doee of the verb/action), and in the genitive مَجْرور (occurring after a preposition):

مَرَّتْ سَيّاراتٌ كَثيرةٌ في هٰذا الشّارع .

"**Many cars** passed in this street."

اِشْتَرَيْتُ سَيّاراتٍ كَثيرةً في حَياتي .

"I bought **many cars** in my life."

مَرَرْتُ بِسَيّاراتٍ كَثيرةٍ في ذٰلكَ الشّارع .

"I passed by **many cars** in that street."

Note: For examples of all other reasons given for the use of case endings in Table 22.2, see respective chapters and sections for specific examples: for (B)–(E), see 4.2; for (F), see Chapter 9; for (G), see Chapters 8 and 10–12; for (H), see 7.1.10; for (I), see Appendix E; for (K), see 3.3; and for (L), see Appendix E. For other reasons use of case endings not listed in Table 22.2, see also Chapters 16 and 18–21.

22.2.3   Diptotes المَمْنوع مِنَ الصَّرْف

Unlike triptote مُنْصَرِفة words, which constitute the majority of nouns and adjectives, diptote مَمْنوعة مِنَ الصَّرْف words (nouns and adjectives) have two endings, subject to three rules: (1) their nominative مَرْفوع case ending is ُ [u], (2) their accusative مَنْصوب and genitive مَجْرور case ending is َ [a], and (3) they do not exhibit nunation تَنْوين when used in the indefinite. Hence, they are called *diptotes*, allowing for only two endings. Below are examples of a diptote noun تَلاميذ "students/pupils" occurring in the nominative مَرْفوع (as the subject/doer of the verb/action), accusative مَنْصوب (as the object/doee of the verb/action), and genitive مَجْرور (occurring after a preposition):

حَضَرَ تَلامِيذُ جُدُدٌ .

"New (male) students came."

قابَلْتُ تَلامِيذَ جُدُداً .

"I met **new** (male) students."

سَلَّمْتُ عَلىٰ تَلامِيذَ جُدُدٍ .

"I greeted **new** (male) students."

Note: As the examples show, a diptote noun may not be followed by a diptote adjective.

Diptote مَمْنُوعَة مِنَ الصَّرْف words (nouns and adjectives) belong to at least 11 classes, as follows:

(1)   feminine proper names consisting of more than three letters (consonants and long vowels) used for females, whether or not they end with a feminine suffix:

إليزابيث	صَباح	زَيْنَب
"Elizabeth F"	"Sabah F"	"Zaynab F"

عائِشَة	فاطِمَة	مَرْيَم
"Aishah F"	"Fatimah M"	"Mariam/Mary F"

(2)   feminine-sounding proper names used for males and ending with a feminine suffix:

طَلْحَة	أُسامَة	حَمْزَة
"Talhah M"	"Usamah M"	"Hamzah M"

(3)   foreign proper names (of Semitic or non-Semitic origin):

جورج	يوسُف	إبْراهيم
"George M"	"Yusuf/Joseph M"	"Ibrahim/Abraham M"

بَغْداد	بَيْروت	دِمَشْق
"Baghdad"	"Beirut"	"Damascus"

(4)   compound proper names consisting of two names merged together:

سَمَرْقَنْد   بَعْلَبَكّ   حَضْرَمَوت
"Samarkand [city]"   "Baalabak [region]"   "Hadramawt [region]"

(5)   proper names that have the pattern فُعَل :

زُحَل   عُمَر   =   فُعَل
"Saturn"   "Omar M"

(6)   proper names ending with ان [aan] beyond the triliteral root consonants:

عُثْمان   عَدْنان   سَلْمان
"Othman M"   "Adnan M"   "Salman M"

(7)   proper names that have verbal patterns such as أَفْعَل and يَفْعِل / يَفْعُل :

أَحْمَد   أَمْجَد   أَكْرَم   =   أَفْعَل
"Ahmad M"   "Amjad M"   "Akram M"

يَشْكُر   يَثْرِب   يَزيد   =   يَفْعِل /
                                                                          يَفْعُل
"Yashkur M"   "Yathrib/Madinah"   "Yazid M"

(8)   adjectives (and the comparative words) that have the pattern أَفْعَل :

أَبْكَم   أَشْقَر   أَحْمَر   =   أَفْعَل
"mute M"   "blonde M"   "red M"

أَشَدّ   أَصْغَر   أَفْضَل
"more intense   "smaller   "better

(9) words (nouns and adjectives) ending with ء١ [aa'] beyond the tri-literal root consonants, whether or not the ending is a feminine suffix or part of the plural form:

كِبْرِياء	خُنْفُساء	صَحْراء
"pride F"	"ladybug F"	"desert F"

حَمْراء	بَكْماء	شَقْراء
"red F"	"mute F"	"blonde F"

رُحَماء	شُهَداء	أَصْدِقاء
"merciful ones MP"	"martyrs MP"	"friends MP"

(10) words that have broken plural patterns, such as:

مَجانين	مَصابيح	مَفاتيح	=	مَفاعيل
"crazy ones"	"lanterns"	"keys"		

مَساجِد	مَعابِد	مَدارِس	=	مَفاعِل
"mosques"	"temples"	"schools"		

أَعاجيب	أَساليب	أَسابيع	=	أفاعيل
"wonders"	"styles"	"weeks"		

أقارِب	أصابِع	أجانِب	=	أفاعِل
"relatives"	"fingers"	"foreigners"		

تَراكيب	تَمارين	تَلاميذ	=	تَفاعيل
"structures"	"drills"	"students"		

دَكاكين	سَكاكين	شَبابيك	=	فَعاعيل
"shops"	"knives"	"windows"		

		=	فَواعِيل
صَواريخ	طَواحين	قَوانين	
"rockets"	"mills"	"laws"	

		=	فَواعِل
طَوارِئ	فَوارِق	شَوارِع	
"emergencies"	"differences"	"streets"	

		=	فَعائِل
رَسائِل	كَنائِس	جَرائِد	
"letters"	"churches"	"newspapers"	

Note: One can avoid having to remember all these (broken plural) patterns (and others) by remembering that they all: (a) consist of five or six consonants and long vowels and (b) their third letter is an *'alif* [aa].

(11) two common words are treated as diptotes مَمْنوعَة مِنَ الصَّرْف, for no obvious reason:

أَشْياء	أُخَر
"things"	"others FP"

The word أُخَر "others" is the plural of أُخْرى "other" used as an adjective for the feminine plural, whereas أَشْياء "things" is the plural of شَيء "thing" used as a noun, as in:

حَضَرَتْ طالِباتٌ أُخَرُ .
"Other (female) students came."

قابَلْتُ طالِباتٍ أُخَرَ .
"I met other (female) students."

سَلَّمْتُ عَلىٰ طالِباتٍ أُخَرَ .
"I greeted other (female) students."

عِنْدي أَشْياءُ كَثيرَةٌ .
"I have many things."

اِشْتَرَيْتُ أَشْياءَ كَثيرَةً .
"I bought many things."

نَظَرْتُ إلٰى أَشْياءَ كَثيرَةٍ .
"I looked at many things."

22.2.4 Occurrence of Diptotes as Triptotes

Some diptote مَمْنوعَة مِنَ الصَّرْف words (nouns and adjectives) can occur as triptotes مُنْصَرِفَة (i.e., with three different case endings), subject to the following rules:

(1)   feminine proper names consisting of three letters, the middle of which has a *sukuun* or a long vowel, can be used as diptotes مِنَ الصَّرْف مَمْنوعَة or triptotes مُنْصَرِفَة , as in:

ريم	دَعْد	هِنْد
"Reem F"	"Da'd F"	"Hind F"

حَضَرَتْ هِنْدُ .		حَضَرَتْ هِنْدُ .
"Hind F came."	=	"Hind F came."

قابَلْتُ هِنْدَ .		قابَلْتُ هِنْداً .
"I met Hind."	=	"I met Hind."

سَلَّمْتُ عَلٰى هِنْدَ .		سَلَّمْتُ عَلٰى هِنْدٍ .
"I greeted Hind."	=	"I greeted Hind."

(2)   Feminine proper names without a feminine suffix used for males are used as triptotes مُنْصَرِفَة , as in:

سامِر	نَجاح	صَباح
"Samir M"	"Najah M"	"Sabah M"

حَضَرَ صَباحٌ .
"Sabah (M) came."

قابَلْتُ صَباحاً .
"I met Sabah (M)."

سَلَّمْتُ عَلٰى صَباحٍ .
"I greeted Sabah (M)."

(3) foreign proper names (especially of Semitic origin) consisting of three letters, the middle of which has a *sukuun* or a long vowel, can be used as triptotes مُنْصَرِفَة :

لوط   هود   نوح

"Lot M"   "Hud M"   "Noah M"

(4) adjectives that have the pattern أَفْعَل whose feminine counterpart has the *taa' marbuuTa* feminine suffix are used as triptotes مُنْصَرِفَة :

أَرْمَلَة   أَرْمَل

"widow F"   "widower M"

أَرْبَعَة   أَرْبَع

"four F"   "four M"

(5) adjectives that have the pattern فَعْلان , which in CA occur only as diptotes مُنْصَرِفَة or triptotes مَمْنوعَة مِنَ الصَّرْف (as part of the modern standardization trends of MSA), as in:

تَعْبان   جَوْعان   عَطْشان

"tired M"   "hungry M"   "thirsty M"

أَنا تَعْبانَ الآنَ .   =   أَنا تَعْبانٌ الآنَ .

"I am **tired** now."   "I am **tired** now."

كُنْتُ تَعْبانَ أَمْس .   =   كُنْتُ تَعْباناً أَمْس .

"I was **tired** yesterday."   "I was **tired** yesterday."

سَلَّمْتُ عَلى رَجُلٍ تَعْبانَ .   =   سَلَّمْتُ عَلى رَجُلٍ تَعْبانٍ .

"I greeted **a tired man**."   "I greeted **a tired man**."

(6) when a diptote مَمْنوعَة مِنَ الصَّرْف is used definite (with the definite article or followed by a possessive pronoun) or as the first noun of an 'iDaafa phrase إضافة , it is treated as a triptote مُنْصَرِفَة with a *kasra* [i] as the genitive case ending, as in:

أَتَنَزَّهُ في الحَدائِقِ الكَبيرَةِ .   ←   أَتَنَزَّهُ في حَدائِقَ كَبيرَةٍ .

"I picnic in **the big parks**."   "I picnic in **big parks**."

أَتَنَزَّهُ في حَدائِقِ المَدينَةِ / في حَدائِقِها .   ←   أَتَنَزَّهُ في حَدائِقَ .

"I picnic in **the parks of the city/ in its parks**."   "I picnic in **parks**."

22.3 Summary

This chapter discussed the formal grammatical features of case and mood endings. Remember:

- certain parts of speech (including past/perfect verbs, pronouns, prepositions, question words, conditional particles, vocative particles, certain nouns and adjectives, and compound numbers 11 and 13–19) do not have grammatical endings, and therefore their endings do not change (except for a few slight sound changes for ease of pronunciation)
- words and particles whose endings do not change are called "invariable" or "indeclinable" مَبْنِيَّة words; although a distinction can be made between words with complete invariable endings and words which take the ending ً [an] when used indefinite and do not take such an ending when used definite
- most Arabic words, including present/imperfect verbs, nouns, and adjectives, have three different grammatical endings; these words are called declinable مُعْرَبَة or (in the case of nouns and adjectives) مُنْصَرِفَة "triptotes"
- present/imperfect verbs have three *mood* endings: مَرْفُوع indicative, مَنْصوب subjunctive, and مَجْزوم jussive
- nouns and adjectives have three *case* endings: مَرْفوع nominative, مَنْصوب accusative, and مَجْرور genitive
- certain nouns and adjectives have two grammatical endings, one distinct ending for the nominative مَرْفوع and an identical ending for both the accusative مَنْصوب and genitive مَجْرور , and, in addition, none has a *nunation* تَنْوِين ending when used in the indefinite; these words are termed diptotes مَمْنوعَة مِنَ الصَّرْف
- diptotes belong to certain categories of proper names (including feminine and foreign proper names); others conform to certain patterns, such as أَفْعَل , فُعَل , يَفْعِل , يَفْعُل , فَعْلان , مَفاعيل , مَفاعِل , and ; and others have the feminine suffix اء [aa'] or the ان [aan] endings beyond their triliteral root consonants
- diptotes مَمْنوعَة مِنَ الصَّرْف can be treated as triptotes مُنْصَرِفَة when they occur definite (i.e., with the definite article) or as the first noun of an إِضافة 'iDaafa phrase; in this case, when they occur with the genitive مَجْرور case, they have the distinct *kasra* [i] rather than *fatHa* [a] ending, which is the diptote مَمْنوع مِنَ الصَّرْف ending for both the accusative مَنْصوب and genitive مَجْرور case.

References and Further Reading (in Arabic)

Al-Afaghānī, Saīd. 1981. *Al-Mūjaz fī Qawā'id Al-Lugha Al-'Arabiyya*. Damascus, Syria: Dār Al-Fikr.

Al-Ghalayyīnī, Al-Sheikh Muṣṭafā. 2000. *Jāmi' Al-Durūs Al-'Arabiyya*. Sidon, Lebanon: Al-Maktaba Al-'aṣriyya.

Al-Hamalāwī, Ahmad. 1975. *Shadhā Al-'urf fī Fann Al-Ṣarf*. Cairo, Egypt: Maktabat Mustafā Al-Bābī Al-Halabī.

Al-Hāshmī, Ahmad. 2002. *Al-Qawā'id Al-Asāsiyya li-llugha Al-'Arabiyya*. Beirut, Lebanon: Mu'ssasat Al-Ma'ārif.

Al-Hulwānī, Muhammad Khayr. 1997. *Al-Naḥw Al-Muyassar*. Damascus, Syria: Dār Al-Ma'mūn li-lturāth.

Al-Hulwānī, Muhammad Khayr. 1978. *Al-Wāḍiḥ fī Al-Ṣarf*. Damascus, Syria: Dār Al-Ma'mūn li-lturāth.

Al-Hulwānī, Muhammad Khayr. 1972. *Al-Wāḍiḥ fī Al-Naḥw wa Al-Ṣarf*. Aleppo, Syria: Al-Maktaba Al-'Arabiyya.

Al-Makhzūmī, Mahdī. 1986. *Fī Al-Nahw Al-'Arabī*. Beirut, Lebanon: Dār Al-Rāid Al-'arabī.

Al-Shuwayrif, Abdullatīf Ahmad. 1997. *Taṣḥīḥāt Lughawiyya*. Tripoli, Libya: Al-Dār Al-'Arabiyya li-lkitāb.

Barakāt, Ibrāhīm I. 1988. *Al-Ta'nīth fī Al-Lugha Al-'Arabiyya*. Al-Manṣūra, Egypt: Dār Al-Wafā'.

El-Dahdāh, Antoine. 1991. *Mu'jam Taṣrīf Al-Af'āl Al-'Arabiyya*. Beirut, Lebanon: Librairie du Liban.

Hasan, Abbās. 1998–9. *Al-Nahw Al-Wāfī*. Cairo, Egypt: Dār Al-Ma'ārif.

Majma' Al-Lugha Al-'Arabiyya Bimiṣr. 1984. *Majmū'at Al-Qarārāt Al-'ilmiyya fī Xamsīna 'āman*. Cairo, Egypt.

Nāṣir Al-Dīn, Nadīm. 1997. *Mu'jam Daqā'iq Al-'Arabiyya*. Beirut, Lebanon: Librairie du Liban.

Ṣaydāwī, Yusuf. 1999. *Al-Kafāf*. Damascus, Syria: Dār Al-Fikr.

'Uḍaymah, Muhammad Abd Al-Khāliq. 1962. *Al-Mughnī fī Taṣrīf Al-Af'āl*. Cairo, Egypt: Dār Al-Hadīth.

Modern Standard Arabic Grammar: A Learner's Guide, First Edition.
© 2011 Mohammad T. Alhawary. Published 2011 by Blackwell Publishing Ltd.

Appendix A

The Geometric Basis of Arabic Numerals

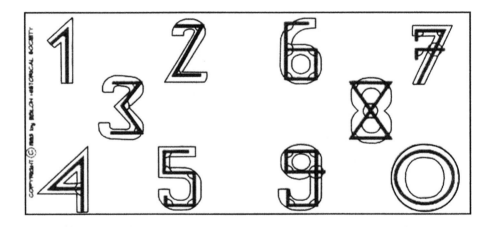

The Arabic numerals as reconstructed by the Eblon Historical Society. Each number is represented by a geometric form, where the number of angles corresponds to the value of the number it represents (from the *ADC Times*, February 1994).

Appendix B
The Writing of the *hamza*
كِتابة الهَمْزَة

1. *hamza* in Initial Position

Any English word which starts with a vowel must start with a *hamza* to make it possible/easier to pronounce the vowel in initial position. However, English does not have a symbol for the *hamza* "glottal stop," since it mostly occurs in this position. In Arabic, two types of *hamza* occur in word initial position which differ in orthographic representations but not in pronunciation: (1) a strong *hamza* هَمْزَة القَطْع which is always retained and pronounced and comprises the vast majority of cases of the *hamza* in initial position; and (2) a light or eliding *hamza* هَمْزَة الوَصْل which is dropped in speech when preceded by a word or particle ending with a vowel, hence "eliding." Both types are written with a silent *'alif* ا as a seat. The strong *hamza* is represented by the shape ء above or under the silent *'alif* (together with the short vowel), while the light *hamza* is not represented by a shape but by the *'alif* (and the short vowel above or under the silent *'alif*).

Note: The *hamza* in medial and final position belongs restrictively to هَمْزَة القَطْع which is always retained and pronounced.

Strong *hamza* هَمْزَة القَطْع written above or under the silent *'alif* ا seat					
"father"	*'ab*	أَب	←	ءَ + ب	followed by a *fatHa* ´ [a]
"mother"	*'umm*	أُمّ	←	ءُ + مّ	followed by a *Damma* ´ [u]
"if"	*'in*	إن	←	ء + ن	followed by a *kasra* [i]

The occurrence and writing of the light/eliding *hamza* هَمْزَة الوَصْل (written above or under the silent *'alif* ا seat)					
"the"	*'al*	الـ	←	ءَ + ل	first part of the definite article (see 1.17)
"Write!"	*'uktub*	أُكْتُب	←	ءُ كْ تُ ب	imperative of Form I verbs (see 13.5.1)
"Sit!"	*'ijlis*	اِجْلِس	←	ءِ جْ لِ س	imperative of Form I verbs (see 13.5.1)
"he started"	*'inTalaqa*	اِنْطَلَقَ	←	ءِ نْ طَ لَ قَ	past tense of Form VII–X verbs (see 13.1.2)
"Start!"	*'inTaliq*	اِنْطَلِق	←	ءِ نْ طَ لِ ق	imperative of Form VII–X verbs (see 13.5.5)
"starting"	*'inTilaaq*	اِنْطِلاق	←	ءِ نْ طِ ل ا ق	verbal nouns of Form VII–X verbs (see 14.2.2)
"name"	*'ism*	اِسْم	←	ءِ سْ م	certain words
"son"	*'ibn*	اِبْن	←	ءِ بْ ن	
"daughter"	*'ibna*	اِبْنَة	←	ءِ بْ نَ ة	
"person M/ man"	*'imru'*	اِمْرُؤْ	←	ءِ مْ رُ ؤْ	
"person F/ woman"	*'imra'a*	اِمْرَأة	←	ءِ مْ رَ أ ة	
"two M"	*'ithnaan*	اِثْنان	←	ءِ ثْ ن ا ن	
"two F"	*'ithnataan*	اِثْنَتان	←	ءِ ثْ نَ ت ا ن	

1.1 Dropping the Light/Eliding *hamza*

The light or eliding *hamza* هَمْزَة الوَصْل is dropped in speech together with the short vowel with which it occurs when it is preceded by a word or particle that ends with a vowel, whether short or long. Additionally, the long vowel of the preceding word is shortened (see also 1.9–10), while the short vowel is retained without any change.

Dropping the light/eliding *hamza* هَمْزَة الوَصْل and shortening the preceding long vowel					
"in the house"	*fi-lbayt*	في الْبَيْت	←	*'al-lbayt* الْبَيْت + *fii*	في
"in the house"	*bi-lbayt*	بالْبَيْت	←	*'al-lbay* الْبَيْت + *bi*	بِ
"and he started"	*wa-nTalaqa*	وَ انْطَلَقَ	←	*'inTalaqa* انْطَلَقَ + *wa*	وَ
"what is the name"	*ma-sm*	ما اسْم	←	*'ism* إسْم + *maa*	ما

Note: When the eliding *hamza* هَمْزَة الوَصْل is dropped in speech, no vowel appears with the silent *'alif* ا , since that vowel is also dropped.

2. *hamza* in Medial Position

When it occurs in medial position, the *hamza* is written on a silent long vowel seat homogenous with the (short or long) vowel that precedes or follows it; accordingly: (1) a silent *'alif* seat is used when it occurs with a *fatHa*, (2) a silent *waaw* seat is used when it occurs with *Damma* [u] or *waaw* [uu], and (3) a silent *yaa'* seat (without dots under the *yaa'*) is used when it occurs with a *kasra* [i] or *yaa'* [ii]. When the *hamza* occurs between two different vowels, a scale of strength is applied, where the stronger vowel provides its homogenous seat according to the following scale of strengths among the vowels:

strongest: *kasra* and *yaa'*
strong: *Damma* and *waaw*
weak: *fatHa* and *'alif*

Medial *hamza* written on a silent (medial) *'alif* ـا / ا seat				
"he asked"	*sa'ala*	سَأَل	← سَ ءَ لَ	occurring with a *fatHa* ´ [a]
"he roared"	*za'ara*	زَأَر	← زَ ءَ رَ	
"hardship"	*ba's*	بَأْس	← بَ ءْ س	occurring with a *fatHa* ´ [a] and *sukuun*
"full F"	*mal'aa*	مَلْأَى	← مَ لْ ءَ ى	occurring with an *'alif* [aa] following it

Exceptions where medial *hamza* does not require a silent *'alif* ا seat				
"he held accountable"	*saa'ala*	سَاءَل	← س ا ءَ لَ	if preceded by *'alif* [aa] and followed by a *fatHa* [a] ´
"reading"	*qiraa'a*	قِرَاءَة	← قِ ر ا ءَ ة	

Medial *hamza* is written on a silent (medial) *waaw* و/ـو seat				
"misery"	*bu's*	بُؤْس	← بُ ءْ س	occurring with a *Damma* ´ [u] and *sukuun*
"heads"	*ru'uus*	رُؤُوس	← رُ ءُ و س	occurring with a *Damma* ´ [u] and *waaw* [uu]
"question"	*su'aal*	سُؤَال	← سُ ءَ ا ل	occurring with a *Damma* ´ [u] and *'alif* [aa]
"merciful"	*ra'uuf*	رَؤُوف	← رَ ءُ و ف	occurring with a *fatHa* [a] and *waaw* [uu]

Exception where medial *hamza* not requiring a silent *waaw* و/ـو seat				
"chivalry"	*muruu'a*	مُرُوءَة	← مُ ر و ءَ ة	if preceded by *waaw* [uu] and followed by a *fatHa* [a]

Medial *hamza* written on a silent (medial) *yaa'* ـئـ / ئـ seat (without dots under *yaa'*)				
"how bad"	*bi's*	بِئْس	←	بِ ءْ س	occurring with a *kasra* [i] and *sukuun*
"he got bored"	*sa'ima*	سَئِمَ	←	سَ ء مَ	occurring with a *fatHa* [a] and a *kasra* [i]
"driver"	*saa'iq*	سائِق	←	س ا ء ق	occurring with *'alif* [aa] and a *kasra* [i]
"friendliness"	*wi'iaam*	وِئام	←	وِ ء ام	occurring with a *kasra* [i] and *'alif* [aa]
"president"	*ra'iis*	رَئيس	←	رَ ء ي س	occurring with a *fatHa* [a] and a *yaa'* [ii]
"he was asked"	*su'ila*	سُئِلَ	←	سُ ء لَ	occurring with a *Damma* [u] and a *kasra* [i]
"youths"	*naash'uun*	ناشِئون	←	ن ا ش ء و ن	occurring with a *kasra* [i] and a *waaw* [uu]

3. *hamza* in Final Position

When it occurs in final position, the *hamza* is subject to two sub-rules: (1) it requires no seat when preceded by a *sukuun* or a long vowel and (2) it is written on a silent *'alif, waaw,* or *yaa'* seat following a *fatHa, Damma,* and *kasra,* respectively.

Final *hamza* requiring no seat after a *sukuun*				
"burden"	*'ib'*	عِبْء	←	ع ب ء	whether the *sukuun* follows a connector letter
"part"	*juz'*	جُزْء	←	جُ ز ء	or the *sukuun* follows a non-connector letter

Final *hamza* requiring no seat after a long vowel					
"water"	*maa'*	ماء	←	م ا ء	following *'alif* [aa]
"seeking refuge"	*lujuu'*	لُجُوء	←	لُ ج و ء	following *waaw* [uu]
"slow"	*baTii'*	بَطِيء	←	بَ ط ي ء	following *yaa'* [ii]

Final *hamza* written on a silent (final) *'alif* ـا / ا seat					
"port"	*marfa'*	مَرْفَأ	←	مَ ر ف ء	following *fatHa* [a]
"he read"	*qara'a*	قَرَأ	←	قَ ر َء	

Final *hamza* written on a silent *waaw* و/ـو seat					
"slowing down"	*tabaaTu'*	تَباطُؤ	←	تَ ب ا طُ ء	following *Damma* [u]
"audacity"	*tajarru'*	تَجَرُّؤ	←	تَ ج رُّ ء	

Final *hamza* written on a silent *yaa'* ي/ـي seat (without dots under the *yaa'*)					
"beach"	*shaaTi'*	شاطِئ	←	ش ا طِ ء	following *kasra* [i]
"reader"	*qaari'*	قارِئ	←	ق ا رِ ء	

4. *hamza* in Final Position Following a Grammatical Ending or a Suffix

When the *hamza* occurs in final position written on a silent *'alif*, *waaw*, or *yaa'* seat (because it follows a *fatHa*, *Damma*, and *kasra*, respectively) and is followed by the accusative case مَنْصوب ending أ [an] or the dual number ending انِ [aani], the same regular rules for adding the grammatical endings and the writing of the *hamza* in medial position are followed (i.e., adding a silent *'alif* for the accusative مَنْصوب case ending except when the *hamza* is already written on a silent *'alif*) (see 1.2.1).

Final *hamza* written on a silent *waaw* و/ـو seat and when followed by the accusative مَنْصوب case ending ً or the dual number suffix requiring a silent *'alif* ا seat for the accusative ending				
"slowing down"	*tabaaTu'-an*	تَباطُؤاً	←	تَ ب ا طُ ء ً	following *Damma* [u]
"two acts of slowing down"	*tabaaTu'-aani*	تَباطُؤانِ	←	تَ ب ا طُ ء انِ
"audaciously"	*tajarru'-an*	تَجَرُّؤاً	←	تَ جَ رُّ ء ً
"two acts of audacity"	*tajarru'-aani*	تَجَرُّؤانِ	←	تَ جَ رُّ ء انِ

Final *hamza* written on a silent *yaa'* ـِ / ـئ seat (without dots under *yaa'*) and when followed by the accusative مَنْصوب case ending ً or the dual number suffix انِ requiring a silent *'alif* ا seat for the accusative case ending				
"reader"	*qaari'-an*	قارِئاً	←	ق ا رِ ء ً	following *kasra* [i]
"two readers"	*qaari'-aani*	قارِئانِ	←	ق ا رِ ء انِ
"caring person"	*ʿaabi-'an*	عابِئاً	←	عـ ا بِ ء ً
"two caring persons"	*ʿaabi-'aani*	عابِئانِ	←	عـ ا بِ ء انِ

Final *hamza* written on a silent *'alif* ـا / ا seat and when followed by the accusative مَنْصوب case ending ً requiring no additional seat				
"port"	*mirfa'-an*	مَرْفَأً	←	مَ رْ فَ ء ً	following *fatHa* [a]
"principle"	*mabda'-an*	مَبْدَأً	←	مَ بْ دَ ء ً

In addition, in *verbs* ending with a *hamza* on *'alif* preceded by a *fatHa*, the dual is formed by simply adding the dual suffix without any changes, but in *nouns* ending with a *hamza* on *'alif*, the *hamza* is converted into a *madda* written on *'alif* → آ ['aa].

Final *hamza* written on a silent *'alif* ـا / ا seat in *verbs* followed by the dual second-person suffix				
"they both sought refuge"	*laja'-aa*	لَجَأا	←	لَ ء جَ ا ← *preceded by fatHa [a] and followed by the dual suffix*
"they both seek refuge"	*yalja'-aani*	يَلْجَأانِ	←	يَ لْ جَ ء ان
"they both read"	*qara'-aa*	قَرَأا	←	قَ رَ ء ا
"they both read"	*yaqra'-aani*	يَقْرَأانِ	←	يَ قْ رَ ء انِ

Final *hamza* written as a *madda* on a silent *'alif* ـا / ا seat in *nouns* followed by the dual number suffix ان				
"two ports"	*marfa'-aani*	مَرْفَآنِ	←	مَ رْ فَ ء انِ ← *following fatHa [a]*
"two principles"	*mabda'-aani*	مَبْدَآنِ	←	مَ بْ دَ ء انِ

On the other hand, when the final *hamza* requires no seat (i.e., when it follows a *sukuun*) and when it is followed by the accusative مَنْصوب case ending آ [an] or the dual number suffix انِ [aani], the writing of the *hamza* is subject to three sub-rules, depending on whether it follows a non-connector letter, a connector letter, or an *'alif*:

Final *hamza* after a *sukuun* written on a silent *yaa'* ـئ seat (without dots under *yaa'*) and when followed by the accusative مَنْصوب case ending ً or the dual number suffix انِ requiring a silent *'alif* ا seat for the accusative ending				
"burden"	*ʿib'-an*	عِبْئاً	←	عِ بْ ء ً ← *if hamza follows a connector letter*
"two burdens"	*ʿib'-aani*	عِبْئانِ	←	عِ بْ ء انِ

Final *hamza* after a *sukuun* requiring no seat and when followed by the accusative مَنْصوب case ending ً or the dual number suffix اِن requiring a silent *'alif* ا seat for the accusative ending				
"a part"	*juz'-an*	جُزْءاً	←	ج ز ءً	if *hamza* follows a non-connector letter
"two parts"	*juz'-aani*	جُزْءانِ	←	ج ز ء انِ	

Final *hamza* after an *'alif* requiring no seat and when followed by the accusative مَنْصوب case ending ً or the dual number suffix اِن requiring no seat for the accusative ending				
"water"	*maa'-an*	ماءً	←	م ا ءً	if *hamza* follows an *'alif* [aa]
"two waters"	*maa'-aani*	ماءانِ	←	م ا ء انِ	

Note: The final *hamza* after a *sukuun* is written on a silent *'alif* seat when it is followed by the dual accusative مَنْصوب ending يْنِ [ayni], since the *hamza* in this case is followed by a *fatHa* – following the media *hamza* rule when occurring with a *fatHa*:

Final *hamza* after *sukuun* written on a silent *'alif* ﺎ / ا seat when followed by the dual number suffix in the مَنْصوب accusative يْنِ				
"two burdens"	*'ib'-ayni*	عِبْأَينِ	←	ع ب ء يْ نِ	occurring with a *fatHa* [a]
"two parts"	*juz'-ayni*	جُزْأَينِ	←	ج ز ء يْ نِ	

Appendix C
The Phoenician Alphabet

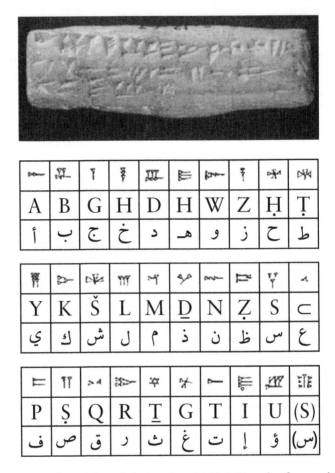

A	B	G	H	D	H	W	Z	Ḥ	Ṭ
أ	ب	ج	خ	د	هـ	و	ز	ح	ط

Y	K	Š	L	M	D̲	N	Ẓ	S	⊂
ي	ك	ش	ل	م	ذ	ن	ظ	س	ع

P	Ṣ	Q	R	T̲	G	T	I	U	(S)
ف	ص	ق	ر	ث	غ	ت	إ	ؤ	(س)

The oldest extant Phoenician alphabet (ca. 1400 BC) – the first real phonetic alphabet – excavated from the Phoenician city of Ugaret on the Syrian Coast (from http://www.utexas.edu/courses/classicalarch/images1/ UgaritAlphabet1400.jpg).

Modern Standard Arabic Grammar: A Learner's Guide, First Edition.
© 2011 Mohammad T. Alhawary. Published 2011 by Blackwell Publishing Ltd.

Appendix D

Identifying the Root الجَذْر and Looking up Words in the Dictionary

1. Triliteral Roots

The vast majority of Arabic words have triliteral (i.e., three-letter) roots. Identifying the root of a given word requires the dropping of certain consonants and vowels in the sequence provided here, each step being inclusive of the previous ones. Words can then be looked up alphabetically according to the order of the letters within the root.

Root		Retained letters		Dropped letter/s	Word

1. Prefixes (e.g., definite-article and present-tense prefixes) and suffixes (e.g., gender, number, past-, present-tense, and adjective suffixes) are dropped:

Root		Retained letters		Dropped letter/s	Word
ب - ي - ت	←	بَيْت	←	الـ ____	البَيْت
و - ر - د	←	وَرْد	←	الـ ____ ة	الوَرْدَة
و - ل - د	←	وَلَد	←	____ انِ	وَلَدانِ
ح - ج - ر	←	حُجْر	←	____ تانِ	حُجْرَتانِ

Modern Standard Arabic Grammar: A Learner's Guide, First Edition.
© 2011 Mohammad T. Alhawary. Published 2011 by Blackwell Publishing Ltd.

Root		Retained letters		Dropped letter/s	Word
ح - ج - ر	←	حُجْر	←	____ تَيْنِ	حُجْرَتَيْنِ
ح - ج - ر	←	حُجُر	←	ات ____	حُجُرات
ك - ت - ب	←	كَتَب	←	____ وا	كَتَبوا
س - م - ع	←	سْمَع	←	تَـ ____ ونَ	تَسْمَعونَ
م - ص - ر	←	مِصْر	←	____ يّ	مِصْريّ
خ - ض - ر	←	خَضْر	←	____ ء	خَضْراء
ج - و - ع	←	جَوْع	←	____ ان	جَوْعان
ج - د - د	←	جَدَّ / جَدد	←	____ ة	جَدَّة
ك - ت - ب	←	كَتَبَ	←	-	كَتَبَ

2. Long (pure) vowels ا [aa], و [uu], and ي [ii] in words consisting of more than three letters are dropped; otherwise, the و [uu] and ي [ii] are part of the root:

Root		Retained letters		Dropped letter/s	Word
ش - ر - ع	←	شرِع	←	ـ ا ____	شارع
ص - ف - ف	←	صُفف	←	____ و ـ	صُفوف
ص - د - ق	←	صَدق	←	____ يـ ـ	صَديق
و - ز - ر	←	وِزر	←	____ ا ـ ة	وِزارة
ي - س - ر	←	يَسر	←	____ ا ـ	يَسار
ك - ت - ب	←	كِتب	←	ـ ا ____ ونَ	كاتِبونَ
س - ي - ر	←	سَيْر	←	-	سَيْر
س - و - ق	←	سوق	←	-	سوق

3. The initial *hamza* in words consisting of more than three letters is dropped; otherwise, the *hamza* in words consisting of three letters is part of the root unless the last of the two letters is doubled (i.e., with a *shadda*):

Root		Retained letters		Dropped letter/s		Word
ص – ح – ب	←	صُحب	←	أ __ ا _	←	أَصْحاب
ك – ر – م	←	كَرَمَ	←	أ ___	←	أَكْرَمَ
ء – س – ر	←	أُسر	←	___ ة	←	أُسْرَة
م – ث – ل	←	مْثِل	←	أ __ ة	←	أَمْثِلة
م – ث – ل	←	مْثِل	←	أ __ ا _	←	أَمْثال
ص – غ – ر	←	صْغَر	←	أ ___	←	أَصْغَر
ح – ب – ب	←	حَبّ / حَبب	←	أ ___	←	أَحَبَّ
ء – ل – ف	←	أَلَفَ	←	–	←	أَلَفَ
ء – س – د	←	أَسَد	←	–	←	أَسَد

4. The initial ـتـ in words consisting of more than three letters is dropped; otherwise, the initial ـتـ in words consisting of three letters is part of the root:

Root		Retained letters		Dropped letter/s		Word
ك – ر – م	←	كَرَّم	←	تَـ ___	←	تَكَرَّمَ
د – ر – س	←	دْرس	←	تَـ ___ ـيـ _	←	تَدْريس
ر – ك – م	←	ركُم	←	تَـ __ ا _ ات	←	تَراكُمات
ط – و – ر	←	طْور	←	تَـ ___ ـيـ _	←	تَطْوير
و – ض – ع	←	وضُع	←	تَـ _ ا __	←	تَواضُع
ت – ح – ف	←	تُحْف	←	___ ة	←	تُحْفة
ت – خ – ت	←	تَخْت	←	–	←	تَخْت

5. The initial ـم in words consisting of more than three letters is dropped unless they contain a long vowel; otherwise, the initial ـم in words consisting of three letters is part of the root:

Root		Retained letters		Dropped letter/s	Word
س – ج – د	←	سْجِد	←	ــَـــ مَ	مَسْجِد
د – ر – س	←	دْرَس	←	ة ـــــ مَ	مَدْرَسَة
ج – هـ – د	←	جهِد	←	ـ ا ـ مُ	مُجاهِد
م – ث – ل	←	مثل	←	ـ ا ــ	مِثال
س – ل – م	←	سْلِم	←	ونَ ـــــ مُ	مُسْلِمونَ
ن – ط – ق	←	نْطِق	←	ــــــ مَ	مَنْطِق
م – د – د	←	مُدَّ / مُدد	←	ة ــــ	مُدَّة
م – ث – ل	←	مِثْل	←	-	مِثْل

6. The initial ا and/or medial ـن in words consisting of more than three letters are dropped:

Root		Retained letters		Dropped letter/s	Word
ك – س – ر	←	كَسَر	←	ـنْ ـــــ إ	إنْكَسَر
ك – س – ر	←	كْسِر	←	ـنْ ـــــ مُ	مُنْكَسِر
ط – ل – ق	←	طلْق	←	ـ ا ـــ نْ إ	إنْطِلاق

7. The initial ا and/or medial ـتـ in words consisting of more than three letters are dropped:			
Root	*Retained letters*	*Dropped letter/s*	*Word*
ع - م - د ←	عَمَد ←	ا _ تَـ __ ←	اِعْتَمَد
ع - ل - م ←	علِم ←	مُتَـ ا __ ←	مُتَعالِم
ح - ر - ق ←	حْرِق ←	مُـ _ تَـ __ ←	مُحْتَرِق
هـ - م - م ←	هْمم ←	اِ _ تِـ ا _ ←	اِهْتِمام

8. The initial ا and/or medial ـستـ in words consisting of more than three letters are dropped:			
Root	*Retained letters*	*Dropped letter/s*	*Word*
ع - م - ر ←	عْمَر ←	اِسْتَـ ___ ←	اِسْتَعْمَر
ق - ب - ل ←	قْبَل ←	مُسْتَـ ___ ←	مُسْتَقْبَل
ل - ز - م ←	لْزَم ←	مُسْتَـ ___ ات ←	مُسْتَلْزَمات

2. Triliteral (Hollow and Defective) Roots

A smaller number of words, in particular hollow and defective verbs, contain a long vowel as part of the root in medial and final position, respectively. In the past tense, their medial and final long vowel is 'alif [aa] and in the present tense their medial and final long vowel is either *waaw* و [uu], *yaa'* ي [ii], or 'alif [aa], although 'alif [aa] is never a root vowel. The root vowel in this case is either a *waaw* و [uu] or *yaa'* ي [ii]. The correct root vowel can be identified through the present tense and/ or the verbal noun (see also 13.4).

Root		Retained letters		Dropped letter/s	Word
The root of hollow and defective verbs/words identified through the present tense and/or verbal noun:					
ق - و - ل	←	قول	←	ـ / ــــ يَـ	قالَ ← يَقولُ / قَوْل
س - ي - ر	←	سير	←	ـ / ــــ يَـ	سارَ ← يَسيرُ / سَيْر
ن - و - م	←	نَوْم	←	ـ / ــــ يَـ	نامَ ← يَنامُ ← نَوْم
د - ع - و	←	دَعو	←	ى / ــــ يَـ	دَعا ← يَدْعو / دَعْوىٰ
م - ش - ي	←	مْشي	←	ـ / ــــ يَـ	مَشىٰ ← يَمْشي / مَشي
ن - هـ - ي	←	نَهي	←	ـ / ــــ يَـ	نَهىٰ ← يَنْهىٰ ← نَهي

Note: If we do not know the present tense or the verbal noun, we must hypothesize that either *waaw* و [uu] or *yaa'* ي [ii] is the root vowel and look up both roots for the proper meaning in light of the context in which the word is used. Fortunately, the two vowels are next to each other in alphabetical order, and so are the two sections in the dictionary. Similarly, the root long vowel of derived hollow and defective verbs and words derived from them can be identified after being reduced to Form I or a triliteral, related word (see also 13.4).

Root		Retained letters		Dropped letter/s	Word
The root of derived hollow and defective verbs identified through Form I or a triliteral-related word:					
ع - و - د	←	عود	←	ـــ يَـ	أَعادَ - يُعيدُ ← عادَ - يَعودُ
ب - ي - د	←	بيد	←	ـــ يَـ	أَبادَ - يُبيدُ ← بادَ - يَبيدُ
ق - و - د	←	قود	←	ـــ يَـ	إقْتادَ - يَقْتادُ ← قادَ - يَقودُ
خ - ي - ر	←	خير	←	ـــ يَـ	إخْتارَ - يَخْتارُ ← خارَ - يَخيرُ

ن – س – ي	←	نسي	←	–	تَناسىٰ – يَتَناسىٰ ← نَسِيَ – يَنْسىٰ
د – ع – و	←	دعو	←	ـَ	تَداعىٰ – يَتَداعىٰ ← دَعا – يَدْعو
د – ع – و	←	دعو	←	ـَ	اِسْتَدْعىٰ – يَسْتَدعي ← دَعا – يَدْعو
ث – ن – ي	←	ثني	←	ـَ	اِسْتَثْنىٰ – يَسْتَثْني ← ثَنىٰ – يَثْني

3. Triliteral with a Geminate Root Letter

Some Arabic words have geminate triliteral (i.e., three-letter) roots with fewer than three letters, with the second and third letters being doubled (i.e., identical with a *shadda*). Hence, the root of such words consists of the letters after the gemination is broken (i.e., the identical letters separated) and after prefixes and suffixes have been eliminated.

Gemination in roots consisting of fewer than three letters separated:					
Root		Retained letters		Dropped letter/s	Word
ص – ف – ف	←	صَفف	←	–	صَفّ
ج – د – د	←	جَدد	←	–	جَدّ
ء – م – م	←	أمم	←	–	أُمّ
ث – م – م	←	ثَمم	←	–	ثَمّ
ث – م – م	←	ثَمم	←	–	ثَمّة
ع – م – م	←	عُمم	←	–	يَعُمّ

4. Monoliteral and Biliteral Roots

A very small number of Arabic words or particles may belong to mono-
literal or biliteral roots, and consist of fewer than three letters.

Monoliteral and biliteral roots consisting of fewer than three letters:						
Root		*Retained letters*		*Dropped letter/s*		*Word*
و	←	وَ	←	–		وَ
فَ	←	فَ	←	–		فَ
ف-ي	←	في	←	–		في
ع-ن	←	عَنْ	←	–		عَنْ
ك-م	←	كَمْ	←	–		كَمْ

5. Quadriliteral

Some words in Arabic may belong to quadriliteral roots, consisting of
four root letters. To identify the root of a word containing four root letters, the same rules (1–8 in Section 1 above) for identifying triliteral roots
are followed for eliminating non-root letters, except for eliminating
initial ﺕ and medial ﻨ , which have to be applied cautiously.

Quadriliteral roots consisting of four letters (rules 1–8 above are applied):			
Root	Retained letters	Dropped letter/s	Word
د - ر - هـ - م ←	دَرِهِم ←	الـ ا ←	الدَّراهِم
ش - ي - ط - ن ←	شَيْطن ←	ة ا ←	شَيْطانة
ط - م - ء - ن ←	طْمَأَنّ ←	اِ ←	اِطْمَأَنّ
ع - س - ك - ر ←	عَسْكَر ←	مُـ ات ←	مُعَسْكَرات
م - س - ك - ن ←	مَسْكِن ←	مُتَـ ←	مُتَمَسْكِن
د - ح - ر - ج ←	دَحْرَج ←	تَـ ←	تَدَحْرَج
ت - ر - ج - م ←	تَرْجَم ←	تْ ←	تَرْجَمْتْ

6. Quinqueliteral

A small number of words in Arabic have quinqueliteral roots, consisting of five root letters. To identify the root of a word containing five root letters, the same rules (1–8 in Section 1 above) for identifying triliteral roots are followed for eliminating non-root letters.

Quinqueliteral roots consisting of five letters (rules 1–8 above are applied):			
Root	Retained letters	Dropped letter/s	Word
س - ف - ر - ج - ل ←	سَفَرْجَل ←	الـ ←	السَّفَرْجَل
خ - ز - ع - ب - ل ←	خُزَعْبِل ←	ات ←	خُزَعْبِلات
ع - ن - د - ل - ب ←	عَنْدَلب ←	ـ ي ←	عَنْدَليب

Appendix E
The Number Phrase العَدَد والمَعْدود

There are three rules involved in the use of both parts of the number phrase العَدَد والمَعْدود or the "number/numeral" العَدَد and the "counted noun" المَعْدود with respect to:

(a)   whether the counted noun following the number is singular, dual, or plural
(b)   the type of case ending on the number
(c)   the type of case ending on the counted noun.

The numbers 1–2: the two parts are identical in gender, number, and case			
سَلَّمْتُ عَلَى طالِبٍ واحِدٍ	رَأَيْتُ طالِباً واحِداً	حَضَرَ طالِبٌ واحِدٌ	١
سَلَّمْتُ عَلَى طالِبةٍ واحِدةٍ	رَأَيْتُ طالِبةً واحِدةً	حَضَرَتْ طالِبةٌ واحِدةٌ	
سَلَّمْتُ عَلَى طالِبَيْنِ اثْنَيْنِ	رَأَيْتُ طالِبَيْنِ اثْنَيْنِ	حَضَرَ طالِبانِ اثْنانِ	٢
سَلَّمْتُ عَلَى طالِبَتَيْنِ اثْنَتَيْنِ	رَأَيْتُ طالِبَتَيْنِ اثْنَتَيْنِ	حَضَرَتْ طالِبَتانِ اثْنَتانِ	

Modern Standard Arabic Grammar: A Learner's Guide, First Edition.
© 2011 Mohammad T. Alhawary. Published 2011 by Blackwell Publishing Ltd.

The numbers 3–10:

  (a) the number and the counted noun have reversed gender

  (b) the counted noun is in the plural

  (c) the case ending of the number depends on its position in the sentence; the counted noun has the genitive مَجْرور case ending

٣	حَضَرَ ثَلاثَةُ طُلّابٍ	رَأَيْتُ ثَلاثَةَ طُلّابٍ	سَلَّمْتُ عَلىٰ ثَلاثَةِ طُلّابٍ
	حَضَرَ ثَلاثُ طالِباتٍ	رَأَيْتُ ثَلاثَ طالِباتٍ	سَلَّمْتُ عَلىٰ ثَلاثِ طالِباتٍ
٤	حَضَرَ أَرْبَعَةُ طُلّابٍ	رَأَيْتُ أَرْبَعَةَ طُلّابٍ	سَلَّمْتُ عَلىٰ أَرْبَعَةِ طُلّابٍ
	حَضَرَ أَرْبَعُ طالِباتٍ	رَأَيْتُ أَرْبَعَ طالِباتٍ	سَلَّمْتُ عَلىٰ أَرْبَعِ طالِباتٍ
٥	حَضَرَ خَمْسَةُ طُلّابٍ	رَأَيْتُ خَمْسَةَ طُلّابٍ	سَلَّمْتُ عَلىٰ خَمْسَةِ طُلّابٍ
	حَضَرَ خَمْسُ طالِباتٍ	رَأَيْتُ خَمْسَ طالِباتٍ	سَلَّمْتُ عَلىٰ خَمْسِ طالِباتٍ
٦	حَضَرَ سِتَّةُ طُلّابٍ	رَأَيْتُ سِتَّةَ طُلّابٍ	سَلَّمْتُ عَلىٰ سِتَّةِ طُلّابٍ
	حَضَرَ سِتُّ طالِباتٍ	رَأَيْتُ سِتَّ طالِباتٍ	سَلَّمْتُ عَلىٰ سِتِّ طالِباتٍ
٧	حَضَرَ سَبْعَةُ طُلّابٍ	رَأَيْتُ سَبْعَةَ طُلّابٍ	سَلَّمْتُ عَلىٰ سَبْعَةِ طُلّابٍ
	حَضَرَ سَبْعُ طالِباتٍ	رَأَيْتُ سَبْعَ طالِباتٍ	سَلَّمْتُ عَلىٰ سَبْعِ طالِباتٍ
٨	حَضَرَ ثَمانِيَةُ طُلّابٍ	رَأَيْتُ ثَمانِيَةَ طُلّابٍ	سَلَّمْتُ عَلىٰ ثَمانِيَةِ طُلّابٍ
	حَضَرَ ثَماني طالِباتٍ	رَأَيْتُ ثَماني طالِباتٍ	سَلَّمْتُ عَلىٰ ثَماني طالِباتٍ
٩	حَضَرَ تِسْعَةُ طُلّابٍ	رَأَيْتُ تِسْعَةَ طُلّابٍ	سَلَّمْتُ عَلىٰ تِسْعَةِ طُلّابٍ
	حَضَرَ تِسْعُ طالِباتٍ	رَأَيْتُ تِسْعَ طالِباتٍ	سَلَّمْتُ عَلىٰ تِسْعِ طالِباتٍ
١٠	حَضَرَ عَشَرَةُ طُلّابٍ	رَأَيْتُ عَشَرَةَ طُلّابٍ	سَلَّمْتُ عَلىٰ عَشَرَةِ طُلّابٍ
	حَضَرَ عَشْرُ طالِباتٍ	رَأَيْتُ عَشْرَ طالِباتٍ	سَلَّمْتُ عَلىٰ عَشْرِ طالِباتٍ

Note: in the nominative case, the verb حَضَرَ is in the singular masculine with both masculine and feminine nouns, agreeing directly with masculine counted nouns (when used with masculine nouns; e.g., طُلّاب) and with the masculine number (when used with feminine nouns; e.g., ثَلاث) (see also 4.1.2 and 16.1).

The numbers 11–12:

(a) both digits of the number phrase and the counted noun have the same gender

(b) the counted noun is in the singular

(c) both digits of the number phrase and that of the counted noun have the accusative مَنْصوب case ending for the number 11. However for the number 12, the case ending of the first digit depends on its position in the sentence while the second digit has the accusative مَنْصوب case ending

١١	حَضَرَ أَحَدَ عَشَرَ طالِباً	رَأَيْتُ أَحَدَ عَشَرَ طالِباً	سَلَّمْتُ عَلىٰ أَحَدَ عَشَرَ طالِباً
	حَضَرَتْ إِحْدىٰ عَشْرَةَ طالِبَةً	رَأَيْتُ إِحْدىٰ عَشْرَةَ طالِبَةً	سَلَّمْتُ عَلىٰ إِحْدىٰ عَشْرَةَ طالِبَةً
١٢	حَضَرَ اثْنا عَشَرَ طالِباً	رَأَيْتُ اثْنَيْ عَشَرَ طالِباً	سَلَّمْتُ عَلىٰ اثْنَيْ عَشَرَ طالِباً
	حَضَرَتِ اثْنَتا عَشْرَةَ طالِبَةً	رَأَيْتُ اثْنَتَيْ عَشْرَةَ طالِبَةً	سَلَّمْتُ عَلىٰ اثْنَتَيْ عَشْرَةَ طالِبَةً

The numbers 13–19:

(a) the first/right digit of the number and the counted noun have reversed gender

(b) the second/left digit for "ten" has the same gender as the counted noun

(c) the counted noun is in the singular

(d) both digits of the number phrase and that of the counted noun have the accusative مَنْصوب case ending

١٣	حَضَرَ ثَلاثَةَ عَشَرَ طالِباً	رَأَيْتُ ثَلاثَةَ عَشَرَ طالِباً	سَلَّمْتُ عَلىٰ ثَلاثَةَ عَشَرَ طالِباً
	حَضَرَ ثَلاثَ عَشْرَةَ طالِبَةً	رَأَيْتُ ثَلاثَ عَشْرَةَ طالِبَةً	سَلَّمْتُ عَلىٰ ثَلاثَ عَشْرَةَ طالِبَةً
١٤	حَضَرَ أَرْبَعَةَ عَشَرَ طالِباً	رَأَيْتُ أَرْبَعَةَ عَشَرَ طالِباً	سَلَّمْتُ عَلىٰ أَرْبَعَةَ عَشَرَ طالِباً
	حَضَرَ أَرْبَعَ عَشْرَةَ طالِبَةً	رَأَيْتُ أَرْبَعَ عَشْرَةَ طالِبَةً	سَلَّمْتُ عَلىٰ أَرْبَعَ عَشْرَةَ طالِبَةً

سَلَّمْتُ عَلَى خَمْسَةَ عَشَرَ طالِباً	رَأَيْتُ خَمْسَةَ عَشَرَ طالِباً	حَضَرَ خَمْسَةَ عَشَرَ طالِباً	١٥
سَلَّمْتُ عَلَى خَمْسَ عَشْرَةَ طالِبَةً	رَأَيْتُ خَمْسَ عَشْرَةَ طالِبَةً	حَضَرَ خَمْسَ عَشْرَةَ طالِبَةً	
سَلَّمْتُ عَلَى سِتَّةَ عَشَرَ طالِباً	رَأَيْتُ سِتَّةَ عَشَرَ طالِباً	حَضَرَ سِتَّةَ عَشَرَ طالِباً	١٦
سَلَّمْتُ عَلَى سِتَّ عَشْرَةَ طالِبَةً	رَأَيْتُ سِتَّ عَشْرَةَ طالِبَةً	حَضَرَ سِتَّ عَشْرَةَ طالِبَةً	
سَلَّمْتُ عَلَى سَبْعَةَ عَشَرَ طالِباً	رَأَيْتُ سَبْعَةَ عَشَرَ طالِباً	حَضَرَ سَبْعَةَ عَشَرَ طالِباً	١٧
سَلَّمْتُ عَلَى سَبْعَ عَشْرَةَ طالِبَةً	رَأَيْتُ سَبْعَ عَشْرَةَ طالِبَةً	حَضَرَ سَبْعَ عَشْرَةَ طالِبَةً	
سَلَّمْتُ عَلَى ثَمانِيَةَ عَشَرَ طالِباً	رَأَيْتُ ثَمانِيَةَ عَشَرَ طالِباً	حَضَرَ ثَمانِيَةَ عَشَرَ طالِباً	١٨
سَلَّمْتُ عَلَى ثَماني عَشْرَةَ طالِبَةً	رَأَيْتُ ثَماني عَشْرَةَ طالِبَةً	حَضَرَ ثَماني عَشْرَةَ طالِبَةً	
سَلَّمْتُ عَلَى تِسْعَةَ عَشَرَ طالِباً	رَأَيْتُ تِسْعَةَ عَشَرَ طالِباً	حَضَرَ تِسْعَةَ عَشَرَ طالِباً	١٩
سَلَّمْتُ عَلَى تِسْعَ عَشْرَةَ طالِبَةً	رَأَيْتُ تِسْعَ عَشْرَةَ طالِبَةً	حَضَرَ تِسْعَ عَشْرَةَ طالِبَةً	

The numbers 20, 30, 40, 50, 60, 70, 80, 90:
  (a) the number is the same for both the masculine and feminine gender
  (b) the counted noun is in the singular
  (c) the case ending of the number depends on its position in the
      sentence; the counted noun has the accusative مَنْصوب case ending

سَلَّمْتُ عَلَى عِشْرينَ طالِباً	رَأَيْتُ عِشْرينَ طالِباً	حَضَرَ عِشْرونَ طالِباً	٢٠
سَلَّمْتُ عَلَى عِشْرينَ طالِبَةً	رَأَيْتُ عِشْرينَ طالِبَةً	حَضَرَ عِشْرونَ طالِبَةً	
سَلَّمْتُ عَلَى ثَلاثينَ طالِباً	رَأَيْتُ ثَلاثينَ طالِباً	حَضَرَ ثَلاثونَ طالِباً	٣٠
سَلَّمْتُ عَلَى ثَلاثينَ طالِبَةً	رَأَيْتُ ثَلاثينَ طالِبَةً	حَضَرَ ثَلاثونَ طالِبَةً	
سَلَّمْتُ عَلَى أَرْبَعينَ طالِباً	رَأَيْتُ أَرْبَعينَ طالِباً	حَضَرَ أَرْبَعونَ طالِباً	٤٠
سَلَّمْتُ عَلَى أَرْبَعينَ طالِبَةً	رَأَيْتُ أَرْبَعينَ طالِبَةً	حَضَرَ أَرْبَعونَ طالِبَةً	
سَلَّمْتُ عَلَى خَمْسينَ طالِباً	رَأَيْتُ خَمْسينَ طالِباً	حَضَرَ خَمْسونَ طالِباً	٥٠
سَلَّمْتُ عَلَى خَمْسينَ طالِبَةً	رَأَيْتُ خَمْسينَ طالِبَةً	حَضَرَ خَمْسونَ طالِبَةً	

٦٠	حَضَرَ سِتّونَ طالِباً	رَأَيْتُ سِتّينَ طالِباً	سَلَّمْتُ عَلىٰ سِتّينَ طالِباً
	حَضَرَ سِتّونَ طالِبةً	رَأَيْتُ سِتّينَ طالِبةً	سَلَّمْتُ عَلىٰ سِتّينَ طالِبةً
٧٠	حَضَرَ سَبْعونَ طالِباً	رَأَيْتُ سَبْعينَ طالِباً	سَلَّمْتُ عَلىٰ سَبْعينَ طالِباً
	حَضَرَ سَبْعونَ طالِبةً	رَأَيْتُ سَبْعينَ طالِبةً	سَلَّمْتُ عَلىٰ سَبْعينَ طالِبةً
٨٠	حَضَرَ ثَمانونَ طالِباً	رَأَيْتُ ثَمانينَ طالِباً	سَلَّمْتُ عَلىٰ ثَمانينَ طالِباً
	حَضَرَ ثَمانونَ طالِبةً	رَأَيْتُ ثَمانينَ طالِبةً	سَلَّمْتُ عَلىٰ ثَمانينَ طالِبةً
٩٠	حَضَرَ تِسْعونَ طالِباً	رَأَيْتُ تِسْعينَ طالِباً	سَلَّمْتُ عَلىٰ تِسْعينَ طالِباً
	حَضَرَ تِسْعونَ طالِبةً	رَأَيْتُ تِسْعينَ طالِبةً	سَلَّمْتُ عَلىٰ تِسْعينَ طالِبةً

The numbers 21–22 (and 31–32, 41–42, 51–52, 61–62, 71–72, 81–82, 91–92):

(a) the first/right digit of the number and the counted noun have the same gender

(b) the counted noun is in the singular

(c) the case ending of both digits of the number phrase are the same and it depends on the position of the number phrase in the sentence; the counted noun has the accusative case مَنْصوب ending

٢١	حَضَرَ واحِدٌ وَعِشْرونَ طالِباً	رَأَيْتُ واحِداً وَعِشْرينَ طالِباً	سَلَّمْتُ عَلىٰ واحِدٍ وَعِشْرينَ طالِباً
	حَضَرَتْ إحْدىٰ وَعِشْرونَ طالِبةً	رَأَيْتُ إحْدىٰ وَعِشْرينَ طالِبةً	سَلَّمْتُ عَلىٰ إحْدىٰ وَعِشْرينَ طالِبةً
٢٢	حَضَرَ اثْنانِ وَعِشْرونَ طالِباً	رَأَيْتُ اثْنَيْنِ وَعِشْرينَ طالِباً	سَلَّمْتُ عَلىٰ اثْنَيْنِ وَعِشْرينَ طالِباً
	حَضَرَتِ اثْنَتانِ وَعِشْرونَ طالِبةً	رَأَيْتُ اثْنَتَيْنِ وَعِشْرينَ طالِبةً	سَلَّمْتُ عَلىٰ اثْنَتَيْنِ وَعِشْرينَ طالِبةً

The numbers 23–29 (and 33–39, 43–49, 53–59, 63–69, 73–79, 83–89, 93–99):

(a)   the first/right digit of the number and the counted noun have reversed gender

(b)   the second/left digit is the same for both masculine and feminine

(c)   the counted noun is in the singular

(d)   the case ending of both digits of the number phrase are the same and it depends on the position of the number phrase in the sentence; the counted noun has the accusative مَنْصوب case ending

سَلَّمْتُ عَلىٰ ثَلاثَةٍ وَعِشْرينَ طالِباً	رَأَيْتُ ثَلاثَةَ وَعِشْرينَ طالِباً	حَضَرَ ثَلاثَةٌ وَعِشْرونَ طالِباً	٢٣
سَلَّمْتُ عَلىٰ ثَلاثٍ وَعِشْرينَ طالِبَةً	رَأَيْتُ ثَلاثاً وَعِشْرينَ طالِبَةً	حَضَرَ ثَلاثٌ وَعِشْرونَ طالِبَةٌ	
سَلَّمْتُ عَلىٰ أَرْبَعَةٍ وَعِشْرينَ طالِباً	رَأَيْتُ أَرْبَعَةَ وَعِشْرينَ طالِباً	حَضَرَ أَرْبَعَةٌ وَعِشْرونَ طالِباً	٢٤
سَلَّمْتُ عَلىٰ أَرْبَعٍ وَعِشْرينَ طالِبَةً	رَأَيْتُ أَرْبَعاً وَعِشْرينَ طالِبَةً	حَضَرَ أَرْبَعٌ وَعِشْرونَ طالِبَةٌ	
سَلَّمْتُ عَلىٰ خَمْسَةٍ وَعِشْرينَ طالِباً	رَأَيْتُ خَمْسَةَ وَعِشْرينَ طالِباً	حَضَرَ خَمْسَةٌ وَعِشْرونَ طالِباً	٢٥
سَلَّمْتُ عَلىٰ خَمْسٍ وَعِشْرينَ طالِبَةً	رَأَيْتُ خَمْساً وَعِشْرينَ طالِبَةً	حَضَرَ خَمْسٌ وَعِشْرونَ طالِبَةٌ	
سَلَّمْتُ عَلىٰ سِتَّةٍ وَعِشْرينَ طالِباً	رَأَيْتُ سِتَّةَ وَعِشْرينَ طالِباً	حَضَرَ سِتَّةٌ وَعِشْرونَ طالِباً	٢٦
سَلَّمْتُ عَلىٰ سِتٍّ وَعِشْرينَ طالِبَةً	رَأَيْتُ سِتّاً وَعِشْرينَ طالِبَةً	حَضَرَ سِتٌّ وَعِشْرونَ طالِبَةٌ	
سَلَّمْتُ عَلىٰ سَبْعَةٍ وَعِشْرينَ طالِباً	رَأَيْتُ سَبْعَةَ وَعِشْرينَ طالِباً	حَضَرَ سَبْعَةٌ وَعِشْرونَ طالِباً	٢٧
سَلَّمْتُ عَلىٰ سَبْعٍ وَعِشْرينَ طالِبَةً	رَأَيْتُ سَبْعاً وَعِشْرينَ طالِبَةً	حَضَرَ سَبْعٌ وَعِشْرونَ طالِبَةٌ	
سَلَّمْتُ عَلىٰ ثَمانِيَةٍ وَعِشْرينَ طالِباً	رَأَيْتُ ثَمانِيَةَ وَعِشْرينَ طالِباً	حَضَرَ ثَمانِيَةٌ وَعِشْرونَ طالِباً	٢٨
سَلَّمْتُ عَلىٰ ثَمانٍ وَعِشْرينَ طالِبَةً	رَأَيْتُ ثَمانِيَ وَعِشْرينَ طالِبَةً	حَضَرَ ثَمانٍ وَعِشْرونَ طالِبَةٌ	
سَلَّمْتُ عَلىٰ تِسْعَةٍ وَعِشْرينَ طالِباً	رَأَيْتُ تِسْعَةَ وَعِشْرينَ طالِباً	حَضَرَ تِسْعَةٌ وَعِشْرونَ طالِباً	٢٩
سَلَّمْتُ عَلىٰ تِسْعٍ وَعِشْرينَ طالِبَةً	رَأَيْتُ تِسْعاً وَعِشْرينَ طالِبَةً	حَضَرَ تِسْعٌ وَعِشْرونَ طالِبَةٌ	

The numbers for hundred, thousand, million . . . :
   (a)   the number is used for both the masculine and feminine
   (b)   the counted noun is in the singular
   (c)   the case ending of the number depends on its position in the
        sentence; the counted noun has the genitive مَجْرور case ending

سَلَّمْتُ عَلىٰ مِئَةِ طالِبٍ	رَأَيْتُ مِئَةَ طالِبٍ	حَضَرَ مِئَةُ طالِبٍ	١٠٠
سَلَّمْتُ عَلىٰ مِئَةِ طالِبَةٍ	رَأَيْتُ مِئَةَ طالِبَةٍ	حَضَرَتْ مِئَةُ طالِبَةٍ	
سَلَّمْتُ عَلىٰ أَلْفِ طالِبٍ	رَأَيْتُ أَلْفَ طالِبٍ	حَضَرَ أَلْفُ طالِبٍ	١٠٠٠
سَلَّمْتُ عَلىٰ أَلْفِ طالِبَةٍ	رَأَيْتُ أَلْفَ طالِبَةٍ	حَضَرَ أَلْفُ طالِبَةٍ	
سَلَّمْتُ عَلىٰ مَلْيونِ طالِبٍ	رَأَيْتُ مَلْيونَ طالِبٍ	حَضَرَ مَلْيونُ طالِبٍ	١٠٠٠٠٠٠
سَلَّمْتُ عَلىٰ مَلْيونِ طالِبَةٍ	رَأَيْتُ مَلْيونَ طالِبَةٍ	حَضَرَ مَلْيونُ طالِبَةٍ	

Compound numbers of hundreds and thousands:
(the same rules above apply)

ثَلاثُ مِئَةٍ	٣٠٠	مِئَتانِ	٢٠٠	مِئَةٌ	١٠٠
سِتُّ مِئَةٍ	٦٠٠	خَمْسُ مِئَةٍ	٥٠٠	أَرْبَعُ مِئَةٍ	٤٠٠
ثَلاثَةُ آلافٍ	٣٠٠٠	أَلْفانِ	٢٠٠٠	أَلْفٌ	١٠٠٠
سِتَّةُ آلافٍ	٦٠٠٠	خَمْسَةُ آلافٍ	٥٠٠٠	أَرْبَعَةُ آلافٍ	٤٠٠٠

Definite number phrase:
   (a)   the number in the definite alone can make the whole phrase definite
   (b)   the counted noun in the definite can make the whole phrase definite
   (c)   the entire number phrase definite makes the whole phrase definite

حَضَرَ الثَلاثَةُ الطُّلَّابِ	=	حَضَرَ ثَلاثَةُ الطُّلَّابِ	=	حَضَرَ الثَلاثَةُ طُلَّابٍ
حَضَرَ الثَلاثُ الطالِباتِ	=	حَضَرَ ثَلاثُ الطالِباتِ	=	حَضَرَ الثَلاثُ طالِباتٍ

Ordinal numbers (1st, 2nd, 3rd–23rd . . .):

(a)   the two parts are identical in gender and number

(b)   the two parts are identical in case ending, except the numbers 13–19, which have the accusative مَنْصوب ending

سَلَّمْتُ عَلى الطّالِبِ الأَوَّلِ	رَأَيْتُ الطّالِبَ الأَوَّلَ	حَضَرَ الطّالِبُ الأَوَّلُ	1st
سَلَّمْتُ عَلى الطّالِبةِ الأُولى	رَأَيْتُ الطّالِبةَ الأُولى	حَضَرَتِ الطّالِبةُ الأُولى	
سَلَّمْتُ عَلى الطّالِبِ الثّاني	رَأَيْتُ الطّالِبَ الثّانيَ	حَضَرَ الطّالِبُ الثّاني	2nd
سَلَّمْتُ عَلى الطّالِبةِ الثّانيةِ	رَأَيْتُ الطّالِبةَ الثّانيةَ	حَضَرَتِ الطّالِبةُ الثّانيةُ	
سَلَّمْتُ عَلى الطّالِبِ الثّالِثِ	رَأَيْتُ الطّالِبَ الثّالِثَ	حَضَرَ الطّالِبُ الثّالِثُ	3rd
سَلَّمْتُ عَلى الطّالِبةِ الثّالِثةِ	رَأَيْتُ الطّالِبةَ الثّالِثةَ	حَضَرَتِ الطّالِبةُ الثّالِثةُ	
سَلَّمْتُ عَلى الطّالِبِ الرّابِعِ	رَأَيْتُ الطّالِبَ الرّابِعَ	حَضَرَ الطّالِبُ الرّابِعُ	4th
سَلَّمْتُ عَلى الطّالِبةِ الرّابِعةِ	رَأَيْتُ الطّالِبةَ الرّابِعةَ	حَضَرَتِ الطّالِبةُ الرّابِعةُ	
سَلَّمْتُ عَلى الطّالِبِ الخامِسِ	رَأَيْتُ الطّالِبَ الخامِسَ	حَضَرَ الطّالِبُ الخامِسُ	5th
سَلَّمْتُ عَلى الطّالِبةِ الخامِسةِ	رَأَيْتُ الطّالِبةَ الخامِسةَ	حَضَرَتِ الطّالِبةُ الخامِسةُ	
سَلَّمْتُ عَلى الطّالِبِ السّادِسِ	رَأَيْتُ الطّالِبَ السّادِسَ	حَضَرَ الطّالِبُ السّادِسُ	6th
سَلَّمْتُ عَلى الطّالِبةِ السّادِسةِ	رَأَيْتُ الطّالِبةَ السّادِسةَ	حَضَرَتِ الطّالِبةُ السّادِسةُ	
سَلَّمْتُ عَلى الطّالِبِ السّابِعِ	رَأَيْتُ الطّالِبَ السّابِعَ	حَضَرَ الطّالِبُ السّابِعُ	7th
سَلَّمْتُ عَلى الطّالِبةِ السّابِعةِ	رَأَيْتُ الطّالِبةَ السّابِعةَ	حَضَرَتِ الطّالِبةُ السّابِعةُ	
سَلَّمْتُ عَلى الطّالِبِ الثّامِنِ	رَأَيْتُ الطّالِبَ الثّامِنَ	حَضَرَ الطّالِبُ الثّامِنُ	8th
سَلَّمْتُ عَلى الطّالِبةِ الثّامِنةِ	رَأَيْتُ الطّالِبةَ الثّامِنةَ	حَضَرَتِ الطّالِبةُ الثّامِنةُ	
سَلَّمْتُ عَلى الطّالِبِ التّاسِعِ	رَأَيْتُ الطّالِبَ التّاسِعَ	حَضَرَ الطّالِبُ التّاسِعُ	9th
سَلَّمْتُ عَلى الطّالِبةِ التّاسِعةِ	رَأَيْتُ الطّالِبةَ التّاسِعةَ	حَضَرَتِ الطّالِبةُ التّاسِعةُ	
سَلَّمْتُ عَلى الطّالِبِ العاشِرِ	رَأَيْتُ الطّالِبَ العاشِرَ	حَضَرَ الطّالِبُ العاشِرُ	10th
سَلَّمْتُ عَلى الطّالِبةِ العاشِرةِ	رَأَيْتُ الطّالِبةَ العاشِرةَ	حَضَرَتِ الطّالِبةُ العاشِرةُ	

سَلَّمْتُ عَلَى الطَّالِبِ الحادي عَشَرَ	رَأَيْتُ الطَّالِبَ الحادِيَ عَشَرَ	حَضَرَ الطَّالِبُ الحادي عَشَرَ	11th
سَلَّمْتُ عَلَى الطَّالِبةِ الحادِيةَ عَشْرَةَ	رَأَيْتُ الطَّالِبةَ الحادِيةَ عَشْرَةَ	حَضَرَتِ الطَّالِبةُ الحادِيةَ عَشْرَةَ	
سَلَّمْتُ عَلَى الطَّالِبِ الثّاني عَشَرَ	رَأَيْتُ الطَّالِبَ الثّانيَ عَشَرَ	حَضَرَ الطَّالِبُ الثّاني عَشَرَ	12th
سَلَّمْتُ عَلَى الطَّالِبةِ الثّانيةَ عَشْرَةَ	رَأَيْتُ الطَّالِبةَ الثّانيةَ عَشْرَةَ	حَضَرَتِ الطَّالِبةُ الثّانيةَ عَشْرَةَ	
سَلَّمْتُ عَلَى الطَّالِبِ الثّالِثَ عَشَرَ	رَأَيْتُ الطَّالِبَ الثّالِثَ عَشَرَ	حَضَرَ الطَّالِبُ الثّالِثَ عَشَرَ	13th
سَلَّمْتُ عَلَى الطَّالِبةِ الثّالِثةَ عَشْرَةَ	رَأَيْتُ الطَّالِبةَ الثّالِثةَ عَشْرَةَ	حَضَرَتِ الطَّالِبةُ الثّالِثةَ عَشْرَةَ	
سَلَّمْتُ عَلَى الطَّالِبِ الرّابِعَ عَشَرَ	رَأَيْتُ الطَّالِبَ الرّابِعَ عَشَرَ	حَضَرَ الطَّالِبُ الرّابِعَ عَشَرَ	14th
سَلَّمْتُ عَلَى الطَّالِبةِ الرّابِعةَ عَشْرَةَ	رَأَيْتُ الطَّالِبةَ الرّابِعةَ عَشْرَةَ	حَضَرَتِ الطَّالِبةُ الرّابِعةَ عَشْرَةَ	
سَلَّمْتُ عَلَى الطَّالِبِ الخامِسَ عَشَرَ	رَأَيْتُ الطَّالِبَ الخامِسَ عَشَرَ	حَضَرَ الطَّالِبُ الخامِسَ عَشَرَ	15th
سَلَّمْتُ عَلَى الطَّالِبةِ الخامِسةَ عَشْرَةَ	رَأَيْتُ الطَّالِبةَ الخامِسةَ عَشْرَةَ	حَضَرَتِ الطَّالِبةُ الخامِسةَ عَشْرَةَ	
سَلَّمْتُ عَلَى الطَّالِبِ السّادِسَ عَشَرَ	رَأَيْتُ الطَّالِبَ السّادِسَ عَشَرَ	حَضَرَ الطَّالِبُ السّادِسَ عَشَرَ	16th
سَلَّمْتُ عَلَى الطَّالِبةِ السّادِسةَ عَشْرَةَ	رَأَيْتُ الطَّالِبةَ السّادِسةَ عَشْرَةَ	حَضَرَتِ الطَّالِبةُ السّادِسةَ عَشْرَةَ	
سَلَّمْتُ عَلَى الطَّالِبِ السّابِعَ عَشَرَ	رَأَيْتُ الطَّالِبَ السّابِعَ عَشَرَ	حَضَرَ الطَّالِبُ السّابِعَ عَشَرَ	17th
سَلَّمْتُ عَلَى الطَّالِبةِ السّابِعةَ عَشْرَةَ	رَأَيْتُ الطَّالِبةَ السّابِعةَ عَشْرَةَ	حَضَرَتِ الطَّالِبةُ السّابِعةَ عَشْرَةَ	
سَلَّمْتُ عَلَى الطَّالِبِ الثّامِنَ عَشَرَ	رَأَيْتُ الطَّالِبَ الثّامِنَ عَشَرَ	حَضَرَ الطَّالِبُ الثّامِنَ عَشَرَ	18th
سَلَّمْتُ عَلَى الطَّالِبةِ الثّامِنةَ عَشْرَةَ	رَأَيْتُ الطَّالِبةَ الثّامِنةَ عَشْرَةَ	حَضَرَتِ الطَّالِبةُ الثّامِنةَ عَشْرَةَ	
سَلَّمْتُ عَلَى الطَّالِبِ التّاسِعَ عَشَرَ	رَأَيْتُ الطَّالِبَ التّاسِعَ عَشَرَ	حَضَرَ الطَّالِبُ التّاسِعَ عَشَرَ	19th
سَلَّمْتُ عَلَى الطَّالِبةِ التّاسِعةَ عَشْرَةَ	رَأَيْتُ الطَّالِبةَ التّاسِعةَ عَشْرَةَ	حَضَرَتِ الطَّالِبةُ التّاسِعةَ عَشْرَةَ	
سَلَّمْتُ عَلَى الطَّالِبِ العِشْرينَ	رَأَيْتُ الطَّالِبَ العِشْرينَ	حَضَرَ الطَّالِبُ العِشْرونَ	20th
سَلَّمْتُ عَلَى الطَّالِبةِ العِشْرينَ	رَأَيْتُ الطَّالِبةَ العِشْرينَ	حَضَرَتِ الطَّالِبةُ العِشْرونَ	
سَلَّمْتُ عَلَى الطَّالِبِ الحادي والعِشْرينَ	رَأَيْتُ الطَّالِبَ الحادِيَ والعِشْرينَ	حَضَرَ الطَّالِبُ الحادي والعِشْرونَ	21st
سَلَّمْتُ عَلَى الطَّالِبةِ الحادِيةِ والعِشْرينَ	رَأَيْتُ الطَّالِبةَ الحادِيةَ والعِشْرونَ	حَضَرَتِ الطَّالِبةُ الحادِيةُ والعِشْرونَ	

22nd	حَضَرَ الطَّالِبُ الثَّانِي وَالعِشْرونَ	رَأَيْتُ الطَّالِبَ الثَّانِيَ وَالعِشْرينَ	سَلَّمْتُ عَلَى الطَّالِبِ الثَّانِي وَالعِشْرينَ
	حَضَرَتِ الطَّالِبَةُ الثَّانِيةُ وَالعِشْرونَ	رَأَيْتُ الطَّالِبَةَ الثَّانِيةَ وَالعِشْرينَ	سَلَّمْتُ عَلَى الطَّالِبةِ الثَّانية وَالعِشْرينَ
23rd	حَضَرَ الطَّالِبُ الثَّالِثُ وَالعِشْرونَ	رَأَيْتُ الطَّالِبَ الثَّالِثَ وَالعِشْرينَ	سَلَّمْتُ عَلَى الطَّالِبِ الثَّالِثِ وَالعِشْرينَ
	حَضَرَتِ الطَّالِبَةُ الثَّالِثَةُ وَالعِشْرونَ	رَأَيْتُ الطَّالِبَةَ الثَّالِثَةَ وَالعِشْرينَ	سَلَّمْتُ عَلَى الطَّالِبةِ الثَّالِثةِ وَالعِشْرينَ

Reading numbers consisting of more than two digits:

From left to right: (more common)	=	From right to left: (less common)	
حَضَرَ أَلْفٌ وَسَبْعُ مِئَةٍ وَسِتَّةٌ وَخَمْسونَ طالِباً	=	حَضَرَ سِتَّةٌ وَخَمْسونَ وَسَبْعُ مِئَةٍ وَأَلْفُ طالِبٍ	١٧٥٦
رَأَيْتُ أَلْفاً وَسَبْعَ مِئَةٍ وَسِتَّةً وَخَمْسينَ طالِباً	=	رَأَيْتُ سِتَّةً وَخَمْسينَ وَسَبْعَ مِئَةٍ وَأَلْفَ طالِبٍ	
سَلَّمْتُ عَلَى أَلْفٍ وَسَبْعِ مِئَةٍ وَسِتَّةٍ وَخَمْسينَ طالِباً	=	سَلَّمْتُ عَلَى سِتَّةٍ وَخَمْسينَ وَسَبْعِ مِئَةٍ وَأَلْفِ طالِبٍ	
حَضَرَ أَلْفٌ وَسَبْعُ مِئَةٍ وَسِتٌّ وَخَمْسونَ طالِبَةً	=	حَضَرَ سِتٌّ وَخَمْسونَ وَسَبْعُ مِئَةٍ وَأَلْفُ طالِبَةٍ	
رَأَيْتُ أَلْفاً وَسَبْعَ مِئَةٍ وَسِتّاً وَخَمْسينَ طالِبَةً	=	رَأَيْتُ سِتّاً وَخَمْسينَ وَسَبْعَ مِئَةٍ وَأَلْفَ طالِبَةٍ	
سَلَّمْتُ عَلَى أَلْفٍ وَسَبْعِ مِئَةٍ وَسِتٍّ وَخَمْسينَ طالِبَةً	=	سَلَّمْتُ عَلَى سِتٍّ وَخَمْسينَ وَسَبْعِ مِئَةٍ وَأَلْفِ طالِبَةٍ	

Reading the date: preceded by the masculine word عامَ "in the year of"

From left to right: (more common)	=	From right to left: (less common)	=	
عامَ أَلْفٍ وَتِسْعِ مِئَةٍ وَأَرْبَعَةٍ وَثَمانين	=	عامَ أَرْبَعَةٍ وَثَمانينَ وَتِسْعِ مِئَةٍ وَأَلْف	=	١٩٨٤
عامَ أَلْفَيْنِ وَتِسْعة	=	عامَ تِسْعةٍ وَأَلْفَيْنِ	=	٢٠٠٩

Reading the date: preceded by the feminine word سَنَة "in the year of"				
From left to right: (more common)	=	From right to left: (less common)		
سَنَةَ أَلْفٍ وَتِسْعِ مِئَةٍ وَأَرْبَعٍ وَثَمانين	=	سَنَةَ أَرْبَعٍ وَثَمانينَ وتِسْعِ مِئَةٍ وَأَلْف	=	١٩٨٤
سَنَةَ أَلْفَيْنِ وَتِسْع	=	سَنَةَ تِسْعٍ وَأَلْفَيْن	=	٢٠٠٩

English Index

Modern Standard Arabic Grammar: A Learner's Guide, First Edition.
© 2011 Mohammad T. Alhawary. Published 2011 by Blackwell Publishing Ltd.

فِهْرِس المَوْضوعات